Navigating the Sermon

*for Cycle C
of the Revised Common Lectionary*

A Compilation of "Charting the Course" Columns from
Emphasis: *A Preaching Journal for the Parish Pastor*
a Component of **SermonSuite.com**

CSS Publishing Company, Inc.
Lima, Ohio

NAVIGATING THE SERMON

FIRST EDITION
Copyright © 2012
by CSS Publishing Co., Inc.

Published by CSS Publishing Company, Inc., Lima, Ohio 45807. All rights reserved. No part of this publication may be reproduced in any manner whatsoever without the prior permission of the publisher, except in the case of brief quotations embodied in critical articles and reviews. Inquiries should be addressed to: CSS Publishing Company, Inc., Permissions Department, 5450 N. Dixie Highway, Lima, Ohio 45807.

Scripture quotations are from the New Revised Standard Version of the Bible. Copyright 1989 by the Division of Christian Education of the National Council of the Churches of Christ in the USA. Used by permission.

Some scripture quotations marked RSV are from the Revised Standard Version of the Bible, copyrighted 1946, 1952 ©, 1971, 1973, by the Division of Christian Education of the National Council of the Churches of Christ in the USA. Used by permission.

Some scripture quotations marked NIV are taken from the Holy Bible, New International Version. Copyright © 1973, 1978, 1984 International Bible Society. Used by permission of Zondervan Bible Publishers. All rights reserved.

For more information about CSS Publishing Company resources, visit our website at www.csspub.com, email us at csr@csspub.com, or call (800) 241-4056.

ISBN-13: 978-0-7880-2676-8
ISBN-10: 0-7880-2676-3

PRINTED IN USA

Table of Contents

Introduction — 7

Advent 1 — 9
While you wait by David Kalas

Advent 2 — 14
A man for one season by David Kalas

Advent 3 — 19
Songs of joy by Wayne Brouwer

Advent 4 — 24
The Christmas visitor by David Kalas

Christmas Eve / Christmas Day — 29
Night of light by Timothy Cargal

Christmas 1 — 34
Wise child by Wayne Brouwer

New Year's Day — 39
God's gift of time by Mark Molldrem

Epiphany of Our Lord — 43
Has it dawned on you? by Craig MacCreary

Baptism of Our Lord / Epiphany 1 / Ordinary Time 1 — 48
Returning from exile by Timothy Cargal

Epiphany 2 / Ordinary Time 2 — 53
Wedding bells by Wayne Brouwer

Epiphany 3 / Ordinary Time 3 — 58
Primal urge by Craig MacCreary

Epiphany 4 / Ordinary Time 4 — 63
Blocking and tackling by David Kalas

Transfiguration of Our Lord (Last Sunday after the Epiphany) — 68
The picture Bible by David Kalas

Ash Wednesday — 73
Love that hurts by Wayne Brouwer

Lent 1 78
Getting started on the right foot by Craig MacCreary

Lent 2 83
God of the ages by David Kalas

Lent 3 88
Tumbling towers by Timothy Cargal

Lent 4 93
Always wanting more by Mark Molldrem

Lent 5 97
Christian (version 7.0) by David Kalas

Passion / Palm Sunday (Lent 6) 102
The tipping point by Wayne Brouwer

Maundy Thursday 107
Dutiful servants of all by Mark Molldrem

Good Friday 111
The people nearby by David Kalas

Easter Day 116
Back to the garden by Wayne Brouwer

Easter 2 121
Witness: suffering and rejoicing with hope by Mark Molldrem

Easter 3 125
Finding ourselves in being found in Jesus by Mark Molldrem

Easter 4 130
How can the dead testify? by Mark Molldrem

Easter 5 134
All things new and improved by David Kalas

Easter 6 139
Guess who's at the door by David Kalas

Ascension of Our Lord 144
Jesus rules! by Mark Molldrem

Easter 7 148
Locked in a room with open doors by Craig MacCreary

Pentecost Sunday 153
The day the Spirit moved in by David Kalas

Holy Trinity Sunday 158
One God: Father, Son, and Holy Spirit by Mark Molldrem

Proper 4 / Pentecost 2 / Ordinary Time 9 162
The united colors of faith by Wayne Brouwer

Proper 5 / Pentecost 3 / Ordinary Time 10 167
Distinguishing features by David Kalas

Proper 6 / Pentecost 4 / Ordinary Time 11 172
Preaching to the choir by David Kalas

Proper 7 / Pentecost 5 / Ordinary Time 12 177
Searching for truth in all the wrong places by Mark Molldrem

Proper 8 / Pentecost 6 / Ordinary Time 13 182
A share of the Spirit by Timothy Cargal

Proper 9 / Pentecost 7 / Ordinary Time 14 187
What must I do? by David Kalas

Proper 10 / Pentecost 8 / Ordinary Time 15 192
Living forward in the present by Mark Molldrem

Proper 11 / Pentecost 9 / Ordinary Time 16 196
After the handshake and the hug by Mark Molldrem

Proper 12 / Pentecost 10 / Ordinary Time 17 200
Fullness by any other name... by Mark Molldrem

Proper 13 / Pentecost 11 / Ordinary Time 18 204
"Up" is not the only heavenly direction by Mark Molldrem

Proper 14 / Pentecost 12 / Ordinary Time 19 208
The goodness that roared by Mark Molldrem

Proper 15 / Pentecost 13 / Ordinary Time 20 212
Hall of fame game by David Kalas

Proper 16 / Pentecost 14 / Ordinary Time 21 217
Mixed reactions by David Kalas

Proper 17 / Pentecost 15 / Ordinary Time 22 222
Etiquette for God's realm by Timothy Cargal

Proper 18 / Pentecost 16 / Ordinary Time 23   226
Life with attitude by Mark Molldrem

Proper 19 / Pentecost 17 / Ordinary Time 24   231
But what if it is broken? by David Kalas

Proper 20 / Pentecost 18 / Ordinary Time 25   236
From lamentation to larceny by Mark Molldrem

Proper 21 / Pentecost 19 / Ordinary Time 26   240
Blessing the rich man's proceeds by Mark Molldrem

Proper 22 / Pentecost 20 / Ordinary Time 27   244
System requirements by David Kalas

Proper 23 / Pentecost 21 / Ordinary Time 28   249
Christianity, the basic course by Craig MacCreary

Proper 24 / Pentecost 22 / Ordinary Time 29   254
The easiest way to lose by David Kalas

Proper 25 / Pentecost 23 / Ordinary Time 30   259
Keep looking up by Wayne Brouwer

Reformation Day   264
Forming, deforming, reforming by Wayne Brouwer

All Saints   270
The twilight zone by Craig MacCreary

Proper 26 / Pentecost 24 / Ordinary Time 31   275
Encouragement by Wayne Brouwer

Proper 27 / Pentecost 25 / Ordinary Time 32   280
A bright forecast by David Kalas

Proper 28 / Pentecost 26 / Ordinary Time 33   285
What's new? by Craig MacCreary

Christ the King (Proper 29)   290
A week to preach up by David Kalas

Thanksgiving Day   295
The secret of a perfect Thanksgiving by Wayne Brouwer

About the Authors   301

If You Like This Book...   303

Introduction

Over forty years ago, CSS Publishing Company was founded by two pastors and a Sunday school superintendent who had a vision to assist pastors "on the front lines" in their efforts to share the gospel of Jesus with people over the entire United States. The lectionary was taking hold over the country in an effort to bring a common message to people, no matter where they worshiped.

Over the years, CSS has published many different products. Of the more than 1,700 publications that have been produced in the history of the company, **Emphasis: A Lectionary Preaching Journal** has been one of the most popular. In its history, thousands of pastors and their congregations have benefited from the commentaries and insights found within its pages.

Navigating the Sermon is a collection of commentaries from "Charting the Course," which is at the core of what **Emphasis** is about. For each Sunday in the Cycle C lectionary, the writers who contributed to these columns have provided thematic guidance drawing together the lessons for each Sunday in the church year. Not only have they provided one idea for each Sunday, but most days have multiple themes from which to choose.

We are excited to offer this new resource to the readers of **Emphasis**, both old and new, and pray that this book will be a blessing to you and an invaluable aid to your preaching ministry.

The editors of CSS Publishing Company

Advent 1
Jeremiah 33:14-16
1 Thessalonians 3:9-13
Luke 21:25-36
David Kalas

While you wait

What is the relationship between waiting and probability?

If I am waiting for someone to meet me at a particular place and time, then my sense that he could walk through the door any minute increases as the appointed hour grows nearer. And, if he is not there on time, my expectation continues to grow for several minutes after the set time. "He really should be here by now," I say to myself. "I'm sure he will arrive any moment."

At some point, however, the line on the graph of my expectation turns downward. I daresay, for example, that if a person is more than an hour late for an appointment, my anticipation that he will walk through the door diminishes rather than increases with every passing minute. Eventually, I will assume that something must have happened. I conclude that he is not coming at all.

The first-century Christians eagerly awaited Christ's return. After all, the other major events — Jesus' birth, death, resurrection, ascension, and the coming of the Holy Spirit — had happened in such a relatively short period of time. Surely Jesus' return was imminent.

Some of Jesus' own teachings and promises encouraged the belief that he would return sooner rather than later. In our gospel lection for this Sunday, Jesus says that "this generation will not pass away until all things have taken place," which surely led his disciples to conclude that he would return during their lifetimes.

The genuine sense of expectation within the early church is further evidenced by their confusion about his delay. Paul had to address for the Thessalonians the unexpected theological conundrum of what happens to believers who die prior to Christ's return (1 Thessalonians 4:13ff). Peter had to explain that the Lord was not, in fact, slow to fulfill his promise (2 Peter 3:1ff).

Now so many years, generations, and centuries have come and gone. It may be that, for many twenty-first-century Christians, we are no longer looking at our watches and wondering why he isn't here yet. Perhaps the graph of our expectation has turned downward, and we secretly doubt that he is coming at all — at least during our lifetime.

Advent is the right season for us. It is a season of waiting for a "long-expected Jesus."

Jeremiah 33:14-16

"The days are surely coming, says the Lord." If the season of Advent had a motto, this would be it.

Life includes a certain amount of waiting. During Advent, we focus on a certain kind of waiting. Waiting that is deliberate, faithful, and hopeful. Waiting for what God has in store and waiting that is confident in his promises.

Waiting does not come easily for us, even in the best of circumstances. It is more difficult when the timing is unknown and it is hardest of all when we become discouraged: discouraged that the good thing for which we wait may never come.

The people of Jeremiah's day had good reason to be discouraged. By the time of our selected passage, many Jews were already in exile in far-off Babylon. Judah and Jerusalem had no remnants of their former glory. The king on David's and Solomon's throne was a weak puppet. The land had been ravaged. The temple and palace had been stripped bare — left in an alley sitting on blocks without hubcaps.

For all the devastation that had already occurred, the worst was still right around the corner. Like a neighborhood picking up the pieces from one tornado only to look up and see another one descending from a menacing sky, the Jews in Jerusalem were on the verge of seeing their city decimated, their king humiliated, and the temple destroyed.

In the midst of that, Jeremiah proclaims the Lord's assurance that days of safety, justice, peace, and righteousness are ahead. Just when David's line seems about to be cut off for good, God promises "a righteous branch." Just as Jerusalem faces unprecedented danger comes God's guarantee that "Jerusalem will live in safety."

Jerusalem living in safety doesn't happen in Jeremiah's day, though. Neither does it come in Nehemiah's day, nor in Jesus'. Not in our day, either, for that matter.

The temptation during Advent may be for us to adopt an "it's all good" posture. We understandably emphasize the promises fulfilled and the messianic hope realized. But we are challenged to consider honestly the promises that are not yet fulfilled — the divine checks that are still in the mail. The Jeremiah passage can help us do that.

God made his promises through Jeremiah in the midst of an era of divine judgment. That is not an inconsistency, a schizophrenia, in God. On the contrary, it is profound proof of his marvelous consistency. For in spite of his people's notorious wickedness, his will and his plan for them remains one of goodness, blessing, and peace.

Furthermore, inasmuch as we recognize the identity of the "righteous branch" who is the centerpiece of this prophecy, we see that God's promises are fundamentally about what God will do. His people have not done their part in his perfect plan but still he will do his part.

If our observance of Advent is only the artificial, anachronistic period of waiting for Jesus' birth, then we shortchange God, his word, and his people. For we, like the people of Jeremiah's day, are in a genuine period of waiting. It is a time of great turmoil in the world around us. It is an era when we can't deny that God's own people have failed him. Still, in the midst of that, we affirm the unchanging goodness of God's will and the certainty of his promises. And thus we wait with faith, hope, expectation, and confidence.

1 Thessalonians 3:9-13

The passage is an excerpt. Not just an excerpt from a letter, but an excerpt from a relationship.

That's true in a measure, of course, of any passage from any of the New Testament epistles. It is especially so here, though, for this passage is particularly personal.

Pastors and preachers know that there is nothing that seems quite so fragile and improbable as a brand-new convert. A baby Christian seems so unlikely to survive its first days in this fallen world. It is astonishing to consider, therefore, that that is essentially what Paul was leaving behind in virtually every city he evangelized. He did not have the luxury of entrusting one or two new Christians to an established congregation of mature saints. Rather, he so often left behind a brand-new congregation of brand-new believers. He could only entrust them to God himself.

So, when Timothy returned to Paul from Thessalonica with a good report (3:6, 8), Paul must have been profoundly encouraged and grateful. He expresses his gratitude to God (v. 9), as well as his passionate concern for them while he is separated from them (v. 10).

I have noticed in myself, as a parent, a strange bit of unintended theology. I am inclined to pray more fervently for the safety, protection, and welfare of my children when I am away from them. Perhaps that reflects — rightly or wrongly — an unstated assumption on my part that when I am there to take care of my children myself, God need not be so attentive.

In this passage, Paul shows a parental attitude toward the Thessalonian Christians. He is worried about them while he is absent, prays "most earnestly" about them, and is almost impatient to be back where he can take care of them himself. Through it all, though, Paul continues to entrust the Thessalonian believers to God.

Paul's ultimate prayer for his spiritual children is that God "would so strengthen your hearts in holiness that you may be blameless before our God and Father at the coming of our Lord Jesus with all his saints." Here we meet our Advent theme of Christ's coming. And here we get another angle on what is to take place in our lives while we wait.

Luke 21:25-36

In each of the three synoptic gospels, sayings and parables about the end-of-time pepper Jesus' final week in Jerusalem. In the gospel of Luke, our selected passage comes in the midst of a chapter devoted almost entirely to the eschaton. (In Matthew, the same passage appears in the midst of nearly two full chapters of teachings about the end.)

The end, according to Jesus, will be marked by signs. As suggested by the term given them, these events will be, literally, significant — that is to say, they will be important and informative.

The interesting thing about Jesus' brief fig tree parable to illustrate the signs is the issue of cause and effect. The leaves appearing on the fig tree are reckoned by Jesus as a sign that summer is near, just as the dramatic and cosmic signs he described may be understood as a sign that his coming is near. But note that the leaves on a fig tree are not the cause of summer's coming; rather, the cause-and-effect relationship works the other way around.

Can we draw the same conclusion about the second coming of Jesus? What is the cause-and-effect relationship between his return and the signs of his return? Can it be that his advent prompts the dramatic occurrences that are said to precede it? A great deal of wind and water batter the coastline before the eye of the hurricane actually hits land. Perhaps, too, Christ's coming is so potent that it is necessarily preceded by an entourage of cosmic and cataclysmic events.

If that is the case, then isn't it ironic that Jesus should have to warn his disciples to be careful, lest "that day catch you unexpectedly" (v. 34). How is it that such a day could catch us unexpectedly? What Jesus described was not like a supersonic jet — no warning that it's coming but just a massive boom when it arrives. No, this coming day will be preceded by all kinds of rumbling.

Still, many a person has chosen to ignore a symptom in his or her body. Denial, too-busyness, and a kind of anti-alarmist tendency can prompt an individual to dismiss a sign that something serious might be wrong. Christ's followers are challenged not to be so myopically preoccupied with the present that we miss the universe's symptoms.

Meanwhile, our text presents us with an interesting juxtaposition of things passing away and not passing away. The present generation, according to Jesus, would not pass away before "all things have taken place." Heaven and earth, by contrast, will pass away. Still, on the other hand, his words will not pass away. It is an unexpected redefinition of permanence and stability. Heaven and earth, which seem everlasting, will pass away. Indeed, the beginning of their end has already begun. Words — which don't seem to exist in reality beyond the moment they are spoken — the words of Jesus will endure forever.

Finally, as we consider verse 32, we must assume that Jesus was incorrect about "this generation," or that there is some meaning other than the plain meaning to "this generation" or "pass away," or that "all things have taken place." If it is the latter, then suddenly a great many folks are unemployed who have made a career out of reading the signs of the times. It also begs the question: If all things have already taken place, then why hasn't Christ returned yet?

Perhaps that is the question Peter answers in 2 Peter 3. Wouldn't it be ironic if, while we sat here thinking that we are waiting for him, it turns out that he is actually waiting for us?

Application

What do you do while you wait?

We do a fair amount of waiting during an average week. We wait in traffic. We wait on hold on the telephone. We wait in checkout lines. We wait for the server to take our order or bring our food. We wait for folks to respond — to our phone message, to our letter, to our email. We wait for things to download, to boot up, and to print.

And what do we do while we wait?

The proliferation of cell phones have made waiting easier for many of us. We feel we can at least get something done while waiting in traffic or in line. Many folks also turn waiting into an opportunity to check their calendars and lists of things to do. For years businesses have tried to improve our experience of waiting on hold by playing music, promoting products, and offering recorded assurances that our call is important to them and that the next available agent will be with us shortly.

The irony with most of what we do while we wait is that it usually has nothing to do with the thing we're waiting for. I may make some calls on my cell phone while waiting in traffic, but the calls don't alleviate the traffic or increase my speed. I may take a moment to look ahead on my calendar while waiting in the line at the grocery store, but my calendar does not assist my grocery shopping.

Have you ever waited in a grocery line behind people who seem unprepared when it's their turn to check out? They get to the front of the line and fumble for their wallet or coupons. They only then begin to fill out the check that could have been mostly completed during the wait.

That is the irony — the tragedy, really — of so many Christians in our present waiting. We are busy about many things while we wait, but so often the stuff we're doing has no relation to or impact on the thing we're waiting for. So, when that day comes, we stand a very good chance of being unprepared.

Being prepared is a central theme in Jesus' teachings about the end of time, and the first key to preparedness is to "be alert at all times" (21:36). Jesus identifies the commonplace things that threaten to dull and distract us so that we will not be alert. Hearts that are "weighed down" and "the worries of this life" — these are not extraordinary things. Quite the contrary, they conspire to blind us to what is extraordinary.

Perhaps the average parent often wishes that the child in the backseat would just go to sleep and stop asking, "Are we there yet? How much longer?" Our heavenly Father, on the other hand, may grieve the fact that so many of his children are asleep and seemingly disinterested in "how much longer."

The writer of Hebrews says that Jesus will return "to save those who are eagerly waiting for him" (Hebrews 9:28). I wonder if that might be a frighteningly small group. If he returns to save those who believe in him, then the raptured crowd will be much larger. But I'm afraid that "those who are eagerly waiting for him" is a small minority of the former group.

So we are presented with the challenge to wait eagerly. And just how eager we are will be determined and reflected by what we do while we wait.

An Alternative Application

Luke 21:25-36. In the 1988 movie *Rain Man*, one scene features Raymond, an autistic man who had lived most of his life in the protective environment of an institution, trying to cross a street at a busy intersection. He waits patiently for the sign to give him the cue to "Walk," but before he has reached the other side of the street the instruction changes to "Don't Walk." So Raymond stops, right there in the middle of the street.

There is much consternation and honking among the drivers who are being inconvenienced. Raymond, meanwhile, is confused and troubled, for he was only following directions. We recognize that "Don't Walk" is not to be taken literally when you've already begun to cross the street. But Raymond, in his innocence and inexperience, read the sign differently.

Jesus' teaching about the end of time in this passage suggests that his followers, too, might read signs differently than the rest of the world. Not traffic signs, but signs of the times.

Consider the signs predicted by Jesus. In our selected passage, as well as in the verses immediately preceding, it seems that the signs of the end times will be tumultuous developments, both in the world and in the cosmos. Any one of the several dramatic, and in some cases cataclysmic, events would be front-page stories. Any one of those signs would dominate the "news talk" on radio and television.

Jesus predicts the understandable reaction of the world to these kinds of signs. Nations will be confused and distressed. People will faint, filled with fear and dread.

What about Jesus' followers? Apparently they are expected to read and respond to the signs quite differently. "Stand up and raise your heads," Jesus says, "because your redemption is drawing near" (21:28).

While everyone else runs for cover, Jesus' disciples greet that day with gladness. While the rest of the neighborhood heads for shelter in their basements, Jesus' followers climb up on their roofs to welcome his return.

Of course, that distinction is not limited to the big day. The distinction between how Jesus' followers live and how the rest of the world around them lives should be apparent every day.

In this respect, Jesus' teachings about the end of time are natural extensions of his earlier ethical teachings about how to live in the meantime. For whether it is the big day or just another day, his followers respond differently. We respond differently than the world around us because we are responding to something different than the world is. While the fallen world lives in response to appetites and affections, to flesh, to money, and to ego, the followers of Jesus Christ live in constant response to him and that makes all the difference.

Advent 2
Malachi 3:1-4
Philippians 1:3-11
Luke 3:1-6
David Kalas

A man for one season

In 1967, the Academy Award for Best Picture was awarded to *A Man for All Seasons*, a movie based on the life of Sir Thomas More.

Perhaps we might preach a sermon this week with a variation on that title. It would be a sermon based on the life of John the Baptist. In contrast to Sir Thomas, John is a man for one season. He is a man for this season: Advent.

Advent doesn't get any attention outside the church and often it does not get much attention within the church. But Advent is the theme of these weeks, and John the Baptist is the person who exemplifies the season.

In truth, of course, Advent is a season that our broader culture observes and experiences but does not acknowledge. They call those weeks leading up to Christmas "the Christmas season." But inasmuch as those weeks are characterized by looking forward, counting down, and preparing, it truly is the Advent season.

On the church calendar, the Advent season is just over four weeks long. In our culture at large, the Advent season may be longer, for the Christmas displays and advertisements appear earlier and earlier. The longest Advent season, however, was the historical one: that is, the centuries of looking forward, waiting, and preparing that the people of God — indeed, the whole world — experienced prior to Christ's coming.

Advent is the season that comes before and John is the man who comes before. Advent is the season of looking forward to Christ's coming; John is the man who points forward to that coming. Advent is the season of preparation; John is the man who prepared the way.

In our Old Testament lection, Malachi anticipates the "messenger to prepare the way before" the Lord. In our gospel lection, John is introduced to us as that one who comes to prepare the way, as predicted by the prophet Isaiah. John is, therefore, the embodiment of Advent. He is the man for this season.

Malachi 3:1-4

I have in my mind an image of a relay race. As one runner approaches the end of his leg of the race, he reaches to hand the all-important baton to his successor. A successful transition at full speed can be the key to victory.

So it is when we come to the book of Malachi. The canon is coming to the end of its second leg: namely, the prophets, which had succeeded the law. And now, Malachi is the man who stretches out his message, reaching well beyond the confines of his own time, to hand off the pen to the New Testament writers. As it happens, of course, Matthew doesn't come along for nearly four centuries after Malachi's time. But the prophet's message manages to span the distance.

No sooner have we turned the page from Malachi to Matthew than we find this sense of continuity between prophecy and fulfillment. The messenger anticipated by Malachi — John the Baptist — is on the scene a few chapters into Matthew. Then there is the coming of the Lord himself.

Our people may be more or less well acquainted with the prophecies about Jesus. They may not be so familiar, however, with prophecies about John. The fact is that John the Baptist is a more important character in scripture — and in the work of God — than we generally recognize. Perhaps a Sunday in Advent would be an effective time to observe, for example, that the Christmas story does not appear in all four gospels, but John the Baptist does. Jesus himself makes this dramatic statement about John: "Truly I tell you, among those born of women no one has arisen greater than John the Baptist" (Matthew 11:11a).

As we consider this "man for one season," we may want to spend a few minutes acquainting our people with his unique role and importance, including his predicted coming here in Malachi.

The exact nature of the Lord's coming, meanwhile, is a matter of broad interpretation. We instinctively expect that the Christmas message of his coming will be marked by gentleness. Gentleness, to be sure, is a part of the story but it is not the whole story.

John the Baptist knew that the Lord's coming was not all peaches and cream. "I baptize you with water for repentance," he said, "but one who is more powerful than I is coming after me; I am not worthy to carry his sandals. He will baptize you with the Holy Spirit and fire. His winnowing fork is in his hand, and he will clear his threshing floor and will gather his wheat into the granary; but the chaff he will burn with unquenchable fire" (Matthew 3:11-12).

That message from John is consistent with the picture anticipated by Malachi. This prophet did not paint a picture of a baby in a manger. Rather, Malachi's portrait is of a man whose skin is dark with dirt and soaked with sweat from his labor. The muscles in his hands and forearms are taut and his face intense with concentration on the task at hand. He scrubs with abrasive soap. His face glistens from perspiration in the glow from the fire with which he works, handling silver in an intensely heated furnace. Who can endure the day of this one's coming? Surely no dirt and no dross will endure it.

Malachi's picture reminds us of the broader theme of "the day of the Lord." The prophets look for that day, which has the explicit virtue of being the day when the Lord comes to set things right. But in order to make things right, it is necessarily a day of conflict, judgment, and cleansing. The prophets portray the day as a dreadful one (see, for example, Isaiah 13:6-10; Joel 2:1-11; Amos 5:18-20; Malachi 4:1-6).

That picture of Jesus is perhaps best exemplified by his cleansing of the temple. He comes in and makes things right — violently and disruptively, he makes things right. Yet that does not seem to be the primary mission of his first coming. The New Testament writers also pick up the theme of "the day of the Lord," and they, too, see the dreadfulness of it (see, for example, 1 Thessalonians 5:2-3; 2 Peter 3:10-13). But it is a day yet to come (2 Thessalonians 2:1-4). It is mostly the province of Christ's second coming.

Finally, throughout his book, Malachi shows a particular interest in the temple and the priesthood. Not surprisingly, therefore, his anticipation of the Lord's coming has a kind of temple-centricity to it. The Lord "will suddenly come to his temple." A particular feature of his work will be to "purify the descendants of Levi," and the result of his work will be that they will "present offerings to the Lord in righteousness" and "the offering of Judah and Jerusalem will be pleasing to the Lord."

With the exception of a brief allusion in "Angels from the Realms of Glory" by James Montgomery ("suddenly the Lord, descending, in his temple shall appear"), such an emphasis is not typically part of our association with Advent or the coming of Jesus. We may have so accentuated the notion that Christ's coming did away with the need for temple, priests, and offerings that we neglect Malachi's expectation that the Lord will reform (rather than eliminate) these things.

Even so, the image remains a powerful and a helpful one. Inasmuch as the temple, priesthood, and offerings all represent the worship of God, we welcome the promise that the Lord will come to refresh the purity and renew the acceptability of those things. We are duly instructed by Malachi's emphasis on God coming to set right his own house and his own people. It is not the pagan, outside world that this refiner comes to purify; it is the temple and the Levites. As such, we are reminded of Peter's counsel to the persecuted Christians of his day: "For the time has come for judgment to begin with the household of God" (1 Peter 4:17a).

Philippians 1:3-11

We remember from our seminary studies that this section of Paul's epistle to the Philippians falls into a very definite category, a genre, for this is the "thanksgiving section" of the ancient epistle.

We have conventions in our letter writing, too, of course. The location of the return address, the salutation "Dear" that we use even with strangers, the variety of traditional closings that appropriately reflect the relationship between the sender and the recipient, and so on — these are all fairly standardized elements in letter writing in our culture.

Likewise, there were some standard conventions for the letters written in Paul's time and place. Following the greeting and preceding the body, there was commonly a thanksgiving section. Paul observes that convention in most of the letters we have from his hand, with the notable exception of his angry letter to the Galatians.

Paul gladly reports to the Philippians that he thanks God every time he remembers them. We have people like that in our lives: folks whose mere memory brings a smile to our face and joy to our heart. And given the tone of gratitude and joy that characterizes this letter — and this relationship — it's easy for us to imagine how precious and delightful to Paul the Philippians are.

Such memories and such relationships may be particularly important to Paul just now as he writes from prison.

Most of us, and most of our members, don't know what it is to sit in prison. But even a more common experience like a hospital stay can give us some insight into Paul's circumstance. We know that, sitting alone in a place we would rather not be, surrounded by some hazards, experiencing some pain, and haunted by some uncertainty, the visits, calls, and cards of dear friends are especially precious to us.

In confinement and isolation, it's a great blessing to know that you are not forgotten. Paul knew that the Philippians had not forgotten about him. They had responded to his work in the beginning, and they had shared in his work since. Now, even in prison, he had received support from them, both in the person of Epaphroditus and the gift that he brought. Paul is assured, therefore, that "you hold me in your heart."

The apostle's grateful reflections on what the Philippians have been lead him to think also of what they should be and shall become. Even in chains, one senses that Paul is always on the move. He is not a static guy. He is always pressing on toward the goal (Philippians 3:14). As surely as he keeps his goal in clear view in his own life, he cherishes a goal for his people as well. They have been and are marvelous, no doubt, but they have not yet fully arrived.

He prays for their completion: "That your love may overflow more and more with knowledge and full insight to help you to determine what is best, so that in the day of Christ you may be pure and blameless, having produced the harvest of righteousness that comes through Jesus Christ for the glory and praise of God."

I don't know what your experience is in your congregation, but in most churches I have attended and served, our prayers for one another do not rise to this level. We seem most inclined to be concerned about and to pray for one another's physical health. Then there are financial concerns. But Paul challenges us to aim so much higher: full insight, pure and blameless, and a harvest of righteousness.

Finally, Paul's confidence "that the one who began a good work among you will bring it to completion by the day of Jesus Christ" is reminiscent of the Malachi passage we explored earlier. Paul's image is of a perfecting process that has "the day" as its deadline, just as "the day of his coming" in Malachi will be characterized by a purifying and refining process.

Luke 3:1-6

When Luke introduces his gospel, he reports, "I too decided, after investigating everything carefully from the very first, to write an orderly account for you, most excellent Theophilus" (Luke 1:3). And the author lives up to his stated purpose here in this passage, for his storytelling is well-researched and well-organized.

Luke expertly sets the stage for us as he introduces us to John the Baptist. He places John for us on a time line in history: "In the fifteenth year of the reign of Emperor Tiberius." He further locates John geographically within that larger context of the Roman Empire, identifying the local potentates in the region of Palestine. Then Luke gives us a fix on John's location that is not merely a point on a time line or a map, but rather an environment, a distinctive setting: "in the wilderness." Next, Luke places John in the context of scripture, associating him with an Isaiah prophecy. And that, in turn, leads to the most important context of all: Luke locates John in the framework of God's will and plan — the voice in the wilderness, the one who prepares the way.

The movement from the beginning of the passage to the end is significant. At the outset, the camera is focused on the humans of earthly significance, but at the end, by contrast, our attention has been turned to a human of divine significance. The distance between the manicured Tiberius in the pillared courts of the seat of power, on the one hand, and the dusty prophet in the middle of nowhere, on the other, couldn't be greater. Yet, we know in retrospect that the actual importance, impact, and lasting significance of the two men belie their appearances and settings at the time.

Though Luke is not Jewish — indeed, he is probably the only Gentile writer in the entire Bible — he employs a traditional Old Testament image in introducing John. "The word of God came to John." This was the hallmark of the Old Testament prophets: that the word of the Lord came to them. And it was an image that bore witness to both the true source of prophecy, the initiative of God in communicating with his people, and the vitality and activity of the word.

That the word of God came to John "in the wilderness" is significant. The wilderness is the distinctive setting for John's ministry and it becomes a pivotal detail in how John is understood by the New Testament writers.

All four gospels employ at least the first verse of this Isaiah prophecy in reference to John the Baptist (Matthew 3:3; Mark 1:3; Luke 3:4-6; John 1:23), although Luke is the only one who sees a usefulness in quoting subsequent verses from that section of Isaiah. In the fourth gospel, "The voice of one crying out in the wilderness" is part of John's self-identification (1:23). Its ubiquitous gospel use in reference to John surely suggests that that is how the early church understood him.

In Francis Ford Coppola's 1974 movie, *The Conversation*, the plot turns on a slightly different hearing of a single line of conversation. The words are exactly the same each time, but the understanding of the inflection is just slightly different and it changes the meaning of the line dramatically.

A similar thing happens to one line of text from Isaiah.

The standard New Testament interpretation of the phrase from Isaiah is an interesting one since it differs from what is plainly understood to be the meaning of the phrase in its original context. The NRSV translates Isaiah 40:3: "A voice cries out: 'In the wilderness prepare the way of the Lord, make straight in the desert a highway for our God.'" But the New Testament usage of the same scripture is translated: "The voice of one crying out in the wilderness: 'Prepare the way of the Lord, make his paths straight.'"

For Isaiah, "in the wilderness" was where the way of the Lord was to be prepared. For the New Testament writers, "in the wilderness" was where the voice cried out. And with that slight variation in the understanding of a single phrase, the prophecy goes from an exilic-era anticipation of the captives' return to a foreshadowing of John the Baptist.

Application

We have identified John the Baptist as the man for this season. John is the embodiment of Advent. He is the one who comes before and he is the one who prepares the way.

Our particular concern this week might be just what those preparations look like.

We know all about pre-Christmas preparations. The decorations hung on the street lamps and telephone poles along Main Street, the lights and figurines adorning houses and yards around the neighborhood, the hanging of the greens at church, and the family's traditional ways of decorating the house back home. In addition to the decorating, there are the other preparations: the baking, the writing of Christmas cards, and all of the shopping.

Those are our familiar and sentimental ideas of Christmas preparations. They hardly match John's preparation for the Lord's coming. John "went into all the region around the Jordan, proclaiming a baptism of repentance for the forgiveness of sins."

Perhaps, amidst all of the festivity and busyness of the season, we might remind our people about the best and the most biblical Christmas preparation: "repentance for the forgiveness of sins."

An Alternative Application
Malachi 3:1-4. "Dreaming of a White Christmas." Our images of Christmas are largely tame ones. Chestnuts roasting and silver bells ringing. The peacefulness of Christmas Eve and the festivity of Christmas Day. The beauty of angels, the simplicity of Bethlehem, the humbleness of the stable, and the sweetness of a baby.

In the midst of all that loveliness, Malachi's note seems quite discordant. "Who can endure the day of his coming, and who can stand when he appears?" That's hardly the stuff of Bing Crosby and Nat King Cole.

Malachi is not picturing jolly snowmen or eight tiny reindeer. Rather, he anticipates who "will sit as a refiner and purifier of silver." The hero of Malachi's Christmas does not come with a sack full of presents; he comes with "a refiner's fire" and with "fuller's soap."

I believe that Malachi *was* dreaming of a white Christmas. Not merely some sentimental and fleeting snowfall, but a true cleansing by the one who comes to refine and purify. And, deep down inside, that is the kind of white Christmas we truly need and want.

Advent 3
Zephaniah 3:14-20
Philippians 4:4-7
Luke 3:7-18
Wayne Brouwer

Songs of joy

A colleague of mine once decried the way that people in his congregation wished to sing only Christmas songs during Advent. They had been so captured by the commercial culture that they no longer knew how to wait and wonder and wish and weep during Advent. My friend said that he refused to allow the singing of Christmas hymns or carols before the third Sunday of Advent.

Well, the third Sunday of Advent has arrived, and the Old Testament and epistle lectionary passages are indeed a call to sing — with joy, with gusto, with hope, with expectation and faith. The gospel reading also ends on a brief note of joy: The people, we are told, received John the Baptist's words as "good news." But there is a darker quality about the rest of that passage we will have to explore with care.

Nevertheless, today is a good day to sing and to sing with joy. Even as we wait in Advent expectation, we live in Easter hope and pentecostal promises. The Lord has come and the Lord will come again!

Zephaniah 3:14-20

When the Ayatollah Khomeini returned to power in Iran decades ago, one of his first decrees was to ban music from the airwaves. No music on the radio, none on television. "Music," he said, "makes the brain inactive."

It is no wonder that the Ayatollah was no friend to Christianity. Music grows naturally in the heart of the child of God. "Speak to one another with psalms, hymns, and spiritual songs," says the apostle Paul. "Sing and make music in your heart to the Lord" (Ephesians 5:19 NIV). The Old Testament heritage of faith is filled with the majestic splendor of choral celebration.

Today, we are invited to share in ancient Israel's prophetic song. Zephaniah, who lived in the tumultuous seventh century BC, felt the collapse of the political and economic systems and shouted loudly that the great and terrible day of the Lord was about to come (see ch. 1). Along with others of the prophets he knew that this "day" would bring three things: divine judgment on the evil of all nations, including Israel/Judah (see chs. 1-3); the sparing of a remnant of God's covenant people (see ch. 3); and the ushering in of the messianic age. This third element of prophetic insight is the key to today's lectionary reading from the prophet.

The words of Zephaniah's song would nurture the religious confidence of his countrymen who were about to be exiled to Babylon. They would find hope in a future beyond the destruction when their God would restore the national identity and prosperity. But Zephaniah's words have continuing promise for all who sing in New Testament eschatological expectation of the return of the once and coming messiah king.

As we sing our Advent carols it might be well to remember the judgment of American philosopher, George Santayana. "Music is essentially useless," he said, "as life is!" Perhaps that will remind us why music remains essential to the life of faith, and why Zephaniah couched his prophecies in poetic song. It is a sorry world that buys into Santayana's judgment. Think of Robert Ingersoll, who spent his life caustically denying God and defying God's power. After he died, the funeral invitations went out according to his instructions. They carried this pathetic line: "There will be no singing."

Tom Prideaux, then entertainment editor of *Life* magazine, once wrote about hearing Irving Berlin perform. A vast host of vocalists had sung Berlin's music over the years, but here was the great one bringing his own tunes to life as no other could. "It wasn't a man singing a song," said Prideaux. "It was a man singing his autobiography!"

That is true of Zephaniah and it is just as true of Christians who are fighting their way to Christmas. A friend once asked Franz Joseph Haydn why his church music was always so full of gladness. "I cannot make it otherwise," he replied. "I write according to the thoughts I feel. When I think upon my God, my heart is so full of joy that the notes dance and leap from my pen!"

In one congregation I served, a young woman used to come with her friends. She was a nursing student, full of zest, the life of every party, but she was bored at our worship services. She would settle in at the edge of the bench and yawn through the whole message. When everybody stood to sing, she'd stand and look around, just waiting for it all to be finished.

One Sunday when we started singing, she literally beamed! Her face shone as she made music more energetically than anyone else. "What happened, Chris?" I asked. "You're different today!"

Quickly, she told me about her family. Her parents had been divorced years before. Afterward things remained bad between her mom and dad. They hurt each other a lot and never forgave each other.

Then her dad got cancer. He had died the week before. Chris and her mom flew out to see him just before the end. He told them he had become a Christian. He said he was sorry for all the grief he had put them through and asked for forgiveness. When they started to cry together, suddenly it all made sense to Chris. That's why she was singing that Sunday. Jesus touched her father's life, and now Chris knew his love too.

"On that day," wrote Zephaniah, and then he announced the theme of the songs the redeemed people of God would sing. Those who know both the judgment tragedy and the eschatological expectation of the Day of the Lord worship well during Advent.

Philippians 4:4-7

Philippians is one of Paul's "prison epistles," sent out during the two years Paul waited in Rome under house arrest until he could gain an audience with the emperor (see Acts 28). While the other prison epistles — Ephesians, Colossians, and Philemon — appear to have been sent out in a single group (having common themes and identical delivery personnel), Philippians is unique. More often than not it is referred to as the "epistle of joy," and today's lectionary reading is a case in point. Paul fairly jumps with delight and sends an infectious word to the church whose strange and wonderful origins are spelled out in Acts 16. "Rejoice!" Paul shouts several times. Certainly we, who anticipate and celebrate the coming of the Messiah, should respond well to his coaching. This is especially true because, as Paul notes, "The Lord is near!"

An ancient story tells of an extremely wealthy king who ruled a vast domain from magnificent palaces. He had the respect of his citizens and peace within his borders. But for some perplexing reason he was very unhappy. The king's doctors could find no medical problem. Neither could psychiatrists figure it out. Finally, one old, wise man, an advisor to the king's late father, had this advice: "There is but a single cure for the king. Your majesty must sleep one night in the shirt of a happy man!"

Strange advice, to be sure! But the desperate king needed only a hint of finding release from his malady to command that the search begin. His messengers scoured the land, looking for one truly happy person. The messengers could find no one. Not one happy person! Everyone had experienced days of sorrow and times of mourning. Many could laugh for a moment but sooner or later each person would settle back to reflect on the pain in his or her life.

Finally, the messengers happened upon a beggar next to the road leading back to the palace. He wore a smile. He giggled uncontrollably. He laughed at life as it surrounded him. Here was a truly happy man! "Give us your shirt," the messengers demanded. "The king has need of it!"

That only caused the fellow to double over with spasms of hilarity. "I'm sorry!" he gasped, between fits of laughter. "You see, I have no shirt."

Paul knows that we need more than just the shirt of another person in order to find joy. Our language has a number of similar words that relate to good feelings inside. *Pleasure*, for instance, reflects our delighted response to sensations that stimulate us. *Happiness* surrounds us because of certain happenings in our lives. And then there's *joy*.

In a sense, *pleasure* is an "it" word; it mostly has to do with *things* that touch our senses. And *happiness* is a "me" word; its primary focus is *my* response to events that come and go in my life. But *joy* is really a "we" word; it usually reflects what happens between people, between me and you, between me and God.

Joy starts in the heart. It's a relational word. Robert Rainy, one-time head of New College in Edinburgh, Scotland, used to say, "Joy is the flag that is flown from the castle of the heart when the king is in residence there!" Paul would agree.

If joy starts in the heart, it is refined in the mind. It is more than an emotion that comes and goes. It is deeper than a reflexive response that needs the right kind of stimulation. It is an act of the will. "Rejoice *in the Lord*!" commands Paul. Joy grows from heartfelt relationships.

But it is also a choice of the mind. In 1769, Alexander Cruden, who was one of the most meticulous Bible students of his day, wrote: "To laugh is to be merry in a sinful manner." John Wesley was more on track with Paul's injunctions when he said, "Sour godliness is the devil's religion." Such an attitude doesn't belong in a heart responsive to God's love. It has no place in a mind that hears Paul's command.

One Sunday, a woman came to our church for the very first time. She had never been to a Christian worship service before in her life. What struck her most? "You sing so much!" she said.

Exactly!

Luke 3:7-18

There is a strange irony in today's gospel lesson. It ends with the phrase: "And with many other words John exhorted the people and preached the good news to them." Yet, most of the words Luke reports to us from John's preaching hardly sound like "good news." John seems to rant in anger. John is judgmental. John accuses and is caustic. He uses threats to cajole religious devotion out of these folks. We do not sit well with John, particularly this close to Christmas.

Sometimes people put this sticker on the bumpers of their cars: "I don't get mad; I get even!" If a big, burly fellow with a grim-looking face says something like that, we don't challenge whether he really means it. A man who had tipped the bottle a few times before jumping in his car followed me into a parking lot one day and stumbled out with a string of curses about someone cutting him off. He was not a man to be reasoned with. He spoke threats very colorfully. I didn't doubt that he could act on them.

When John uses similar tones in voicing the divine message, we who listen get queasy. Psychologists say threats aren't the best motivation technique. Company supervisors who intimidate their workers don't draw out the full potential of employees' skills or energy. Instead, they tend to create an atmosphere of hostility and resentment. They breed factions and bitterness, the kind of thing the apostle Paul calls "the works of the flesh" in Galatians 5:19.

Threats usually challenge us to become more defiant. When King Philip II of ancient Macedonia couldn't win a diplomatic alliance with Sparta, he sent this note: "You are advised to submit without further delay, for if I bring my army into your land, I will destroy your farms, slay your people, and raze your city."

The Spartans weren't easily threatened. They sent back a single word in reply: "If!" And Philip decided to back down.

If threats have any legitimate place in our communication, it may be in an emergency. Once, when George Frideric Handel had trouble getting a rather temperamental soprano to sing a piece as he had written it, he picked her up, carried her over to an open window, and threatened to throw her out unless she did as she was told. It worked. She sang beautifully!

John's preaching is something like that for us. God is love. God's wish for us is life and peace and joy. In fact, God's goodness is our primary understanding of what this Advent season is about. After all, Jesus himself says, "I have come that they may have life, and have it to the full" (John 10:10 NIV). But sometimes we're too blind or ignorant or willful or stupid to know that. Sometimes we're lost in the quick fixes of our drugs or schemes or ladders to success. Sometimes we're drunk with an inflated sense of our own self- importance. And then John's words to us are a shocking threat that we desperately need. They demand attention. They force us to reevaluate where we're at and what we're doing. If it takes those words to keep me from committing spiritual suicide, maybe they will be the only expression of love I will be able to hear at the time. Perhaps that is why, to the people in John's day, waiting almost in despair for Messiah to come, these were words of "good news."

Application

There is a profound illustration of the meaning found in all three lectionary passages in Marcelle Maurtette's 1954 play, *Anastasia*. It was based on the true story of a woman named Anna Anderson who claimed to be the long-lost daughter of the last emperor of Russia, Czar Nicholas II, and his wife, Aleksandra. During the Revolution, the royal family was held hostage in the palace and then executed as the Bolsheviks bathed the countryside with blood.

Rumors persisted that little Anastasia, the youngest of the Romanovs, somehow survived. Enter Anna — a nameless, homeless, memoryless wanderer, prone to suicidal fits at the "insane asylum" where she was brought. Nobody knew where she came from. They gave her the name Anna because she had none of her own.

One day, Anna's doctor came across a picture of the last Russian royal family. Anna bore a striking resemblance to little Anastasia, and she seemed to know more about the Russian noble house than one would expect. When hypnotized, her subconscious knew even more.

Newspapers picked up the story. Was this really Anastasia? By some miracle was her life spared, only to be thrown into this new and dismal tragedy? Or is she only a hoax, a scoundrel, a publicity-seeker? The controversy sold millions of papers and so the press hyped it to the limit.

The old empress, mother of Nikolas, had not been in Russia at the time of the murders and now lived in exile. She, if anyone, should know whether Anna was truly her granddaughter. The two women talked for a long time. Then the elderly woman told the world: "Anna is my granddaughter Anastasia!"

Suddenly Anna began to change. She blossomed as a person. She took hold of her life. The suicide threats were gone. She washed herself and combed her hair. She looked after herself and dressed in style. She stood up straight in a crowd and carried herself with dignity when walking.

The rumors followed her for the rest of her life. The courts in West Germany debated the issue of her identity for years. But Anna — Anastasia — had a new lease on life. She started over. She learned to live again. She left the past behind and found herself with a future.

One line in the play carries the heart of the story. How did Anna climb from the pit of her insane asylum and walk again in the land of the living? What transformed Anna the nobody into Anastasia the princess? This is her secret: "You must understand that it never mattered whether or not I was a princess. It only matters that... someone, if it be only one, has held out their arms to welcome me back from death!"

Someone gave her a new identity. Someone gave her a reason to live. Someone gave her a vision and a purpose and a hope and a goal. In the unsettling and changing and tumultuous wanderings of her existence, someone gave her something to live for.

That is the secret of joy and renewal we preach on this Advent Sunday. Surrounded by the ominous and glittering powers of our age, each of us warty toads becomes a handsome prince or princess in the choir of the coming king!

An Alternative Application
Luke 3:7-18. While it is not the easiest to preach, the dark message of John in Luke's gospel may well be most needed in today's consumerist culture. The idea of a threat could be couched in terms that bring a smile before punching home. For instance, Henry Camille was a feisty, pint-size professional hockey star of the 1950s. During one ice battle, he lost his temper and lashed out at a big, tough defenseman named Fernie Flaman, who was feared for the cruelty of his fists. As they pounded each other, the outmatched Henry yelled up at his opponent: "Watch out, Fernie, or I'll bleed all over you!" They both sank to the ice, laughing.

It might be possible to talk about the threats issued by God through the voice of John and use them to call out a religious revival that would make Christmas celebrations this year more meaningful. God did, in fact, come to us in Jesus to "bleed all over us" until we could enjoy the laughter of salvation.

Advent 4
Micah 5:2-5a
Hebrews 10:5-10
Luke 1:39-45 (46-55)
David Kalas

The Christmas visitor

If some visitor from another part of the universe came to earth during the Christmas season, I wonder what he would make of our holiday. I can't speak for other parts of the world, but I daresay that in most North American cities he would receive mixed messages about the exact nature of our celebration.

How would he put together the pieces of our Christmas puzzle? A jigsaw puzzle that includes pieces ranging from a baby in a manger to a red-nosed reindeer; from a stingy Scrooge to a grouchy Grinch; from a bearded, heavyset man bearing gifts down chimneys to an animated snowman.

How would the alien decipher the relationship between the three great sites of Christmas: Bethlehem, the North Pole, and the shopping mall?

What kind of riddle would our Christmas songs present to a stranger? He'd hear us sing the glories of a newborn king, the sentimentality of a white Christmas, the achievements of Frosty, the merits of Rudolph, and the surprise of seeing mama kissing Santa Claus.

How might our visitor from another world reconcile the angels with the elves? The three wise men with the three French hens? The poor baby in a barn with the middle-class shoppers in the mall?

As it happens, our celebration is precisely about a visitor to earth at Christmastime. But the growing numbers of unchurched in our communities are receiving mixed messages about the exact nature and meaning of this season of the year.

It is expressly our business to tell them all about it.

Micah 5:2-5a

Tucked away in the midst of a book from an Old Testament prophet who doesn't get as much attention as some others, this might easily have been an unfamiliar passage. As soon as the chief priests and scribes highlighted this passage for the visitors from the East in the days of Herod the Great, however, it became a passage of special importance.

We are sentimental about the "little town of Bethlehem," and we recognize the messianic fulfillment of this prophecy. In Micah's day, however, it may have seemed an odd, even disturbing, prediction.

Judah at this time was ruled by a monarchy. Specifically, Micah's prophetic ministry took place during the reigns of three kings of Judah: Jotham, Ahaz, and Hezekiah (Micah 1:1). Hezekiah was the son of Ahaz, and Ahaz was the son of Jotham. Likewise, Jotham had succeeded his father on the throne, just as his father had succeeded his father before him. They were all descendants of David — it was a dynastic line.

Micah's prediction that a ruler would come from Bethlehem, therefore, was a provocative one. Ever since David established Jerusalem as the capital of Israel (and later Judah), that was where each new ruler was born. Each new ruler was expected to be the son of his father, who was king in Jerusalem. The very promise of a ruler coming out of Bethlehem, therefore, suggests some disruption. Would the royal line be broken? Why wouldn't this new ruler come out of the palace in Jerusalem?

Micah's prophecy must have seemed anachronistic, at best. Israel's greatest ruler had, indeed, come from Bethlehem. That was David's hometown. But ever since David's time, the future kings had been born in Jerusalem.

A great many disruptions did occur in the seven centuries between Micah's prophecy and Christ's birth. The Assyrians had ravaged the land. The Babylonians had taken their booty and their captives. Alexander the Great had come and gone, along with his successors. The Jews had enjoyed a brief period of independence during the days of the Hasmoneans. But now, 700-plus years since the days of Micah, Judah was no longer ruled by a monarch descended from David. Rather, Judah was occupied by Rome and ruled by an Edomite (or Idumean), Herod the Great.

In the light of the events between the time of Micah and the time of Herod, this prophecy suggested another disruption: this time, it suggested a disruption in Judah's favor, and a disruption Herod feared. The advent of this new and eternal ruler from Bethlehem — the city of David — spelled the beginning of the fulfillment of God's special plans for his people and for the whole world.

Hebrews 10:5-10

This is the season when we recall Christ coming into the world. Our recollection and celebration tend to be all about the incarnation (that is, the Christmas event). This passage from Hebrews, however, takes a different tack. "When Christ came into the world, he said, 'Sacrifices and offerings you have not desired....' " That won't sound like part of the Christmas story to most of the people in our pews.

In the Old Testament lection for this Sunday, we are reminded that Christ's birth fulfilled Micah's prophecy concerning Bethlehem. And that is a familiar part of the Christmas story and celebration. The writer of Hebrews reminds us, though, that Christ's coming also fulfilled other prophecies (specifically, in this case, Psalm 40:6-8).

Hebrews' hermeneutic may be unfamiliar to the people in our pews. We are perhaps more accustomed to Old Testament prophecies that are plainly and deliberately predictive. When Isaiah, for example, says that a girl will conceive, give birth, and name her child Emmanuel (Isaiah 7:14), we easily recognize that as a prophecy. Or when Micah declares that a ruler will come forth from Bethlehem, that too has the traditional sound of a prophecy. But the writer of Hebrews is taking the words of the psalmist from a thousand years BC and putting them in the mouth of Jesus. That may be a different use of scripture and a different understanding of prophecy than is familiar to us.

Perhaps the crux of the matter is this: Does a statement have to be a prediction in order for it to be fulfilled? Can a statement that does not consciously anticipate a future event somehow still be fulfilled by a future event? The early church clearly thought so, for they saw Christ all through the Old Testament, even in places, people, and statements that do not overtly look ahead.

In this case, as is the case for so much of the epistle, the writer of Hebrews uses an Old Testament passage to shed light on the cross of Christ.

During this quintessentially New Testament event — Christmas — the flesh-and-blood details of the Old Testament law's animal sacrifices seem far away and irrelevant. Yet the writer of Hebrews intrudes into our nativity scene and points back to the old, bloody altar in the tabernacle.

During the innocence, sweetness, and sentimentality of Christmas, Good Friday seems like a long way away. Yet the writer of Hebrews interrupts the happy, harmless scene and points ahead to the old, bloody cross.

It seems almost ghoulish to gaze at a newborn baby and give thought to how that baby will one day die. Of course, that is very much the spirit of Simeon's sober warning to Mary (2:34-35). It may be implicit in the gift of myrrh and it strikes at the heart of the gospel message. Not every gospel writer tells about Jesus' birth, but every gospel writer tells at length about Jesus' death.

In our proclamation of Christ's coming into the world, we mustn't neglect the reason that he came. "Christ Jesus came into the world to save sinners" (1 Timothy 1:15) and that by means of the sacrificial, atoning death described in our Hebrews passage.

Luke 1:39-45 (46-55)

Luke's gospel is well-known for its attention to women and children. Luke seems to recognize characters and players in the story that the other gospel writers miss or ignore. This passage is a lovely example of a scene we only do — only could — find in Luke: an episode with no men involved; just a friendly meeting of two women.

At the surface, it seems a very ordinary event: one woman visiting an out-of-town friend and relative and the two sharing the mutual joy of their pregnancies. In fact, however, the event is quite extraordinary, for the babies they carry together represent the inauguration of the coming kingdom of God.

Elizabeth was well along in her pregnancy when Mary came to visit and so her baby's movements were unmistakable. And when Elizabeth's baby heard Mary's voice, Elizabeth clearly sensed his reaction. The scene becomes marvelously celebrative, as the infant John leaps, Elizabeth gives voice to his joy with her exclamation, and Mary breaks into a song of praise.

How different was this scene from the one Mary left behind in Nazareth? One can only imagine that this happy greeting — and this recognition of the child she carried — was a refreshing change from the understandable skepticism of the folks back home. How much murmuring and finger-pointing had Mary begun to endure back in Nazareth? How much speculation? How much condemnation?

We may get a sense for Mary's experience in Nazareth when Luke writes that "she set out with haste." We might also surmise that she went to Elizabeth as perhaps the only person Mary knew who would naturally understand a miraculous pregnancy. And we may get a sense for what a refreshing change Elizabeth's response was for Mary when we read Mary's ebullient reaction. Note that she had not responded with such enthusiasm a few verses earlier in the event we call the Annunciation (1:26-38). Her response to the angel is brave and obedient but not enthusiastic.

As I consider Elizabeth's emotional importance to Mary, I am reminded of Paul and Barnabas. Immediately following his conversion, Paul remained an object of scorn and suspicion among the early Christians. How much finger-pointing and speculating did he suffer? And how refreshing to have Barnabas step forward to recognize and believe what God had done in Paul's life, and to welcome him in.

Elizabeth (and her baby!) believed and confirmed what God was doing in Mary's life and in Mary's body. She was Mary's Barnabas, Mary's "son of encouragement."

Application

There are other new and interesting directions a preacher might go with the selected passages for this Sunday. Still, as our people come to church on this Sunday before Christmas, surely our primary calling must be to declare the person and work of Christ. Who he is and what he did are central to all three of this week's lections.

The three selected passages set side by side might be treated as separate eyewitnesses, each giving a description to a police sketch artist. Would the three resulting sketches look like the same person?

Micah describes a king whose strong reign is marked by peace and security. Hebrews, by contrast, shows a person whose body is offered as a sacrifice. And Elizabeth's testimony in Luke ("the mother of my Lord") confirms the angel's word to Mary that the baby she carries is God himself.

The pictures seem quite different, yet they all bear witness to the same person and therein lies some of the beauty of the gospel.

The classic Epiphany hymn, "We Three Kings," captures the multifaceted truth nicely. After offering a poetic explication of each of the three gifts, the hymn summarizes the person and work of Christ as "king and God and sacrifice." This is the combined testimony of the three scriptural witnesses we have before us this week. And this is the marvelous visitor to our world whom we celebrate at Christmastime. Our world still needs to hear the whole truth about him proclaimed clearly by you and me.

Alternative Applications
Micah 5:2-5a; Luke 1:39-45 (46-55). Matthew's gospel records the arrival of the Magi in Jerusalem (Matthew 2:1-8). They had followed the star for so many miles, all the way from their far-off homes in the East. When they arrived in Jerusalem, however, their pilgrimage hit a snag. Where was the one born to be king of the Jews?

Bethlehem is just a few miles from Jerusalem. The wise men were very near their destination, but they weren't quite there yet. Was the star an imprecise guide and is that why they came up short of the actual place where Christ was? Or was it their own preconceived notions that prompted them to stop in Jerusalem — after all, the capital and throne of the present king (Herod the Great) were in Jerusalem and so surely that must be the place where the new king of the Jews would be born.

Whatever the reason, the wise men, with their mixture of science and astrology, had gotten most of the way to Christ but they had not found him yet.

Once in Jerusalem, making their provocative inquiries, the wise men were brought before Herod and his court. They asked where the baby was who was born to be king of the Jews. Herod shows a startling understanding of what is going on, asking the chief priests and scribes where the Messiah was to be born. In response, they cite the Micah passage and that bit of guidance is just enough to complete the quest of the Magi.

It is a significant point for us as preachers that these men, who enjoyed guidance that was either divine or scientific or both, still needed scripture and other people in order to find Christ.

Moreover, the Micah passage (with its Magi usage) and the Luke passage combine to illustrate again the poignant reality of how much we human beings need one another in our relationships with God. Mary had heard God's plans for her directly from an angel, but her response to the angel was rather muted in comparison to the song she burst into at Elizabeth's house. How essential it was for her to have that flesh-and-blood confirmation of God's plan for her. And, likewise, the Magi had come so far on their own, but they could not complete their journey without the aid of those anonymous Bible experts in Jerusalem.

From the Garden of Eden where it was not good for Adam to be alone, to Jesus' promises for two or three gathered in his name, to our own experience of nurture and fellowship, the lovely reality is that we need other human beings. Even in what seems to be the exclusively vertical relationship we have with God, still we need the horizontal relationships with other people. They introduce us to him, they teach us about him, they inform our understanding of his will, and they share our journey with him. The Magi needed the scribes, Mary needed Elizabeth, and we need one another.

Luke 1:39-45 (46-55). A brief reference in Luke's account of Mary's encounter with Elizabeth reminds us of the most forgotten and overlooked character in the Christmas story. He does not appear in our nativity scenes or our Christmas pageants. In preaching the Christmas story year after year, we consider, examine, and imagine every other player in the Christmas event. Songwriters, preachers, and the authors of children's books have even given lengthy consideration to the animals that may have been part of the Christmas story. Meanwhile, one of the most important persons in the Christmas story remains largely neglected: the Holy Spirit.

Elizabeth is filled with the Holy Spirit (1:41) when Mary came to visit and that prompted her critically important proclamation about Mary and her child. Later, Elizabeth's husband, Zechariah, is filled with the Holy Spirit (1:67), and he spoke of God's plan and the role of his newborn son. Later still, Simeon is led by the Spirit (2:25, 27) to the Christ Child, and he, too, makes a proclamation about God's salvation.

Most important of all, it is the Holy Spirit who makes Christmas happen (see 1:35). The angel explains it to Mary, and we affirm it each time we recite the Apostles' Creed ("conceived by the Holy Spirit").

Luke makes a point of including the Holy Spirit in his telling of the Christmas story and so should we.

Luke 1:39-45 (46-55). The Christmas event opened to mixed reviews. Matthew reports that Joseph had early misgivings. We see that Mary, too, was at least perplexed, if not worse. The shepherds' initial reaction was fright. And Herod was tragically violent in his response.

On the other hand, of course, there was the adoration of the Magi, the eventual joy of the shepherds, and the delight of Simeon and Anna.

However, the first person to recognize Jesus with rejoicing was John the Baptist. While others in the audience looked about nervously, John was the first to applaud. Others took a while to warm up to the good news, but John recognized it immediately.

The sage observation is that we do not judge truly great art; it judges us. If I say that I am not impressed by a masterpiece, that is not a reflection on the art; it is a reflection on me. So it is that John's *in utero* reaction to Jesus tells us something not only about Jesus, but it tells us also something about John.

We come to discover later in the gospel accounts the importance of John. Indeed, his significance may be indicated in part by the fact that all four gospel writers include him in their story (though not all four tell about Christmas). Still, his strange role in Luke's Christmas story makes him a kind of example for us.

Herod stands for those in every generation who outright oppose Jesus. His scribes represent those religious folks who manage to know about Jesus and yet remain essentially indifferent to him. And Joseph's early reaction reminds us of the people whose first instinct is to calculate the embarrassment and inconvenience Jesus will cause. But John is the exemplary one — the Christmas hero — who, upon hearing, "leaped for joy." May his example be our pattern, both at Christmas and throughout our lives.

Christmas Eve / Day
Isaiah 9:2-7
Titus 2:11-14
Luke 2:1-14 (15-20)
Timothy Cargal

Night of light

One of the great cultural traditions of modern American Christmas observance is the use of lights. Everything that doesn't move is decorated with lights. Christmas trees are recognizable by their lights, and indeed as more and more types of trees are used as Christmas trees, the more it is the presence of the lights that identifies them as such. Lights are put around lampposts. We hang lights from the eaves and awnings of our homes and around windows and doorframes. Lighted fixtures and images are arrayed in front yards, and those that are not self-lighted are bathed in spotlights. Without a moment's embarrassment at the brazen self-interest, electrical power companies promote contests for the best and most elaborate seasonal displays. Terms like "Sparkle Christmas" are entering the vocabulary of some regions, and almost everyone would recognize "the Season of Light" as a non-sectarian — indeed secular — term for Christmas time.

The tremendous irony of calling Christmastide "the Season of Light," at least in the northern hemisphere, is that it is of course the darkest time of the year. Shifts and adjustments in the western calendar system have only slightly obscured the fact that Christmas Day originally coincided with the date of the winter solstice, the date with the longest period between sunset and sunrise in the entire year. It seems more than likely that one reason that we so eagerly embrace all this use of artificially generated light for a celebration during this particular season of the year for us is in order to deal with the depression in energy and often in mood that accompanies the shortening of daylight hours.

Yes, the association between light and Christmas is tremendously ironic when considered in the context of the calendar in the northern hemisphere. But the Old Testament and the gospel lessons appointed for Christmas Eve emphasize an important spiritual reason for the association of Christmas, light, and the deepest of darkness. It was precisely because of the tremendous darkness that the light of Christ needed to shine into the world. Even though it is impossible to know the time of year at which Jesus of Nazareth was actually born, from a spiritual perspective, nothing could better capture the significance of the time of Christ's birth than to call it "the Night of Light."

Isaiah 9:2-7

This oracle attributed to Isaiah of Jerusalem was not originally a prophecy at all, at least not in the sense that we typically now use the word "prophecy." That is to say, Isaiah did not compose this poem in order to predict long distant events (the birth of Jesus lay some seven centuries in the future) or even for that matter to predict events in the much shorter term of his own lifetime. Rather, this oracle is properly a celebration of the coronation of a new Judean king. Given Isaiah's close relationship with the Davidic house during the reign of four such kings (Uzziah [6:1], Jotham, Ahaz, and Hezekiah), it is difficult to know which king is being celebrated. Clearly the Book of Isaiah and the relevant portions of 2 Kings indicate Isaiah was most supportive of Hezekiah, and so he would be the most likely candidate. But given the general nature of the references to the Davidic house within the oracle (see especially v. 9), certainty is impossible.

If Isaiah was most likely writing about Hezekiah in this oracle, why do Matthew (see Matthew 4:12-17) and later Christian tradition associate it with Jesus? The answer to that question lies in a proper understanding of how Matthew and his contemporaries understood the relationship between ancient prophecies and their own time. First, Matthew would have been the first to admit that Isaiah's words did not refer exclusively to Jesus. Isaiah spoke God's word to his own contemporaries and did so to help them understand what was happening in their own lives and not what would happen centuries later. But Matthew would also have argued that Isaiah's oracle was just as helpful to people of the first century in understanding what God was doing in their own time through Jesus. For Matthew, the oracle did not refer either to Hezekiah or to Jesus; it referred to both Hezekiah and to Jesus. What God had done for God's people in the eighth century BC, God was now doing again (in a deeper and fuller way, Matthew would no doubt have argued) for God's people in the first century AD. The same pattern of interpreting prophetic oracles can be found in the pesher commentaries from Qumran.

One clear indication that Matthew indeed took the original context of Isaiah's oracle very seriously (and in some ways more so than later Christian writers who began the association of this oracle with the circumstances of Jesus' birth) lies in where he places the "fulfillment" of the oracle in Jesus' life. Although the oracle specifically refers to a birth ("a child has been born for us, a son given to us," v. 6), Matthew said that the oracle's relevance to Jesus was fulfilled not at his birth but at the beginning of his ministry (see again Matthew 4:12-17). Thus, just as Isaiah's oracle was originally associated with a king's coronation and the beginning of his reign, Matthew associates it with the beginning of Jesus' reign through his ministry.

The historical setting and background to this celebration of the coronation of a southern, Judean king is the fall of the northern Israelite kingdom to the Assyrian empire. The imagery of "deep darkness" (v. 2) is then used to express their desperation and hopelessness. That they have "seen a great light" that has shined upon them is that they have witnessed the survival and continuation of the Davidic dynasty despite the subjugation of their own homeland. Isaiah's hope and expectation was that these members of the northern tribes would see in this God's faithfulness to the covenant with David and all the Israelites more generally. He also apparently hoped that Judah would be able to roll back the Assyrian hegemony over the region and bring it back under Davidic rule (see especially vv. 4-5), but alas, despite Judah's continued existence for another century (until its own subjugation to Babylon), it was never able to reincorporate the northern tribal areas into a reunited kingdom. That harsh reality became itself a reason why latter Jews would look for a fuller and more complete "fulfillment" in a future messianic figure.

As already noted, the reference to the child's birth in verse 6 does not indicate the actual occasion for the writing of the oracle. Following a standard practice of Hebrew poetry, there is a synonymous parallelism between "a child has been born for us" and "a son given to us," and here it is the second line that has the primary emphasis. The sense is essentially that at the moment of the king's coronation, the people look back upon his birth as a time of special blessing.

The more modern translations have properly recognized the pairing of qualifiers with each title and so corrected the translation of the old and still quite familiar King James Version. Thus, the king is "Wonderful Counselor, Mighty God, Everlasting Father, Prince of Peace." If it should be objected that some of these titles are not appropriate to a purely human regent, then the objection is to be answered by noting their original context. The king is "mighty God" not because he is himself divine, but because he was thought of as God's earthly co-regent over the people. He is "everlasting Father" because he is the latest heir to the everlasting covenant with David regarding the right to rule over God's people. The imposition of later Trinitarian concepts to these terms is not so much wrong as applied to fulfillment in Christ (as explained above) as it is anachronistic as applied to the Judean king about whom the oracle was originally composed.

To summarize, the point is not that this oracle is only improperly applied to Jesus as opposed to say Hezekiah. Rather it is to stress that properly understanding its relation to Hezekiah is key to understanding its application to Jesus. The evangelists and others are telling us that what God had said in the past is an important lens for understanding what God has done in Christ. But if that lens is to provide clarity rather than distortion, then we must understand its original context rather than imposing on it our yet later ideas about Jesus Christ.

Titus 2:11-14

One of the great values of the epistle lesson assigned by the lectionary for Christmas Eve is that it reminds us that this night stands as the threshold between Advent and Christmastide. As more and more congregations adopt the practice of only Christmas Eve services rather than both Eve and Christmas Day services (Christmas morning being considered first and foremost "family time"), the Christmas Eve service is having all the liturgical functions of Christmas Day foisted upon it. Whatever one's feelings about that development, it is good to be reminded that Christmas Eve is also about the final preparations to make ourselves ready for Christ's advent.

Those preparations are in this passage understood primarily in terms of repentance. Even as we recognize that "the grace of God has appeared, bringing salvation to all" (v. 11), the lesson we are to draw from that grace is that we need to "renounce impiety and worldly passions, and... to live lives that are self-controlled, upright. and godly, while we wait for the blessed hope and manifestation of the glory of our great God and Savior, Jesus Christ" (vv. 12-13). The stance taken in this text is one that simultaneously looks back to Christ's first advent ("grace... has appeared") and forward to his second advent ("while we wait"). It is thus the perfect stance for the threshold that is Christmas Eve in the life of the church.

But the end purpose of our repentance and redemption is not merely personal piety or even salvation understood as escape from God's eternal judgment. Christ has redeemed and purified us so that we might become "a people of his own who are zealous for good deeds" (v. 14). Christmas is not supposed to be just a time to recognize and celebrate God's gift to us. That gift is always to be a challenge to act in such ways as to extend God's grace to others. Even as we are busy driving back the physical darkness with all our decorations, we need to be busy driving back the spiritual, emotional, and social darkness from the lives of others. Doing so requires eager actions to accomplish good things and not simply season's greetings for best wishes.

Luke 2:1-14 (15-20)

The difficulties with correlating the various historical allusions in this gospel lesson with the records of Greco-Roman history and the account in Matthew are by now well-known. Quirinius became "governor" (legate) of the Roman province of Syria about a decade after Herod the Great's death, and there is no evidence that the Romans ever required people to return to their ancestral homes to be registered in a census (then as now, the point of a census was to determine current population patterns for taxation and other purposes). Matthew 2 has Mary and Joseph living in Bethlehem at the time of Jesus' birth with special circumstances leading to his being raised in Nazareth, whereas in Luke 2 Mary and Joseph's relations to Bethlehem and Nazareth are reversed. Here in Luke, shepherds visit Jesus on the night of his birth in response to an angelic visitation; Matthew recounts a visit by Magi approximately two years later (see Matthew 2:16) in response to an astral event.

For those interested in delving into the details and some of the suggestions for sorting out this tangle, almost any recent critical commentary will suffice. The Christmas Eve service, however, is probably not the occasion for exploring these matters. It is best to do that in Christian education settings, or if you must treat them homiletically, to do so when the Matthean texts are appointed for the First Sunday after Christmas in Year A or at Epiphany. Without suggesting that these problems do not exist (remember, they are well-known even to people without seminary training), simply stay with the details of the Lukan text. Don't homiletically re-create the crèche in your sermon. The preacher's task is to preach the gospel lesson, not some hybrid story that exists only in our minds.

Most of the historical problems in this lesson arise in verses 1-7. What is most important homiletically in this passage, however, is really not affected by any of those difficulties. Luke has set up a marked contrast between where the focus of attention lies in the world and where it should properly lie. Caesar Augustus decides he wants some information, and "all the world" is set in motion to respond to his whim. The Savior of the world is born to two Galilean peasants, and "there was no place for them in the inn." In the juxtaposition of that use of imperial power and the inability to recognize God's presence with and for the powerless (see Luke 1:46-55), there is a vivid description of the darkness that has blinded the world.

God pierces the darkness with the blinding light of the glory of the Lord (v. 9). The angel announces to shepherds that a new shepherd-king like David has been born. This child will be the "Savior" (one of a number of titles that Gaius Octavius had appropriated for himself along with Augustus ["revered"] and Pontifex Maximus [the bridge between the material and spiritual worlds]) whose coming is "good news of great joy for all people," not a threat. They must be told precisely where they will find the child because he is in fact in the last place that anyone would look for newborn royalty ("lying in a manger"). The angel is then joined by a multitude of angels who proclaim to the physical world what only the spiritual realm can yet recognize: God is to be praised because the Lord has favored the world with peace.

While it is still night ("Let us go now," v. 15b), the shepherds go to seek out the child and his parents and discover them in precisely the circumstances that the angel announced. That fact is not coincidental. If the angel's message has been demonstrated true in the details that could easily be confirmed, then all of the message is to be accepted — even those parts that still seem to verge on the outlandish. The message was trustworthy beyond all reasonable expectation in announcing where the child would be found, and so the message is trustworthy in announcing what the child will ultimately accomplish. And so those of the physical world who have seen the light shining in the darkness join in the praises with the spiritual realm (v. 20).

Application

For many who gather for worship on Christmas Eve, Christmas is a time of joyous light literally and figuratively. They have the material resources to join in our cultural "Season of Light" by decorating their homes if they wish, sharing in the parties, traveling to be with family members, exchanging gifts — all the things we do to brighten our lives in the midst of the onset of winter. The fact that they make the commitment to attend church in this prime "family time" shows that they understand as well that a spiritual light has shined into their lives. They have seen the light of the glory of the Lord and have felt the warmth of God's grace and peace.

All of that is as it should be. Those who have been blessed by God should recognize and rejoice in that blessing and share its benefits with others. To paraphrase the first question and response of the Westminster Catechism, the highest purpose of human life is to glorify God and to enjoy God forever. But truly understanding and appreciating the light that God has shined on our lives requires that we never forget as we bask in its warmth that "the people who walked in darkness have seen a great light" (Isaiah 9:2a) and "the light shines in the darkness" (John 1:5).

We remember and celebrate Christ's birth in the midst of one of the longest nights of the year. We drive back the darkness with candlelight services and every manner of lighting we can devise. But it is still in the night that we cause all this light to shine. Like the Christmas house lights that are hard to see in the full sun of day but illuminate our yards in the blackness of night, we only can see the light because we see it shining in the night.

In the same way, we need to see the figurative and spiritual night that still shrouds the world. There are still burdensome political and social structures that oppress people. There are still people shrouded in the darkness of depression rather than bathed in the light of joy. There are still people whose lives are more characterized by what they genuinely need — not just what they lack — than by what they have. As the letter to Titus challenges us, we have received the blessings of God to make us "zealous for good deeds." Just as we use our resources to drive back the darkness of the longest nights, so we need to use our spiritual and material resources to drive back the darkness of these nights as well. Then Christmas Eve will truly be a night of light.

An Alternative Application
Luke 2:1-14 (15-20). The praise of the angelic multitude is only one of several poems in the Lukan infancy narrative that have been construed liturgically as songs. There are as well Mary's *Magnificat* (1:46-55), Zechariah's *Benedictus* (1:68-79), and Simeon's *Nunc Dimittis* (2:29-32). Taking the *Gloria*, then, as a point of departure, one might construct a sermon on the "songs of the season" comparing and contrasting these songs from the gospels not only with the themes of secular Christmas carols but even with the carols of the church. What are the different Christmases that are reflected in the lyrics of these songs?

Christmas 1
1 Samuel 2:18-20, 26
Colossians 3:12-17
Luke 2:41-52
Wayne Brouwer

Wise child

Often a child's perspective is uncannily wise because his/her logic is so direct. A woman was working her flower garden under the intense scrutiny of her four-year-old neighbor. As they got into a conversation, the young girl suddenly gave out this startling revelation: "When I grow up, I'm going to marry Danny." Danny was a six-year-old boy living in the house just down the street.

The woman was curious. "Why are you going to marry Danny?" she asked.

"I have to," said the little one, "I'm not allowed to cross the street to where the other boys live."

While we know that circumstances, including street-crossing permissions, would change radically before either of the minor citizens was ready for marriage, there is a wonderful simplicity in this view of life as seen through four-year-old eyes. Two of today's lectionary readings focus on the wisdom that came through children — Samuel and Jesus — and the third reading expresses wisdom portrayed in a marvelously simple way.

1 Samuel 2:18-20, 26

When Ryan, son of "Focus on the Family" ministry founder, James Dobson, was young, he had a knack for getting into trouble. If there was something to break, chances are he smashed it. If there was something to get into, he was like a weasel. If there was something to mess up, he was the devil's whirlwind.

After a while, the Dobsons got rather exasperated. Shirley would shake her head and frequently say to her husband, "Somebody better do something about that boy!"

One day they were working around the house when both suddenly had the same feeling of uneasiness. They looked around for Ryan but couldn't find him. They scrambled and searched with growing fear: What had he gotten himself into now?

Finally, Dr. Dobson looked out the kitchen window. There was Ryan. Somehow, he had climbed onto the back of a big truck parked out on the street. Before he knew it, he had managed to get high enough to scare himself. When he tried to find his way down, his shirt got caught. Now he was swaying back and forth, hanging from the rear of the truck.

Dr. Dobson was in a bit of a panic. He wasn't quite sure how to help Ryan. He was afraid that if he shouted or ran up to him suddenly, the boy might be startled and fall to the pavement and hurt himself. So very quietly, but very quickly, he sneaked up to Ryan from the side of the truck. He thought it was a little strange that Ryan wasn't crying or calling out for help. As he got closer, though, he heard his son muttering very emphatically to himself, "Somebody better do something about that boy! Somebody better do something about that boy!"

If you can see that picture in your mind, then you've got a good feeling for the background behind the early chapters of 1 Samuel. Like a boy who's been playing where he shouldn't, the nation of Israel was messing with fire. Like a person who has pushed her luck just a little too far, the Israelites were hung up on a situation they couldn't escape. And like the child in each of us, the only thing they could think about was this: "Somebody better do something!"

Power politics was the name of the game in Israel's world. It wasn't much different from today, actually. The Philistines, latecomers to Canaan as farming colonies from the Aegean Greeks, were pushing inland from the coast. The Plain of Sharon, next to the Mediterranean Sea, was too sandy to be a great agricultural investment. Inland, however, were the five valleys of the Shephelah fingering into the hills of Judah. Both the Israelites and the Philistines wanted these. This was the beginning of the Iron Age, as archaeologists now name it, and the Philistines had brought that metallurgical technology with them across the sea. The Israelites, however, were still living in the Stone Age, and therefore quickly lost control of the valleys to the better-armed invaders.

However, there was more that played on the mind of the devoutly religious in the land. Not only was this the latter part of the Stone Age, it was also the last ugly gasp of the era of the Judges. Israel was a weak nation of superstitious suspicions, dividing the people into a poorly stitched patchwork of bickering clans barely covering the hills of Ephraim. Most had forgotten the ways of Moses and Joshua, and now wandered in a fearful daze. If there was any prayer left, it was the kind that Ryan muttered that day: "Somebody better do something about that boy!" They certainly couldn't help themselves. They were really beyond prayer, in a sense. They had lost their religion. For a long time now, they had pretended that God didn't exist, and that the Sinai covenant didn't really have a place in their world. So, when they needed divine intervention most, they couldn't find it.

It is like the story of a father who came home one day to find his nine-year-old daughter crying her heart out. When he asked what was wrong, she managed to blurt out between sobs that she and her friend had been playing hide-and-seek. When it was her turn to hide, she had hidden so well that her friend had finally given up and gone off to play another game. At last, when she came out of her hiding place, she was all alone.

The stories of Israel in the book of Judges are a lot like that. First, Israel would hide from God. Then God would hide from Israel. And somewhere along the way, they both started playing different games. That is the tragedy surrounding the family of Eli and the nation of Israel in the first several chapters of this book. That is why reproach hangs over the land. There, swinging on the hook of judgment, sways little Israel. One can almost hear the mutter: "Somebody better do something!"

But in the stories of Samuel comes a new word of grace. God will not allow this special people to hang on the hook of their own making forever. In the prayers of Samuel's mother (see chs. 1-2) is the confidence that God is already raising a deliverer to make things right. This is why Samuel is a type of the other great Israelite who was prayed into this world by a loving mother, the one whose birth we celebrated last Sunday. Out of the mouths of young children, divinely sent and appointed by the sovereign of Israel, would come the word of life for God's people. One day, somebody did take Israel (and us) off the hook, even allowing himself to be caught up there in the process.

Colossians 3:12-17

Paul was under house arrest in Rome around 59-60 AD when he sent out this letter together with those to the Ephesians and Philemon. Philemon's slave, Onesimus, had run away from the Lycus Valley estate near Colossae. Eventually he made his way to Rome and somehow had connected with Paul. For a while they enjoyed a growing camaraderie, but guilt at the overall deception of harboring a friend's runaway caused Paul to send Onesimus back to Philemon. Since Paul himself was still unable to travel, due to the restrictions of the Roman penal system, he entrusted the safe passage of Onesimus to another friend named Tychicus. Paul sent along a letter of explanation and exhortation to Philemon and penned the other two letters for area churches.

So the story of a young person was on Paul's mind as he wrote Colossians. It seems, from the letter to Philemon, that Paul learned a good deal from Onesimus, even as Onesimus received great grace from Paul. When Paul's Colossians letter is read during worship on a Sunday morning, it is likely that Tychicus would be the reader and that both Philemon and Onesimus would be in attendance, for this was their closest city church (Philemon probably served as house church pastor for the gathering on his own estate). The wisdom that Paul gives is aimed not only to life in general, but also to the specific situation of Onesimus' and Philemon's differing socioeconomic situations and the manner in which these are to be minimized in the fellowship of the faith. Furthermore, the call to forgiveness would surely have been targeted at least to these two who had much to grieve about — Onesimus in the bitterness that caused him to run away, and Philemon in the righteous judgment a slave owner could have against a rebelliously disobedient servant.

Paul's words are rooted in transcendent perspective. If we are to see one another through the eyes of compassion and commitment, they can only be first received by us when we follow Jesus to the observation deck of heaven (3:1). Furthermore, the call to "clothe yourselves" in verse 12 is a direct follow-through of the earlier injunction to "put to death" the variety of social sins listed in the preceding verses. Paul was using a rhetorical devise made popular by one of the Greek philosophers who developed a habit of telling people to put off the old man and put on the new.

Paul's list of characteristics and traits to be newly worn by believers is a marvelous and poetic compendium of social graces and Christian ethics. While it is possible to talk about each of these in serial fashion, there is a holistic quality that might be missed if the passage is broken into too many parts. Perhaps a better approach might be to make a comparison with new clothes that may have been received as Christmas presents. When these new garments are worn, the old clothes seem ill-fitting and out of fashion. So with the new character developed through the gifts of the Christ Child, one cannot display them to their advantage until one gets rid of all that conflicts with them, and then begins to make these new blessings a living part of one's daily wardrobe.

The qualities of behavior elicited by Paul are not mere niceties to be added like marketplace deceptions. When Henry Higgins sought to make a case study of Liza Doolittle in *My Fair Lady*, his goal at first was merely to dress up a cockney waif in the pseudo-sophistication of the cultured elite and show that together they might fool everyone with their pretense. What actually happened, however, is that Liza and Henry changed in the process until each was a different person than either had been at the start. This gets at the heart of what Paul is trying to communicate. If one is "in Christ," one should begin to act and live in a different manner than one did before one was "in Christ." At the same time, as one begins to act and live in this new way, the sense of being "in Christ" deepens until it is a whole new expression of life and not just a propagandist customer service veneer.

Luke 2:41-52

Madeleine L'Engle's fine story, *Dance in the Desert*, combines elements of Matthew's infant narratives and those of this passage. It begins with a caravan of people traveling in hurried fear through a trackless wilderness. They seem to be running from something and turn furtively to check the movement of shadows at the edge of their peripheral vision. Particularly noticeable among them is a young family, a husband and wife along with their tiny boy.

Night falls and the travelers establish a camp. All gather around the huge bonfire that is lit as a repellent to the darkness and whatever beasts and demons it might hold. From huddled security near the flames, the community shivers at growls and hisses that emanate from the unseen world beyond the licking of the fire. Now and again the piercing reflection of strange eyes looks at them out of the black void, and they quickly turn back to comforting small talk, which helps them pretend at safety.

But they will not be left alone. The shrieks and warning snarls edge closer. Then a paw appears, or a sniffing nose, only to be withdrawn before spears can poke or arrows be aimed. More sticks are thrown on the fire. Yet the beasties and wild things will not be stopped. Growing more daring, a bear steps into their circle and a bold viper slithers in from the other direction. There is panic in the camp as all scatter and leap and search for weapons. In the commotion, the young husband and his younger wife are separated, each believing the other has grabbed their little boy to safety.

However, the child was left behind. He faces the wolf and the lion and the bear and the snake and the other wilderness creatures alone. Only there is no distress in his voice and no panic in his cry. Instead, he coos and clucks with delight at these mighty furry and scaly toys that have come to play. He claps his hands and bounces his feet and giggles with animation.

As the watchers are suddenly pulled from their panicked zigzagging by the tinkle of the child's good humor, all the adults stop and turn, expecting the wild things to tear limb from limb and demolish this human plaything they have abandoned. But it is not so. Instead, the child has brought some kind of intelligent direction to its strange play. His chubby arms are actually orchestrating a symphony of animal cries, and his hands are directing the choreography of a marvelous beastly dance. The bear is on its hind legs, not to swipe and strike but to gyrate with the tempo of the child's clapping. The snakes slither in pairs forming artistic designs in the desert sands. Above, the vultures and hawks swoop and turn, bank and dive in aviary formation. The lions and tigers nod their heads as if in rhythm to celestial instrumentation.

Slowly, and with mesmerizing fascination, the adults creep back to their places by the bonfire. They become the audience in the greatest show on earth. The child whoops and tips and giggles and sways and claps his hands in time with the music of heaven, and the animals of earth dance around him with delight. Even the big people begin to hear transcendent melodies, and the night has become as friendly as dawn or daylight.

Eventually the child tires, as all children do, and the cooing stops, the clapping ceases, and the animals slink away. But they are no longer predators and the fear of both man and beast has vanished. All that is left is the child and those who linger in awe know that there is a new center of gravity in the universe.

This might be a grand parable of the day, described by Luke, when Joseph and Mary took young Jesus to be *bar mitzvahed* at the temple and celebrate his first pilgrim feast there. While they traveled with others, fearful of things that went bump in the night, the child left by heaven in their care was actually orchestrating the sounds of life around them. Left behind at the fire (the temple, which housed the glory of God) to be attacked and ravaged by the fearsome beasts of theology, the child instead claps his hands, sways his arms, speaks the cooing of heaven's wisdom, and the animals dance around him. And we, who live in other times and places, peek out from behind the shadows and listen to his voice.

Application

In the early church, there was a tale told of a young girl who lived with her parents in a cottage at the edge of a dense forest. "Don't wander too far into the woods," they told her. "You might get lost."

A warm summer's day with birds singing and winds calling, however, carried the girl's feet deeper and deeper into the cool underbrush. The shadows were long before she realized how lost she was. Yelling and crying, she dashed one way and the next, not finding home and working herself into convulsions of panic.

Meanwhile, her parents were worried as well. In the dusk of evening they called her name and made forays into the woods. As thoughts of all the worst fates attacked them, they organized villagers and other neighbors into search parties.

By dawn the young girl was sleeping exhaustedly on a bed of pine needles, and only her father was left of the many searchers. As he stumbled into the clearing and saw her, his footsteps broke branches and sent birds twittering. The noise awoke her and she saw him. Jumping to her feet she ran toward him, arms outstretched, "Daddy! Daddy!" she cried. "I found you!"

So it is with us on this Sunday after Christmas. We are children who have torn open our presents and wandered far into dark places. Lost and lonely, we fall exhausted in alien places. But our Father comes looking for us, sending one who is like us and who loves us, into the dark forests that surround us. When we see him this Sunday morning we start up with delight and cry out, "I found you!" But the story of Christmas is actually a rescue tale in which we discover that we are found by the one sent into our world to call us by name.

An Alternative Application
Colossians 3:12-17. The Colossians lesson can be used well by itself. It is a quick tie from the idea of getting clothes as Christmas gifts to now wearing them. The biblical clothes may form an alliterative chain — Paul calls on us to wear what is helpful, humble, happy, and holy. These can be wonderfully illustrated in marvelous ways and can also point to the transition from one year to the next: by the grace of God — put off the old and put on the new.

New Year's Day
Ecclesiastes 3:1-13
Revelation 21:1-6a
Matthew 25:31-46
Mark Molldrem

God's gift of time

Every January 1 there is a sense of freshness. It is the first day of the first month in the new year. The eve before, and perhaps the entire previous week, people have tried to set the past behind, forget the regrets, celebrate the triumphs, and anticipate a clean slate to fill with new year's resolutions. Time stands before the reveler like an open door. To walk through invites one onto new stages of life. Of course, once over the threshold, it does not take long to realize that the year gets old rather quickly. Much of what we thought we left behind in the old year is still packed in the baggage we carry into the new. One of the blessings that can come from a New Year's Day worship experience, however, is a deeper understanding of God's gift of time — how to receive it, how to value it, how to use it.

Ecclesiastes 3:1-13

Imagine the son of an exiled Hebrew, born at the close of the sixth century BC, listening to the tales of his father and grandfather about times of war, times of exile, and times from before when there was plenty in the homeland and then poverty. A desire mounts to write down intuitions and observations about all the stories. Yet, to recount the history of God's people is like riding a roller coaster. There are ups and downs, horizontal curves and vertical curves, slow climbs to the summit and fast falls to the bottom. Reflecting on the positive and negative aspects of this history would take a supple mind and a clever pen. Consider the range that had to be taken into account. There were good kings, like Jehoash and Hezekiah; there were bad kings, like Ahaz and Menasseh. There were times of blessing, and there were times of judgment. There were times of planting and times of plucking. Weeping and laughing, mourning and dancing tumbled over one another, creating a love/hate relationship to the heritage from which one emerges. Dickens' *A Tale of Two Cities* could have been written about one and the same Jerusalem: "It was the best of times. It was the worst of times." As the heart searches for faith and the mind for understanding in all this jumbled story, it is no wonder that expressions from the writer of Ecclesiastes are rather fragmented and disjointed, a collection of thoughts and observations held together only by the soul's probing desire to grasp a meaning in it all.

The opening line in chapter 3 has caught the imagination of many, whether it be for interpreting the topsy-turvy world created by the '60s through folk rock music ("For everything turn turn turn; there is a season turn turn turn; and a time for every purpose under heaven") or picking out a funeral text. The wisdom of this literature is that it simply identifies the reality that there will be a mix of opposite forces that vie for their time in the spotlight. No matter what we may try to do to shape our world or control its movements, we will be the ones caught up in the seasons of birth and death, killing and healing, breaking down and building up. This is true for personal lives as well as community growth/decay cycles.

The reader should be cautioned that the litany of opposites set up with their respective "times" is not a nod to Eastern philosophy. Lao-tzu writes in the *Tao Te Ching*, "Once it began, the universe had two parts..." (for example: day and night, calm and fright, blindness and sight, loose and tight) "... these two parts make up the Way of Nature. It is the blending of these parts that gives the universe its breath. It is the ending of these parts that creates violence and death." To recognize this and then to live in harmony is the enlightened goal of the student of life. Heaven and earth are really one dynamic, interactive whole and it is the human purpose to discover the "dance of Shiva." Fritjof Capra, in his work *The Tao of Physics*, explains how this is reflected in the concept of God: "The Eastern image of the Divine is not that of a ruler who directs the world from above, but of a principle that controls everything from within."

Yet, for the preacher, the seasons run their cycles "under heaven." There is a great distinction between the author of life and time and the created order *and* the human creature. "Be not rash with your mouth, nor let your heart be hasty to utter a word before God, for God is in heaven, and you upon earth..." (5:2 RSV). Time is God's valuable gift in which the mix of life happens. This mix is not the divine in its dynamic unity of opposites. It is in and through the mix in time that the human creature is to find relationship with God, who is in heaven. "God has made it so, in order that men should fear before him" (3:14 RSV). God has put eternity into the human consciousness (3:11 RSV) but not to the extent that the creature can become "one" with the creator. There will always be what Kierkegaard said, an "infinite qualitative difference" between God and the man and woman. Yet, apart from God, life is experienced as a "vanity of vanities." Therefore, it behooves the creature to understand the times, especially in the context of the relationship with God, who ultimately desires the crown of creation to "eat and drink and take pleasure in all his toil" (3:13 RSV).

Revelation 21:1-6a

Four times in these few verses the adjective *kainoz* (new) is used. God's touch with newness reaches heaven and earth, Jerusalem and all things. With God, life does not remain the same. It is not just that with the passing of time, like the turning of the calendar to January 1, everything will change for the better, as if there were some magic, anticipatory longing to make it so. It is clear in this passage that God is the actor, shaping the script of newness for heaven and earth, Jerusalem and all things, according to his inscrutable will. "Behold, *I* make all things new" (21:5). The placement of *kainoz* right after the interrogative at the beginning of the sentence emphasizes the *new* reality that comes from the hand of God.

What is new is that the reconciliation between God and humanity will be complete. The image of God living with humanity evokes the tenting of God with the nomadic tribes of Israel before they became a settled kingdom in Palestine and also the incarnation of God in Jesus. The Greek word *skhnh* (tent, booth) makes this perfectly clear (see John 1:14). The separation between God, who is in heaven, and humanity on earth is no more. The marriage bond is secured and cohabitation with the harlot has resumed for eternity. The prophet Hosea would be pleased (Hosea 14:7), as well as Malachi (Malachi 2:16).

Also what is new is that death is finally overcome. The mortal blow to death was inflicted from the cross; but, not until the consummation will death itself be dead. When Ernest (in the comic strip *Frank and Ernest*) is asked by Frank what he would like his epitaph to say, he responds, "To be continued." The good news in this text is that God will see to it. The anguish of God's people will be a *former* thing, now passing away, because God is doing a *new* thing, which is God's prerogative to do, since God is the beginning and end of all things. Old and new are in God's hand to discard and shape at will. It is God's will to be about new things that will be a blessing for the beloved of God in Christ Jesus. Eternal life is the heritage promised (21:7). What a pastoral word of encouragement and hope for a people suffering persecution then (first century *anno domini*) or any oppression now (twenty-first century *anno domini*)!

Paul makes bold comment on this, proclaiming that this newness is already happening to us as we live in Christ by faith now (2 Corinthians 5:17). The reality of the eschaton bubbles like a fountain from the future into the present providing a satiating drink for those parched by the deathly dryness of the old. "These words are trustworthy and true," Revelation says. Therefore, seize these words in faith and be seized by the promised future from God so that now you may know the wholeness of life through all the various seasons and times.

"The New is in the Old contained; the Old is by the New explained." This little rhyme can be applied to these verses from Revelation that are part of the lectionary for today. Like with Matthew and Hebrews,

Revelation relies on and takes so much from the Old Testament to make a *new* point. Isaiah 65:17f is the ground on which the seer of Revelation stands to catch the vision of a new heaven and a new earth, a new Jerusalem and all things new. Out of the cycles of judgment, the prophet Isaiah perceives God spinning a future full of goodness for his people, characterized as the messianic age. So, when the Messiah indeed comes, it is only natural that this text is picked up and spun afresh in light of what Jesus accomplished upon the cross and through the resurrection.

Matthew 25:31-46

If the nature of religious language is metaphor, this story of judgment is a superb example. As Lakoff and Johnson explain in their book *Metaphors We Live By*, "The essence of metaphor is understanding and experiencing one kind of thing in terms of another." It is difficult to conceive of judgment day and imagine what it must be like to stand on the threshold of eternity. Yet, imagination is one of God's gifts to probe understanding that is beyond understanding, to speak of those things that are so difficult to render into words.

Jesus takes a familiar image of a king and a shepherd and blends them into the judge who will determine the fate of the nations. The king has authority to do what he wills. The shepherd understands the difference between the sheep and the goats. This shepherd king, who is judge, brings to mind none other than David, the shepherd boy made king, who was "a man after God's own heart" (1 Samuel 13:14). The eternal covenant made with him (and before with Abraham, his ancestor) will come to fruition through Jesus, the descendent of Abraham and David, Son of Man, who will come again in glory to judge the world he came to save (see John 3:16-21).

By stretching our understanding of metaphor, we can get deeper into the text and see how it relates to the other texts, specifically in regards to time. Again, Lakoff and Johnson make the argument respective to philosophy and linguistics that "most of our ordinary conceptual system is metaphorical in nature... and we act according to the way we conceive of things." Using this as a springboard to catapult us deeper into the pool of understanding, let us consider the metaphorical concepts *Time is a Limited Resource and Time is a Valuable Commodity*. Lakoff and Johnson identify the following expressions as representative of these metaphorical concepts:

> *I don't have enough time to spare for that.*
> *You're running out of time.*
> *You don't use your time profitably.*
> *Thank you for your time.*

The righteous ask Jesus, "*When* did we see thee hungry...?" They are asking the question of time. Because time is a limited resource, it becomes a valuable resource. Therefore, *how* that time is spent becomes a matter of value. This is precisely the point the king makes. Compassion characterizes the actions of feeding the hungry, giving drink to the thirsty, welcoming the stranger, clothing the naked, visiting the sick and those in prison. The Christ-like quality of compassion is what the king notices. Concomitant with that is the recognition that true compassion is extended to "the least of these." Jesus sharpens the servant nature of compassion, when he says elsewhere (Luke 6:27-36) that one should act not expecting anything in return. This would be the case when relating to one's enemies and "the least of these." Jesus demonstrated what he meant when he reprimanded his follower for lopping off the ear of the high priest's slave during the garden fiasco.

Unfortunately, we are left wondering if Jesus may have healed the man. Or, perhaps Jesus seized the moment as exemplary of the preacher's seasons: a time for war and a time for peace, a time to hate and a time to love. In a split second, Jesus changed the seasons through the power of his person and commitment to establish the time of God's kingdom. Rather than being an all-too-familiar killing time, he would usher in the new healing time, which will be a gift to all people. This gift would inspire the gifted to share themselves and their time, limited and valuable as they are, in ways that will please the one who ultimately rules the cosmos.

In the aftermath of the rebellion of 66-70 AD, when Titus led the legions of Rome through the bloodied streets of Jerusalem and destroying the temple, this metaphor of judgment challenges the followers of Jesus to keep asking the right question of themselves. The king, who commands his army of the faithful, will not ask, "Did you fight for me?" He will ask instead, "Did you live for me? Did you serve me?" The litmus test for this will be the way we act in our daily life relationships.

Application

Abraham Maslow's hierarchy of needs reminds us that issues of food, clothing, and safety are fundamental. When these are adequately met, a person has the freedom and focus to develop upward into fuller humanity: belongingness/love, esteem, and finally self-actualization. Christians have been, are, and will continue to be involved in the nitty-gritty needs of people who are simply struggling to survive. This is as it should be; this is how it must be. As Jesus said, "The poor you always have with you" (Matthew 26:11). The inspiration for rolling up our sleeves and getting our hands dirty with "the least of these" is the hope that this is exactly what the shepherd king wants us to do. He will reward us with the eternal life that has already been birthed in our souls by the power of the Holy Spirit (Romans 5:1-5), issuing the offspring of faith, hope, and love.

Hope is a powerful force. It has been said that there is no such thing as a hopeless situation unless we become hopeless people. We need hope! Not just the bland, superficial pop-optimism that says, "This is going to be the best year ever. I know I am going to do everything in my power to make it so. If we all were positive and contributed to the common good, there is no telling what we could accomplish together." We need a hope that can look into the darkest storm approaching and still have the confidence that "in everything God works for good with those who love him, who are called according to his purpose" (Romans 8:28 RSV). If Strauss and Howe are correct in their historical analysis of the American cycles and we are heading into "the fourth turning," a cycle of crisis (as were the years of Revolutionary War, Civil War, Depression, and World War II), we need to prepare our congregations with a grounding in biblical hope.

Time will ultimately give way to eternity; but, in the meantime, to assure heavenly goals assume earthly responsibilities. This is not to say one earns entrance into heaven by what is done on earth in terms of good deeds. Rather, it is to say that good deeds take on the character of the heavenly goals themselves. As we want to be with Jesus in heaven, live like him on earth. Be a "little Christ" to the neighbor. Jesus will recognize his own by the way their behavior imitates his. He did command his disciples to "love one another as I have loved you" (John 15:12 RSV). As we so identify our lives with his, the power of his promises will be manifested in the present, empowering the believer to live confidently in the hope of new things to come from the hand of God, meliorating even the worst that evil can conjure up against us.

As we begin the new year, it is good to be reminded that this new time is a gift from God to be used wisely, invested prudently, in ways that enhance our relationship with God. Soon enough there will be things happening to tempt us away from experiencing the holy in life. Our relationship with God will continue to be tarnished. But the new cannot be constrained by the wiles of the serpent. What was said in the garden is reverberating down through history since the cross of Christ: "He shall bruise your head, and you shall bruise his heel" (Genesis 3:15b). The head of the serpent is being bruised already and will effectively be dealt the final mortal blow when the Son of Man returns. In the meantime, hope on, act on for "It is done!" What God says will be, will be. In fact, it is already beginning. Enter into the new day, the new year to "eat and drink and take pleasure in all your toil, which needs to include compassion."

Epiphany of Our Lord
Isaiah 60:1-6
Ephesians 3:1-12
Matthew 2:1-12
Craig MacCreary

Has it dawned on you?

Over the years, though I am from a low church tradition, I have come to appreciate Epiphany more and more. It gives us a second shot at revisiting the Christmas story to ponder whether the secular celebration has done too much damage to what God intended us to be about. In recent times there has been some evidence that our problems might not be too much darkness; rather the light God intends seems to have a hard time making its way through the bright lights of our world. If you live near or in a city, light pollution has a way of limiting your view of the heavenly hosts. Epiphany provides some possibility, with less glare from holiday lights and expectations, to understand just what God might have accomplished or what we may have missed in the recent round of holiday merrymaking.

It is a fearful thing to imagine that if the wise men showed up on our doorsteps we might find ourselves in the same position as Herod — frightened, confused, and unable to be much help in locating where the child was born. It was no less disturbing for Herod to discover the sky was full of messages in bright lights that he could not figure out. A puppet of the Romans yes, but this is the kind of thing that he ought to be on top of. After all, it has spooked all of Jerusalem, which is bound to put the culture and the corporate powers that be on edge. It has not quite dawned on the Jerusalemites just what God is up to. This is not the kind of thing that the people of the capital ought to be mistaken about.

If you had been living in exile as the Hebrews had and found yourself returning from the far country you could begin to wonder what God was up to in bringing you back from Babylon. What will the role of the returnees be? What role is God counting on them to play in the scheme of things? As they surveyed the ruins of Jerusalem and the temple, they must have asked themselves whether their task was to put it all together in the way things had been. If not that, then what was to be their part in God's plan? Was it all about them returning, setting up shop, and settling in so that they could live happily ever after in the land of milk and honey?

Only slowly, it seems, did it begin to dawn on at least some of the Israelites that this was not going to be about restoring past certainties, but God was doing a new thing here. While it did not abolish the old, it certainly meant going beyond some of their usual thinking. Read the Isaiah passage assigned to this day and get beyond the familiar Christmas images they evoke as it slowly dawns on you the breadth and depth of the new thing that God is doing here. With serious political, social, and theological ramifications, the Christian scripture claims that this new thing is most completely fulfilled in events that we have just celebrated.

The letter to the Ephesians points to the mystery that Paul lived out and embodied. The inclusion of the Gentiles in the promises of God changed everything for the early church. Inclusion always rearranges things. Many of us can remember the last vestiges of segregation. James Carroll, in his history of the Pentagon, recounts how the building is filled with restroom facilities because it was built in the days when segregation was the law in Virginia. A few years ago, the run of the Connecticut women's basketball team easily pushed the men's team right off the front of the sports pages. Reporters who never imagined themselves hanging around a women's locker room found that they had to accommodate to the dynamics of a different news beat.

I am told that in the town where I reside, Manchester, New Hampshire, over seventy languages are spoken! Who would have ever thought it? It takes a while for it to dawn on you just what the dimensions are of what God is up to in the world and just what you deem is an epiphany.

Was all this what we celebrated through the holidays? It may take a while until it dawns on us. Of course, the gospels tell us that much of this will be cleared up with the dawn of Easter morning.

Isaiah 60:1-6

The closing episode of the television series, *M*A*S*H*, featured the return home of the characters from years at war in Korea. Of course, the characters can barely believe that they are going home. "Rise and shine for your light has come" is not all that easy. Things have happened while they were in exile that makes the homecoming difficult. Indeed, the lead character, Hawkeye, is in a mental hospital unable to resolve all the issues that have developed in his life from the exile. There must have been a similar set of difficulties in the return of the Israelites. Some had kept the faith; some had not done so well. Others had gone over the line in their compromises to a Babylonian system. Perhaps some did not see this as light for their journey at all for they had done well in the new land and had hopes for their children. This proposition might not offer an easy way up a career ladder.

As I consider this text, it dawns on me that I might not be ready to return from the exile that the Christmas celebrations can often be. Where have things been left unsaid or undone? Did we compromise too badly with the culture? Did the family celebrations cover what should have been said and shared? Was my holiday mostly about feeling good or getting a feel for the kingdom of God? Did I allow people to live in exile in the kitchen or working long hours while I enjoyed the fruit of their labors?

God seems to be up to quite a feat here as the text describes the nations and the wealth of the world streaming toward Jerusalem. At first glance, I blush at the prospect of this moment. This seems to be a whole different kind of globalization than we read about in the newspapers. Of course, that just might be the point. It dawns on me that the text bears more relevance than ever before, for we can now see how the world's wealth can come under one umbrella serving the aims of a free market and free trade. "They shall bring gold and frankincense and shall proclaim the praise of the Lord." It seems that in our world, tied in with the praise of the Lord, is the proclamation that neither free market nor free trade are in and of themselves gods to be worshiped. They may be good things but when they become objects of our worship, we are getting in the way of the plan and purpose of God. Yes, the world often beats a path to our door to see our wealth, yet does it leave praising the Lord?

It often dawns on me that the coming of sons and daughters from far away can be quite challenging. Sometimes it can be quite difficult when Zion's children start showing up. It seems that there are some challenges ahead for the worldwide church as the center of the Christian population moves toward what is called in the first world, "the third world." Different understandings of human sexuality in the churches in other countries have left many liberals in economically advanced nations confused, offended, and challenged. Conservatives find themselves challenged by the understanding of the root causes of economic disorder in the world by those who do not share in the economic prosperity of so-called first-world nations. It dawns on me that the coming of Zion's children into their own from far away will pose more challenges than many had anticipated.

While there are more challenges to be met if Zion's children are to praise the Lord, it is also clear that those who return from exile are to undertake this work. "Be radiant, your heart shall thrill and rejoice." Actually, I find myself doing so because the light calls us from exile, calls us to put aside false gods, and calls us together. Darkness does cover the earth, a thick darkness, when we try to make it in the land of exile. We were not meant to live there, where we support temples to false gods. It will be quite a day when the day of the Lord dawns. When it dawns on us that the day has already come, then "we shall arise and shine... for the glory of the Lord has risen upon us."

Ephesians 3:1-12

Gentiles included. The struggle of the early church to include and accept the Gentiles on an equal footing was worked out in many places. We are given in the Christian scripture, through the various narrations of the process, a fairly sophisticated version of what took place. We have the high-powered reflections of serious theological minds as in the book of Acts, Paul's letters, and in all the gospels. No doubt there is the reified, high level, intense serious aspect to that struggle. However, it appears to me that something simpler, more humble was at work as the church faced the issue. The early church was overwhelmed by these new people so different in customs and their approach to life. Who was Paul, a latter-day persecutor of the church, to be taking up their cause? It appears obvious to us a few centuries later that engrafting the Gentiles was the way to go. Certainly, Judaism suffered in the midst of the first-century upheavals by turning inward rather than turning outward. It is clear that there were Jewish communities scattered around the world and many God fearers who might have been a source of vitality and growth. The early church decision to expand into new areas certainly seems, in retrospect, a no-brainer.

Yet it was a struggle, and for Paul this was a mystery that remained hidden for all ages in God who created all things. As we sit on this side of the divide, it remains a mystery why this was so puzzling. Yet closer to home, many of us have lived through times when we could not fathom how it would be possible for white people and black people to walk together in anything that looks like equality. I suspect that some of the fears that retarded the inclusion of all Americans in the fulfillment of the American creed also frustrated Paul: What if we must eat with them, what if one of them wants to marry my daughter, what if one of them is ordained, and on and on. These things tend to be the default position for some of us. An African-American friend tells of sitting through a speech in which every negative reference was to blackness in some form. The speaker was just reflecting the default position with which he had grown up.

Some of the mystery is how the early church made the choice to go against the cultural, social, and religious grain to invite Gentiles to be full participants in the life of the church as Gentiles. There was no clear model as to how to go about this. In the end, as Paul does, the corpus of scripture can only attribute this to divine activity.

It dawns on me that as I look at my holiday celebration, I wonder if they proclaimed the boundless riches of God that Paul announces to the Gentiles. Rather than a source of unity, the holiday celebration is a source of clumsiness with Jewish friends, and a source of division, as some Christians demand that store Santas must wish shoppers Merry Christmas rather than happy holidays. The Feast of Kwanzaa seems to be a recognition that the spirituality behind Christmas for many is the "White Christmas" that some folks are not dreaming about. If nothing else, the economic tie of Christmas means for many a disappointing realization that the wall between people grows higher at a time when it ought to come down. Needless to say, many find the season of good cheer and fellowship a burden hard to bear in the midst of their sorrow and depression. This does not sound to me like the boundless riches of Christ who embraces all.

I have no model for this. I wonder what it would be like if the season of joy became more a source of unity — an opportunity to find out where we find joy and what it is like to live without it in our various traditions. It seems that, at its core, the story of Epiphany is the celebration of the gifts that the Gentile wise men brought. Our celebration might be the dawning of a new Epiphany of the boundless riches of God that we know in Christ Jesus.

Matthew 2:1-12

Here they come again. In most churches, the wise men have already made their appearance in the manger scene, and the Christmas pageant would not be complete without the royal retinue. Of the pageants I have seen, including major productions with camels and sheep, the object is to get them to the manger scene as fast as we can for the major dénouement, when in royal reverence they deposit their gold, frankincense, and myrrh. The rest of it all seems to fall to the cutting room floor as it were. We just might have missed out on something here in our obsessing with this one scene in their story.

What was that moment like when they observed his star for the first time at its rising? For people in their position, this must have provoked a variety of reactions. No doubt the standard theatrical version of the tale would include wide-eyed amazement at this new addition to the heavens. Of course, these are the people who are supposed to know about such things. Clearly, early on, they understood these events as tied to what will be authoritative Judaism.

The scene that ought to be part of every Christmas pageant is the one when Herod got wind of what was going on. According to the word on the street, there were Gentile authorities asking questions that he did not have an answer for. Not only Herod, but all of Jerusalem, was afraid. If the Gentile wise men have it right, this cannot be good.

At the end of the first scene, what we know is that there is something that the Gentiles get in understanding what God is birthing into the world and there is something that all Jerusalem along with Herod misses completely. That ought to be reason for some fear and trembling on our part. Who knows when some Gentiles may show up, and we will have to pay attention to what insights they might bring to us as to what is going on in our world? They do not know the full extent of what is happening here, and what it will lead to, but they know something. The lesson is that it is worth paying attention to the outsider. Indeed, the outsider may have something to offer that the insider misses and cannot fathom. The churches could learn from this: recognizing that insiders will often miss things that others see. It might be interesting to invite folks from other religious traditions or no tradition to come and worship and offer their reactions as to what they experienced in our praise and singing. All Jerusalem might tremble but there might also be an epiphany of the first order. It might be interesting to ask some of those who came as a part of the somewhat larger than normal crowds who followed the star to Christmas Eve why they came. What is it that seems to inhibit their return: again, fear and trembling, but potential epiphany?

It seems that Herod comes up fairly short in the streetwise department. He makes arrangements with the wise men to find the exact location of the place. Does he really expect the wise men to buy his story that he, too, wishes to pay homage to the child? Get a grip here. These are people who have discerned in the heavens the plan of God and does Herod think that they will not see through him? This scene would definitely be in my Christmas pageant. There is no epiphany for Herod. There tends not to be an epiphany for those who spend their day putting people in their place as opposed to learning to put themselves in other people's places.

Then comes the great scene in which they kneel before the babe. They leave with no stars in the sky but they leave starry-eyed at the prospect of what God is up to in the world. Herod has had his eye out for trouble, opposition, and anything that might get in his way. He is not likely to have an epiphany that will leave him starry-eyed.

Application

As a child, I always had trouble with the account of "the wise men." We sang the Christmas carol, "We Three Kings of Orient Are." There comes a time in a young person's life when you discover that some of the Christmas stories that surround the holiday just might not be true. A precocious encounter with the Christmas classic, *Yes, Virginia, There Is A Santa Claus*, suggested that there was a problem. Now I am told via a casual encounter with public radio that in all probability Clement Moore did not write *'Twas The Night Before Christmas*. Does this never end? It begins to all feel like a scandal revealed on a *60 Minutes* episode. Notations in history books that Jesus was probably born in 4 BC only make matters worse.

That the names of the wise men came from *Ben Hur*, a novel written by a Civil War general, Lew Wallace, adds to the confusion. Finding out that even the notion of the three comes from the number of gifts and not the number of people, did not make things better. Who were these people — kings, astrologers, or the proverbial wise ones?

Then it dawns on me that one might take the liberty to say that they were all three. Like government types, they had power that came as much from defining the future as anything else. The story invites us to consider the minority report that is rendered through their dream life. There is another tale being told here other than the official government version of things. The conventional notion of the heavens is challenged by a star that requires them to redo their charts.

Their role in the story of how God is entering into the world may tell us that we need to redo our charts, rethink our sense of what the future holds, and revisit our understanding of what is for the sake of what might be; that we, too, might come and worship him.

An Alternative Application
Ephesians 3:1-12. Epiphany celebrates in part the entry of the Gentiles into the fellowship of Christian believers. They come not as ones who bring a great background in the scriptural saga. You know you are moving into modern-day Gentile territory when the local athletic association schedules a soccer tournament to start at 10 a.m. Sunday morning, when the local radio stations announce that there will be a congressional meeting of your congregation, or the music selection the wedding couple has chosen will take the assembled gathering to places you may not want them to go.

No doubt about it — we are in Gentile territory now. How do we plan to share the boundless riches of Christ with this new crop of Gentiles? I suspect that we might do it in some measure by sharing how we live with the mystery of life that we and others are. How do we cherish the mystery that we cannot fully explain? Paul himself did write, "Behold I show you a mystery." It seems that the level playing ground in facing the mystery of life is where we and the Gentiles can find common ground.

In many ways, we are at the same place as Paul. We have been overtaken and captured by events. No longer operating from the center of the culture, we are one among many spiritual options for the Gentiles of our time that have little or no church experience. How do we walk in the way Paul walked in Gentile territory that we might further the kingdom of God?

Baptism of Our Lord / Epiphany 1 / Ordinary Time 1
Isaiah 43:1-7
Acts 8:14-17
Luke 3:15-17, 21-22
Timothy Cargal

Returning from exile

Recent biblical scholarship has placed tremendous emphasis on the ways that the scriptural traditions of both Christian testaments were formed and shaped by the experiences of foreign invasion and exile. What we know as the Old Testament is in many ways, both in its parts and as a whole, a response to the experience of the Babylonian exile and the attempts of the people of God to re-establish themselves in their homeland. Similarly, the New Testament bears the clear marks of the shaping forces of Jewish and Christian self-identity formation in the wake of the Jewish war against Rome and the second destruction of Jerusalem and its temple.

But in the American church we generally do not find ourselves in a cultural location that easily resonates with these shaping experiences of the scriptural tradition. We live in the nation that is now more widely regarded globally as the empire rather than the colonies (a self-concept kept alive for us by retelling the story of our nation's founding), and the sole remaining "hyper-power" following the end of the "superpower" struggle of the Cold War. We are part of a society that sends others into exile; not one that lives at the whims of other more powerful nations.

Nevertheless, many of those same biblical scholars who emphasize the shaping influence of the exile experience on the scriptural tradition contend that "exile" can be an important theological category for the contemporary church. Not only does it open our awareness to what it means for others to be on the "wrong side" of the so-called American empire, but it provides an invaluable resource for the church as it loses its privileged position within American culture. The end of Christendom in Western culture marks, in some senses, the sending of the church into cultural exile. Yet churches are so accustomed to privileged status, it will require some real imagination to not only see ourselves as exiles but also to claim for ourselves the promises of the God who delivers from exile.

Isaiah 43:1-7

Imagine yourself as a foreign exile, living your whole life without ever having seen your homeland. Oh, you have heard all the stories from your parents and grandparents about how things used to be. Your family was one of the most important in your nation's capital city. Perhaps your grandfather was a courtesan in the royal court — probably not a direct advisor to the king, but certainly an advisor or assistant to the king's advisors. Or perhaps your grandfather was a priest and your father (much younger then, of course) had been training for the priesthood. Maybe your family had controlled a key economic sector, involved in the very difficult business of international trade in a world that would not know even a steam engine for more than two millennia. Whatever the particulars, you had been raised on the memories of your family's social influence, wealth, and power. But these were your father's and grandfather's memories and not your own.

No, your only memories were of exile. Even before you were born, an invading army had captured your homeland's capital and stripped your family of its wealth and prestige. Nor were they content to leave them dispossessed; they had brought your family back to their own capital city so they could keep an eye on things. Your family had hardly been enslaved or relegated to a life of abject poverty. You had been born into a family ensconced in the skilled castes, but just how much wealth and control they had been allowed to accumulate was carefully monitored and limited. You and your family were reminded at every turn that this was not *your* land. Your land, your ancestral home, had been conquered and humiliated.

How had this happened? What could have caused such great social, financial, and even geographic dislocation? Well, the only thing your people and those who had forced them into exile could agree on was that the ultimate answers were theological. They said it was because the patron god of your ancestors simply had been unequal to the task of protecting you from the powers of their empire and the supernatural exploits of their patron gods. Not too different than the playground taunts of children — "My dad can beat up your dad!" — they taunted that their gods had overpowered your god. But your father and grandfather had raised you on another explanation. The problem was not in the might and grandeur of your God — the only real God in a universe populated with supernatural beings, some of whom were pretenders to the title. No, the problem was with your ancestors and even still with you and your peers. It was because of disobedience and faithlessness that God had punished you, your family, and your countrymen. Your enemies were just pawns of your own God, but pawns nevertheless used to bring destruction on you. It was a fundamentally different explanation, yet one that offered no comfort or reassurance in your exile.

Now that you have children and maybe even grandchildren of your own, there comes a prophet, one of your own countrymen likewise exiled far from home, announcing that God's anger is sated. God had finally, after more than a generation, "redeemed you; [God had] called you by name," and declared that you belonged to the divine. The prophet proclaimed God's recognition of your hardship and promise for your deliverance: "When you pass through the waters, I will be with you; and through the rivers, they shall not overwhelm you; when you shall walk through the fire you shall not be burned, and the flame shall not consume you." Having suffered God's wrath, now "you are precious in [God's] sight," honored and loved. God having used other nations as instruments of punishment against you now "give[s] people in return for you, nations in exchange for your life." God promises you a return from exile. If only you could believe, for you remain far from your homeland, an exile in a foreign land.

Acts 8:14-17

Imagine yourself as an exile but having lived your whole life in your homeland. It is an exile not of geography or politics but of minor ethnic differences inflamed by major prejudices and bigotries. You live in the same land that your ancestors have lived for centuries, but your neighbors never tire of telling you that you just don't belong there. Sure, you have tried to dish out as good as you get and the feelings of animosity and even hatred have been mutual for longer than anyone can remember. Yet you have not had the upper hand for generations, and they won't let you forget that although you may have once shared common ancestors, heritage, and land, they now consider you "half-breeds" at best, or complete foreigners at worst.

Now comes this character named Philip. It is a name that doesn't quite seem to fit. "Philip" is after all a Greek name — the very name of Alexander the Great's father — but this particular man who carries it is clearly of Jewish ethnicity. He must be one of those "Hellenists," those collaborators first with the Greeks and now with the Romans, a "wanna-be" equally ridiculed by "real" Jews and Gentiles alike and even by Samaritans like yourself. But if he is a Roman wanna-be, he sure has a strange way of going about it. He keeps talking to everyone he meets about some guy named Jesus who, he claims, is the long-awaited Messiah.

You want to believe him. After all, Samaritans have long been waiting for the Messiah as well. They were Israel, at least until the Assyrians had conquered their homeland centuries earlier and forced their assimilation with peoples transplanted there from throughout the empire. If anyone could end the animosity between the children of Abraham, Isaac, and Jacob, then surely it would be the Messiah. Here at last was someone announcing the Messiah's arrival. Maybe it was because of that Hellenistic name and the cosmopolitan upbringing it revealed (or is it "betrayed"?), but here also was a Jew proclaiming the arrival of the Messiah to Samaritans — and not in a vindictive, judgmental, "Now-you're-going-to-get-yours" tone either. No, he talked about this Jesus the Messiah as a certainty of joy for Jews and Samaritans alike. If only you could believe him, for you are a Samaritan surrounded by Jews and Romans.

Maybe it is because he senses your hesitation; maybe it is because God's blessings simply cannot be contained in the messianic age. Whatever it is, wonderful things are following in Philip's wake. People were being delivered from things that had long tormented them. Others were being healed of what everyone considered incurable diseases. "So there was great joy in that city." It all seems too good to be true and surely too good to last. Your fears suddenly seem confirmed. Word has spread back to Jerusalem, back to the ones who have considered you half-breeds and treated you dismissively. They simply can't believe that you — Samaritans of all people! — could have "accepted the word of God." So they have sent Peter and John on a fact-finding mission. Is all this joy really from God, or is it yet another Samaritan trick, the work of the devil in religious guise? There is only one way to find out. Peter and John pray, and in response to their prayer the Holy Spirit of God comes and lays claim on your lives so plainly, so obviously that everyone can see it. Your exile in your own homeland has ended. There are no longer Jews and Samaritans, only people of the Messiah.

Luke 3:15-17, 21-22

The crowds that crossed the Judean wait to hear John the Baptist preach on the banks of the Jordan made the arduous journey with their hearts filled with messianic hopes. But John told them the Messiah had yet to be revealed. Moreover, John, in tones that must have sounded threatening, promised that the Messiah would baptize not with water but with "the Holy Spirit and fire. His winnowing fork [would be] in his hand, to clear his threshing floor and to gather the wheat into his granary; but the chaff he [would] burn with unquenchable fire." God's judgment was coming upon the world, and these people were not ready.

What is most amazing about this story, however, is not its portrayal of an apocalyptic prophet out in the wilderness preaching the coming destruction. No, such figures continue to be known to us even in the modern world. What is truly amazing about this part of our story is how Luke characterizes the episode. He wrote, "So, with many other exhortations, [John] proclaimed the good news to the people." The *good news*? The promise of being "baptized with fire" — of being immersed and overwhelmed by the "unquenchable fire" of God's judgment and wrath — this promise was the *good news*? If divine judgment was the "good news," then I am sure the crowds on the banks of the Jordan did not want to hear the "bad news."

Were the imminence of divine judgment the only news, we could scarcely call it "good news." John's full message is that the one who would come to baptize us in the unquenchable fire of God's judgment would also baptize us with the Holy Spirit. As Luke recounts the story of John's ministry, before the coming Messiah can baptize anyone with anything — whether water, spirit, or fire — the Messiah himself must first be baptized with the Holy Spirit who descends as a dove. Yes, the sky is torn open, and yes, the voice of God is heard from the heavens. But the sound that is heard is not the battle cry announcing the arrival of judgment. The voice of God doesn't shout condemnation or recrimination, but rather whispers words of acceptance and affection: "You are my Son, the Beloved; with you I am well pleased."

What are we to make of this situation? John tells his audience to expect apocalyptic judgment with the coming of the messianic age, but when the skies open to announce the dawn of that age, we hear from the heavens only terms of endearment and words of acceptance. Was John wrong? Or was it that while God loved and accepted the eternal, divine Son, only God's wrath was to be bestowed upon all the children whom God had created? Maybe the lesson to be learned from this story is that if you are as good and sinless as Jesus, then God will accept and love you, but otherwise expect only judgment.

That would not, however, be very "good news." None of us can claim to be without sin. No, the good news promised in this story is that God accepts and loves each of us even as God loved Jesus. In our own baptism, God speaks to us the same promise: "You are my child, my beloved; with you I am well pleased."

Application

Imagine yourself as an exile but this time it may take a bit more effort. You see, you don't feel like an exile. Exiles are people who are forced from their homes by others or circumstances beyond their control. You are right where you have been for years. True, you have felt increasingly isolated, even somewhat threatened. But the pressure has not been on you to leave; the pressure has built up from the fact that fewer and fewer have come to join with you as the world around you has changed more and more and has become more and more alien. You can remember a time when it was not this way, a time when it was simply expected that people living in your culture would share your faith, would join with you in worship and service. But as you look around at the surrounding culture you realize that those days are gone. Suddenly you are not sure whether you feel more like Samaritans who had been exiled and marginalized in their own land or Judahites who had found themselves exiled in a strange and foreign land.

Like all exiles, you are sometimes overwhelmed by feelings of despair. You have tried to return back to your home, to make things once again like they were before. But as the years pass you realize that there is no home in which to go back. Things will never be just as they were before, never as they still exist in your parent's and grandparent's memories and maybe even your own. You recognize these are at best your memories, not your children's and certainly not your grandchildren's.

Just when despair begins to descend into hopelessness, you begin to see signs of the Spirit's activity. Long ago, the prophet of Judah's exile had announced God's promise to bring "sons from far away and... daughters from the end of the earth." Now you regularly hear children's rambunctious laughter, a sound that had grown infrequent. You see signs that God is again drawing "offspring from the east" gathering people "from the west" as the long-dominant Euro-American church is broadened both in its scope *and* expression in global, multicultural ways. There is a new sense of the Spirit's presence that brings some excitement and some renewed energy. You want to believe that these signs are indeed indications that your exile is over.

However, returning from exile is not the same as going back to the way things were. God is active but God is not overturning our cultural aphorism that "you can't go back home again." Yet the reason we cannot go back is not one of despair but one of hope. There is no going back to the old things because God is doing a new thing. Like the Samaritans' experience with Philip, the signs and wonders of this age of Spirit and Messiah cannot be contained. It takes faith and courage to return from exile. History tells us that not all the Jews who had been exiled to Babylon found the courage to return to the new beginning God was making in Jerusalem. History tells that not all the Samaritans and Jews of the first century embraced Philip's message about the Messiah. History tells us that those who were the first exiles to return were often confronted with uncertainty and even struggle. But God was with those who returned to Jerusalem to join in building God's future. The Holy Spirit was undeniably with those who accepted the call to join with the Messiah and the same Spirit of God awaits us if we will return from our exile.

An Alternative Application

Luke 3:15-17, 21-22. You don't hear much about divine judgment in some parts of the church anymore. There are enough problems and threats in our lives. There is tension and war rather than peace among the nations of the world as they wrestle with one another over the disparate distribution of resources and power. The willingness of nations to build and stockpile weapons of mass destruction or to engage in acts of terrorism cause us all to live under a cloud of suspicion and threat. There is the social unrest of our communities brought on by poverty and crime. In far too many cases, some can no longer retreat into the shelter of their homes, for even there, threats and recriminations erupt into domestic violence. So pervasive are the perceived threats of modern life that the only thing we want to hear about God is the constant surety of divine love and grace.

Whether we want to hear it or not, Luke was right when he wrote that the prophecy of God's impending judgment is an essential part of the "good news," the gospel of Jesus Christ. We need to recall what God's judgment upon the world was expected to accomplish, for the wrath of God is not after all a senseless temper tantrum or a groundless pique of anger. God's judgment does not target all of humanity indiscriminately but rather is a tool for accomplishing divine justice. If we fear the coming of God's judgment, if the promise that divine justice is to be restored in the world does not strike us as "good news," then truly the announcement of its impending arrival is a warning to us that we are not prepared. If we are afraid that we will be the objects of God's wrath, then it can only be because we recognize that we have adopted the standards of those who oppress others to advance themselves. Exhortations to repent and become people who seek God's justice for the world can indeed be "good news," for those who heed this call to prepare themselves for the time of God's judgment through repentance and service to accomplish that justice.

Epiphany 2 / Ordinary Time 2
Isaiah 62:1-5
1 Corinthians 12:1-11
John 2:1-11
Wayne Brouwer

Wedding bells

A former US president and his wife were reputed to have visited their old hometown and stopped for gas. The attendant happened to be an old acquaintance who had once taken the wife to a high school dance. Driving away, the president remarked, "Aren't you glad you didn't marry him, honey? You'd never have gotten out of town."

His wife flashed a saccharine smile and retorted, "If I had married him, he would be president today and you would still be washing dishes!"

We influence one another, especially in the deep commitments of marriage. Neither of us would be the same had we connected so significantly with a partner of a different character.

One priest remembers a wedding rehearsal where the bride was obviously distraught. She had a hard time focusing while her emotions played bumper cars in her mind and heart. So he took her aside and gently instructed, "Tomorrow don't try to get your head around everything at once. Just take it a step at a time and you will be okay. First concentrate on the aisle. You've walked it so many times with your family; imagine that it's just another Sunday service. Then focus on the altar where you've knelt for communion; that should settle your nerves. Finally, when you get to the front, look at him — he is your friend and your greatest support. When you see him you won't have to think about anything else. There it is in a nutshell — aisle, altar, him. Just think of those three things over and over and you will be fine."

The priest's advice seemed to work. At the ceremony, the bride was almost relaxed. People who gathered in the benches along the processional walkway marveled at her poise. They did, however, wonder about the words she muttered as she passed: "I'll alter him! I'll alter him!"

We do, indeed, alter one another in marriage. Today's passages are all about that. Isaiah pictures a wedding in which Israel regains her royal bearing in the rocky relationship she has had with God. Paul reminds us that the Spirit of Christ lives in the church, and it changes and alters us in order that the bride of Christ might thrive in a relationship with her divine husband. John brings us to a wedding with Jesus and uses the occasion to explore the transforming power of divine love.

Several times, as I officiated at marriages, the fathers of the brides were handing out "business cards" that read: "I am the father of the bride. Nobody seems to be paying much attention to me today, but I can assure you there are several banks and credit card companies that are watching me closely!" Too true!

The richest treasure at any wedding is the strength of character that alloys the bride and groom into a team stronger than their individual resources. In marriage, divine math always projects that one plus one equals far more than two.

Isaiah 62:1-5

Today they are a gracious couple in their senior years who seem absolutely right for each other. They defer to one another in conversation, yet often finish each other's thoughts. They enjoy taking early evening walks and not infrequently passers-by notice that they are holding hands. They travel some, and golf a bit more, and appear to have the same tastes in food and fun. Around them circles a group of friends who share coffee dates and Bible studies. This could be a textbook marriage success.

But it isn't. Years ago, I took him home several times when he was completely and utterly drunk. On one occasion, he slammed his car into a building and would have done more damage had it not been for a snowdrift that cushioned the impact. His car was totaled and he was slobbering pathetic apologies. After several times of watching him, suspicious that he was trying to drive under the influence, I even called the police and had him arrested.

His wife was exhausted from attempting to mind his childish alcoholic tantrums, hiding their dysfunctional relationship, and working part-time jobs to cover expenses for booze and broken things and high-risk car insurance. He only made things worse by becoming religiously righteous and attacking every heresy and social ill very publicly and with much noise. Often this involved berating women who didn't mind their places as obedient servants to obviously superior males. With quiet shame, his wife filed for divorce.

Somehow, it never came about. Friends stood by both of them. Together we got him into a crisis substance abuse program. He repented and made a slow series of amends to his wife and family. Through it all, the grace of God once again weaved reconciliation and renewal.

None of us who were on the painful inside of his catastrophic self-destruction imagined this man's sanity or this couple's marriage could be saved. Yet it was. By grace alone, it was.

In truth, their affair was another retelling of ancient Israel's religious soap opera. The pages of Isaiah's prophecy tell an amazing story of tender love between Israel and God, couched in the language of youthful passions and marriage analogies. They also describe Israel's abysmal failure paralleled by God's faithful pleading for her to come to her senses and return home to their children.

Unfortunately, Isaiah would never see God's desire for marriage recovery with Israel become reality. Too soon, Israel would take spiritual adultery and prostitution too far and be lost forever from the ties of covenant troth.

Still, Isaiah's prophecy lingers in scripture as a testimony of God's faithful love and as a model for the best of what marriage can be. Those who find a way to imitate God's long-suffering spousal patience and the best of Israel's too infrequent repentance may experience the recovery of a marriage even when it has been written off as compromised beyond reason and damaged in excess of recovery.

Not every broken partnership can be saved. Nor should foolish, scandalous, hurtful, or destructive behavior be ignored or condoned simply to keep a religious pretense of marital faithfulness. Yet the best remedy to infidelity or other attacks on marriage is repentance, reconciliation, and renewal. These, after all, as Isaiah indicates, are very much God's desire.

1 Corinthians 12:1-11

When we built our first home, after years of living in parsonages, we talked with many people before signing the contract with a particular developer. We wanted a house that was planned well to suit to our family needs, located in a neighborhood that reflected our values, and sturdily assembled through construction methods and materials that were in relative harmony with the creation.

We loved that house. It had a soft sandalwood-colored brick front and a great big forest green door, welcoming all who shared our hospitality. Yet, while my wife and I retain vivid memories of the exterior appearance and internal layout of that house, our daughters' recollections have dimmed greatly. Not surprising, I guess, since the oldest was only twelve when we moved.

What intrigues me, though, are the things our daughters *do* remember. They recall sitting on my lap (all three at the same time!) while I read to them the entire *Narnia Chronicles* series by C.S. Lewis. They talk about several birthday parties we had in that house. They know the names of their friends from down the street and the games they played together. They can still recite the prayers we prayed with them at their bedsides and they remember where the family meal table was and what our conversations were while around it.

My wife and I recall a fine house; our daughters remember a warm, loving, and spiritually rich home. In this they are in tune with the religion of Paul as he opens this teaching on spiritual gifts. The church, he reminds us, is not about buildings or blueprints or bureaucracy. It is rather about expansive faith that establishes symbiotic blessings among people who are vitally connected to one another by a marriage made in heaven. It is about laughter that lights up faces and turns hands into helpers. It is about conversations through which children are nurtured and learn to breathe spiritually, old folks are respected for their wisdom, and those new to faith are encouraged.

During the horrible 1940s wartime bombing of London, England, air raid sirens too often prevented sleep, and children were bundled away into shelters for fear of the savage destruction that fell from the skies. In an instant, a street could become a junkyard, with flames gobbling the leftover carnage.

One family has carried with them a powerful scene from those days. The bombs fell and their house was obliterated. For nearly half an hour, the parents screamed hoarsely until they found all four children. Some had cuts and bruises but all were alive. In mixed anguish and appreciation, they hugged each other among the ruins. Sobbing, the mother complained, "We've lost our home!"

But the nine-year-old daughter thought otherwise. "No we haven't, Mummy," she said, "we've got our home right here! All we need to do is find another house to put it in."

So it is with the church when it is functioning according to the lifeblood of its richly diverse spiritual gifts.

John 2:1-11

This is the first of Jesus' "miraculous signs," according to John. We need to pay attention to that note as we craft our homilies and sermons. John gives us several clues as to what we can tell others in describing this scene.

First, he pins the wedding celebration in Cana to "the third day" (John 2:1). By itself, this locative phrase means little. When it is tied to the clues John gives in chapter 1, it is truly illuminating. John carefully links his story of Jesus to the creation story of Genesis (see John 1:1 and Genesis 1:1, and note John's identification of Jesus "the word" as the Creator). Furthermore, the incarnation of Jesus is a renewal of the original creation of light. So it is that when John tells us of Jesus' coming, it is a remanifestation of what took place on the first day of creation, according to the book of Genesis.

This becomes evident in the chronological sequences noted by John in the verses preceding today's text. Jesus' early actions mimic the revelations of God through the primary days of the creation story. If one follows them along, "the third day" mentioned in 2:1 turns out to be the seventh day of John's record of Jesus. It was on the seventh day, according to Genesis 1, that God rested from creative work in order to enjoy the intimacy of a relationship with the people God created. John is telling us here that Jesus has arrived to share the full intimacy of God with us on planet earth.

Second, the fact that Jesus performs his first miraculous sign at a wedding feast is instructive. We don't know who the bride and groom are, but it was likely that they were relatives of Mary, Jesus' mother, and that she had been asked to serve as caterer for the event. That was the typical way of providing food for the celebration in first-century Palestine. So it was natural for Mary and Jesus to be there and for Mary to assume that Jesus would help out with the supplies for the party.

The added link is that John ties each of the seven "miraculous signs" of Jesus to an Old Testament reference. Here the connection appears to be made with the story of Adam and Eve. Since it was within the marriage relationship of the first couple, according to Genesis, that the cancer of sin appeared, so Jesus restores the celebration to the wedding party. Marriages were first to fall prey to the debilitating effects of evil; now Jesus comes to bring restoration and wholeness to a couple whose carefree intimacy is already in danger of compromise even in the first hours of their wedded life.

Third, the method Jesus uses to accomplish this feat is that of taking the symbols of the Old Covenant Age and transforming them into the bearers of blessing for the New Covenant Age. The rituals and ceremonies of Israel's existence were meant to be caretakers and teachers of the provisions of God yet to come. If indeed, in the person of Jesus, the new age has dawned and the light of the world has returned, then the old forms must give way to the new, and the vessels of ritual need to become resources of grace.

This understanding of Jesus' first miraculous sign is confirmed by John's placement of the temple-cleansing scene immediately afterward. The temple was the most complete and complex of the symbols deriving energy from ritual. Jesus steps in to cut through the ceremonial red tape and make it possible for people to connect directly with God once again.

Application

I've beaten the national average but I'm still not batting 1,000. More of the weddings at which I officiate result in seemingly healthy or strong marriages than do those which end in divorce, at least as far as I know. I assume that my "success" is based in part on my commitment to never officiate at any marriage where both partners could not openly declare their trust in God and common faith commitments, and in my insistence that all must go through significant pre-marriage counseling before the knot is tied.

However, that has resulted in neither a perfect track record for me nor perfect marriages for those I blessed. One couple lasted a mere fourteen weeks before he didn't match up to her romantic ideals, and she spent far more money than he was accustomed. Another stuck together for a decade before his hyper-controlling tendencies asphyxiated the thing. Two children were bitterly scarred in that one.

While the failures of these marriages are bothersome, what scares me more is when couples call it quits after twenty, thirty, or forty years. Once you get past the "seven-year-itch" and the "eleventh-year-fear" it would seem that some deep interconnectedness would have set in to provide a greater stability for the onslaught of the years. Like the old John Deere tractors I farmed with as a boy, there was more work in getting the thing going than there was in keeping it running. The secret was the massive flywheel. I had to strain in order to turn it over the first time, but once the magneto caught and the pistons popped and the flywheel gained some momentum on its own, it almost took an act of God to kill the thing!

But God is not in the business of killing a good thing. He "gives strength to the weary and increases the power of the weak," as Isaiah once put it. Even in marriages. Perhaps especially in marriages, since God thought that one up in the first place. In fact, according to the passages in today's lectionary readings, God is the best source of flywheel power to keep a good thing going.

How do we get the power to see it through? How can we find the grace to run the race and not trip at the last lap? How can we go the distance and make it to the top and complete the journey?

The Bible is not about magic. Its verses recall the stumbling and sinfulness of God's people, as the Isaiah pericope notes. They speak also about the warm and compassionate heart of God, displayed by Jesus at the wedding in Cana, and infused by the life-giving Spirit that stimulates vitality, as in the words of Paul to the Corinthian congregation. Spiritual health, like careers or characters, is not made overnight. It happens when we dig in for the long run and keep our eyes on the prize.

M. Scott Peck, the psychiatrist who became a Christian through his observations of human behavior while counseling, said that the scariest people on earth were not those who had quirky personalities or relational scars. The most threatening folks, he wrote in *The People of the Lie*, were those who did not believe in a higher power, a God or gods beyond themselves. Peck noted that when we stop praying and begin to assume an attitude of belligerent self-sufficiency, we shrink the world to our perspectives and seek to control it according to our whims. The result is always horrifying.

Spirituality that goes the distance is inevitably built on trust — trust in others who share the journey and trust in God. An 81-year-old man sat in his oversized chair and slapped his hands against the top of the armrests and said to me with a wistful smile, "We're sixty years married this week and mighty proud of our family. But it's not us... It's the grace of God. It's the grace of God."

An Alternative Application
1 Corinthians 12:1-11. The Corinthians lesson can be used well by itself. It is practical and easily illustrated, especially when taken in consort with the "body life" passage that follows. One way to think of the Spirit as Paul portrays it is to imagine a reservoir of clean, clear water, high in the mountains beyond the range of human contamination. Engineers (think "apostles" and "church structures") have managed to channel a flow from that lake down to the valley below. It surges through pipes that drive generators to create electricity that radiates out into the community as the source of power to drive many devices. It also pulses into a stream of water that sustains life for those living in the valley.

In this way, the power of God, originating from heaven's throne, is communicated to a world in need. The Spirit is the link and energy, channeled through the teachings and ministry connections of the church, and bringing vitality to the neighborhood.

Epiphany 3 / Ordinary Time 3
Nehemiah 8:1-3, 5-6, 8-10
1 Corinthians 12:12-31a
Luke 4:14-21

Craig MacCreary

Primal urge

The texts set before us all have to do with encountering the primal and basic core of religious faith. Increasingly, I find a desire to identify what is primal in our lives. When I went to seminary some thirty years ago there was an inherent suspicion of the primal. The text was to be demythologized, psychologized, deconstructed, or mined for its moral maxims, and its capacity to deal with everyday human problems. It is not to say that these efforts did not bear fruit or bring many to faith. It did leave many of us viewing the unreconstructed primal as primitive and in need of putting some distance between it and ourselves.

No doubt there is truth to be had in the historical, critical scrutiny of scripture. I cannot imagine myself reading any text without the contextual, historical, and literary questions that my training calls me to deal with. However, I have increasingly wondered whether the historical critical method can generate passion, intensity, and vision through all the filters it creates.

In each of the texts, the reader is called to understand their life in the face of some primal understandings. In the Nehemiah text, the returned exiles are called to struggle with the rule of law, God's law, as they rebuild the nation and its institutions. The returnees must be schooled in the primal intentions of God as commanded in the law and the foundational events of their history. Judging by the people's reaction, the encounter with the primal was very intense. Paul gives us a central metaphor for the church that is primal enough that it informs nearly all understandings of the nature of the church. Paul has come in for a lot of deconstructing in recent years but not here. Of course, the reaction to Jesus' reading of the prophet and his claim that it was fulfilled in their hearing resulted in everyone fixing their gaze on Jesus in anticipation of what he might say or do next.

Here is religious and theological writing that could not be easily ignored by its readers. Indeed it is the people who called for the reading of the law. I believe that the people hunger for the kind of organic understanding of the church that Paul lifts up. Who does not long for community that rejoices and suffers together? The "What Would Jesus Do" movement embodies a desire to have a relationship with Jesus that enables the church to have the mind of Christ amongst its members. Here we have evidence of what was at the core of that mind. Of course, on the other hand, what is at the center of his thinking has earth-shattering implications, which are a bit more than some had bargained.

The texts address the questions: Where do we come from; who are we now; and where do we think we are headed? I look at how my ancestors worshiped and the fervor with which they believed and I can understand why many in the crowd beneath Ezra's feet wept when what many believe to have been an early form of the Pentateuch was read. My direct spiritual ancestors founded institutions like Harvard and Yale and Dartmouth, pioneered in the expansion of human rights, and proportionally gave unbelievable sums of money to evangelize throughout the world. I am sure the readers of this journal have similar tales to tell of the people from whom they are spiritually descended. The sense of distance between that vitality and where we seemingly are these days is a bit more epiphany than we want to have. Certainly, Paul's primal understanding of church was written in light of cracks in the spiritual and theological facade of the early church that threatened its unity. It is an ideal that we have not attained in an era of private, do-it-yourself, consumer-driven, age-segmented religious experience. Jesus' words come as an epiphany of purpose and vision as to his direction. Yet, it also comes as quite a revelation of the distance between us and the fulfillment of the year of the Lord's favor.

The primal brings tears and joy. Joy as to what God is about and tears that too many of us have lost touch with the primal aims of our God.

Nehemiah 8:1-3, 5-6, 8-10

Most of our generation must surely find the story of the returned listening to the reading of the law near fanciful at best. Their fervor and desire for the law seems quaint. Moderns might sit down and consider, given our changed circumstance, what approach should be taken toward establishing a controlling legal authority. That people would stand for this hour after hour seems to be a quaint sort of religious enthusiasm. Surely in the retelling of this, we must be hearing the self-interest of the central authority and the elite seeking to establish its control over the nation — perhaps.

Yet, anyone who has raised children knows that this explanation does not exhaust the possible meanings here. There comes a time when children begin to ask the questions about where they have come from — more accurately from what sort of people have they come from. Is there anything in my family that I must live up to or live out? Is there somewhere in the past a curse, a failing, that must be lived down? Is there a great cloud of witnesses looking down upon me now that I somehow must not let down in my journey? Children search for epiphany — as defined by the dictionary "the sudden manifestation of the essence or the meaning of something." In their own way they ask, "What did our people believe and what was it like for them to believe?" that they might find some clue as to who they are and what they should be.

They also long for the law. The developmental theorists remind us of what every parent knows: there is a stage where a child's black-and-white thinking can be quite legalistic. Certainly it is not a stage to be mired in, but one to build on; to be adjusted and matured. It is not one to be avoided. Indeed it may need to be revisited as one grows and matures. Children want to know where they stand and where the boundaries will be established and what boundaries will be defended. They seem to know better than their parents sometimes that God, as a smiling grandpa without norms, does not work.

In exile, far from home, there was much pressure and many benefits to forget who you were and to routinely cast aside the law. It can be quite a revelation how far one has gone off the path of moral development when you are far from the constraints of home. It is quite a revelation that the longest of the Ten Commandments is the commandment about remembering the sabbath to keep it holy. With attendant explanations it takes up over 50% of the words devoted to all of the commandments — an epiphany. What seems to have been a unique contribution to the world's ethical thinking by the Israelites was the notion of sabbath. You would never know it from what passes for ethical conversation in the media. Perhaps, because of living in exile, as we do in many ways, this is the most readily violated of all the commandments. Certainly it is the one we believe has the least consequences for being broken — a revelation of how far we may be from our origins.

Of course, the reading of the law does not take place in the context of a courtroom or a classroom but in the context of worship. Then Ezra blessed the Lord, the great God, and all the people answered, "Amen, amen," lifting up their hands. Then they bowed their heads and worshiped the Lord with their faces to the ground. It is worship because this is not merely about laying down the law but laying open the law and an opening to the heart of its author. More than intellectual ascent is required here.

It was quite a day for the Israelites: an epiphany of lost origins and newfound commandments. A day of understanding that came through communal discernment. It was a day of the primal in preparation for their work.

1 Corinthians 12:12-31a

Paul seems to engage in some fantasy here as he has talking feet, hands, eyes, and ears to illustrate his main point. However the older I get the more I appreciate the metaphor. There are days when my various body parts are a cacophony of messages. Some are clearly of the first kind that Paul mentions in verses 14-16. There are times when there are various parts of me that try to make their move toward secession. If they do not completely secede the individual body parts put forth the notion that their various needs are privileged over others. This results in the various parts trying to run the whole show. In the churches I have served, this shows up in the ever-popular phrases "We have never done it that way before" and "We know how things are done around here, so it is my way or the highway." It also shows up in the idea since the young people and the young parents are the future of the church, they have a blank check to do any fool thing no matter how tasteless. So the various parts, believing that they do not belong to the body try to rearrange everything according to their own desire. This results in taking the next step of the various parts attempting to say to each other that there is no place for the other parts in the new order of things. I have no need of the social gospel people, the ladies' circle, or whatever. Paul is trying to strike a balance where all parts of the body are honored but none is privileged.

I recently had a graphic illustration of this. I try to run about six miles every day. I am not particularly adept at this, yet I found myself trying to push hard to, at least at the age of 57, be able to run a 10k in under 57 minutes. I pulled it off. I accomplished my goal by running my distance in 56 minutes. I was rather proud that I had 56-minute legs at the age of 57 and was quite solicitous of their care. However, the rest of my members have started a fairly serious conversation to the effect that that the wear and tear indicates that I am not at the 56-minute level. If I expect to continue running, we will have to have a major summit meeting as to what running should be about in my case. All parts will be honored and none privileged.

How do we go wrong in the church such that we wind up privileging some while not honoring all? Indeed, to do the former is to do the latter and vise versa. Paul implies that where we go wrong is baptism. If we get it right, then we understand that at baptism we become members of this mystical body where all parts are honored but none are privileged. He points out that some of the major differences that divide Paul's world are overcome by the Holy Spirit. Like the Orthodox church of today, the Spirit was bestowed as a gift shortly after baptism. I suspect that we are less than fully versed in covering this meaning of baptism with either parents or adults who are about to undergo the rite.

In the Corinthian church, communion became a source of spiritual illness because the members did not discern the Lord's body. Those who had much showed up early and, believing that it was their privilege, went ahead with the meal, whether there was enough to go around or not. Speaking in tongues had become an occasion for self-glorification rather than mutual edification. The Corinthians made just about anything and everything an occasion to pull rank rather than pull together.

It might be quite an epiphany if we came to understand the divisions in the church that have lead to divisiveness because of our failure to understand the primal meaning of our baptism.

Luke 4:14-21

The reports about him do spread throughout the land as Luke recounts, and can there be any doubt that for the most part he does earn the praise of everyone? I have yet to read any bad press on Jesus, and I have seen plenty of attempts to get on the bandwagon. Jesus, from day one, is the hot topic of conversation. Yet here we are given a story where Jesus seems to have left people in a stunned silence. People always seem to have something to say about Jesus. The gospel recounts that it seems in general people could not shut up around Jesus. They sought to speak with him or about him. What was going on as the folks stared at Jesus? Were the preachers and pontificators in the crowd wondering what to say next? Did those idle curious, looking for something more spectacular for the moment, say to themselves, "So this is it. Isn't something more supposed to happen?" Did the regulars think, "I better look this up?"

It does seem that we have here a fragile moment, for it does not take too long as the dust settles for people to seem unsettled at what has happened. While all speak well of him, they wonder just how it is that a local boy could be saying such things. You have the feeling that things could break down as they eventually do, for by the end of the encounter they are ready to throw him over a cliff.

In a way, we do to Jesus what Paul experienced among the Corinthians. We dissect him and find that we have no use for the aspects of Jesus that we have grown uncomfortable with. The Jesus that prays and ponders puts off those who say that Jesus is a social revolutionary. The Jesus that tells the lepers to go show themselves to the priest offends those who say, "Is not this the Jesus who has come to confound and challenge conventional religion?" Jesus the healer and miracle worker irritates those who have come because of the ethical insights of the Sermon on the Mount.

Yet here we are presented with one Jesus. He whose birth angels heralded, whose prenatal history is the fulfillment of Jewish history, and whose birthing has brought blindness to some and new sight to others is standing in the synagogue reading the morning lesson. The local folk who have their slice of Jesus can't get over it, "Is this not Joseph's son standing here with us reading the morning lesson?"

Quite an epiphany we have here. The teaching is told in the context of the miraculous. The fulfillment of history is told in the midst of the traditional being confounded. Luke tells his story of the implementation of God's plan from Jerusalem to Rome in the context of the prayer and the leading of a personal spirit. No wonder all eyes are fixed on him.

There is a unity of being in Jesus that the centrifugal forces of life want to pull apart. Unlike Jesus, when I am in overdrive it is all about my plan, not God's plan. Unlike Jesus, I struggle to cast out the demons without demonizing. Unlike Jesus, I seek healing without being open to having the conventional meaning of the term confounded. I join Paul in his plea for the unity of the church, yet I carry on inside me titanic battles that leave Jesus in bits and pieces.

Perhaps it is impossible to ever have the unity of spirit that Jesus brought to that synagogue meeting. Perhaps, at best, I can do this serially. Yet my primal understanding of Jesus is the one who is saving because he lifts up the sides of me that are underdeveloped and the parts of me that are overdeveloped. This scripture has been fulfilled in my hearing of it.

Application

These texts chart a course toward a primal sense of our origins, our unity, and our sense of direction as God's people. Yes, we do need to be reminded that we are descended from prophets, law givers, and missioners. We have a large history to draw upon and guide our steps and steady our living. We are people who are the expression of a unity of spirit that has survived through the centuries. We are a people that in the Spirit has quite a destiny set before us. A friend of mine reminds me that we are God's gift to the world; don't hide it, don't deny it, just act like it.

I suspect that this comes for many in the pew as quite a revelation. The community we enter into through baptism changes our history, status, and destiny. I do not see that written on many baptismal certificates. This is the season of Epiphany, a time to consider what is revealed and how the meaning and essence of things is made known to us. It is also a time to consider how Christ Jesus is the fulfillment of what we understand to be God's ways in the world and how we become part of the meaning and essence of things.

An Alternative Application

1 Corinthians 12:12-31a. It seems one experience that is featured in the Christian scriptures is beyond the imagining of most of us, a term in prison as an inmate or a jailor. For many of us, the idea of being a captive freed is well beyond our experience. Yet many of us are captive to bad marriages or arid living, jobs that provide little sense of vocation, patterns of living that get us in deep trouble, and troubled pasts that will not let us go.

Yes, all eyes are on him as we wonder how this can be the year of the Lord's favor. It seems to me it won't be if we merely plan a change in jobs, a new spouse, winning the lottery, leaving town, or any of the other things that humans change that often brings no real change to their lives.

It will be the year of the Lord's favor if we allow Jesus to touch those places in our lives where we need to be changed, freed, released, or take a second look. It is not too late in the new year to make another resolution. Only this time, it will not be so much about what I need to change but what will I allow Jesus to change in my life. When he releases me from captivity, I resolve to march through the open door no matter where the road may lead. I will allow him to bring me his riches no matter what it may cost me. I will allow him to open my eyes no matter how much it changes my view of me and others.

Epiphany 4 / Ordinary Time 4
Jeremiah 1:4-10
1 Corinthians 13:1-13
Luke 4:21-30
David Kalas

Blocking and tackling

On a typical NFL football team, there are some players who get all the attention and glory, and other players who are nearly anonymous. That line is typically drawn according to position.

On offense, for example, the quarterback, the running back, and the star wide receiver are traditionally the players who get all the hype. These are among the so-called "skill" positions. These are the players focused on by fantasy football fans. And these are the guys who, at the end of the day, have the capacity for flashy statistics: yards passing, yards rushing, yards receiving; completion percentage; yards after catch; rushing average; and, most important, how many touchdowns.

Meanwhile, among the players and positions traditionally overlooked are the offensive guards and tackles. Everything that the stars achieve depends on these anonymous and unheralded big men, but they still fly below the radar of appreciation and applause.

The running back says, "I carried the ball 23 times for 136 yards and 2 touchdowns." He had a good day. The receiver says, "I caught 8 passes for 120 yards and 2 touchdowns." He had a good day. The interior lineman says, "I blocked my guy all day long." He, too, had a good day, but who cares? He is not swarmed for post-game autographs and interviews.

The church in first-century Corinth may have suffered a bit from that same phenomenon. Fascinated by the flashy, they needed to be reminded about the fundamentals. We gather from Paul's first epistle to them that they had their own notion of the "skill" positions in the church: tongues, healing, miracles, and such. The apostle had to remind them about the basic blocking and tackling of the Christian life — such as love — without which all the rest would amount to nothing.

Jeremiah 1:4-10

We are fortunate to have in scripture the accounts of a number of different people being called by God. Moses, Gideon, Isaiah, Peter and Andrew, James and John, Matthew, and Paul are among them. We see different individuals respond to God's call in very different ways. Moses is famously reluctant. Isaiah volunteers. Peter and company are immediately responsive.

Here in this episode, we catch a glimpse of Jeremiah's call from God and we sense that Jeremiah is reticent. In the spirit of Moses at the burning bush, Jeremiah feels quite unqualified and he expresses that hesitation to God. The Lord, however, is quick to dismiss Jeremiah's objection.

We see in this single episode several themes that are woven throughout scripture.

First, there is the divine employment of the unqualified. As we mentioned above, Jeremiah's response is reminiscent of Moses, who also tried to point out to God that he was, in some way, not the right man for the job. Gideon (Judges 6:15), Saul (1 Samuel 9:21), and Peter (Luke 5:8) all registered similar objections. Add to those instances the old, barren woman from whom God intended to generate whole nations; the overmatched boy with a sling; and the small, improbable band of men charged with taking the good news to the whole world; and we see God's proclivity for hiring unqualified workers. The one whose "power is made perfect in weakness" (2 Corinthians 12:9) seems to delight in winning with lousy teams.

Second, there is the gracious stubbornness of God. Jeremiah voices his hesitation but neither the form nor the content of Jeremiah's response makes God go away. He is not driven off by Jeremiah's reluctance; neither is he repelled by Jeremiah's inadequacies. Instead, he persists with Jeremiah, in spite of both his disinclinations and his disqualifications. And that is gospel for us, for you and I need God to be persistent. If he were easily discouraged or quickly dissuaded, we would all be lost. Every saint is a testimony to God's stubborn grace: the God who begins a good work in us and who is faithful to complete it (Philippians 1:6).

Third, there is God's engagement with youth. We do not know how old Jeremiah was, but he was young enough to say, apparently with a straight face, "I am only a boy." The Hebrew word used by Jeremiah is "imprecise." On the one hand, Abraham uses the same word to refer to young men who accompanied him in battle (Genesis 14:24); on the other hand, the writer of Exodus uses it to describe the baby, Moses, when he was found by Pharaoh's daughter (Exodus 2:6).

Whatever the exact age and stage of Jeremiah, it is certainly true that God willingly engages and effectively uses the very young. In the New Testament, we are fond of the image of Jesus welcoming the children, and we are reminded of Paul's challenge to young Timothy (1 Timothy 4:12). In the Old Testament, meanwhile, we see baby Moses providentially spared, young Samuel called at night, and the shepherd boy, David, used in battle: all while they were still quite young.

Fourth, and quite prominent within this passage, is the theme of God's preordained will for people. This is a perilous path to go down as we soon find ourselves in the deep waters of many complex theological issues and questions. Foreknowledge, election, and predestination; the relationship between God's sovereignty and human freedom; Calvinism vs. Arminianism; the implications of double predestination; this is the difficult terrain we encounter when we venture down this path. At a minimum, however, we can cheerfully affirm the beautiful image of God's prenatal call and claim on Jeremiah's life. Whether one emphasizes God's sovereign choice or God's prevenient grace, the fact and the testimony remains that he is interested in us before we are interested in him, and he is at work in our lives before we recognize it.

1 Corinthians 13:1-13

Our epistle lection for this Sunday is one of the most famous, familiar, and fond passages in all of scripture. Often called "the love chapter," 1 Corinthians 13 is a staple at wedding ceremonies, as well as a common text for posters, bulletin covers, and needle points. After only the Lord's Prayer and Psalm 23, 1 Corinthians 13 may be the best-recognized and most-recited passage in the Bible. And yet, for all of its familiarity, it may not be widely understood.

The first issue, as always, is context but this passage has been so frequently excerpted that it is, in so many minds, completely independent of its context. That original context may be a necessary place for us to begin in preaching this passage.

The larger discussion at this point in 1 Corinthians is the gifts of the Spirit, both in the lives of individuals and in the life of the church. The true significance of love is only evident within that larger context. At the same time, it is worth noting that what has happened to chapters 12 through 14 of 1 Corinthians does, in some way, prove Paul's point. He asserts that the rest of the gifts are temporal and will come to an end but that "love never ends." Sure enough, the discussion of the other gifts in which the love chapter is found is generally eclipsed by — sometimes even forgotten because of — the power and beauty of love.

The chapter also suffers somewhat from the fact that it is associated with wedding ceremonies. It has become, as a result, something of an adornment. It is a thing of beauty, like the flowers or the dresses, but not a thing of great meaning. And what meaning it has is often misunderstood as romantic in nature.

See what has happened to our popular understanding of this passage. We have taken it out of its original context — a discussion of the gifts of the Spirit — and reestablished it in a new context — wedding ceremonies. So Paul's grand explication of love now has, for many, all the profundity of a Barry Manilow song.

Romance, of course, is not at all the style or content of 1 Corinthians 13, and we do well to distance ourselves and our people from such a reading and hearing of this text. The word "love," along with our understanding and our exercise of it, has become so devalued in our culture. It is confused (at least by the young, if not more) with enthusiasm. And it has become the word to articulate how much I want a person or thing, when of course what "I want" has nothing whatever to do with the profound love that Paul describes here.

The initial point Paul makes, dovetailing with his preceding discussion of the gifts of the Spirit, is that the other gifts are proven to be empty and lifeless without love. Then, having established the essential importance of love, Paul follows with a several-verse description of what love is and what it is not.

Perhaps you have been in class or retreat settings, as I have, where those selected verses (4-7) are excerpted and turned into a two-part exercise. First, each individual in the group is asked to replace the word "love" (or its pronoun) in each phrase with his or her own name. Since I am supposed to be characterized by this quality of love, using Paul's description of love to describe me becomes a powerful diagnostic to show specifically where I fall short. Second, each individual is asked to replace the word "love" in each phrase with Jesus' name. This is a devotional sort of exercise, inviting us to meditate on him, his nature, and his love.

Finally, Paul argues for the eternal quality of love. The rest of the gifts are temporal in their necessity and usefulness but this love "never ends." It is one of a very few things that abides, and it is the greatest of even those.

Luke 4:21-30

Our gospel lection comes from Jesus' return to his hometown, Nazareth. A homecoming ought to have a certain warmth and happiness to it. This particular episode, however, turns ugly fast.

Every preacher knows that there are the passages folks love to hear preached, and then there are others that are not so welcome. It is human nature to prefer a sermon on "Come to me, all you that are weary and are carrying heavy burdens, and I will give you rest" (Matthew 11:28) over one on "If any want to become my followers, let them deny themselves and take up their cross daily and follow me" (Luke 9:23). They are both teachings of Jesus. They are both relevant to us. They are both invitations. But they are not equally welcome words.

Jesus went before a congregation in Nazareth and preached an unwelcome message.

Selecting two stories from the people's scriptures that, taken together, were sure to tweak their noses, Jesus proposed an offensive thesis: namely, that God sometimes chooses to do his work, not among his own chosen people, but among the Gentiles. Indeed, that God's own people are sometimes the ones least receptive to his work and his word.

It was an unthinkable proposition, and while he clearly had texts to support his hypothesis, his conclusion was most unorthodox — perhaps even heretical. And the people responded with a kind of righteous indignation.

Beyond that, their response was also one of personal animus. For Jesus was not just making an unorthodox observation from scripture; he was also pointing the finger at them. If the discussion could have remained a theoretical and arm's-length debate about the ministries of Elijah and Elisha, it might have been tolerable. But the thrust of Jesus' message was not theoretical and historical; instead, the application of it was present and personal. It was about them and him and their failure to respond properly to him.

Then the improper response begins.

The final line from this episode is striking. Luke describes a mob scene that, under other circumstances, would have been lethal. We have, on our television screens, seen occasional incidents in which an angry crowd has gotten hold of an individual, an automobile, a piece of property, or a section of a town, and done devastating damage. Here in Nazareth, an incensed mob manhandles Jesus out of the synagogue and to the very edge of the cliff on which the town was built. They meant to throw him over. They meant to kill him; yet, Luke reports, "He passed through the midst of them and went on his way."

No evidence of a struggle. No Chuck Norris or Arnold Schwarzenegger heroics to burst out of the crowd. Not even Samson's jawbone of a donkey or David's slingshot is employed. He simply walks through the midst of the crowd.

How does that happen? You and I sometimes find it difficult — in a mall at Christmas or outside the stadium after a game — to work our way through a crowd that doesn't even know or care who we are. But when the crowd is focused on you — out to get you — how do you just pass through the midst of it?

The same one who eluded Herod's death decree in Bethlehem; the same one who walked on stormy waters; the same one who had the authority to say a word and cast out a demon, heal at a distance, and call a corpse out of a tomb; that one can walk through the midst of a crowd intent on killing him. The episode here, in Luke, offers additional meaning and credibility to Jesus' strong claim in John: "No one takes (my life) from me, but I lay it down of my own accord. I have power to lay it down, and I have power to take it up again. I have received this command from my Father" (John 10:18).

Application

If the gifts of the Spirit were a spectator sport, you can imagine which players would get the applause and be hounded for autographs.

Here is this two-man team that does a tongues-and-interpretation combo. The crowds cheer.

Here is a player with a gift of healing: one disease and disability after another is thwarted by his God-given gift. The fans are really on their feet now.

Here is a spiritual athlete whose faith is so strong that he moves mountains before our eyes. The crowd goes absolutely wild — they're doing "the wave"!

Meanwhile, in a far corner of the field, there is another player, who is hardly noticed. He is surrounded by irritations, yet is dealing with each one patiently. He is being fouled by other players, yet he keeps no record of it. When he does something well, he does not spike the ball, dance, or draw attention to himself. He does not seek the spotlight or insist on things going his way, and when his teammates get all the glory, he is happy for them, and cheers for them as loudly as anyone.

The other players — the flashy ones, the especially gifted ones — get all of the attention and accolades. Yet, at the end of the season, when God designates the MVP, the fans are surprised by his decision: "the greatest of these is love."

Alternative Applications
Jeremiah 1:4-10. "The Case of the Cautious Candidate." I had a friend who was considering a job offer. He wanted the job and he applied for it. He went through the whole application and interview process quite successfully, and in the end, the company offered him the job. But he hesitated to take it.

As we talked about it, he shared with me that he had doubts about his qualifications.

"Do they think you're qualified?" I asked.

"Yes."

"Well, that's their call," I said. "You only need to make your decision for you. You don't have to make their decision for them."

Jeremiah felt unqualified for what God was calling him to do. But qualifications are for the employer to judge. That's God's call. He knows the job and he knows which prospect he wants to hire. I'm not sure that there has been a reluctant candidate yet who has talked him out of his personnel decision: who has made God say, "I was wrong; you are right."

Likewise with us. There's a good chance God will call each of us to do for him something that we will feel unqualified, under equipped, or overmatched to do. But that's his call to make and not ours. It's his work and if I am the one he has chosen to do this particular segment of it, then I can be assured that the same one who was with Jeremiah will be with me.

Jeremiah 1:4-10; Luke 4:21-30. "Tough Appointment." I am a United Methodist clergy and so I live my life under appointment. In our system, a pastor is appointed to a church by the presiding bishop for one year at a time. While many of our churches, frankly, operate with a more congregational mentality, the fact remains that the bishop decides which pastors will be appointed to serve which churches.

I don't think I would reveal state secrets to say that not every United Methodist clergyperson is equally thrilled with the appointment he or she receives.

The Old Testament and gospel lections this week, however, remind us that the servant of God receives his or her appointment from God. And, it is often an inhospitable assignment.

God's instructions to Jeremiah are blunt and no-nonsense: "You shall go to all to whom I send you." Jeremiah is not encouraged to pick and choose. He is not applauded for hitting 75 or 80% of his targets. He is to go wherever God sends him. And, on top of that, he is to say, "Whatever I command you." That, we know from the rest of his story, is an unsavory task. And God's next imperative — "Do not be afraid of them" — drives home the prospect of a hostile audience.

We are reminded of Jeremiah's tough assignment and experience when we get to Jesus' appointment at the Nazareth synagogue. He recounts the truth of God's own people being antagonistic toward God's prophets and then he experiences it himself, firsthand.

In a consumer culture, where our parishioners are conditioned to eschew uncomfortable messages and assignments, God's tough appointments will be unwelcome news. It is a part of discipleship that we should preach to them, however. (And it is a part of discipleship that we should model for them too.)

Transfiguration of Our Lord
(Last Sunday of Epiphany)
Exodus 34:29-35
2 Corinthians 3:12—4:2
Luke 9:28-36 (37-43)
David Kalas

The picture Bible

Big events in our culture are generally accompanied by much picture taking.

If you've watched the initial kickoff at any year's Super Bowl, you've seen how the occasion is marked by thousands of flashes around the stadium, as people capture the moment. So, too, with a major press conference, a bill signing, or a summit: big events in our culture are always surrounded by cameras, whirring and clicking away.

Big events in our families work the same way. We always take lots of pictures at our personal big events: weddings, birthday parties, anniversaries, baptisms. You and I have been part of that picture taking as one of the family members and we have also been part of a lot of those pictures as the officiating minister.

For myself, I have had the privilege along the way of attending the eightieth and ninetieth birthday celebrations for several different family members and parishioners. These are festive occasions with plenty of food, endless storytelling, and lots of kids. The better part of a century is a long time for a family tree to be able to grow, and so there are children, grandchildren, great-grandchildren, and even great-great-grandchildren.

One inevitable part of such an occasion, of course, is the big family portrait. All the offspring group together (usually arranged in family units) around the matriarch or patriarch who is being honored and celebrated. There, smiling and proud, we see the three, four, or possibly five generations of a family represented in a single moment.

Perhaps you've been part of such a group picture.

The Bible has a group picture like that. In this instance, we might say that Luke is the photographer: He is the one who captures the moment for us in our gospel lection. The setting is a mountain in northern Palestine, and the occasion — the big event where the picture was taken — is the Transfiguration of Jesus.

Exodus 34:29-35

As a matter of trivia, it may be worth noting that this is the passage that gave rise to numerous artistic depictions of Moses with horns. When the text reports that "the skin of his face shone," the Hebrew word that is used (*qaran*) for "shone" can mean: "to shine," "to send out rays," and "to display or grow horns." The Greek Septuagint more properly translated the tense of the original Hebrew verb and opted for a word that suggested Moses' face was glorified. The Latin Vulgate, however, used a word for "horned" and out of that came the popular convention in art to portray Moses with horns.

On the other hand, perhaps the matter is not so trivial, for it serves as a metaphor for a rather common problem. The face of Moses shone with the glory of God, and yet it has been perceived and portrayed by some as horns. The misapprehension recalls the folks who thought the disciples were drunk on Pentecost (Acts 2:12-13) and the leaders who reckoned that Jesus' miracles were Beelzebul's doing (Matthew 12:24). Misreading and misunderstanding the work of God is not a trivial matter, at all.

The reaction to Moses' radiance by his own contemporaries represents another sort of misunderstanding. When Aaron and the people saw his glowing countenance, the Bible reports that "they were afraid to come near him." When we see in the next verse that Moses had to call to them and that then they "returned to him," we are given the impression that they may actually have run away at first.

Aaron and company did not misunderstand and think that Moses had horns. No, for they could see quite clearly that he was shining. Even so, they misunderstood and responded improperly.

Think of the other kinds of people and situations that would have made those people shy away or flee. They might run from a leper. They might run from the pharaoh or some other enemy. They might run from some dangerous creature (such as the poisonous serpents that later invaded their camp). But juxtaposed with these other things that might make them turn and run, see how silly it is to react the same way to Moses: a man who was simply aglow from the presence of God.

A better reflex would have been to run to Moses, but people are different in this regard. For some, the instinct is to draw near to the mysterious and glorious. For others, the reflex is to cower and shy away. From the burning bush on, we see Moses as the kind of person who is always pursuing God, always drawing nearer. Indeed, in the chapter preceding our lection, Moses literally seeks God's face. With his epitaph in Deuteronomy, Moses is distinguished for the closeness of his relationship with God: "Never since has there arisen a prophet in Israel like Moses, whom the Lord knew face-to-face" (Deuteronomy 34:10). No doubt it was that sort of face-to-face contact with God that so transformed Moses' own face.

2 Corinthians 3:12—4:2

In our Old Testament reading, we were introduced to Moses' veil. Now here, over a millennium later, the apostle Paul borrows the image of that veil and uses it as a metaphor for a larger spiritual problem.

The analogy is an imperfect one — every analogy is — inasmuch as the veil has changed its location. In the original story from Exodus, Moses is the one who has seen the glory and who has come to reflect that glory. He chooses to put the veil on himself, apparently for the sake of the Israelites.

In Paul's application of the image, however, it is the Jews themselves who have the veil over their faces. It keeps them, indeed, from seeing the glory. But, this is not the fading glory of Moses' face that they are missing; it is the glory of the Lord. The present opportunity, therefore, is greater and so the veil is more tragic.

Paul says that the glory associated with Moses was "being set aside." His point is not merely that the shine on Moses' face faded over time. Rather, he implies a broader point about law and gospel, about the old covenant and the new. That old glory was good but incomplete, and so we have the hope now of seeing a greater glory.

Ambrosiaster, a fourth-century church father, identified the greater glory that is available for us to see, and he ties together all three of our lections in his commentary on this passage: "Paul is saying that we have a hope of seeing glory, not the kind that was on the face of Moses but the kind which the three apostles saw on the mountain when the Lord revealed himself" (Ambrosiaster, *Ancient Christian Commentary on Scripture, New Testament VII* [Downers Grove, Illinois: InterVarsity Press, 1999], p. 221).

Paul's picture of the Jews is a poignant one: They "hear the reading of the old covenant, (yet) that same veil is still there." These were Paul's own people. Though he recognized that his peculiar calling was to the Gentiles, the fact is that he routinely began his missionary work in each place by teaching in the synagogue there. On a regular basis, he saw the very thing that he describes here: The people sitting there, hearing the old covenant being read, but not seeing or recognizing the glory to which it points.

Remember Paul's heart for these people. In his letter to the Romans, he reflects at length on how they have largely rejected the good news about Christ. With powerful language, he expresses his grief and his heartfelt longing on their behalf: "I have great sorrow and unceasing anguish in my heart. For I could wish that I myself were accursed and cut off from Christ for the sake of my own people, my kindred according to the flesh" (Romans 9:2-3).

Many preachers with all-Gentile congregations have seen the same terrible sight. I have looked out on the people in my pews and felt a great pity and frustration for some that I see. They have been sitting in church almost every Sunday of their lives; they have heard the scriptures read and preached; and yet, still, it seems there is some veil that keeps them from understanding and receiving the truth.

Paul says that "only in Christ is (the veil) set aside." When a person turns to him, "the veil is removed." Although it seems that Paul has discovered no surefire way to make that happen for anyone, he has proclaimed the opportunity in every place he has been, but he cannot lift and remove another person's veil. In that sense, it is a voluntary condition — to whatever extent ignorance can be voluntary.

Luke 9:28-36 (37-43)

The story of Jesus' transfiguration appears in all three synoptic gospels (Matthew, Mark, and Luke), though it does not appear in John. In all significant details, the three accounts are the same: Jesus' three human companions are Peter, James, and John; the event occurs on a mountain; Jesus' appearance is altered, becoming dazzlingly white; Moses and Elijah appeared with him and spoke with him; Peter speaks up to suggest erecting three dwellings; a cloud overshadowed them; and a voice from the cloud spoke of Jesus as "my Son."

The several differences between the three accounts are not significant and taken together they give us a fuller picture of the occasion. Mark adds to our understanding of Jesus' appearance that his clothes were white "such as no one on earth could bleach them" (Mark 9:3). Luke is the one who expands on the nature of the conversation between Jesus, Moses, and Elijah. Luke is also the gospel writer who notes that the disciples were sleepy. Mark reports that the disciples were terrified. Matthew concludes with the disciples falling down on their faces, filled with awe, until Jesus touched them and told them to get up and not to be afraid. Luke also observes that the disciples did not tell anyone at that time what they had seen.

We should give some attention to the particular men who were with Jesus on that mountain.

Luke reports that Jesus took just three of his disciples up this mountain with him to pray. We do not have any details in scripture to explain why these three men — Peter, James, and John — were apparently Jesus' inner circle, but the textual evidence clearly suggests that they were. In addition to this occasion, those are also the three disciples that Jesus separated out to go into the house with him when he raised Jairus' daughter (Luke 8:51); and it is the same three Jesus took with him deeper into the Garden of Gethsemane on the night he was betrayed (Mark 14:32-33).

In addition to being Jesus' inner circle of disciples during his earthly ministry, Peter and John went on to become pillars of the church. James was an early martyr. John was prominent first in the Jerusalem church, and then became the patriarch of an entire community of believers — traditionally associated with the church at Ephesus — and the source of perhaps five of the books in the New Testament. Peter, meanwhile, was the spokesman and leader of the Jerusalem church beginning on the Day of Pentecost and tradition traces his missionary work all the way to martyrdom in Rome.

In addition to these contemporaries of Jesus, Moses and Elijah — great figures from the Old Testament — also appeared on the mountain.

Moses was Israel's first leader. When the people first went to Egypt, they were just a large family. During their centuries of slavery, their only real "leadership" was their Egyptian overseers. When they emerged from their bondage as a small nation of nomads, Moses was their leader and he led them for an entire eventful generation.

Moses was the one who was God's instrument of deliverance from bondage in Egypt. He was the point man in negotiations with the pharaoh. He was the one who led the Israelites from Egypt to Canaan, suffered their complaints, endured their assorted rebellions and surrenders, and interceded on their behalf before God.

Perhaps most significant of all, Moses was the agent through whom God gave his law to his people. It is difficult to overstate the importance of the law to the Old Testament people of God. The placement of the Ten Commandments within the Ark of the Covenant, which in turn resided in the holy of holies, gives some indication of the central importance and theological significance of the law. And while the casual reader today might dismiss so much of the material as harsh, repetitive, or irrelevant, the undeniable fact is that the devout Jews welcomed the law as a great gift from God. (Psalm 119, the longest chapter in the Bible, offers a tremendous glimpse into how God's people, at their best, cherished God's law.)

Finally, there was Elijah. He was the spectacular ninth-century prophet, who embodied power and boldness from God. He spoke out against a wicked king and queen, he challenged a foreign god and his clients to a showdown of divine proportions, and he exhorted his fellow Israelites to an undiluted allegiance to God.

While Elijah does not have a book named after him — like Isaiah or Jeremiah or others — he came to a place of special significance by the end of the Old Testament era. In the book of Malachi, his return is anticipated as an antecedent to the coming of the day of the Lord (Malachi 4:5-6) and that expectation concerning Elijah is echoed in the gospels (as in Matthew 11:14).

Application

See the portrait provided by Luke: the photograph of the big event there on the mountain. In the foreground, there are three men — from left to right: Peter, James, and John. In the back row, high and aglow, we see two other men: Moses and Elijah. And there, in the center of the picture, is Jesus, the Christ.

See the picture snapped there on that mountain, for it is a "picture Bible" — that is, the whole Bible contained in a single scene. There is Moses, representing the law. Next to him is Elijah, representing the prophets. Then come Peter, James, and John, representing the apostles and the church. The Old and New Testaments stand together on that mountain: the old covenant and the new, meeting, intersecting, overlapping.

There, in the center of it all, is Jesus. He is the star of the show, the first cause, the reason for being. He is the one whose sacrifice and blood was required by the law. He is the one whose coming, suffering, and reign the prophets promised. He is the fulfillment of all that had come before and he is the one whose gospel the apostles proclaimed.

Alternative Applications

Exodus 34:29-35. "Whatever Miss T. Eats." Walter de La Mare's familiar children's poem makes this simple observation: "It's a very odd thing / As odd as can be / That whatever Miss T. eats / Turns into Miss T" (Walter de La Mare, *Peacock Pie, A Book of Rhymes* [Oxford: Kessinger Publishing, 2004], p. 15).

It's a very sweet picture and a rather innocent notion. The simple observation is that this young girl sits down at the table to eat her meals; and whatever it is that she eats — "porridge and apples, / mince, muffins, and mutton, / jam, junket, jumbles" — becomes part of her; and so, in a sense, it becomes her.

In point of fact, however, we know that in the long run there is another effect. It is not only true that whatever Miss T. eats turns into Miss T.; it is also true that, as the old saying goes, "You are what you eat." Lean or fat, nutritious or junky, healthy or harmful: Miss T. does not merely absorb what she eats into an unchanging self; she is affected by what she eats.

What is true of our bodies is true of our minds, hearts, and souls, as well. What we consume, what we take in, what we feed on does not merely submit to becoming part of us. It influences and changes us. And over the long haul, we become what we digest.

If one person is routinely exposed to language that is crude, while another person is exposed to more refined and articulate ways of expressing oneself, the effects on each will be quite predictable. So, too, we see in our children and teenagers the fruits of a popular culture that is relativistic in its philosophy, superficial in its emphasis, dismissive of authority, and generally oversexed. We become the inevitable products of what we are exposed to and immersed in. We are what we eat.

In our Old Testament lection, meanwhile, we are given a positive, alternative picture. It is the marvelous picture of Moses aglow. Here is a man who had been so exposed to God that he himself became radiant. As routinely as the rest of us show in the tan (or the burn) of our skin that we have been out in the sun, so Moses' skin showed that he had been in the presence of God. It is a remarkable story and a beautiful prospect.

You and I become a product of what we "eat" — i.e., what we take in, absorb, immerse ourselves in, and expose ourselves to. We may become trite, crass, conscientious, or erudite through our exposures. Moses has blazed for us the best trail of all: that we should be so thoroughly exposed to the presence of God that we ourselves would reflect his glory.

Exodus 34:29-35; Luke 9:28-36 (37-43). "What Happens Next?" Our Old Testament lection begins with this blunt report: "Moses came down from Mount Sinai." On the surface, it is a simple statement of fact: namely, the next thing Moses did. In the larger scheme of things, however, it is also a profound statement of truth: namely, this is always what we are required to do.

At the top of the mountain, Moses stood in the blazing presence of God. At the foot of the mountain, there were the same old frail, blemished, unreliable people with whom he constantly had to deal.

At the top of the mountain, Jesus spoke with the now-heavenly figures of Moses and Elijah; he was radiant and the voice of his Father spoke. But, at the foot of the mountain, he encountered again the screaming human needs, the demons, and the "faithless and perverse generation" (v. 41).

"Moses came down from Mount Sinai." Of course, he did. Jesus came down from the mountain too. And we always do. What comes next does not need to negate the reality of what happened on the mountain. But we follow, after all, the God who became incarnate. We are always called to leave the mountaintop glory in order to meet and minister to the needs down below.

Ash Wednesday
Joel 2:1-2, 12-17
2 Corinthians 5:20b—6:10
Matthew 6:1-6, 16-21
Wayne Brouwer

Love that hurts

The story is told of a young girl whose very best friend lived just down the street. They were playmates and almost sisters, with visits back and forth nearly every day.

When Jennifer was killed in an automobile accident, Tracie and her family were drawn through the same trench of grief. Two families were heartbroken and shared the awful blackness of funeral clothing together.

The day after the funeral, Tracie disappeared for a few hours. Her mother was worried and searched the house and yard in growing concern. When she went out to the street in front of their home she saw Tracie at a distance, slowly meandering toward her on the sidewalk, oblivious to her surroundings.

"Where were you, Tracie?" her mom asked as she strode toward the young girl. "I was worried about you."

"I was at Jennifer's place," Tracie replied. "I was helping her mom."

"What were you helping her with?"

"Well, neither of us felt like doing much, so I just crawled up into her lap and helped her cry."

Sometimes we all need to cry, and now and again we need help to do it. In the passages for today, on this Ash Wednesday, tears and repentance, sorrow, and prayer and fasting and pain are the order of the day. Joel helps ancient Israel cope with a devastating famine that hints as a harbinger to God's greater judgments. Paul reminds the Corinthian congregation of his pain on their behalf, hoping to move them to tears of repentance. And Jesus simply assumes that we will give, pray, and fast, for in these disciplines our hearts become more fully aligned with the values of the kingdom of heaven.

Joel 2:1-2, 12-17

It was a plague of locusts that set the context for Joel's prophecy of judgment day. While farmers watched their crops sliced away by the unstoppable insect horde, cultural uneasiness set in and the prophet linked this disaster to God's ultimate punishment on sin. No illustrated message has ever been more graphic.

It has been repeated 1,000 times. One college professor presented his class syllabus on the first day of the new semester. He pointed out that there were three papers to be written during the term, and he showed on which days those assignments had to be handed in. He said that these dates were firmly fixed and that no student should presume that the deadline did not apply to her or him. He asked if the students were clear about this, and all heads nodded.

When the first deadline arrived, all but one student turned in their papers. The one student went to the professor's office and pleaded for more time — just a single day! The student spoke of illness and hardships that had prevented him from completing the assignment, but all the research was finished, and a few more hours would allow the paper to be ready. The professor relented and granted a one-day extension without penalty. The student was extremely grateful and sent a note thanking the professor profusely.

When the second deadline arrived, three papers were missing from the pile of student productions. The student who had previously asked for an extension was back, and so were two others. As before, all the reasons expressed for failure to complete the assignment were touching and moving and tear-jerking, and the professor again allowed some latitude. The deadline was set aside, and the papers were required by the end of the week. A veritable chorus of praise filled the professor's small office, and blessings were heaped upon him.

When the third due date arrived, the professor was inundated with requests for extensions. Nearly a quarter of the class begged for more time — many other assignments and tests were due, many books still needed to be read, much work was required this late in the semester. But this time the professor held firm. No extensions were to be given. Grades would be marked lower for tardiness. Stunned silence filled the classroom.

The large delegation that met the professor in the hallway near his office was very vocal in their anger. "You can't do this to us! It isn't fair!"

"What isn't fair?" asked the professor. "At the beginning of the term you knew the due date of each paper and you agreed to turn in your work at those times."

"But you let so-and-so have extensions. You can't tell us now that we can't have a few extra days."

"Maybe you are right," said the professor. He opened his grade book and made a rather public subtraction from the grades given to the four formerly late papers. Each of those students, now also in this group, protested loudly. "You can't do that, professor! That's not fair!"

"What's not fair?" asked the professor. "Justice or mercy?" The question blanketed them heavily as each student silently slipped away. And the professor? When he reported the incident to others, he simply concluded (paraphrasing Henry Higgins from *My Fair Lady*), "They'd grown accustomed to my grace!"

We grow easily accustomed to God's grace. We need to become "Wow!"ed again by the amazing thing that happens when God chooses to start over in love toward us, even after the "great syllabus" demands a divine reckoning. No partnership can stretch forever to cover bad behavior or infidelity. Judgment day invariably comes.

Yet the prophecy of Joel carries with it more than warnings of God's grim reaping. In the divine matrix, justice is always wedded to mercy. The prophet, therefore, includes a call to a day of fasting, a solemn assembly in which hearts are turned and consciences cleansed before the Holy One. While the actual response of the people in Joel's day is unknown, the prophet ends his short messages with scenes of refuge and pledges of a world renewed. This is not only a theological promise for the future of humankind; it is also the hope we cling to when our relationships wander through rough places. God will guard the hearts that trust him even in the difficult times. Those who hear the warnings of a prophet like Joel can also be surprised by the miracle of a lover's care.

2 Corinthians 5:20b—6:10

Second Corinthians is actually the fourth of Paul's letters that we know about posted from Ephesus to the Peloponnesian Peninsula in the middle years of the 50s AD. Paul had stationed himself for three years in Asia Minor, working from Ephesus as a base of operations. But Corinth, the city that was his home for the bulk of his second mission journey, was much on his mind. Early in Paul's time at Ephesus, he heard news of gross immorality afflicting the congregation he loved deeply and sent a harsh letter of reproof.

The response was underwhelming. Some in Corinth held up his scathing indictment as the letter of the law, but many questioned and challenged Paul's right to meddle in their affairs now that he was no longer a pastor-in-residence. Divisions and jockeying parties sprang up in the church until it looked like the United Nations on summer recess.

Those still in leadership positions were worried. They decided to send a letter and a delegation to Paul, hoping that a personal visit would take the edge off Paul's passionate anger, and a few theological questions would turn everyone's attention away from the ethical and moral morasses in which they were stuck. In fact, it seemed to make a difference. The outcome was another letter from Paul, but this one more focused on the big picture issues of church development. It enters our New Testament as 1 Corinthians.

The success of that encounter seemed to give Paul reason to believe he had regained a place of authority in speaking to the problems of the Corinthian congregation. Therefore, he wrote another letter and sent it under the personal care of Titus. This epistle, however, was evidently vitriolic, for Paul himself acknowledged that it caused the congregation great sorrow and deeply hurt them (2 Corinthians 7:8). His words here in 2 Corinthians 5-6 are an attempt to explain more carefully that what he hoped would happen is a show of repentance among the Christ-believers in Corinth and a renewal through reconciliation.

Paul's litany of hardships is designed to show the depth of commitment he has for the Corinthian congregation. If he were not so deeply tied to them in love he would not care so ponderously for their welfare. It is like the parent who tells the child before a punishment, "This hurts me more than it hurts you." No child believes it, of course. Not until that child has grown and brought other children into this world. Then, suddenly, the full awareness of parental care floods home, and the tears of a child gush fountains from the eyes of a father. Paul hopes that something of this testimony of love will be reciprocal, and that those who write him off too quickly as a lame-duck departed authoritarian fool will peer into his heart and know that his call to repentance and renewal is rooted in the twin bonds that bind God and Paul to this rascally but revered church.

Matthew 6:1-6, 16-21

The Sermon on the Mount is the longest teaching of Jesus recorded in the gospels. By way of a number of clues, Matthew gives clear indication that he wants us to see Jesus as the new Moses, bringing the deepened word of God to a new age of the kingdom. Jesus goes up the mountain (5:1) as did Moses, and the major elements of the original covenant document in Exodus 20-24 are restated and then deepened and broadened in impact. Even at the close of the sermon in chapter 7, Matthew tells us that people marveled at Jesus' teachings, finding them more authoritative than those of the scribes. The implication is clear: The scribes only interpret the teachings of Moses, but Jesus brings a new word like Moses.

In the verses for today, Jesus addresses public acts of kingdom living — almsgiving, prayer, and fasting. It is interesting to note, first of all, that Jesus expects these practices to be part of the lifestyle of those who are his disciples and citizens of the kingdom of heaven. These are not optional activities but essential behaviors. To be a follower of the ways of the God of the covenant is to care for the poor, to pray, and to fast.

Almsgiving requires at least three stages of investment. The first is awareness. One cannot give alms without having the eyes to see where the need is and who personifies that impoverishment. This is illustrated by a fascinating incident from early in the church's history. According to Edward Gibbons, in his masterful treatise, *The Decline and Fall of the Roman Empire*, Antonius Pius, who ruled from 138-161 AD, was one of the best of Rome's rulers. During his days there was more wealth, business success, and domestic peace than most civilizations have known.

Antonius Pious was a good ruler, and his people knew it. In fact, one of his biggest supporters was the Athenian philosopher Aristedes, who lauded the emperor on many occasions. One day, however, Aristedes sent Antonius Pious a letter in which he urged the ruler to observe and imitate a particular group of people in the kingdom. "In all your grand empire they are the only ones who make it a habit to see the needs of the poor and do something about it," wrote Aristedes. Who was he referring to? Christians — disciples of Jesus who had learned to see.

A second dimension of almsgiving is the actual sharing of substance. Fiorello La Guardia was a police court judge before he became mayor of New York during the Great Depression. One cold winter's night, a man was brought to him charged with stealing a loaf of bread. The man acknowledged his guilt, noting that it was the only way he could provide food for his family. La Guardia pronounced judgment and fined the man $10, knowing that the thief could not possibly pay up.

Instead of sending the guilty party to jail, La Guardia pulled $10 out of his own wallet to pay the fine. Then he took back the $10, suspended the sentence, and fined everyone in the courtroom 50¢ for living in a city where a man has to steal bread in order to eat. When the man left the courtroom that day he had light in his eyes and $47.50 in his pocket.

Thirdly, almsgiving involves compassion, the quality of sharing in the plight of another with more than flippant handouts. Said Ralph Waldo Emerson, "Rings and jewels are not gifts, but apologies for gifts. The only gift is a portion of thyself."

Jesus' words about prayer remind us to ask ourselves why we want to pray in the first place. Bill Keane, in one of his delightful *Family Circus* comic strips, once showed little Jeffy picking up his football and looking forlorn because it was flat. A car had run over it. Little Jeffy says to himself, "I need a new football. I don't know if I should send up a prayer, write a letter to Santa Claus, or call Grandma." We may laugh at his dilemma, but it digs deeper into most of our psyches than we would care to admit. Jesus uses the illustration of some who treat prayer as simply another form of getting things we want, whether goods or esteem, even in a religious community. Do we seek the honor or approval of others or is there a ready relationship that is in place with God?

Prayer, according to Jesus, means that we recognize our truest needs and also recognize the one who cares for us more than we can even care for ourselves. One writer tells of a kindergarten class that took a field trip to a fire station. A firefighter told the children what to do in case of fire. "First you go to the door," he said, "and you feel it to see if it's hot. Then you get down on your knees. Does anyone here know why you do that?"

"Sure," said one of the little ones. "You get down on your knees to ask God to get you out of this mess." While not all prayers are made in the heat of fiery conflagrations, there is a refreshing honesty about that child's understanding of prayer.

When Jesus continues and addresses the concept of fasting, he again assumes this practice will permeate the community of his disciples. While we may think of fasting as culturally conditioned and best left in the world of first-century Judaism, it would be well to give it another consideration. In biblical times, people fasted for three specific reasons. The first was repentance: David fasted after he was caught in his sin with Bathsheba; the people of Nineveh fasted when Jonah shouted the impending judgment of God; the Israelites fasted every day of atonement, and many times in between. Second, fasting was a way of remembering: when King Saul and Prince Jonathan died in battle with the Philistines, David called the nation to fast and remember; Daniel fasted when he recalled the destruction of Jerusalem; and in Jesus' day there was an annual fast to remember the holocaust that nearly wiped out the Hebrew race when the hordes of Babylon swept down from the hills of Ephraim. Third, fasting was a way in which people could rivet their attention on God, keeping the body uncomfortable while the mind was clarified. Jesus himself expressed this fasting activity during his forty-day wilderness preparation for ministry. He was only following in the fine footsteps of Queen Esther who readied herself for an encounter with King Xerxes by fasting, and Ezra who joined fasting and prayer as his final act of readying the returning exiles before they took to the wilderness road between Babylon and the ruins of Jerusalem.

Fasting is not dieting. It is, instead, a declaration of the religious truth that we are not mere consumers who live for our bellies. Furthermore, it is a way of saying, "No," so that we can determine where, in fact, we will say, "Yes," and mean it truthfully out of our relationship with God. Those who cannot say, "No," do not know what it means to say, "Yes."

Application

On this Ash Wednesday, there is no greater application than to point people's eyes to the suffering Savior. We begin today the forty-day walk to the cross, sensing anew the growing heaviness in Jesus' heart, the weariness of his shoulders as the burden of the world collapses upon them, the aching of his spirit in the knowledge of what looms ahead, and the resolute resignation of his voice as he speaks increasingly about what will be done to him when he arrives in Jerusalem.

If we keep one eye and ear on Jesus, and then observe Joel and Paul with the other eye and ear, we will have a good stereo effect to elicit the proper pain of those who have a deeply symbiotic spiritual kinship with their Savior.

An Alternative Application

Matthew 6:1-6, 16-21. It might be possible to abstract the verses on fasting from Jesus' words in the Sermon on the Mount and use them as a model for today's demeanor. There is a poem by Edna St. Vincent Millay that brings us into the mood of fasting as we enter our own fasts during this Lenten season:

> *I drank at every vine.*
> *The last was like the first.*
> *I came upon no wine*
> *So wonderful as thirst.*
> *I gnawed at every root,*
> *I ate of every plant.*
> *I came upon no fruit*
> *So wonderful as want.*
> *Feed the grape and the bean*
> *To the vintner and the monger;*
> *I will lie down lean*
> *With my thirst and my hunger.*

Lent 1
Deuteronomy 26:1-11
Romans 10:8b-13
Luke 4:1-13
Craig MacCreary

Getting started on the right foot

We now set sail for Jerusalem, the events of holy week, and the hope of Easter morning. There is the old New England story of the farmer that, in giving driving instructions to the flatlander, informs the person that they can't get there from here. The story's humor revolves around the absurdity of such a statement. Of course you *can* get there from here. However, as I have watched the changing of the guard on Parliament Hill in Ottawa, Canada, I have noticed that before they actually begin there has to be a lot of shuffling and rearranging of ranks. In their case, if they do not start off on the right foot from the right place, they will not wind up where they need to be. Lent is more like the changing of the guard than like the story of the New England farmer.

Each of these texts helps us to identify where we begin our Lenten journey. They help us begin at the right place so that we can come out at a good place and be ready for the good news of Easter.

The text from Deuteronomy gives us our Jewish roots as the starting point for our journey. It is a good place to begin. Often, the Lenten journey has wound up in the bad place of anti-Semitic charges of Christ killer and hideous readings of scripture that imply the events of Holy Week will not only leave Judaism behind but will leave many Christians with a false sense of superiority regarding the Hebrew's story. If this is where we end up, then we certainly have gotten off to a bad start.

The lesson from Deuteronomy reminds us that we cannot get a grasp of what God is setting before us without coming to terms with what the journey has meant up to now. If this is what God has been up to in leading us in the past, then the journey ahead is about more than individual salvation or personal immortality.

The letter to the Romans proclaims that everyone who calls on the name of the Lord shall be saved. As part of the journey, it invites us to consider having our destinies tied to people of different customs and habits. Though the Lord may not make distinctions, we certainly do. If the starting point is that Jesus is Lord, then we are in for quite a journey. The Gentiles are a pretty broad and diverse category of people. If we begin with the lordship of Jesus, the engrafting of people can lead in many directions. However, if we do not begin with this lordship of Jesus, then we may not arrive at the place God intends for us.

The gospel lesson tells the tale of how Jesus' journey began following his baptism. You hardly catch your breath and Jesus barely comes up out of the water when he is plunged into the desert: tempted by the devil, hungry, and on his own. Can you get there from here? The truth is that we often wind up in the wrong place because we have not started with our real hungers and we have often wrongly tried to satisfy them. We often wind up out of step with each other because the steps that we have taken to get power, security, and prosperity are taking us seriously off target on our journeys.

Each of these texts raises the issues of where is the beginning point in my journey and with whom do I share the journey? I believe if these questions are our starting point in the Lenten pilgrimage, then we have an opening to where God wants us to land.

Deuteronomy 26:1-11

The text suggests that our starting point in the journey is "the land that the Lord your God has given you." My traditional faith upbringing tells me the starting point of Lent is my personal sins and what I have given myself over to that is blocking my relationship with God. This text seems to be quite a broad and expansive concept to be part of our Lenten luggage. However, the starting point in arriving at the place God wants us to be is the realization that land has been given as a gift. The starting point is asking, "Has the gift generated appreciation, gratitude, and sharing a sense of abundance?" The starting point may be that land rather than being treated as a gift, becomes something to be fought over. We have been given a place but many are homeless. We do not feel at home because more than 30,000 square feet of living space is needed. We have land issues.

The text makes clear that we were plucked from obscurity by this gift of land. By God's action, we have become a people with a history. Once we were only singular, a wandering Aramean, but by God's action we have become communal with dreams to share and visions to work out and a story to live out. But something happened in Egypt that happens to all who become communal. We become national as well as communal. As part of that system, as run by the Egyptians, we become enslaved to brick making. Education becomes about the number of credit hours you need and the letter grade you get. Medicine becomes mountains of paperwork and number of patients seen. Security becomes more about how high walls can be built rather than how contacts across borders can be made.

More and more bricks are on order to build the edifices of empires but the love of learning takes a backseat. The first brick is put into place by admission to the right preschool that will enable you to matriculate at the right private school and so advance to Skull and Bones at Yale or its equivalent. Healing begins to be second fiddle to cost effectiveness. Taking care of business becomes more important than taking care of yourself or of souls as we work longer hours and give up more vacation time.

That can happen to you in Egypt. By its very nature that is what Egypt and Egyptian thinking can do to you. The next thing you know you are enslaved to the notion that life cannot be good without that 30,000-square-foot house — more bricks. The only reward, as the Hebrews found out, for being able to make more bricks is the demand that you make more bricks. This is what has happened and does happen to us when we live in Egypt.

The story is not all about us. "The Lord, the God of our ancestors, the Lord heard our voice and saw our afflictions." It does not say that this voice was one of prayer. It is not a voice that has gotten its theological i's dotted and t's crossed. It is not a voice that is even directed to God or one that speaks with only one accent. Yet, God hears this voice. At the starting of a Lenten journey, I realize my need to repent for not speaking in this voice. We often try to fancy up our situation with theological language that we think will capture God's attention. The good news is that we already have God's attentiveness; we need only speak in a voice that reflects our genuine anguish.

What is also good news is that God will act on what God sees and hears. This is our story as well. There have been signs and wonders: walls do come crashing down, apartheid and segregation end, empires do not hold on forever. This is good news for the poor, but unfortunate for those who have gone down to Egypt to make their fame and fortune, and for all who are good and tired of making bricks. It is very bad news for those who are building their towers like Babylon or requisitioning more bricks for walls.

Romans 10:8b-13

Confessing that "Jesus is Lord" is one of the hardest things to do as I consider the starting place of my Lenten journey. As I consider Calvin's understanding of Jesus in his *Institutes of Religion*, I find it much easier to confess Jesus as prophet or priest than king. I feel comfortable with the first two roles no doubt because they spring directly out of specific religious connotation. I can see myself in the role of prophet speaking truth to power. I can understand one of the fundamental roles of ministry as priests mediating the presence of God through the rites and rituals of the church. That is as far as it gets. I have real trouble with identifying with the lordly virtues of kingship. I look at the assortment of modern possibilities for naming Jesus and the ones who come to mind feel pretty comfortable: wisdom teacher, therapist, visionary, marginal Jew, and so on. They all have their appeal. However, when it comes to what Paul writes to the Romans, I can feel the mental and spiritual brakes screeching as my faith understanding heads for a derailment.

It is a role that I am uncomfortable giving to Jesus and one that I am uncomfortable taking in ministry. I like Jesus as friend, I like to be friendly. I like Jesus as helper; I like to be thought of as helpful. I like to think of myself as a prophet of justice and I like seeing Jesus in the same way. I even graduated from a seminary, Lancaster Theological Seminary, that had the nickname "The School of the Prophets." It never occurred to anyone that the nickname "School of the Lords" would be appropriate.

Perhaps, however, the starting point for my Lenten journey is the realization that I need to pay attention to what Paul is saying here. Certainly in the Roman world, saying that Jesus is Lord is quite a claim. In our world, making this claim is no less vital. It is not just a claim that challenges Roman gods, it also challenges a world where many would make a god of the free market or anything else that would satisfy human wants.

Theologically, I am comfortable with the Jesus who says that he "stands at the door and knocks" and if anyone would let him come in, he would dine with them. However, I am less sanguine about the Jesus who ignores locked doors, who comes and barges right in and stands in the midst of the disciples after Easter morning. The Jesus who cannot be barred in the exercise of his lordship is, I suspect, somewhat threatening. The Jesus watching and waiting until we are ready is appealing to most. There is hardly a church that could not find in its church building somewhere an artistic representation of these words from the book of Revelation. However, it seems somewhat harder to find any painting or sculpture of the Jesus who comes into the midst of the disciples despite their attempts to wall out the external world.

I, too, wonder if my discomfort with this role for Jesus is really my discomfort with this role in ministry. Where does authority arise and how should it be exercised? Do other factors pretending to lordship creep into our lives so that we find ourselves serving false masters? One wonders what would have happened to the sex scandals among clergy if the churches had responded, "No one who believes in him will be put to shame."

Paul says it is not adequate to make the statement, "Jesus is Lord" only in one's heart. Putting it on your lips has a way of making it real in a way that keeping it inside does not. Putting it on the lips makes it a matter of conversation. No one should offer obedience without some conversation with those who find the concept of kingship and lordship difficult and offensive in their experience. The starting point of my Lenten pilgrimage is in part repentance for not having been more of a part of that conversation.

Luke 4:1-13

He is in the wilderness or the uninhabited place. It is usually in such places that these temptations come at us. However, the kind of temptation that Jesus struggles with seems alien to us. Does it really boil down to this way or that way? In making our life choices, we usually need to balance one interest after another. Can we see where the devil is coming from in this case? Is there not a case to be made here on his behalf? After all, if we could turn the world's stones into bread, we could make quite a dent in world hunger. Is there not a place, despite all the moral compromises involved, for taking charge with authority and power in the world? Is not one of the chief complaints against the peacekeeping capabilities of the United Nations that the UN is nothing but a well-intentioned, weak ineffectual presence in the world? One can certainly make out the case for Jesus being protected from certain death at least for what turned out to be his short life. Wouldn't it have been wonderful if Jesus had been around long enough to keep on as teacher and offering all those wonderful stories? If he had been protected from death if only for a bit longer would we not have had some answers for all those thorny questions that can get raised in confirmation classes? Would it have hurt for just a few more miracles to become the occasion for the miracle of more people coming to faith? There is a case to be made for the devil here.

The problem here is that no matter how eloquently the case can be made, it cannot be squared with the Spirit that has filled Jesus' soul, the scripture that falls from Jesus' lips, or the worship that Jesus' Spirit offers. When I yield to temptation and find myself off course from where God wants me to be, it is the result of failing to make these things the center of my being. Having made most of the headway in my life through using my brain, I am only more than ready to listen to well-reasoned arguments even if they come from the devil. Indeed only when I find myself beginning to listen to devilish arguments do I realize how I have wandered from what ought to be the starting point of my life.

Of course, wouldn't it be wonderful if we could turn stones into bread. However, the problem in the world is not that we do not have an adequate supply of bread. The problem is that we do not have a distribution system that faithfully shares the abundance we do have. The devil has conveniently left this out of the equation. Shall Jesus turn just enough stones into bread to satisfy his own needs? Such basic selfishness seems part of the world's problems right now. Shall he make enough bread from stones to satisfy the world's problems while leaving the distribution network to the devil? That, too, seems to be part of the world's problems as too many have too little, too few have too much, and the price on the wrapper that goes around the bread is more than the farmer gets for the wheat that goes into the bread. If your soul is set on the Holy Spirit, if a knowledge of scripture is at your fingertips, and you engage in holy worship, you tend to pick up on these things.

Of course, all the kingdoms come at a price. All you need to do is to stop worship as we know it and everything will be fine. All you need to do is to no longer make daily bread the aim; stop praying, "thy kingdom come." Make sure those who trespass somehow into your territory know about it in no uncertain terms before you even think of owning up to the number of times you have trespassed against them. Would any of the kingdoms of the world be worth very much if we lived in a world like that? People who are up on their scripture know these things; people who walk in the Spirit see through this offer.

The final temptation offers thoroughgoing protection from all of the exposure that the rest of the world has. Of course, thoroughgoing protection will result in complete disconnection from the reality of life as the rest of us experience it. Who would want to go and worship at that altar? It is tempting to be super human but the promises of God come to a head in the one who is fully human — Jesus the Christ.

People who are filled with the Spirit, have the words of scripture at hand, and who know what right worship is pick up on these things as the starting points for their lives.

Application

Saint Paul wrote that we should run the race that is set before us. A good part of the battle is getting to the starting line. A few years ago, when I ran my first 10k race, I learned what that meant. In the race that is set before us, there are no shortcuts and no getting there without getting to the starting line first. This would seem rather obvious until you realize at Lent how easy it is to wander off the course from the start.

My faith journey is rooted in the sad story of a people who are called out and made a community by the gift of God. Yet, they cave into the temptation of living the "Egyptian" lifestyle. My faith journey begins with the knowledge that God hears their complaints and our complaints when that happens. In my reluctance to give Jesus lordship as much a starting place as his friendship, I wonder how far off course I have become. No doubt about it, reason should be one of the supports of faith, and a faith that defies too much reason can be off the mark. Yet, I wonder how vulnerable I am to temptation when reason — more than right worship, more than the right relationship to the Holy Spirit, and more than the righteousness of God made known in scripture — is my first line of defense.

Lent invites us to ponder these questions in order that we may find ourselves on course for the good news of Easter.

An Alternative Application
Romans 10:8b-13. All my life I have seen signs that say, "Jesus saves." What is behind the signs means many things to many people. There seems to be near unanimity in agreeing with Paul that everyone who calls on the name of the Lord shall be saved — whatever that may mean. I must admit that I come from a tradition that has some skepticism in regard to that language. Putting a sign on the front lawn of our church to the effect that "Jesus saves" would get the phones in our congregation and community buzzing.

We have in the lectionary texts the recitation of great saving moments in the history of the Hebrews, which they owned and celebrated. It might be quite a sermon to celebrate just what have been those times in the life of your congregation when you felt that the "Lord had heard your voice and saw your affliction and acted to free you from bondage." It might make quite a beginning to Lent to gather in stories from church members as to when they have felt such times in their lives and share that testimony with the entire congregation.

It seems particularly true in the kind of New England mainline Protestant church I serve that we need to repent of not telling and sharing these stories. We are particularly vulnerable to devilish temptations when we do not have a narrative that tells our history of salvation experiences.

Lent 2
Genesis 15:1-12, 17-18
Philippians 3:17—4:1
Luke 13:31-35
David Kalas

God of the ages

What is the relationship between the past, the present, and the future? What impact does one have upon the others?

Gamblers carefully review and evaluate the minutiae of a team's past performances in order to wager intelligently on their upcoming game. Investors track the trends in markets and sectors in order to guess what lies ahead for a given company, stock, or fund. And psychologists help troubled souls identify what events and influences in their past continue to impact them in the present.

Just as we ponder the effect of the past on the present and the future, we also discover that the future reaches back to influence the present. The routine business of preparing — whether for school, for an interview, for a trip, for work, or for retirement — demonstrates the impact that the future has on present priorities and decisions.

When we delve into the pages of scripture, however, we are introduced to a whole new understanding of the interrelationship between past, present, and future. Past is not as determinative as we human beings are naturally inclined to think. Instead, we discover that it is the far future that is meant to have the greatest impact on our present.

Genesis 15:1-12, 17-18

One of the great disservices that has been done to so many of the people in our pews is the association of the word "unquestioning" with the word "faith." In some teaching and preaching, the marriage has been explicit. And in many struggling, individual hearts, the connection is simply assumed. *To question is to doubt, and to doubt is to lack faith. Faith, therefore, must never question.* So goes the guilt-ridden logic.

Here in this passage, however, we have the great hero of faith, Abraham, and in one of his most notable moments of faith (see Romans 4). Yet Abraham speaks only three sentences in this episode and two of them are questions.

Many of your people and mine have been led to believe that faith and questions cannot go together, so they may also feel that reverence and candor are mutually exclusive in prayer. A generation or two that is accustomed to dressing up for church may also be in the habit of dressing up for God. They reserve for prayer a formality of language and a kind of filtered content that is directly the opposite of their other most familiar and intimate relationships. The candor of the biblical saints, therefore, can be a lesson to many of the people in our pews.

Abraham, faced with all that the Lord had given him, presumed to point out what God had not given him. What long-term good would additional blessings from God be to Abraham if he had no real heir? And note that Abraham put the matter squarely on God. It was neither chance nor human incapacity that had kept Abraham and Sarah from having children, but rather it was the Lord who had "given me no offspring."

How refreshing Abraham's approach is for many of us. How liberating to be reminded that pretense is not reverence. It is not an act of faith to be dishonest with God. Rather, Abraham had a complaint — or at least a concern — and he was candid with his Lord about it. Surely it is more faithful to be honest with

God. Surely it is more faithful to bring our needs and concerns to him than to grumble about them to ourselves or pretend they don't exist. What so often passes for reverence in our sometimes shallow praying is, in fact, more of an insult to God — an insult because we presume not to be honest with God and an insult because we are afraid to be.

The Lord did not upbraid Abraham for his candor or his questions. Rather, God responded with promises, reassurances, and details. And Abraham believed him.

Abraham believed the Lord and the Lord reckoned it to him as righteousness. Paul regarded this episode as the great Old Testament evidence of his doctrine of justification by faith. In addition to that fundamental matter of our salvation, it is an important episode for us to remember in the midst of our day-to-day circumstances, as well.

See how improbable Abraham's belief was. Our natural tendency is to extrapolate from past trends in order to predict future developments. Because the line on the graph has gone down in each of the preceding eleven months, we expect it to go down further in the twelfth month. That extrapolation is where Abraham began — the concern that Eliezer would be his only heir — but his faith was able to look beyond that. If he had merely extrapolated — only reasoned and reckoned by his own understanding without the benefit of faith — then his calculations would have come up childless. But he believed God. Against all odds, he believed God.

God's essential promise to Abraham was that he would have many descendants who would possess the land. At the time God made that promise, however, Abraham had no natural descendants, no realistic possibility of having any, and the only piece of that land he would legally possess by the time of his death was a field that he purchased for the purpose of a burial ground (Genesis 23). The circumstances were not very promising. The Lord, however, was very promising. And Abraham believed the Lord.

Philippians 3:17—4:1

Television commercials and programs that feature dangerous activities are sometimes accompanied by the warning, "Do not try this at home." This kind of driving is fine for the professional stunt drivers on the closed course, but don't get any ideas. Don't try doing what they do.

Then, in contrast, see the apostle Paul. He is sitting in chains in a foreign prison, possibly facing execution. And from that location, Paul encourages the Philippian Christians, "Join in imitating me."

The man who discovers that he has walked into a minefield doesn't usually call out to those he loves, "Follow in my footsteps!" But from prison Paul urges his brothers and sisters in Christ to follow his example.

This is no case of "misery loves company," however. Quite the contrary: joy loves company and Paul is full of joy. Paul's letter to the Philippians has rightly earned the nickname "the joyful epistle," for his tone and vocabulary are conspicuously joyful, especially given his circumstances. It is the joy of knowing Christ, and Paul had personally discovered that that joy eclipsed all of the attendant difficulties.

This excerpt from the joyful epistle is personal and poignant. Paul's deep love for the Philippians and his heartfelt emotion in writing to them is evident in the warmth and tenderness of his language. He refers to them twice as his "brothers and sisters." He tells them things "with tears." And the final verse of this passage (4:1) is so encumbered with expressions of love that it becomes awkward as a sentence.

The poignancy of the passage lies in the fact that Paul is writing from prison. The issue, though, is not that Paul feels sorry for himself in his present state. Rather, it is the poignancy of being separated from the Philippians. We all know that nothing is quite so frustrating to love as not being able to "be there." It is especially difficult when the ones we love are in the midst of some difficulty or danger.

Truthfully, Paul's own situation was far more difficult than the Philippians'. But the physical pain and peril he faced were not so compelling to Paul as the spiritual challenges facing the Philippians. The confinement and persecution Paul was experiencing did not seem to compare favorably to the self-indulgent hedonism he warns about (3:19) and yet he calls upon the Philippians to imitate him rather than those pleasure-seekers.

Set side by side, Paul's bread-and-water rations behind bars don't look so desirable as the all-you-can-eat-smorgasbord living of those who "live as enemies of the cross of Christ." On the other hand, if we set side by side the glory and beauty of Christ with "their god... the belly," if we set side by side a citizenship in heaven with the dust and disappointment of "earthly things," and if we set side by side "the body of his glory" with "the body of our humiliation," then suddenly there is no comparison. So Paul urges his beloved ones to imitate him and to "stand firm in the Lord."

Luke 13:31-35

It's always a bit suspicious when your opponents offer you advice. We see it routinely in the world of politics, as Democratic operatives give advice on television about what the Republicans should do, and vice versa. Likewise as the Pharisees come and offer ostensibly helpful advice to Jesus.

We don't have any evidence to confirm the report that Herod was eager to kill Jesus. On the contrary, he had long been too afraid to kill John the Baptist, with whom he had more of a personal complaint. After he finally arranged for John's execution, Herod was immediately haunted by the thought that Jesus was John come back to life (Matthew 14:2; Mark 6:16). Furthermore, when Jesus was brought to Herod in custody, Herod "was very glad, for he had been wanting to see him for a long time... hoping to see him perform some sign" (Luke 23:8). And given the opportunity to pass sentence on Jesus, Herod declined, returning Jesus to Pilate.

It seems much more likely, therefore, that the Pharisees were trying to make Jesus go away simply because they wanted him to go away. Just shortly before this episode, Luke reports that "the Pharisees began to be very hostile toward him" (Luke 11:53), and so it seems highly improbable that the Pharisees would try to protect Jesus from Herod.

Jesus was very shrewd about people's motives, and so he likely recognized that the Pharisees were not earnestly trying to protect him from Herod. His "go and tell that fox" statement, therefore, was probably meant as much for the Pharisees as for Herod.

Interestingly, the Pharisees were likely fabricating a death threat in order to scare Jesus away, he still went deliberately on his way toward Jerusalem, and he went precisely for the purpose of dying (see 13:33). In light of the cross and the empty tomb, how pathetic does the Pharisees' threat seem? Jesus had already eluded earlier efforts to kill him when the time was not right (Matthew 2:13-16; Luke 4:28-30; John 7:30, 8:59), and he made it clear even at the time of his arrest that he could be rescued simply by saying the word (Matthew 26:53). While the threat of death is the ultimate weapon the world can wield, it was an inadequate tool against Jesus.

Having expressed aloud his intent to go to Jerusalem to die, Jesus breaks into a lament about Jerusalem. The love-in-pain tone of Jesus' repeated vocatives ("Jerusalem, Jerusalem") might be best understood in light of other biblical examples of the same technique: "Simon, Simon" (Luke 22:31), "Martha, Martha" (Luke 10:41), "O my son Absalom, my son, my son Absalom" (2 Samuel 18:33), and "My God, my God" (Psalm 22:1; Mark 15:34). Facing the prospect of his own death, Jesus laments, but not for himself. Rather, he laments for Jerusalem, the city that not only declines the Lord's overtures but also violently rejects them. It may have been customary in some times and places to kill the messenger who brought bad news. What an irony, though, that Jerusalem chose again and again to kill the messengers who brought good news — loving exhortations and gracious salvation from God.

From the perspective of this side of the empty tomb, we understand better what Jesus said to Herod and to the disingenuous Pharisees. Jesus was not literally going to complete his work in the next 72 hours. Rather, he planted the cryptic seed of this lovely gospel truth that his work would indeed be finished "on the third day."

Application

The older we get, the more we come to recognize the interconnectedness of the past, the present, and the future.

We see the pendulum of fashion trends swing back and reintroduce styles that we remember from thirty years ago. We see how human relationships — whether between individuals, groups, or nations — are sweetened or embittered by the accumulation of past events. And we recognize more and more within ourselves the profound and continuing influence of our childhood experiences on our adult responses and behaviors.

At another level, when a medical doctor offers a patient a prognosis, it may come in the form of odds — say, a 40% chance of recovery. That prognosis for the future, however, is no more than a record of the past. Based on the past results of similar cases, we predict the future outcome of present cases.

At a personal level, you and I experience every day an assortment of common emotions — e.g., worry, hope, dread, regret, nostalgia, anticipation, and such — all of which bear witness to the enormous impact that past, present, and future have on one another.

The three lections we have before us this week also bear witness to the relationship of past, present, and future, but with a twist. The twist is faith. The twist is a recognition that we cannot really calculate the equation of past, present, and future without factoring in the God who is Lord of both time and eternity.

Abraham's past and present did not add up to the future that God had in mind. His past and present, so far as he could tell, added up to some slave from Damascus receiving all of his inheritance. But the sovereign God had a future in store where a whole nation of Abraham's descendants would inherit and settle the land where Abraham lived only as a sojourner. Descendants as many as Abraham could count would spread out over the land as far as Abraham could see. With God, Abraham's future was far more than a simple extrapolation of his past and his present.

Paul, meanwhile, urged the Philippian Christians to let their present be a kind of extrapolation of their future. Paul laid out for them an understanding of what the future held, on the one hand, for those who were "enemies of the cross of Christ" and, on the other hand, for those who were believers following his example. In the present, in a prison, Paul's approach did not look so good. But Paul looked to the future — God's future — and lived toward that.

Jesus predicted that his work would be finished on "the third day." Between that prediction and victory, however, came a lot of seeming troubles, setbacks, and defeats. We, in the midst of troubles, are likely to lose hope about the future. But, like Abraham and Paul, we serve a Lord who will indeed fulfill his promise and finish his work with victory.

Alternative Applications

Genesis 15:1-12, 17-18. Some of the big events in our lives are about plot. We get married, we have children, we move, we change jobs, we experience some loss or tragedy, we retire, and on it goes. The "plot" big events are often the kinds of occasions when we take pictures.

Other big events in our lives, however, are not about plot. They are about dialogue. They are instances when nothing visibly or measurably happens, but they are big events because of what is said.

At the opening of the scene in Genesis, Abraham has just come off of a series of big plot events. First, there was the ugly Egypt episode (12:10-20). Famine had forced a move by Abraham and Sarah, and then fear prompted them to be deceptive about their relationship. When the truth was discovered, they were summarily evicted from the land where they had sought refuge. Next came turmoil between his camp and the camp of his nephew, Lot, leading to their separation. Shortly after their separation, however, Lot's new home found itself in the crossfire of a regional conflict, and Abraham was forced to mobilize for a military rescue operation.

Life had not been peaceful and uneventful for old Abraham since leaving Ur. But then, "after these things," God came and spoke to Abraham. The next big event in Abraham's life was not about plot, it was about dialogue.

God spoke to Abraham. He spoke great promises. He spoke great improbabilities. "And he believed the Lord; and the Lord reckoned it to him as righteousness" (v. 6). It was an all-dialogue event, but it was seminal. Two thousand years later, the apostle Paul pointed to this event as not only pivotal for Abraham, but emblematic of the great pivotal event for all who are saved (see Romans 4 and Galatians 3).

The preacher and his/her people can embrace the truth of big events that are all dialogue. Precisely such events are sprinkled through our testimonies. Prayer itself is usually such an event. Anytime an occasion (like this Sunday morning) features a dialogue with God — his word to us and our faithful response to him — it is a big event.

Luke 13:31-35. From time to time in Bible study settings, I challenge people to make a list of the apparent shortcomings of God's people at the point in time being studied. For example, what were the recurring failures of the Israelites in the wilderness? What were the great sins cited by the eighth-century BC judgment prophets? What did Jesus need to correct and reprove among his disciples again and again? What were the concerns that prevailed in the local churches to which Paul wrote?

My contention is that we will seldom come across a shortcoming or sin that is unfamiliar to us. What we see in the pages of scripture, we are also very likely to see in the mirror. That is not to say that every individual is beset with the whole collage of human sinfulness. It is to say, however, that we don't usually have to look very far to see that the human condition and tendency is always pretty much the same.

Accordingly, it is worth considering at a personal level what Jesus says of Jerusalem. We may distance ourselves from this passage because we haven't stoned any prophets. The underlying issue, though, is how God's people respond to him and to his word.

We, perhaps more than any previous generation of God's people, are inclined to pick and choose what we like from God's word, biblical commands, and Jesus' teachings. We don't need to stone any prophets when we can simply reduce God's word to a smorgasbord for consumers.

Meanwhile, there is this God who seeks to gather his people, like a hen gathers her chicks under her wings. Do we come when he calls? Do we let God draw us near to himself? Or do we ignore his invitations, postpone our response, and resist a closer relationship and deeper discipleship?

Perhaps our own names should be inserted when we hear Jesus lament, "Jerusalem, Jerusalem!"

Lent 3
Isaiah 55:1-9
1 Corinthians 10:1-13
Luke 13:1-9
Timothy Cargal

Tumbling towers

I still remember that morning and I imagine that I will for the rest of my life. I was scheduled to have the first (and hopefully last) significant surgery of my life. I had arrived at the hospital very early that morning and had been taken back into the surgical preparation area. Initially everything was proceeding as scheduled but after a while everything just seemed to come to a halt. Oh, there was plenty of activity buzzing around, but the things I had been told would happen with me just weren't. I was growing impatient and irritated.

Then I began to pick up some buzz about a plane crash. It was hard to pull together details from what I was overhearing (no one was bringing me news directly, and there was no television where I was). It apparently had happened in New York. I could understand why everyone was talking about it, but I didn't see why it should have brought things to a halt in a suburban Washington hospital. Then the buzz seemed to be about a crash here in Washington. Was it a second crash or were they confused about where the crash had been in the first place? All that was clear was that I wasn't on anyone's agenda at the moment.

A short while later my surgeon arrived. All surgeries for that morning had been cancelled. Not one, but two planes had crashed into the World Trade Center Towers in New York, a third had crashed into the Pentagon little more than ten miles away, and a fourth plane was reportedly heading toward Washington. The operating rooms had been closed in order to deal with what was expected to be a flood of emergency cases.

The date, obviously, was September 11, 2001. For me, the events of that day were in some ways up close and personal but still primarily experienced through radio and television news reports. For the vast majority of Americans, that day was lived vicariously through the news media. The ability of millions to simultaneously share in an experience through mass media has created events that became defining moments in our culture. People can replay in intricate detail the circumstances that surrounded them and the emotions they felt when they first heard that news or that the Space Shuttle *Challenger* had exploded on lift-off, the *Columbia* had exploded during re-entry, Martin Luther King Jr., had been shot while standing on a balcony of a motel in Memphis, John F. Kennedy had been shot while riding in a presidential motorcade winding through the streets of Dallas, or Japanese warplanes had just destroyed much of the U.S. Pacific Fleet as it lay at anchor in Pearl Harbor.

Of all the national experiences that have been created by mass media, why is it these catastrophes stay with us so vividly and with such tenacity? It cannot just be their shock value or their overwhelmingly negative impact; we hear about many shocking evils every day. I am convinced that the impact of these events is that they serve as dramatic wake-up calls. Their significance in our minds goes far beyond the particulars of the individual events.

Not a few historians have concluded that the Civil Rights era begun in 1950s died as well on that Memphis balcony, for King's assassination and the rage of the riots that followed in its aftermath fundamentally changed once again the relationship among races in our country. Lee Harvey Oswald's bullet stole life not only from a young president but also from the idealism of America's "Camelot." The bombs dropped by Japanese Zeros not only set ablaze America's Pacific Fleet but left in ashes as well the nation's myth of geographic isolation bolstered and protected by unassailable military might. "9/11" did the same thing for a new generation. The very reason the first shuttle disaster is more etched on our memories than the second is because a whole worldview about the power and precision of technology, a mythology embodied for many by NASA, crumbled along with the *Challenger*, leaving room only for a "not again" reaction at the loss of *Columbia*. Such events lay waste to our carefully constructed worlds of human self-sufficiency.

Isaiah 55:1-9

Sometimes when you read the end of a book first you get a different sense of what it was about than if you had started at the beginning. Knowing how things will turn out and what will be important at the end of the day, as it were, focuses one's attention on different details at the beginning than might have been apparent without those clues. Reading from the end provides an interesting perspective on this particular scripture lesson.

The New Revised Standard Version provides the heading, "An Invitation to Abundant Life" for the oracle by the exilic prophet preserved in Isaiah 55. God's call to satisfy our thirst and hunger "without money and without price" in the opening verse certainly fits with the theme expressed by the heading. Yet the final verses of the reading emphasize lack rather than abundance, at least as regards human wisdom as compared to God's. The oracle insists that our thoughts and actions are as far removed from God's "as the heavens are higher than the earth" (v. 9). Now it could be argued that the prophet invites us to leave behind our lack for God's abundance, to "seek the Lord while God may be found" (v. 6), but one could also argue that the prophet is encouraging us to change our very notion of what counts as abundance.

Returning to the opening verses of the oracle, notice just how different are God's thoughts from the values that dominate our culture. God calls to those who "have no money, Come, buy and eat!" But what can it mean to "buy" if we give neither money nor bartered goods in exchange? To our "free market" world, God calls for everyone to come and receive the necessities of life for free. But we only assign value to things that have a price. Our slogan is, "You get what you pay for," and its corollary is that if you pay nothing then you get nothing of value. We want to be self-sufficient, to make our own way in the world; God calls us who thirst to come to the living waters by which God supplies life (v. 3).

What is God's assessment of the things that we do value? God simply asks each of us, "Why do you spend your money for that which is not bread, and your labor for that which does not satisfy?" (v. 2a). If we are so wise and self-sufficient, then why do we experience so much of life as lack rather than abundance? Our ideas of abundance always leave us hungering and thirsting for more. We need to "listen carefully" to God so that we will know what food is genuinely "good" and can bring "delight" to our lives. We need to elevate our thoughts by replacing our human values and wisdom with God's thoughts.

Such transformation of one's thinking lies at the heart of the biblical concept of repentance, and it is precisely the language of repentance that we find in the final verses of the reading (and the heart of the oracle as a whole). To "seek the Lord," "forsake" wicked ways, and "return to the Lord" (vv. 6-7) are all common expressions of repentance. As long as we think of life primarily in terms of things we can provide for ourselves, then we will be confused by the call to repentance of those who live in want. Those who do return to God and God's ways, however, will receive mercy and abundant pardon — truer marks of abundant life than any material goods one may amass no matter how necessary to physical life.

1 Corinthians 10:1-13

In this portion of his letter, Paul utilizes a classic form of argumentation that is usually referred to as either allegorical or typological. Almost every sentence of the reading bears an allusion to some event from the experience of the Israelites during the Exodus and subsequent period of wilderness wanderings. The specific source references for these allusions can be found in most any study, Bible or commentary, and so will not be repeated here. Paul himself refers to these allusions as "examples," and so we need to ask why he considers these the relevant or appropriate examples (vv. 6 and 11) for his Corinthian readers and what particular function does he hope these examples will play for his readers.

Regarding the initial part of our question, the simple answer as to why Paul chose these particular examples would seem to be that they parallel specific topics that he has already taken up in the letter. Concern with baptism (10:2; cf. 1:11-17), idolatry in the specific context of eating and drinking (10:7; cf. 8:1-13), sexual immorality (10:8; cf. 5:1-13), and complaints within the community and about its leadership (10:10; cf. 3:1-23; 6:1-11; 9:1-18) comprise the bulk of what Paul has written about to this point. Yet examples of all these things abound throughout the Old Testament. Might there be some further reason why Paul chose to cluster all his examples in the experience of Israel in the wilderness?

Perhaps there is one implicit parallel between the Israelites and the Corinthians that Paul wishes to draw out from his choice of these particular examples. Just as all the examples Paul offers are from the earliest period of Israel's communal experience as the people of God, the Corinthians are themselves flush with the experience of being a newly constituted community of God's people. Paul may have wished to suggest that there are particular dangers or risks that accompany a newly experienced awareness of God's grace and acceptance.

The conclusion that Paul draws from his typological argument would seem to support this view. "So if you think you are standing, watch out that you do not fall" (10:12). Those who realize they have been brought into covenant with God as a result of God's grace rather than their own worthiness may be tempted to libertarian excess. God chose us when we were sinners, so would God reject us now if we continue in our sin? But just as the biblical story of the Israelites shows that they put their participation in the covenant at risk by such behaviors, Paul now warns the Corinthians that they run the risk of following exactly the same course.

Beyond providing a warning, Paul also emphasizes "God is faithful" (10:13). The God who brought the Israelites and the Corinthians into covenant will also help keep them within that relationship. The experience of the Israelites and the Corinthians is "common to everyone," and God will intervene to limit the severity of the temptations and to assist in withstanding them. Although the Israelites were tempted to abandon their covenant with God, God would ultimately abandon them. The same would be true for the Corinthians and for us.

Luke 13:1-9

Jesus suggested that two catastrophic events contemporaneous to his own ministry destroyed any sense of self-sufficiency for those who had heard about them. His comments were prompted by a report that the Roman governor Pontius Pilate had ordered the massacre of a group of worshipers from Galilee, mixing their human blood with the blood of the sacrificed animals. The report here in Luke is the only record of this particular atrocity, but it is in keeping with what the contemporary Jewish historian Josephus reports about Pilate's actions against those under his authority (killing Samaritans on their way to worship at Mount Gerizim and diverting funds from the Jerusalem temple's treasury and desolating it with Roman images, provoking riots; *Antiquities* 18.55-62, 85-89).

Jesus related this political tragedy to another recent event where the culpability was hardly obvious. A tower had collapsed, killing eighteen people who were standing nearby. Now there was a widely held view among Jews at that time — a view still found among even some Christians to this day — that physical suffering, whether as a result of illness or disaster, was a direct consequence of sin and a clear indication of divine judgment. Jesus rejected such a simplistic notion outright. Were those who died at Pilate's hand or those crushed by the tower worse sinners than those who escaped with their lives? Jesus answers the question directly: "No, I tell you; but unless you repent, you will all perish just as they did" (v. 5).

If you listen carefully to what Jesus said, it would seem that he takes away with one hand what the other had just granted. No, Jesus insisted, those who died in these disasters were no worse than anyone else. You cannot draw conclusions about a person's morality from the tragedies that occur in their life. "But," Jesus continued, "unless you repent you will all perish just as they did." We are quick to object. "Now wait just a minute, Jesus! If repentance, asking God's forgiveness for our sins, can spare us from perishing as those did in these tragedies, aren't you saying that there *is* a connection between sin and suffering in a person's life?"

It was to head off just such an objection that Jesus immediately related the parable of the fig tree. Jesus wanted to make clear what was wrong with the old way of thinking. The problem was not with the notion of divine judgment. Just as the fig tree, if it failed to produce in response to the gardener's careful attention, would be cut down at the end of the next growing season, so was it true that there will be those who will ultimately suffer God's judgment. Their belief in divine judgment was not the problem; their problem was in their blithe assumption that their comfortable lives were proof they were already immune to such judgment.

The point of Jesus' assertion that the victims were not any worse than the survivors was not to rehabilitate the reputations of the dead but to challenge the living to see that they were no better than those who had been overcome by tragedy. It was not their superiority that had spared them, but God's grace in continuing to care for them, to nurture them like the gardener tending the fig tree. "There, but for God's grace, go I!" Jesus' point in relating the parable in response to the disastrous news that was buzzing about the people was that while they could see what was happening, they were not understanding it correctly (cf. Luke 12:54-56). Where we see divine punishment in the disasters, we should rather see a call to repentance. Where we see divine approval in the care given to the unproductive fig tree, we should actually see divine mercy. Even given God's grace, there are limits to the divine patience. The clock is ticking for the fig tree, and the clock is ticking for each of us.

Application

How are we to respond to this realization? Jesus said that in order to avoid "perish[ing] just as they did" we must repent. Repentance means much more, however, than simply acknowledging that we have done wrong and asking for God's forgiveness. Genuine repentance involves a change of our minds. It only really happens when our view of the world is changed, when we reject the notion of human self-sufficiency in favor of the truth of our dependence upon the divine.

Too often we have watered down repentance in our minds to something like this: "God, I know that you — for some reason — have a problem with this kind of behavior. Now, I don't pretend to understand why you get so upset about this, but I do know that I don't want you mad at me. So please forgive me this time, and I'll try not to do it again." That is not real repentance because that is being sorry that you got caught and being afraid to face the consequences. Real repentance comes when we begin to see the world the way God sees it, to understand the harms God's prohibitions direct us away from and the joys God's commands bring to our lives, to recognize God is not a cosmic killjoy but a loving and patient parent. That is why these events that shatter our preconceived notions about the world — whether towers fall on the unsuspecting, or vibrant, young leaders are felled by assassins' bullets, or technological marvels cataclysmically fail — provide occasions for genuine repentance.

Repentance arises not from fear of punishment but from realization with the prophet that God's wisdom is of an astronomically higher order than human wisdom. Indeed, as Isaiah reminds us, our vaunted wisdom leads to the foolishness of valuing what is ultimately worthless and of despising what has true value. Our problem is not just sins, the numerous ways in which we waste our "money," as it were, buying things that cannot satisfy us and only bring harm to others. Our problem is sin, the inability to recognize the lack of ultimate value in what we desire, the ability to deceive ourselves into thinking we are self-reliant when truly we are dependent upon God. Repentance is replacing human value judgments with divine ones.

Jesus does not call us either to blithely accept suffering as inevitable or to acquiesce to suffering as divine judgment. He calls on us to change ourselves through genuine repentance and to change the world by bearing the fruit of that repentance. They may not have the sudden and dramatic impact upon our emotions and psyches as disasters or assassinations, but in their own ways the disciplines of Lent are also about calling us to reconsider our view of the world. It is a time to ask ourselves if the values that truly govern our lives as we go about our daily business, are the same values that motivate God to action. Lent is a season of repentance, a time not only to seek forgiveness for our failures to God and others, but a time to "be transformed by the renewing of [our] minds, so that [we] may discern what is the will of God — what is good and acceptable and perfect" (Romans 12:2b).

An Alternative Application
1 Corinthians 10:1-13. If the Israelites were an example to the Corinthians of the dangers of an incipient libertinism as they began their communal life as God's people, then both the Israelites and the Corinthians are examples to modern Christians as they continue their Lenten journey. The purpose of Lent is not to raise questions or doubts about our salvation. That is ultimately in God's hands. Lent should remind us of our need to respond to God's grace with faithful lives even as it heightens our awareness of the activity of God's grace in our lives.

Paul's use of a typological argument here also provides good homiletical guidance for modern preachers. He does not so much look for discrete, isolated parallels as for a pattern within the scriptural narrative that is played out again and again in the spiritual lives of God's people. Being able to see that pattern within the Bible helps us to recognize it within our own lives as well. In this instance that pattern serves to underline that such experience is "common to everyone," and then just as God has helped others in the past, so God will give us the assistance we need as well.

Lent 4
Joshua 5:9-12
2 Corinthians 5:16-21
Luke 15:1-3, 11b-32
Mark Molldrem

Always wanting more

With Augustine we can affirm that pride is the fundamental sin and concupiscence is its fundamental fruit. Pride manifests itself in America as we glory in the overall dominance displayed by our athletes during any Olympic games. Our expectations were expanded as athletes excelled and reaped multiple medals for their efforts. Experienced athletes from prior Olympics return to defend their titles. Sportscasters talk just as much about it in anticipation as they did following the competition.

As a human race, we are always striving for more and are usually not satisfied unless we achieve it. Sometimes this striving for more leads to some dire circumstances, like using illegal drugs to enhance physical performance in order to outdo the competition. Our decisions have consequences, some of which cannot be recalled or redeemed. Is this the way it is in terms of our spiritual journey through life — striving for more, but always being left wanting something better? How does this affect our relationship with God? How does God respond to this in us?

Joshua 5:9-12

It is fascinating to note in the Bible how names carry such significance. So often they express the essence of an event or the character in a person and serve as a reminder of the judgments and mercies of God. Gilgal and Gibeath-haaraloth are such names that signify something more than just the mere utterance of the word that is haphazardly attached to a particular place.

Joshua had assumed the leadership of the people after Moses died. He led them into Canaan, crossing the Jordan River. This crossing was a mini-version of the Red Sea episode. There they fled out of Egypt; here they marched into the Promised Land. There the pharaoh was finally impressed; here the kings of the Amorites and the Canaanites were impressed (Joshua 5:1).

A situation developed that needed redress. During the wanderings in the wilderness after the Exodus, a whole generation had arisen who had not been circumcised. Those who had originally come out of Egypt had been circumcised with the sign of the promise. But, because of their disobedience in the wilderness, they were not allowed to enter into the Promised Land. However, the generation born in the wilderness would be allowed to inherit the promise. But, they had not been circumcised. Now was the time to take care of that, so they would bear on themselves the sign of the covenant between God and the people, a sign that was originally given to Abraham (Genesis 17).

To commemorate this event of mass circumcision, the place became known as Gibeath-haaraloth, "the hill of the foreskins." It is a rather graphic name — one that pictures in its utterance what was done at this place to keep in step with God as the people prepared to take possession of the land. It was, however, by the name Gilgal that the place would be called. The word Gilgal comes from the Hebrew word meaning "to roll." As God said to Joshua, "This day I have rolled away the reproach of Egypt from you." God had done a new thing. (Is this, perhaps, a foreshadowing of rolling away the stone of enslavement to death?) Now that the people were poised to inherit the land, they needed to be reminded of what God had done for them. Naming the encampment Gilgal would do just that. The name expressed the meaning of their new status. No longer were they slaves in Egypt. They were a free people, ready to shine among the nations of the world. The reproach of their experience in Egypt was past, rolled away. Newly circumcised, they were ready to march forward into a future God had prepared for them.

The land held that future. Whereas manna had been provided in the wilderness for their daily needs, it was provisional. Now, they needed to settle on the land and work it and from it produce their daily staples. The psalmist would express years later, "Blessed is everyone who fears the Lord, who walks in his ways! You shall eat the fruit of the labor of your hands; you shall be happy, and it shall be well with you" (Psalm 128:1-2).

What is worth noting in all of this is that God is judging his people and showing mercy on them at the same time. The circumcised were brought out of Egypt in a great act of deliverance. When they disobeyed God, they were judged and kept out of the Promised Land. Still, their children would enter to fulfill the promise. Circumcision would continue to be the sign of the covenant to which God would be faithful and the people would be called and recalled to be faithful. The new generation and the generations to come would experience the judgment and mercy of God in different ways as they lived on the creases of an unfolding history that would move the promises of God to greater fulfillment. The people would learn that God was serious about his purposes in the world and their role in bringing them about. The sign of the covenant would forever be before them (Gibeath-haaraloth) and they would roll forward from the place of their encampment (Gilgal), remembering the new chapter that was being written with a new generation.

2 Corinthians 5:16-21

"From now on..." Something has happened to cause Paul to see things very differently. What was it? "From a human point of view..." no longer works to grasp "the breadth and length and height and depth" (Ephesians 3:18) of anything. The psychology of change tells us that people will accept a new paradigm when they have had a *significant emotional experience*. What was this for Paul and the early Christians who were willing to put their lives on the line and behave differently "from now on..."?

The context to understand these words can be found in 1 Corinthians 15 and also the two verses (2 Corinthians 5:14-15) that precede this text for today. Essentially, it was the death and resurrection of Jesus that presented that *significant emotional experience* for Paul and the church, such that "we regard no one from a human point of view." The originator of a *new age* theology is Paul, who announces in his gospel that anyone who is in Christ is a *new creation*. Former things do not count the same way anymore. There is a new paradigm that has seized the imagination. That paradigm is the death and resurrection of Jesus, which announces what God has done and is now doing in the affairs of the world.

First, God has reconciled the world to himself. This has been done through the death and resurrection of Jesus. His "act of righteousness leads to acquittal and life for all men" (Romans 5:18). His obedience reforms and makes righteous those who have been disobedient, but now trust in the unfathomable deeds of God rather than their own doings. The gospel has superceded the law (Romans 3:20-26) as the foundation on which to stand righteous before God. The writer to the Hebrews (9:26b-28) and 1 John (4:10) express this in terms of atonement theology. In Jesus, a new order has been established in which God has revealed his heart for the salvation of the world, definitively creating a new relationship between heaven and earth — the cross of Christ being the new logo.

This opens the door to a new way of relating to one another on a human plane. Paul applies the reconciliation achieved between God and humanity to the purpose of his personal ministry as a follower of Christ. "All this is from God, who... gave us the ministry of reconciliation" (5:18). There has been great dissension in the Corinthian church. Paul has been writing to these folks (probably at least three times!) attempting to iron out the creases that have wrinkled their witness to the gospel. Reconciliation is needed in the church in Corinth. Paul describes himself as an ambassador for Christ, appealing to them on behalf of God to get their act together. Their disagreeableness with one another means that they are at odds with God. As they live in the reconciliation offered by Christ, they will discover a new way to regard one another — no longer from a human point of view!

Paul understands himself as an ambassador for Christ, speaking on his behalf to those who would claim to be followers. Talk about career confidence! Going right to the heart of the matter — that what is at stake is not just one's relationship with brothers and sisters in Christ, but also with Christ himself — Paul beseeches (*doemai*; to entreat, pray; the earnestness of this word is also expressed in 8:4 and 10:2) his Christian friends to "be reconciled to God." That is to say, return to the only ground on which to stand, the ground of Calvary, where Christ worked out the saving reconciliation that makes us right with God! It is from this ground that we can venture forth in right step with one another, modeling ourselves the reconciliation that Christ continues to work in the world.

Luke 15:1-3, 11b-32

Ever since the wilderness wanderings, the people of God have had a fondness for murmuring. There was no exception in Jesus' day. The religious elite, namely the Pharisees and scribes, had a rather snooty attitude toward the more unseemly characters of society. When the tax collectors and sinners were attracted to Jesus so that they might hear him, these religious snobs took notice and immediately criticized Jesus' choice of company. Contrasting these two social groups, one can hear even more the biting irony of Jesus' words, "Whoever has ears to hear, let them hear!"

'*Amartwlov*, which is related to *amartia* — the most frequently used word for sin in the New Testament as well as the Septuagint, designates one who has failed to live up to a standard, whether by action or inaction, intentional or unintentional. The tax collectors, thieves, and prostitutes were numbered among those. If one wished prestige in the community, it would be a social gaff to be associated with the likes of these. How could Jesus make such a politically incorrect move as actually to eat with them?

Later in his gospel account, Luke will quote Jesus as saying, "For the Son of Man came to seek and to save the lost" (Luke 19:10). These are precisely the ones Jesus would want to eat with and talk with and laugh with and cry with and die with. So, it is probably with much glee that Luke clusters three "lost" parables in this "lost" chapter of the Bible. There are two, short anecdotal parables about a lost sheep and a lost coin, to which most people could relate. The gravity of being lost, however, is not fully sensed until the hearer enters the parable of the lost son, the prodigal one. Here Jesus is at his storytelling best.

This story has been worked and re-worked from just about every angle — the most familiar ones being that of the son, the father, and the elder brother. It might provide an interesting stretch of the imagination to relive the parable from the vantage point of the swine who shared the sty with this foreign species; or the harlots who helped him squander his money only to see him leave them more eager than he approached them, because he longed for more of what he truly needed; or the hired servants who observed all this and learned a great lesson on love from their master; or the friends who failed to go after him but were willing to celebrate his homecoming. What insights can be gained from an imaginative exploration of viewing this familiar story through unfamiliar eyes?

Application

It is rather sad to hear the reports on the state of health in America, notably how overweight we have become as a people, younger and older alike. Our consumption shows, in our over-sized garages and our over-sized waists. The manna of which we want more is not the true bread that feeds and nourishes us for life abundant and life eternal. Jesus, as the true bread that comes down from heaven (John 6:32-40), nourishes us in ways that keep us fit for daily life. The love that the father shows the errant son reflects the love of God through Jesus for us erring children; it is this love that fills us full of what we really want more of — acceptance, forgiveness, belonging, joy!

The manna was provisional for God's people as they wandered in the wilderness until that time when they were able to inhabit the land and work it for the fruit of the fields; so too is the Lord's Supper for

God's people as they wander the four corners of the earth until eternity when they will share in the marriage feast of the lamb, the first fruit of all creation (see 1 Corinthians 15:20-28). There will be no need then for "more," because Christ will be all and in all (Colossians 1:15-21; 3:11).

There is a striking monument for peace in Ottowa, Canada. A solid wall rises out of the rubble of conflict. There are three figures on top, keeping vigilant watch. Etched in the stone is the word "reconciliation." Such a monument should be erected in Northern Ireland, Jerusalem, Yugoslavia, Africa, and Indonesia. With hot spots all over the world reminding us of our need for reconciliation, Paul's words strike a very contemporary note. The church can be present in any troubling situation with a clear word about God's intentions for our relationships: reconciliation. "We are ambassadors for Christ [entrusted with the message of reconciliation], God making his appeal through us" (2 Corinthians 5:20). The church today has inherited the mantel that Paul wore in his efforts to bring peace to the Corinthian congregation. We need to wear it boldly. That means publicly! Rather than thinking of our congregations as enclaves to shield us from the world, we should understand our congregations as platforms from which to dive into the affairs of the world with a word that can truly satisfy our concupiscence for more that propels us into power and boundary disputes. Because we know that human reconciliation is rooted in God's reconciliation with humanity (2 Corinthians 5:18), we dare not withhold this truth from the world.

This reconciliation can be worked out between nations as well as between people on the streets or within families. Would it be accurate to correlate the prodigal son's plight in the pig sty with the situation of street people in today's urban centers, whether in the United States, Germany, or Brazil? If so, how is the church today like the father waiting with open arms and an open heart when the lost one comes home smelling like a pig and dirtier than dirt? Are we ready with gospel hospitality to receive whoever comes to the door in whatever condition? Or, is the church like the elder brother with an attitude of preference? Do our congregations truly want to be filled with more "lost souls" or with more people "just like us"?

What good news there is for us all is that no one is so lost or so distant to make it impossible to return home to the heavenly Father! How remarkable upon reflection to be able to look back into our lostness and see how God's providential care was able to provide for us even then — like the nameless citizen who hired the prodigal and stood by him quietly until he came to his senses and then let him go from his hire to find the *more* he had been searching for all along.

Lent 5
Isaiah 43:16-21
Philippians 3:4b-14
John 12:1-8
David Kalas

Christian (version 7.0)

Personality tests, such as the Meyers-Briggs, will place two-word sets side by side and ask the participant to indicate a preference between the two. Without much time to think through all the nuances, the person using the device has to move quickly through the columns of words, sometimes agonizing and sometimes choosing easily.

Relying on reflex more than reflection, which of these two words do you prefer? *New. Old.*

Our preference varies with the situation, of course. We may long for a new house, while cherishing an old chair. We shop for a new computer to replace the old one, but we put it on the same old desk that we would never think of replacing. We buy a new sound system, and then we play our old music on it.

The people of God are always contending with issues of "new" and "old." In one circumstance, "old" means time-tested and proven. In another circumstance, it simply means outdated. For some, "new" means improved. For others, it connotes unorthodox.

Things old and new play major roles in our Old and New Testament lections for this week.

Isaiah 43:16-21

Keynote speakers are introduced by their resumes and bios. Whoever has the job of introducing the main speaker for some event usually has before him a vitae listing that speaker's accomplishments, qualities, and titles. For example:

Our special guest today is a renowned author... is CEO of such-and-such Fortune 500 company... is the pastor of the fastest growing church in America... is one of the foremost authorities on... has achieved unprecedented success in his field....

The audience's pump has been primed, and they wait with anticipation, eager to hear what this remarkable person has to say.

The prophet Isaiah, like a good emcee, has gone out of his way to introduce this word from the Lord by citing God's resume. Unwilling to simply pronounce — as he does in other places — "Thus says the Lord," followed by the prophecy, Isaiah makes a point of reminding his audience of God's past deeds. Specifically, Isaiah calls to mind the deliverance God provided for his people at the Red Sea in the days of Moses.

One would think that was a good approach. Speaking to a people in need of miraculous deliverance, it seems just right for Isaiah to recall aloud God's marvelous acts of deliverance on behalf of the people's ancestors. To a generation in captivity in a foreign land, Isaiah reminds the people how God saved an earlier generation from their captivity in a foreign land. He introduces God's word by citing God's credentials as a deliverer.

And then comes God's surprising word: "Forget about it."

All those past accomplishments, the marvelous stories that are Israel's testimony, the signs and wonders of old — God instructs the people to set them aside and not to give them a second thought.

It's an astonishing command coming from the God who typically exhorts his people to remember — that is, to recall, ritually and regularly, God's saving deeds from days gone by. But not now. Now, in the moment when deliverance is needed again, God urges his people to forget what he has done in the past.

I suppose it is an irksome thing for a musician to have concert crowds wanting only to hear the old favorites. If the artist or band has been around for a while, and if their songs have become cherished oldies to a generation of fans, it is almost impossible to introduce a new song. The concertgoers are so emotionally attached to the old stuff that any new songs are almost unwelcome.

So it is oftentimes between God and God's people. We have so fallen in love with some "hit" from long ago. It meant so much to us at the time and new layers of fond and sentimental attachment have been added with each passing year. We may be unwittingly unwilling, as a result, to let God do a new and different thing in our lives.

And so God urged the people of Isaiah's day to stow away their old 45s — those well-worn records singing of what God had done in the days of Moses, Joshua, or David. He was coming out with a new hit, and he wanted his people to be prepared to hear it and to sing and dance along with it.

Philippians 3:4b-14

The standard magician will startle his audience by seeming to destroy something precious or valuable. Here is a legal tender $50 bill that seems to be torn in pieces or set on fire. Here is an expensive wristwatch or piece of jewelry that seems to have been crushed or to have disappeared altogether. And here is a real, live human being that seems to have been cut in two.

The sleight of hand has more impact because the thing involved has value. Few audiences would watch wide-eyed if a performer appeared to saw a log in two and put it back together. No one would gasp at a cheap thing being set on fire.

Paul invites a gasp from the Philippian audience in this passage. He trots out something of great value, and then seems to make that thing vanish before their eyes.

The thing of value, in this case, is Paul's proud past.

In our materialistic world, where people are judged more by what they have than by who they are, Paul's heritage may go unappreciated. But Paul came from a world — and wrote, at least in part, to a people — for which the great measure in life was not possessions but the law. When Paul set himself against that measure, the measure of the law, the audience was impressed.

On the one hand, there are the matters that Paul could take no credit for personally. His unblemished Jewish pedigree included his tribe, his circumcision according to the law, and his Hebrew parentage.

On the other hand, there were those matters for which Paul could take credit.

First, he was a Pharisee. That does not sound like a favorable claim in the ears of most of our people, for all we know of Pharisees is some of what Jesus said about them. In this context, however, we must recognize that the Pharisees were the most devoutly religious and most carefully obedient men of that day in Israel. Jesus' issue with the Pharisees was their hypocrisy, but there is no indication that hypocrisy was a problem for Paul. He was, we gather, an impeccably pious man.

Second, there was Paul's zeal. His was not a mind-your-own-business religiosity. No, he was a crusader, a zealot, a man of holy indignation who sought to do right and to right wrongs. And, up until his conversion on the road to Damascus, the wrong he sought to right was that seemingly heretical movement within Judaism involving the followers of Jesus. In his passionate obedience to God, Paul endeavored to shut up and shut down the heretics.

Finally, there was Paul's most remarkable claim: he was blameless. Who can make a claim like that? Yet Paul had weighed himself in the balance of the law and found that he was not wanting.

Then comes the moment when Paul takes the saw or the fire to these things of value. "Whatever gains I had, these I have come to regard as loss... I regard them as rubbish." *This thing I treasured...? Watch me crumple it up and throw it away. This thing of great value...? See how I put it down the disposal, run it through the shredder, toss it in the garbage.*

A materialistic world may not value the same things that Paul did, but we do value things. And we can be certain that Paul's response to our things of value would be precisely the same. *Watch me throw it all away.*

The shock and strength of what Paul says is found best in the Greek word *skubalon*, translated here "rubbish." The King James Version translates it "dung." We might think of still other words. The very stuff that Paul was so proud of previously, he can't wait to scrape off the bottom of his shoe. He is eager to shake it loose and leave it behind, for he has found something so much better.

Here is where Paul and the standard magician part company. The audience is shocked when the large bill is set on fire but relieved to find that it somehow survived. The audience is startled to see a living person cut in half but delighted to see that apparent victim in one piece when the trick is over.

Paul, however, does not reassemble the thing of value. He leaves it burned, cut, and shredded. What he wants his Philippian audience to see is not the magic of the valuable thing restored, but the testimony of the valuable thing cast aside — cast aside in favor of "the surpassing value of knowing Christ Jesus my Lord."

John 12:1-8

This dinner must have been a come-as-you-are affair, for that's surely how everyone came. In just a few descriptive verses, John gives us a glimpse around the table, and we discover that everyone looks very familiar.

First, there is Martha being Martha.

Most of us would be able to predict within our own family gatherings who is likely to do what. At our extended family's Christmas celebration, for example, I could predict to you who will arrive early and who will arrive late. We know who is going to carve the turkey, who is going to hand out the presents, and who is going to be continually getting up from the table to make sure that everyone has what he or she needs.

Likewise, when you ate dinner at the home of Mary, Martha, and Lazarus, you could bet that Martha was going to serve. The gospel of Luke (10:38-42) provides us with the famous episode that makes this account ring so true. Martha fusses away at making preparations, while Mary neglects the housework in favor of sitting and listening to Jesus. Martha does not compare favorably in that passage. In the larger business of the kingdom and of Jesus' teachings, however, we must evaluate Martha generously. Serving, after all, is the great hallmark of the follower of Jesus (see Matthew 23:11; Luke 12:35-40, 17:7-10, 22:27; John 12:26; Philippians 2:5-7). Serving is the essence of greatness in the kingdom (Matthew 20:25-28). And serving is how Martha loved — a vital missing element from so much of what passes for love in our day.

Next, there is Mary being Mary.

As we mentioned before, Luke offers the quintessential character profile of Mary and Martha in Jesus' visit to their home in chapter 10. As in that passage, Mary is again at Jesus' feet (Luke 10:39; John 12:3). Mary is the portrait of worship: at Jesus' feet, attentive and adoring.

Next, there is Judas being Judas.

Folks in my generation will likely remember the rock opera *Jesus Christ Superstar*. This episode from John's gospel appears early in that musical account of Jesus' final days. A friend and I were joking recently that *Jesus Christ Superstar* might better have been titled *Judas Iscariot: Tragic Hero*, for the psyche of Judas seems to be the real issue of the piece. Judas is depicted as a tortured but well-intentioned tragic figure, which is a much more flattering portrayal than the one the gospel writer offers us.

John shows us a Judas who is not only a thief, but also a thief who deliberately veils his vice under the guise of humanitarian concern. The embezzler dares to condemn the worshiper for misappropriation of funds. The wicked one pretends the indignation of the righteous.

We are well acquainted with the thirty pieces of silver Judas was paid for betraying Jesus. It's hard to imagine that such an average sum would drive a man to such epic treachery. Such is the intoxication of money, however, and when we live under its influence, we lose our judgment and proper reflexes. So it is that no one can serve both God and money (Matthew 6:24), hard as we may try.

When Judas looks at an act of worship but only sees dollar signs, we simply observe Judas being Judas.

Perhaps the question to ask is whether we also see ourselves.

Next, there is Lazarus being, well, there.

Lazarus is the only individual at this dinner who is named but not described as doing or saying anything. We know what both Mary and Martha did. We know what both Judas and Jesus said. All that we know about Lazarus, however, is that he was there. And that is enough, for he was a living testimony to the power of Christ. It was only one chapter earlier that Lazarus was bound and foul in the tomb, his sisters bereaved, and Jesus at a distance. Now, however, the whole group of friends and siblings is seated together around a table, full of life and joy.

Finally, there is Jesus being Jesus. He is the one who comes and sups with us (Revelation 3:20). He is the one who corrects and challenges us (John 12:7-8). He is the one at whose feet we bow down and worship (John 12:3).

Application

A computerized generation understands the language of upgrades and new versions of old software. The latest Pentium makes us wonder how we ever got anything done with our old computer. The newest, biggest, sharpest flat screen makes our old monitor seem intolerable. All the things that this new version of a program or operating system can do makes the earlier version obsolete.

Why would we choose to hold onto that which is slower, weaker, and less productive? Why wouldn't we toss aside the outdated and inadequate version for the new and improved one?

Historically, however, the people of God have resisted upgrades.

Sometimes the people of God have wanted to retreat to the past because the future seemed too frightening (Numbers 14:3-4). Sometimes they have so cherished the past that it became idolatrous (2 Kings 18:4). Sometimes they have allowed "past good" to morph into "only good" (Luke 5:36-39).

The people of Isaiah's day, however, were challenged not to "remember the former things or consider the things of old." Those former things were not bad, mind you. They were glorious deeds of God and part of Israel's testimony. But with their eyes fixed on the rearview mirror, God's people were apt to miss what he had for them down the road. "I am about to do a new thing; now it springs forth, do you not perceive it?"

Paul, meanwhile, declared that he had indeed set aside the former things. He was no longer finding glory in the old things, but rather "forgetting what lies behind and straining forward to what lies ahead, I press on toward the goal...."

So it is that we are presented with a God who does new things, and who invites us into new things.

Now I believe that the pulpit is too important to be used as a proprietary weapon during in-house battles. The truth at stake in these lections is more profound than local church squabbles between new styles and old traditions. The issue at hand is not superficial questions of style and taste. Rather, the issue is a God who was offering something better than what Isaiah's contemporaries had known to date; a God who offered something better than what Paul had known before; and a God who, very likely, has something better for us — individually and corporately — than what we have experienced thus far. Our scriptural challenge is not to keep up with the times, the fashions, or the technology. Our real challenge is to keep up with God.

Alternative Applications
John 12:1-8. We illustrated above the characteristic differences between the two sisters, Mary and Martha. Differences can be embraced or resisted in our congregations. How you and I are different may be a cherished source of celebration or a bitter point of constant tension.

Our churches will be healthier and happier if we leave room — make room — for the different ways people love and serve the Lord. I'm not a proponent of "anything goes." But one of the lovely truths of this passage is that Mary and Martha were different types of people, and so naturally they manifested their love and service in different ways. Martha was the one always on her feet. Mary, by contrast, was the one always on her knees.

I see Mary and Martha in this scene and I am reminded of the Hebrew word *abad*. A comparison of a few translations of Psalm 100:2 will reveal the beauty of this word. The King James and Revised Standard Versions offer the familiar translation, "Serve the Lord with gladness." The New International and New Revised Standard Versions, meanwhile, translate the phrase, "Worship the Lord with gladness."

What a discovery to find that worshiping and serving God are not separate acts. To worship him is to serve him and to serve him is to worship him. While Martha serves the Lord with gladness, Mary worships him with gladness.

Perhaps in our churches from time to time, Martha needs to be challenged to a deeper devotional life while Mary is encouraged to leave the prayer group and help out in the kitchen every once in a while. Most of the time, though, Mary and Martha should be blessed and embraced for how they each serve and worship the Lord with gladness.

John 12:1-8. Different congregations celebrate the sacrament of communion at different times. If your congregation will be partaking of the sacrament together on this Sunday, perhaps the passage from John would provide a good opportunity to work with the motif of dining with Jesus.

Dining with Jesus is a personal thing — a symbol of his grace toward us and his friendship and fellowship with us. This homey episode with the family of Mary, Martha, and Lazarus is a good picture. So, too, the way Jesus invited himself to eat with Zacchaeus (Luke 19:5) and the way he awaits our invitation to have him sup with us (Revelation 3:20).

Dining with Jesus is also a celebrative thing. Surely it was a happy occasion for Lazarus and his sisters to have Jesus back in their home following the miraculous events of the previous chapter. One senses, too, that the meal with Zacchaeus was a happy occasion. We also see Jesus at the wedding feast in Cana (John 2:1-12). And the dining we do with Jesus here is only a foretaste of the festive celebration that will be the great banquet in the kingdom (see Matthew 26:29; Luke 14:15-24).

Dining with Jesus is also a sacramental thing. It is an occasion of worship for Mary (John 12:3), of epiphany for the disciples in Emmaus (Luke 24:28-35), and of God's presence and grace for his believers in every generation (1 Corinthians 11:23-26).

Passion / Palm Sunday
Isaiah 50:4-9a
Philippians 2:5-11
Luke 22:14—23:56
Wayne Brouwer

The tipping point

In his book, *The Tipping Point*, Malcolm Gladwell shows how some events and activities take on a life of their own when they pass a critical mark. Up until that point, the context can be managed and the outcomes determined. But once something reaches the tipping point, everything changes and energies snowball into effects that cannot be contained.

A friend sent me a series of pictures that displayed the tipping point humorously. At a small seaside town in British Columbia, a small car careened carelessly on waterfront streets and ended ignobly by tipping off a pier into the briny. Rescuers brought in their crane truck to extend its boom over the partially submerged vehicle, planning to winch it up onto the pavement again. A local photographer captured their efforts as the weight of the soggy sedan overloaded the lifting capacity of the crane and it too tipped into the water, landing squarely on top of its object of rescue.

The tale refused to end because town officials gathered in worry and brought in a much larger crane truck from a neighboring village. This behemoth had large extenders that planted stabilizing feet at a secure distance from its frame and a boom built like a giant's claw. With confidence, the operators snaked a hook to lift the fallen smaller truck back from its baptismal shame. Then, just as brutish force seemed invincible, the leeward stabilizers picked themselves up from the pavement and the monster truck gracefully eased into its own tipping point and pirouetted in an arc onto its lesser cousins below. What a tragedy for the machines and their owners but what a terrific day for the photographer!

The lectionary readings for today are all focused on the tipping point of Jesus' final week in Jerusalem. Isaiah pictures it from a distance, anticipating the suffering servant's dialogue with the Father as he enters the dark journey of unjust punishment buoyed only by divine favor. Paul poetically traces the parabola of Jesus' obedient descent to the cross which, in turn, energizes his triumphant ascent back to glory, and Luke takes us from the Last Supper to the supposed last resting place as Jesus is careened among the architects of his death in the final hours of Passion Week. This is the biblical tipping point. Because of it everything changes.

Isaiah 50:4-9a

These verses are found in what is often identified as Second Isaiah (40-55), where judgment and salvation are synthesized in magnificent pictures of grace. These masterpieces are then further interwoven around the mysterious figure of the suffering servant. While it is hard to fully understand Isaiah's vision in his own context (Is the nation of Israel the "suffering servant"? Or perhaps Judah? Is it possibly an enigmatic deliverer from David's royal family? Or even a composite character created for heroic encouragement during Judah's dark times? Is there a historical manifestation of these paradoxical scenes of misplaced identity and deliverance?), there seems to be so much clarity when allowing them to foreshadow Jesus.

There are few good ways to exegete this passage so that it rings true in Isaiah's context and also speaks clearly about the Christ of Passion Week. Perhaps the best homiletic move would be to refer to these verses in snippets of supportive commentary undergirding explorations of Jesus' unjust treatment, using them as insight into the psychological dialogue between the Son and Father. While the world pummels the sinless Christ externally, assuming all manner of self-justified attacks against this outsider, an interior and private conversation might unfold along these lines as Jesus fulfills a redemptive destiny beyond society's ken.

Philippians 2:5-11

Philippians is one of Paul's prison letters, written from Rome around 60 AD while Paul was under house arrest waiting to fulfill his appeal to Caesar (see Acts 26-28). It is one of his most joy-filled letters (along with 1 Thessalonians, written about a decade earlier). This is somewhat amazing since Luke's record of the beginnings of the congregations in Acts 16 would not initially suggest a warm and loving fellowship. Its original members were the strong and independent business woman Lydia, the wispy and spiritually empathic fortune-teller slave girl, and the battle-hardened, retired Roman legionnaire pensioned off to a bit of property in the neighborhood that happened to have a cave he turned into a mercenary incarceration pit. Nevertheless, the congregation that grew from the witness of these became one of Paul's favorites, and he stopped there often in his travels.

Most of our Bibles arrange these verses in poetic form, for the text certainly has the feel of a verse. Scholars often identify this as an early hymn of the church. Perhaps it was written by Paul, or perhaps it was a popular song of faith that he incorporated into his message. In any case it forms a balanced summary of Christ's incarnation and coronation. Care must be taken not to divorce it from its lead-in. Paul uses the hymn in a particular way, as an incentive to mutual submission and humble service within the congregation (vv. 1-4). Thus, while we often abstract the theological statement to confirm our Christological doctrinal statements, we need also to see the ethical impact it has for Christian behavior.

In this way, minor incidents must not detract us from the sweeping momentum of the divine mandate. We view the life of Jesus at the nadir of its parabolic swoop, feeling with him the crunch of a hammer release in full collision with its intended mark. All the energy expended to carry the second person of the Trinity across the gulf between heaven and earth, and raise up this agent of divine grace, is pounding Jesus into the final confines of submission. What began as a shout of angels near Bethlehem is now whimpering into the bloody torment of Calvary. With Paul, we are eager to rush ahead to the victory shout of "Jesus is Lord!"; with Paul, we must also first linger in depths of Jesus' "obedience unto death."

As with the Isaiah passage, this hymn of faith is not so much to be preached but to be sung or emoted. What would one feel while processing through this roller coaster of social upset? How does Jesus find himself fully engaged in the degrading process of betrayal, denial, misunderstanding, and religious ostracism, especially when it appears that he is limited from knowing with clarity the full victory that will come and wrestles painfully with the Father about this challenge while praying in Gethsemane garden?

It is in this context that Paul gives the brief poetic exhortation about the characteristics that mark those on Jesus' team. It is not self-preservation but service that counts. It is not superiority but selflessness that wins points. It is not stridency but sacrifice that finds recognition from the owner of the club. Jesus is building a team that will change the world. Unfortunately on that day, too few people seemed willing to show up at the try-outs.

There is a scene in Tolkien's *The Fellowship of the Ring* where a partnership is forged among those who would accompany Frodo on his journey to destroy the ring of power. The movie version makes for a very gripping visual illustration, and the original literary text is equally as moving. What comes through is a sense of selflessness as the bond that unites these creatures. Furthermore, each subsumes his will to the greater cause and trusts an unseen and transcendent good for an outcome that will bless all of Middle Earth, even if the trek itself causes the demise of any or all of the compatriots.

So it is in Paul's small glimpse of Jesus working out the mission of God. In a world turned cold to its Creator, in an age riddled by Delphic oracles, temple prostitutes, and emperors claiming divinity, in a little corner of geography where messianic hopes ran high, God called together a strange team to make its mark by playing a different game.

Walter Wangerin Jr., in his great allegory, *The Book of the Dun Cow* (along with its wonderful sequel, *The Book of Sorrows*), captures the scope of the divine mission as well as the underrated character of the team. If the focus remains on the team apart from the mission, the point is lost. God is reclaiming God's creation but does so through human agency. The game is fierce and the playing field is rough. Only those who can tear up their personal score sheets in order to get into God's game will make the team. Only they are truly called. Only they are equipped to serve, follow, and play on the greatest winning team of all time.

Luke 22:14—23:56

How should we preach this entire narrative? It is impossible to dwell adequately on each important segment — the table scene with both its Lord's Supper institution and the disciples' self-importance squabbles, prayers in the garden, the betrayal and arrest and denials, the mockings, sham trials, and crucifixion. Either a specific passage has to become the source of homiletic development, or some metaphor needs to cull the main themes and present them in a gripping manner.

One approach that serves the latter method is an allegory developed by Walter Wangerin Jr. in which Jesus is called the Ragman. Wangerin pictures himself in a city on a Friday morning. A handsome young man comes to town, dragging behind him a cart made of wood. The cart is piled high with new, clean clothes, bright and shiny and freshly pressed.

Wandering through the streets the trader marches, crying out his strange deal: "Rags! New rags for old! Give me your old rags, your tired rags, your torn and soiled rags!"

He sees a woman on the back porch of a house. She is old and tired and weary of living. She has a dirty handkerchief pressed to her nose, and she is crying 1,000 tears, sobbing over the pains of her life.

The Ragman takes a clean linen handkerchief from his wagon and brings it to the woman. He lays it across her arm. She blinks at him, wondering what he is up to. Gently, the young man opens her fingers and releases the old, dirty, soaking handkerchief from her knotted fist.

Then comes the wonder. The Ragman touches the old rag to his own eyes and begins to weep her tears. Meanwhile, behind him on her porch stands the old woman, tears gone, eyes full of peace.

It happens again. "New rags for old!" he cries, and he comes to a young girl wearing a bloody bandage on her head. He takes the caked and soiled wrap away and gives her a new bonnet from his cart. Then he wraps the old rags around his head. As he does this, the girl's cuts disappear and her skin turns rosy. She dances away with laughter and returns to her friends to play. But the Ragman begins to moan and from her rags on his head the blood spills down.

He next meets a man. "Do you have a job?" the Ragman asks. With a sneer the man replies, "Are you kidding?" and holds up his shirtsleeve. There is no arm in it. He cannot work. He is disabled.

But the Ragman says, "Give me your shirt. I'll give you mine."

The man's shirt hangs limp as he takes it off, but the Ragman's shirt hangs firm and full because one of the Ragman's arms is still in the sleeve. It goes with the shirt. When the man puts it on, he has a new arm. The Ragman walks away with one sleeve dangling.

It happens over and over again. The Ragman takes the clothes from the tired, the hurting, the lost, and the lonely. He gathers them to his own body and takes the pains into his own heart. Then he gives new clothes to new lives with new purpose and new joy.

Finally, around midday, the Ragman finds himself at the center of the city where nothing remains but a stinking garbage heap. It is the accumulated refuse of a society lost to anxiety and torture. On Friday afternoon, the Ragman climbs the hill, stumbling as he drags his cart behind him. He is tired and sore and pained and bleeding. He falls on the wooden beams of the cart, alone and dying from the disease and disaster he has garnered from others.

Wangerin wonders at the sight. In exhaustion and uncertainty, he falls asleep. He lies dreaming nightmares through all of Saturday, until he is shaken from his fitful slumbers early on Sunday morning. The ground quakes. Wangerin looks up. In surprise he sees the Ragman stand up. He is alive! The sores are gone, though the scars remain. But the Ragman's clothes are new and clean. Death has been swallowed up and transformed by life!

Still worn and troubled in his spirit, Wangerin cries up to the Ragman, "Dress me, Ragman! Give me your clothes to wear! Make me new!"

We know the picture. It is the one Luke unfolds here. Jesus is the Ragman who must touch lives, who must heal wounds, who is bound by necessity to bring relief. This is the pilgrimage of the Ragman to the center of the city, to the garbage heap of society, to the hill called Golgotha — the skull! The place of death! The mountain of the crucifixion! There he must go. Personally.

But so, too, those who are with him, including the disciples in his day and all who come to faith through their testimony. That is why Jesus speaks so pointedly in addressing the squabbles of the Last Supper. Religion is neither an individual game nor a spectator sport. Harry Emerson Fosdick remembered a storm off the Atlantic coast. A ship foundered on the rocks and the Coast Guard was called out. The captain ordered the lifeboat to be launched, but one of the crew members protested. "Sir," he said in fear, "the wind is offshore and the tide is running out! We can launch the boat, but we'll never get back!"

The captain looked at him with a father's eyes, and then said, "Launch the boat, men. We have to go out. That is our duty. But we don't have to come back." This is the tipping point for those who follow Jesus on the road of discipleship.

Application

The Cost of Discipleship, as Dietrich Bonhoeffer noted, is self-denial, and today's lectionary passages clearly point to Jesus' life as a strong call for us to join him in that vocation, not as an end in itself or as a means to a self-help goal (like dieting), but rather as a countercultural missional testimony. Those who travel this road do not get to Easter without first enduring Good Friday; they do not presume a glorious outcome that gathers the media like paparazzi vultures, but sense that the journey of service brings light in darkness, hope in despair, healing for pain, and faith where power corrupts and destroys.

An Alternative Application

Luke 22:14—23:56. The gospel lesson invites us to focus special attention on the person of Peter. Jesus singles him out for a special exhortation. In spite of himself, Peter was about to take the easy way out precisely at the point where Jesus was about to go through the hardest part of his journey. Peter wanted to save his own life, and in so doing deny himself a place on Jesus' team. Yet after these events, Peter learned some great lessons that make a wonderful illustration to bring home the discipleship impact of the Passion story. According to stories from the early church, at the time of the intense persecution under Nero, the Christians of Rome told Peter to leave. "You're too valuable," they said. "Get out of town! Find your safety! Go to another place and preach the gospel."

According to legend, Peter is supposed to have gone from the city. Yet, only a few days later, Nero had Peter in custody. Soon afterward, he was sent out to die. When the soldiers took Peter to the site of execution, Peter begged of them one last request. He asked that he might be crucified upside down. He said he wasn't worthy to die in the same way as his Lord. So they nailed him to his cross inverted.

According to the stories, the crowds of Christians gathered round. They wanted to be with their beloved leader as he died. "Why," they asked him as he hung there upside down on the cross, "why did you come back, Father Peter? Why did you return to Rome? Why didn't you flee into the hills?"

This is what Peter is supposed to have said. "When you told me to leave the city, I made my escape. But as I was going down the road, I met our Lord Jesus. He was walking back toward Rome, so I asked him, 'Master, where are you going?' He said to me, 'I am going to the city to be crucified.' 'But, Lord,' I responded, 'were you not crucified once for all?' And he said to me, 'I saw you fleeing from death and now I wish to be crucified instead of you.' Then I knew what I must do. 'Go, Lord!' I told him. 'I will finish my pilgrimage.' And he said to me, 'Fear not, for I am with you.' "

Maundy Thursday
Exodus 12:1-4 (5-10) 11-14
1 Corinthians 11:23-26
John 13:1-17, 31b-35
Mark Molldrem

Dutiful servants of all

Do we ever really get together anymore? Think about it. Funeral homes are experimenting with drive-through visitation. In order to make an uncomfortable situation less awkward, one can now avoid looking into the eyes of a child whose parents just got a divorce — instead, send them a greeting card designed for just such an occasion. TV trays can be set up more easily than setting the kitchen table, and this way everyone can take care of themselves when it is convenient. Teleconferences give a whole new meaning to "calling a meeting."

Even though services are provided over the phone or on the internet or through the mail to people by people who never meet in person, one still wonders what is missing when we can live so much of our lives without rubbing shoulders with others. As we enter the Triduum of Holy Week, we cannot escape noticing how "hands on" everything becomes for God when dealing with humanity. The incarnation bears its ripest fruit in these final hours of Jesus' lifelong passion.

The gospel writer John does not let us escape noticing that the message Jesus leaves with his disciples is one that can only be expressed when they are gathered together. No memos, instant messaging, or call forwarding are used to convey what is on the heart of God. It is communicated only when the disciples are within reach of Jesus, and then within reach of one another. One may be able to play solitaire with cards but not with Christianity.

Exodus 12:1-4 (5-10) 11-14

When the Lord promised to redeem the 'Apiru slaves in Egypt "with an out-stretched arm and with great acts of judgment" (Exodus 6:6), no one thought of counting just how many acts it would take nor that when the count reached nine, it would only take one more devastating blow to the pride of Pharaoh to make him relent and let God's people go. As with most of the plagues, this tenth one would not touch the Israelites, providing they took drastic action — an action, the likes of which they did *not* need to take to be spared the previous plagues.

A sacrifice needed to be made. A spotless lamb was to be selected for each house. After the lamb was slain, its blood was to be sprinkled over the doorposts and lintel of the house. When the assigned angel of death crossed over the land to execute God's judgment, the angel would pass over the homes of the Israelites on which the blood had been sprinkled. Some important and enduring concepts undergird this requirement and the *eat and run* Passover meal that resulted.

First, a sacrifice was understood as necessary in order to protect God's people from his wrath. Life needed to be shed in order to preserve life. Since "the life is in the blood," it made sense to sprinkle the blood upon the doorposts and lintel as the sign that the appropriate sacrifice had been made. This gesture was sacrificial in that it was substitutionary for the firstborn male, who would be the object of God's wrath due to Pharaoh's hardness of heart.

Second, God himself provided the means of escape from the wrath to come. God would acknowledge and accept the blood of the lamb (or goat) and *pass over* the home that by faith had obeyed the command. God is not capricious or careless when it comes to the implementation of his response to human rebellion or need. The love and care of God for his people is expressed in this arrangement.

Third, the Passover is to be observed as an ordinance forever. The meal not only solemnizes the event at the time; but, for all time, it becomes the means by which future generations are connected to what happened in Egypt at this particular time. In this sense, the meal is a *remembrance*, not just recollecting what occurred as an intellectual exercise, but participating in its meaning and experiencing the power of God's deliverance in the here and now.

Fourth, time itself is reordered based upon this event. "This month shall be for you the beginning of months; it shall be the first month of the year for you" (12:1). Historically, this is the constituting event of the people of God, who from this point in time could reflect back upon the call of Abraham and even creation itself to find the beginnings of all these things that are taking place. See Deuteronomy 6:21-23 and 26:5-9 as examples of creedal/confessional statements of self-understanding. Although a half-century old and firmly couched in the historical-critical method, B. Davie Napier's *Song of the Vineyard* offers a refreshing and insightful explication of this and other first covenant events with their meanings.

1 Corinthians 11:23-26

Paul's discussion of the Lord's Supper is found in the section of his first letter to the Corinthian congregation in which he deals with matters of public worship. There is an issue pertaining to the veiling of women that needs to be addressed. Paul asserts the tradition of women needing to veil their heads when it comes to prayer and prophecy. In a more lengthy treatment, Paul turns his attention to spiritual gifts, which was another source of contention in the congregation. He identifies the source of these gifts in God, their variety for the common good of edification, and the highest gift of all — love. In the midst of these matters, Paul instructs the Corinthians regarding proper behavior at the Lord's Supper.

As with so many other things they did in their Christian life, the Corinthian Christians messed up when it came to their experience with the Lord's Supper. They did not sit at table together, but some ate early. That meant that others, who came in later, went hungry. The ones who started without the others imbibed too much and profaned the meal. The congregation suffered from gluttony and lack of a "potluck" mentality (where there is always enough for everyone because all share what they have!).

It is within this context that the words that come after our assigned text are to be understood. "Discerning the body" (11:29) refers to a healthy appreciation of every member of the congregation and being sensitive to how each is to be included in the meal. The reference to "the body and blood of the Lord" (11:27) refers directly to the elements. Later, Paul mentions frailties of the body (physical; "weak and ill," 11:30), from which some have died. Here are three different senses of the word "body" reflected in these few verses.

These things having been said, we can now look at the core of this section on public worship that deals with the Lord's Supper. Paul reminds the Corinthians what is at the heart of the Lord's Supper. This is not shared as the "correct theology" of the elements, as if what was at stake here was a kind of proper mantra, without which one would participate "in an unworthy manner" (11:27). The matter of unworthiness has already been discussed in terms of their behavior at the meal. What Paul does here in these few verses is ground the meal in Jesus and lift up its intention.

First, Paul makes the claim that what he expresses here now is "received from the Lord" (11:23). Although Paul was not present with the other disciples at the original Maundy Thursday event, he asserts apostolic authority in what he outlines as the *main course* of the meal. Jesus is at the center of the meal, for it is his body and his blood that are shared. In this sense, he is the author of the meal and focus is to be on him. This alone should curb inappropriate behaviors!

Second, the congregation is reminded through the words of Jesus that the meal is indeed "for you" (11:24). Martin Luther personalized this in Latin when he referred so thankfully to the *pro me* nature of the sacrament. What Jesus is doing in the Passover meal is redefining it around the deliverance that he offers God's people (the new Israel represented in the twelve apostles) through his body sacrificed and his blood shed to avert the wrath of God upon the ungodly. To borrow John's words, we discover in Jesus "the lamb of God who takes away the sins of the world" (John 1:29). The writer of the letter to the Hebrews draws the connection between Jesus and the entire sacrificial system with these words: "For if the sprinkling of defiled persons with the blood of goats and bulls and with the ashes of a heifer sanctifies for the purification of the flesh, how much more shall the blood of Christ, who through the eternal Spirit offered himself without blemish to God, purify your conscience from dead works to serve the living God" (Hebrews 9:13-14).

Third, the meaning of the meal is to "proclaim the Lord's death until he come" (11:26). It is not about "getting your fill" or "tying one on at the end of a hard day." The meal is a living, dramatic sermon to the world that "Christ has died, Christ is risen, Christ will come again!" The meal proclaims what God has already done in Jesus Christ (that is why Matthew includes the words "for the forgiveness of sins" in his account; Matthew 26:28!) and what Jesus has yet to do, namely return. In the meantime, the church watches and waits while it works for the kingdom's goals. One might say that this makes the Lord's Supper a *wait and work* meal, rather than the *eat and run* meal of the Passover.

The Words of Institution used in the liturgies of the meal are essentially a compilation of this text in 1 Corinthians 11 and the account in Matthew 26. The Passover meal is transformed into a sacrament for the church with the reinterpretation of its meaning. The deliverance from bondage to Pharaoh presages deliverance from bondage to sin. Blood is present at both events: the first from a spotless lamb and the second from the spotless lamb of God. "Indeed, under the law almost everything is purified with blood, and without the shedding of blood there is no forgiveness of sins" (Hebrews 9:22).

John 13:1-17, 31b-35

The account of Jesus washing the disciples' feet is one of the distinctive features that sets John's gospel apart from the synoptic gospels. Rather than recording the meal in detail, with emphasis on the transformation of the Passover meal to the Lord's Supper, John simply mentions that they ate. In fact, the supper itself is overshadowed by what Jesus does. He disrobes and assumes the role of the servant, washing the disciples' feet.

Surrounding this episode are comments by Jesus on himself as light (12:44-50, before) and "the way, the truth and the life" (14:1-7, after). By washing the disciples' feet, Jesus sought to illuminate their understanding about true love and leadership. It is a matter of humble service (13:16-17). The *doulov* (slave, servant) is under the *kuriov* (master, lord). Therefore, if the master himself, Jesus, whom the disciples call *Kuriov*, washes feet, then, the disciples (as *doulov*) should also do so. Jesus exemplifies how he wants his followers to exercise their love and leadership in the world — through humble service. "I have given you an example that you also should do as I have done to you" (13:15). This is "the way, and the truth, and the life" for anyone who would find themselves in Jesus.

When Jesus defines his commandment given to his disciples in terms of love, the best word to translate that reality is *ûgapj* (13:34-35). Four times this word is used in these two verses. Paul may go on about the qualities of love, as he does in 1 Corinthians 13. John simply portrays it through this simple, yet profound act lived out by Jesus under the shadow of his cross. The foot washing foreshadows the cross because both have to do with cleansing — the one from the dirt of the road and the other from the sin of the journey.

Martin Luther, in his little tract *Christian Liberty*, writes, "A Christian is a perfectly free lord of all, subject to none. A Christian is a perfectly dutiful servant of all, subject to all." As we are free *from* sin, so we are free *for* service. Because we are the lords of life (both with and without the apostrophe), we are called upon to serve the needs of the world wherever we may find them. It is never too humbling a task to "devote all our works to the welfare of others, since each has such abundant riches in his faith that all his other works and his whole life are a surplus with which he can by voluntary benevolence serve and do good to his neighbor," as Luther would write. When one pictures Jesus stooping to wash the disciples' feet in devotion to the mission on which his heavenly Father sent him, these words of Luther apply not only to him, but also to any who would follow him likewise: "By faith he is caught up beyond himself into God. By love he descends beneath himself into his neighbor." This is the witness of love and this is how the Father is glorified.

Application

It is interesting to see that *Habits of the Heart*, published in the mid-'80s, has been reprinted with an extended introduction, claiming that the American ethos of individualism is very much functioning as a defining character of our identity. Once studied, it does not go away. Our sense of "rugged individualism" is ingrained into our character, despite so much of our altruism and education that seeks to balance it. In this context, the Passover meal and Holy Communion provide a story that sets before us a different model with which to understand ourselves. The Passover was a household meal; Holy Communion, where two or three are gathered. The essential social characters of both Judaism and Christianity invite us to be engaged in relationships that are necessary for nurture. The relationships are both to the story itself as participants in faith, as well as to other people who hold the value of the story in expressing the meaning of their lives.

The "for you" aspect of the sacrament emphasizes that something has been done on our behalf. This is something we could not do on our own, namely forgive our sins and overcome death. The crucified and risen Lord Jesus strides to meet us at the communion rail with the assurance that he has done just that "for you." As unilateral as that action of grace is, so too are we invited to receive it in faith. We do this by participating in the meal — from gathering with others, to voicing the liturgical words that articulate the meaning of the meal, to receiving the food itself, to going out into the world together as witnesses of what we have just received from the hand of God.

In the busy routines of daily life where families find precious little time to get together, especially for meals, the church can ring the dinner bell. As the people of God assemble, there is time to hear the story that constitutes faith and life; there is time to build relationships upon the solid foundation, not so much on what we can do for each other, but on what God has done for us all through our Lord Jesus Christ. Because while the meal is *for us*, it is *about* Jesus Christ. As we feast on him and the gospel meat he gives us to savor, we receive each other as fellow servants who have learned from the same Master. Ecumenism, as well as neighborliness, could make great strides forward if we all understood better what it means to wash feet rather than wring necks.

Good Friday
Isaiah 52:13—53:12
Hebrews 10:16-25
John 18:1—19:42
David Kalas

The people nearby

You know the experience of showing photographs to someone who was not part of the trip, or group, or event where the pictures were taken. You walk the other person through each photograph. You describe what the occasion was, where the place was, and who the people were.

Today may offer an opportunity to do just that again. Today, Good Friday, the pictures we sit down and look at together are from the passion of Christ.

We have three different pictures to view. Isaiah, John, and the writer of Hebrews all have their own portraits of the event.

John's camera, if you will, is more a movie camera than a still-shot camera. His pictures move us from place to place, as we follow Jesus from the Last Supper to the garden, then to the trials before the council and the governor, then up to Golgotha, and then to the tomb.

The writer of Hebrews, meanwhile, offers more of a still shot of the event. Specifically, he takes the picture of Christ on Good Friday up against the backdrop of the Old Testament law, with its rituals, priests, sacrifices, and blood.

Finally, the prophet Isaiah's picture of the occasion is sort of a collage. An assortment of images is employed in the Old Testament text: a variety of pieces that are arranged together to form a single whole.

We sit down today to look at these pictures together. We see the occasion: Christ's suffering and death. We also recognize the place involved in these pictures: Jerusalem, Gethsemane, a hill called "skull," and a nearby tomb. Then, finally, there are the assorted people we see in these pictures. Identifying and introducing them might be our special purpose on this day.

Isaiah 52:13—53:12

When Philip caught up with the chariot where the Ethiopian was riding and reading, this was the passage that sparked their conversation. The Ethiopian asked an excellent hermeneutical question: "About whom does the prophet say this, about himself or about someone else?" (Acts 8:34). And Philip responded by proclaiming to him the good news about Jesus (v. 35).

On this Good Friday, we will dispense with the scholarly musings about the possible subjects of this passage, and instead we will follow Philip in his understanding that this prophecy anticipates and describes Jesus Christ.

So many of the Old Testament prophesies that foresee a messianic figure and age are pictures of victory, prosperity, and an everlasting reign of peace by some son of David. This portrait of a tortured victim, an apparently helpless martyr, however, does not seem to square with those other, more potent images of the Messiah. Clearly Jesus' own disciples did not, at first, recognize and understand this part of what it meant for Jesus to be the Christ (see, for example, Mark 8:29-33).

The traditional hero defeats the enemy, and he rescues the innocent and the oppressed at the expense of their oppressor. But the hero of this prophecy is of a very different sort. Consider these against-the-grain statements: "He was wounded for our transgressions, crushed for our iniquities," "the Lord has laid on him the iniquity of us all," and he "made intercession for the transgressors." The people this hero rescues are not at all innocent. He does not rescue at the expense of some antagonist but at his own expense. This is the heroism of self-sacrifice and love.

The so-called suffering servant of this passage is revealed in terms of several relationships. There is a great fluidity in the author's use of personal pronouns, moving freely between first-, second-, and third-person references, both singular and plural, without any deliberate effort to identify the antecedents.

The insights to be discovered in an examination of these pronouns exceed the boundaries of this brief commentary. We could explore the relationships depicted between the servant and God, between the servant and us, between the servant and the unidentified "they" and "them" of the passage. As a starting point, however, I would recommend a careful look at just the first-person pronouns.

The first-person, singular pronouns, we presume, indicate that God is speaking. He is the one who would most naturally say things such as these: "See, my servant shall prosper," "[he was] stricken for the transgression of my people," and "I will allot him a portion with the great." The first-person, singular pronouns, therefore, give us a glimpse into the mind and purpose of God. And on this Good Friday, we may take the first-person, singular statements from this foreshadowing of the cross to explore what it was that God designed to accomplish on that day.

The first-person, plural pronouns, meanwhile, identify the statements that we can own. We may be the "we." One fruitful approach to this passage would be to look for ourselves in it. What part do we play on Good Friday? What is the suffering servant's relation to us, and what is our response to him? The old spiritual asks, "Were you there when they crucified my Lord?" And the first-person, plural pronouns of this suffering servant passage similarly invite us into the event.

Hebrews 10:16-25

When some authority figure walks into an existing situation — especially when that situation is a bit of a mess — and declares, "Now here's the way it's going to be from now on," it's usually a sign of a stricter regime. The fat will be cut. Discipline will be enforced. Heads will roll.

The writer of Hebrews, however, paints a very different picture of God's new regime. The situation is a mess, to be sure: a chronically sinful humanity, including a very disappointing chosen people. Yet, tellingly, when God declares the way it's going to be, it is not a message of martial law. Rather it's a message of love and grace.

Here is a great testimony to the heart of God and to a way in which he is so very different from us. He has not become fed up to the point where he has lost sight of his perfect picture. He has not been so discouraged or angered that he abandons his original plan. Instead, he declares how it's going to be, and the picture he paints is as gracious and perfect as it was at the start.

That God is willing — no, eager! — to make a new covenant, reveals his nature. He does not forfeit us to the sinfulness we have chosen. He does not lock the door behind the runaway child and say, "Good riddance!" Instead, he desires a new start with us, though we do not deserve it. And though we do not make very promising partners in this proposed arrangement, he is very promising.

He promises, first, to make a change within us. Rather than God's law remaining an external thing quite apart from us, he will make it an internal component — a part of us. He promises, second, to forgive our sins in this most remarkable way — a way that we human beings find nearly impossible to achieve in our relationships — he will "remember their sins... no more."

The writer of Hebrews is the great expositor of the gospel according to the Old Testament. After citing those Old Testament promises of God, he turns to the fulfillment of God's good purpose that is afforded us through Christ.

The statement that "we have confidence to enter the sanctuary by the blood of Jesus" will not make immediate sense to most of the people in our pews. Entering into the sanctuary, in our day, is about signage and accessibility. And confidence entering into the sanctuary is about user-friendliness and a welcoming atmosphere. Indeed, in so many churches, even the terminology of "sanctuary" has been abandoned.

Within the context that the writer of Hebrews has in mind, however, the sanctuary is the holy place. And who can enter there with confidence? Indeed, who can enter there at all?

The Old Testament design for regulations about the tabernacle all bear witness to a holy God. And human beings are not to wander casually in and out of the presence of this holy God. When the high priest made his prescribed annual entrance into the holy of holies, he took blood with him.

Now the writer of Hebrews assures us that we are all invited to enter the holy place and to approach the presence of God. We do so with confidence because of the blood by which we are saved, purified, and sanctified — that is, the blood of Jesus.

Indeed, Jesus dominates the entire scene as the writer reflects on that tabernacle and its rituals. Jesus is the new "great high priest." It is his blood by which we enter and it is through the curtain of his flesh that we approach the Father.

John 18:1—19:42

Customarily, we are given a paragraph or two as our gospel lection for an occasion. Not today. For this occasion, no excerpt will suffice. We need to see the whole scene and so we are presented with two entire chapters from John's gospel: his account of Jesus' crucifixion, all the way from Gethsemane on Thursday night to the garden tomb late Friday afternoon.

The gospel reports that Jesus went to a garden across the Kidron valley — a place Judas knew because Jesus had gone there often with his disciples. Here is one of so many pieces of evidence that Jesus was entering voluntarily into what was ahead for him. He knew what Judas was up to, and yet he did not take evasive action. Instead, he went to precisely the place where Judas would find him.

The image of Judas arriving with soldiers, police, and weapons is a preposterous one twice over.

At a human level, it is a massive case of overkill. Jesus had been within their reach day after day in the temple; yet they took no action against him. Did they think that he would resist? Did they think that there would be a great, violent resistance that would need to be overcome by force?

Meanwhile, at a supernatural level, this detachment is equally ridiculous, though in the other direction. While their show of force is laughably excessive, given Jesus' complete lack of resistance, it is embarrassingly paltry given Jesus' capacity. As he said in Matthew's account of the Gethsemane event, it would take just a word from him and the Father would dispatch twelve legions of angels to his aid (Matthew 26:53). How would the local soldiers and police have fared against that?

John's gospel does not give us the glimpse of tortured prayer that we find in other gospel accounts. Jesus is not facedown on a rock, sweating drops of blood, and praying that "this cup" be taken from him. Instead, Jesus stands tall in the face of his tormentors, in control of the entire situation, even though to all outward appearances he is the victim of jealousy, malevolence, and betrayal. He does not pray to have the cup taken from him but rather challenges the sword-flashing Simon Peter: "Am I not to drink the cup that the Father has given me?"

All four gospels record Peter's infamous denial of Jesus. John, however, may do the most artful job with the story, weaving it into the back-and-forth scene changes between Jesus' trial inside and Peter's pressure outside.

Meanwhile, the trajectory of Jesus' ordeal takes him from the garden to the house of the high priest. While Pilate's name is the notorious one, the high priest is the first to have a hand in the death of Jesus. His participation is a significant one, both in the tragic sense of God's own priest opposing his work and in the symbolic sense of the high priest's role in shedding blood to make atonement for the people.

From the high priest's house, Jesus was taken to the Roman governor, Pilate.

The picture of the Jewish leaders refusing to enter Pilate's headquarters in order "to avoid ritual defilement" is emblematic of the very kind of hypocrisy that Jesus so often criticized in them. Here, again, they strain the gnat but swallow the camel, for they are tiptoeing around ritual uncleanness, while running full-speed ahead into conspiracy, injustice, and opposition to God.

Of the four gospel writers, John gives us perhaps the fullest picture of Pilate. We see more of the content of his dialogue with Jesus, in addition to the familiar tug-of-war with the Jewish leaders and with the incited mob. We see here a man perceptive enough to recognize Jesus' innocence, secure enough that he did not seem personally threatened by Jesus or his kingdom claims, and ethical enough that he was not cavalier about the prospect of executing an innocent man. Yet it seems that he was not strong enough to resist being pushed into doing what he did not want to do.

Later, after the Jewish leaders object to the wording of the sign that Pilate had had posted above Jesus' head, he is intractable: "What I have written I have written." It seems, however, that this occasional virtue of not being pushed around, not catering to pressure from the locals in his jurisdiction, came too late.

Nicodemus, whom we met in the shadows of John 3, now reemerges on this grim occasion. He did not know, it seems, how to believe and follow Jesus when he was alive, but as Johnny-on-the-spot, he had to pay his respects to the dead. There may always be some who prefer a dead Lord. It is easier to bring our myrrh and aloes than it is to take up his cross and follow.

The burial of Jesus seems to have been a matter of expediency. "The tomb was nearby." That hasty entombment reminds us of just how quickly these events unfolded. On Thursday afternoon, the disciples were excitedly making preparations for a holiday meal together with Jesus. By Friday afternoon, he was dead. The whole thing was so sudden: his strange predictions at the supper table, the ambush in the garden, the mock trial, the quick sentencing, and then he was gone.

Application

As we weave together three passages — all very different, but which point to and depict the same event — we catch a glimpse of the assortment of people who were nearby.

First, perhaps at the greatest distance, see the antagonists. They are the conspiring Jewish leaders, the Roman governor, the mocking guards and torturing soldiers, and the bloodthirsty crowd. See their pictures in John's gospel as they carry out their wickedness against Jesus. Below those pictures, add the captions from Isaiah: "He was oppressed, and he was afflicted, yet he did not open his mouth." "By a perversion of justice he was taken away." "They made his grave with the wicked... although he had done no violence, and there was no deceit in his mouth."

Focus in more closely on that crowd of antagonists, and see there at the center the high priest. He, who was assigned by God to make atonement for the sins of the people, unknowingly prophesied that "it is better for you to have one man die for the people than to have the whole nation destroyed" (John 11:50). He is the one whose hand was so pivotal in shedding the blood of the once-for-all atoning sacrifice, unaware that his victim would become the new and eternal "great high priest over the house of God."

Now see the inner circle of people — the disciples, followers, and believers. They misunderstand. They run and hide. They deny. See their pictures in John's gospel and beneath their pictures add these captions from Isaiah's prophecy: "He was wounded for our transgressions, crushed for our iniquities; upon him was the punishment that made us whole, and by his bruises we are healed." "All we like sheep have gone astray; we have all turned to our own way, and the Lord has laid on him the iniquity of us all." "Who could have imagined his future?"

Then see the Father and the Son.

There is the Son, who set aside every human reflex in order to submit to the Father's plan so that "through him the will of the Lord shall prosper." And there is the Father, whose will it was "to crush him with pain," to "make his life an offering for sin," and then to "prolong his days." It was the Father "who laid on him the iniquity of us all," and the Father who "will allot him a portion with the great."

Last of all, there is us. We are in the picture because it is our iniquity, our wounds, and our transgressions. We are invited to be nearby, for by this event we are encouraged to "approach with a true heart in full assurance of faith."

An Alternative Application
John 18:1—19:42. "The One that Got Away." It is a natural human reflex to defend oneself. Something comes at your eye, and you blink. It's a natural, physical reflex.

Defending oneself is also the developed reflex of fear. Someone raises a hand to strike you, and you brace yourself. Perhaps you put your own arms up to protect; perhaps even to defend yourself by striking back.

Of course, it is also the unwholesome reflex of the ego to defend oneself too. If someone criticizes me, my instinct is to defend myself verbally. When I am at my worst, I respond by attacking verbally, as well. Someone misunderstands my actions or motives, and I am impatient to set the record straight. Someone finds fault with me, and I want to be able to answer with a reason or at least an excuse.

See how submissive to the Father's will Jesus was. He set aside the physical reflex, the fearful reaction, and the ego's instinct. Both the Isaiah prophecy and the gospel account bear witness to a man who made no natural effort to try to get away.

When he was being pursued, he did not run and hide. When he was surrounded, he did not lash out or resist. When he was accused, he did not defend himself. And when he was attacked and abused, he neither cursed nor cried for mercy, but prayed for the transgressors.

We have seen in other settings (like Luke 4:28-30 and John 8:58-59) that Jesus was able to get away from a physical threat. We have seen in earlier episodes (such as Matthew 21:23-27 and 22:15-22) that Jesus was able to extrude himself from verbal traps, as well. Who can fathom what supernatural aid he had at his disposal (see Matthew 26:52-53). Yet he made no effort to get away.

When it was all said and done, he did get away. He got away in a manner they could never have guessed. While he made no effort to get away from the betrayer, the accusers, the tormentors, or the executioners, on the third day he rose up and got away from the tomb!

Easter Day
Acts 10:34-43
1 Corinthians 15:19-26
John 20:1-18
Wayne Brouwer

Back to the garden

A first-time father glanced over at his wife as dawn began to break. Both were exhausted and had gone sleepless again because of their colicky newborn who cried the night away. "It must be time to get up," he told her, "the baby's finally asleep."

Sometimes it seems as if dawn will never come and the night will be an endless whimpering of pain and suffering. The metaphor is not only for those restless midnight-to-first-light watches but also for the fate of the human race. There is a darkness that surrounds us like oil and seeps through our societies with its vexing blight, filling news reports with violence, and back pages with obituaries. Night is with us always, and it is not our constant friend (see Psalm 88:18).

So it is a wonderful thing to remember on this Easter morning what Clement of Alexandria declared: "Jesus has turned all of our sunsets into sunrises." Similarly, when Houston Smith, the great scholar of religious studies at the University of California in Berkeley, pegged the seven major world religions to the clock (Confucianism at 9 a.m. for its social organizational motifs; Islam at noon when the brightness of the sun casts no shadow and all must bow in obedience; Taoism to the personal path that one begins to meander at 5 p.m. when the obligations of the work day are set aside; Buddhism to the supper hour of 7 p.m. and all the modest pleasures of simple life enjoyment; Judaism to sundown and rest as the reward of God's good favor; Hinduism to the midnight hour when all things merge into oneness), he taught that Christianity was the religion of the dawn. Christianity puts its face to the future and builds its hope from the passing of the dark night of sin into the promises announced by "That Great Gettin' Up Morning" relished in the old spiritual.

All of the gospels tie the importance of today to the garden tomb and the witness of its stark emptiness over against all other cemetery plots on this grave-littered planet. But John increases the impact by linking the garden of the tomb to the garden of Eden. In the most profound of reversals of fortune, according to the fourth gospel, the alienation that closed the garden of paradise at the beginning of our race's history is suddenly undone when Jesus reopens fellowship between God and humanity in the garden of Easter morning.

Peter's testimony to Cornelius resonates with the same historical condensation: a change in divine strategy emerges in the Easter garden and produces the dawning of the new age in which we live. Similarly, Paul's great instruction regarding death and resurrection to the Corinthian congregation is filled with echoes of dawn and morning and a return engagement between the Creator and the creature in the power of Easter's first fruits. Today, to paraphrase T.S. Elliot, we go back to the garden and know the place again for the first time.

Acts 10:34-43

Peter's short recital of salvation history is a gem of condensation and punch. Creation, Israel, Jesus, Pentecost, and the mission of the church are quickly packaged together and tied up with a call to believe.

But the words take on even more significance when understood within the development of the great ripples of grace that eddy outward through the book of Acts. Luke narrates the story of the early church along the pattern set by Jesus in 1:8 — "You shall receive power when the Holy Spirit comes on you and you shall be my witnesses in Jerusalem and in all Judea and Samaria, and to the ends of the world." He adds literary nuances that refine that global spread. Along with the big shift after chapter 12 that vaults Paul to the primary role of gospel presenter after the initial dozen chapters that focused on Peter, there is another, more subtle progression within the tale. The markings of this secondary advancement are noticed particularly in verses 6:7; 9:31; 12:24; 16:5; and 19:20. In each of these a similar refrain recurs. The "word of God" "grows" or "spreads" or "multiplies." These repetitious choruses mark the end of narrative sections in which a successive portion of society is penetrated and transformingly influenced by the message of Jesus and the resurrection. First, it is Jerusalem that revels in the good news (2:1— 6:7), then it is Judea and Samaria (6:8—9:31); later it will be Asia Minor (12:25—16:5) and Europe (16:6—19:20). But in between geographical advances comes the tale of a new harvest leaping beyond the Jewish world and landing feet-first in the kingdom of the Gentiles. 9:32—12:24 forms a section in which Peter becomes the bearer of the gospel across ethnic lines in the first deliberate missionary engagement of the kind.

It is striking to see that the message Peter brings to Cornelius, the Roman centurion stationed at Caesarea, is exactly the same as that announced to the Jews in Jerusalem on Pentecost Sunday. It is all about creation, Israel, Jesus, Pentecost, and the missionary message of the church. The critical junction in the story, as it is always told, is not the ethical wisdom of Jesus or even his healing miracles; rather it is his savage death and amazing resurrection. Easter is the heart of the gospel message. Everything changes because of Easter. When people struggled only to live for the hours of this lifetime they succeeded in various ways and attempted to make it through according to a variety of religious traditions. Now that Jesus has died and come back to life, the very playing field is altered. To make it through this life is not enough. We must also now face our Creator who judges both "the living and the dead" (v. 42). Therefore everyone, Gentile as well as Jew, is forced to deal in some way with Jesus. Religions, as well as life itself, can be favorable to Jesus or antagonistic to Jesus, but they cannot any longer ignore Jesus. Resurrection morning has revised the rules of the game.

Years ago, a newspaper editor assigned one reporter to write a human interest story about David Livingstone, the great pioneer missionary and explorer of Africa. The editor gave specific instructions: "Don't focus your attention on Livingstone's religion. Keep it about the man, the do-gooder, the humanitarian."

This was easier said than done, as the reporter found. For it is not possible to talk about Livingstone apart from his religion. There is no doing good without understanding the source of that good in Livingstone's perceptions. There is no humanitarian kindness apart from the kindness of God to humanity, which became the substance of Livingstone's testimony. Livingstone as a man is God's man. Even the epitaph written to commemorate him in Westminster Abbey subtly suggests the same by making allusions to 1 Peter 2:5: "He needs no epitaph to guard a name / Which men shall praise while worthy work is done. / He lived and died for good, be that his fame. / Let marble crumble; this is living stone."

So it is with Christianity. It can be evaluated on many fronts and understood through multitudinous dimensions. But at its heart, inseparable from any part of it as air is from life, is the resurrection of Jesus. Take that away and you no longer have Christianity. You may have an ethic or a sentiment or a philosophy or a moral code, but you will not have Christianity.

1 Corinthians 15:19-26

This is actually the second of Paul's letters to the Corinthian congregation from his third journey base of operations in Ephesus. Earlier he had sent a nasty scourge (see 5:9) that met with mixed response and resulted in a delegation coming to Paul for further clarification. It is clear to read this history in the language and themes of this letter. Chapters 1-3 address the problem of many competing groups within the congregation, and then tip over into Paul's need to defend his own authority in chapter 4. Paul was, after all, the source of the gospel message for the Corinthian church and the founder of its congregational character. Divisions in the church threatened to turn it into a balkanized amalgam where party politics undermined a unified sense of identity in Christ.

Paul goes on in chapters 5-6 to address the overt sinful behaviors that apparently had been the target of his earlier missal. One case involved a man shacking up with his father's wife in a manner that offended many in the congregation, and even more folks beyond, thus compromising any hope of effective witness about Jesus. The other incident was a public account of fellow church members suing one another in court and scandalizing the unity of the body of Christ. Paul's fingers wag menacingly as he warns the church to deal quickly and appropriately with these blights.

Then, beginning in chapter 7, Paul responds directly to the questions raised by members of the Corinthian congregation, seeking his wisdom and direction:

1. Should we encourage marriages or not (7:1-24)?
2. How should virgins handle their sexuality (7:25-40)?
3. Can we buy and eat the cheap meat in the markets that comes from pagan shrines and has been originally devoted to other gods (8:1—11:1)?
4. Are there any rules for appropriate worship services (11:2-16)?
5. Some are complaining about our Lord's Supper celebrations — what are we doing wrong (11:17-34)?
6. Which are the best spiritual gifts and how should they be used (12:1—14:40)?
7. What will happen to those in our community who have died (15:1-58)?
8. What's this collection you keep telling us about (16:1-4)?

Today's lectionary passage is the heart of Paul's response to the question about death in the early Corinthian congregation. While we enjoy the power of this passage as a strong literary treatise, we are often not aware of the intensity of both its original question or the power of Paul's answer. The idea of "resurrection" erupted as the core and central element of Christian preaching because of the uniqueness of Jesus' return to life on Easter. While there were religions and philosophies that speculated on the immortality of some spiritual inner essence of humankind, few shaped a doctrine of resurrection that was vitally gripping and described a full return to life of the full person. This is what made the message of Christianity stand out among the religions of its time.

Furthermore, there was a very strong sense in the preaching of the apostles that Jesus, who had recently returned to heaven, was about to come back to earth to finish the job of creation's restoration as the messianic age began. Jesus only went to heaven in order to allow time for the apostles to tell everyone about the events of his death and resurrection. Probably next week, or next month at the latest, the missionary blitz will be finished and Jesus will return.

There was a tremendous urgency about the witness of the church and the eschatological expectations of the believers generally. This made the recurring problem of deaths in the community a confusing challenge. Since Jesus was returning so soon, everybody expected to be there when he came, and a transition state for the dead was not even considered at first. But when Jesus delayed his parousia, and as more folks succumbed to illness or age, the cemetery pile-up became a problem. Hence the question of what happens to those who die before Jesus returns?

This question gives Paul the opportunity to restate the evidence of Jesus' resurrection and then go on to talk about the powerful change wrought by Easter. Death is our human lot. But Jesus shifts us into a parallel humanity, founded not only on the terminal resources of the first Adam, but on the eternal energies of the first fruits of the kingdom of God.

Death challenges us all, ever since it laid waste to the garden of Eden. But Jesus brings us back to the garden and offers us the antidote to the deadly virus that has ruled too long unchallenged. This time those who linger in the garden find life instead of death.

John 20:1-18

The two scenes in this lectionary passage are powerful in themselves, but take on extra significance when viewed within the framework of John's carefully crafted gospel presentation. First, John's commitment to reporting the details of events goes beyond merely stating the obvious. Already in the prologue to the gospel (1:1-18), two guiding principles become apparent — John is casting this story of Jesus as a deliberate corollary to the original creation account of Genesis 1, and "light" and "darkness" will therefore become key criteria by which to interpret what takes place.

Here these themes erupt into action. Jesus' resurrection takes place on "the first day of the week," both chronologically and symbolically. It is the calendar day of Sunday, as we call it. But it is also the theological day of creation when by divine fiat God dispels the chaotic darkness through the declaration that light shall overcome it. So John tells us that it is not only "early" on that first day of the week but that these things took place "while it was still dark." In other words, the gloom that had settled over planet earth as a shroud of sinful deception (see 1:1-18) still lingers, although God's new (re)creative work in Jesus is about to blast it away.

Second, when Mary looks into the empty tomb, she sees two angels at the place where Jesus' body had been laid. Here again, however, John adds important interpretive details. The two angels are not standing next to one another but are positioned at either end of the flat surface where Jesus' body had rested. Thinking back to chapter 1 we are reminded that when Jesus appeared, "We have seen his glory," according to John. This "glory" was one with that of the Father and is a clear reminder that when God appeared to God's people in Old Testament times, there was an expression of the *shekinah* glory that pervaded tabernacle and temple and took up residence on the mercy seat of the Ark of the Covenant. This mercy seat was the portable throne of Yahweh on earth and was guarded at either end by cherubim — angels who stood at attention. What John wishes for us to see as Mary looks into the tomb is that the "glory" of God as revealed in Jesus is no longer here, nor will it any longer be confined or localized to an earthly shrine. God has come to earth to create and re-create, bringing the light of heaven; now that work is accomplished, and we may live in the light wherever we go. And as John shows us next, follow that light eventually back into heaven itself.

Third, while Mary is weeping at the tomb, John reminds us that this all takes place in a garden. Furthermore, when Mary is approached by a man, she believes him to be the gardener. Why does John make a big deal of this? Because, in the early days of the original creation as recounted in Genesis, humans lived in a garden and the true "gardener" came to walk and talk with them there. After the divisive acts of sinful disobedience, the humans were thrust out of the garden and the days of intimate fellowship with the "gardener" were ended. Now, however, as re-creation begins to reshape life on planet earth, the "gardener" returns to the garden and pauses for conversation with those who too long have been alienated from him.

Fourth, this is confirmed in the fact that Mary is confused and doesn't understand anything until Jesus speaks her name. When Jesus says "Mary," everything suddenly falls into place. Mary knows who she is and begins to understand who Jesus is. Notice that John never denies or challenges the notion that this figure looming into Mary's sight range is the gardener. Instead, John allows that perception to stand but fills it with all its theological significance. As the true gardener speaks her name, Mary comes to life. Just as in the Genesis story where the Creator/gardener calls Adam by name and thus brings him into being.

Clearly, John is telling us of events that took place on the first Easter Sunday morning. Just as convincingly, John is calling our attention to those details that help us see the significance of all this as a renewing of the creation by the Creator who comes to restore light and life in a world that has been too long under the sway of darkness and death.

Application

Our cemeteries tend to look like gardens. Perhaps a play can be made on the idea of those who are entombed there as "Planted for Life." Of course, this planting is after the manner of Christian faith; not the irrevocable lostness of death without hope.

Dr. Alexander Simpson, who invented chloroform in his Edinburgh laboratory in 1847, was asked later in life what he considered his most valuable discovery. He astounded reporters by declaring that it was in finding the love of God. As testimony to this, when he and his wife buried their young daughter whose illnesses refused to be tamed even by her father's great skills, the gravestone contained only one word beside the typical name and dates: "Nevertheless..." It was Simpson's assurance that death had already been trumped by life.

An Alternative Application

John 20:1-18. While there is punch in the Acts reading and power in the epistle text, it is the gospel story that begs to be treated by itself this morning. Let Mary's experiences remind us of what Easter gives back to us: our friend Jesus, our very selves, and the lives of our loved ones lost during the years past.

Easter 2
Acts 5:27-32
Revelation 1:4-8
John 20:19-31
Mark Molldrem

Witness: suffering and rejoicing with hope

Is the church living post-Christendom or post-Easter? Are Christians today discouraged by the world in which they live? Or are Christians excited by the world in which they live? It is said that perception is everything. While this is a business/public relations/advertising mantra that caters to the subjective, it may be useful for a moment to make a point.

How do Christians perceive the world in which they believe and witness? As we take our cues from the New Testament, we must concede that we live as a post-Easter people, which should excite us to the third heaven (as it did an acquaintance of Paul). Whatever we want to say about our post-Christendom world (i.e., the church can no longer be taken for granted as the cultural center of our society, nor can we expect the society in general to reflect the particular Christian ethos), this is only the context in which we witness. It is not the formative ground from which we view the world. The formative ground on which we stand and from which we view the world is located just outside the empty tomb down the road from Calvary.

In a sense, we should neither decry nor applaud the fact that we live *in* a post-Christendom context. For, in truth, we *live* post-Easter! This perception is everything! It shapes the witness of the believer, who suffers the misperceptions of a sinful world while rejoicing in the marvelous manifestations of the love of God through Jesus' life, passion, crucifixion, and resurrection.

Acts 5:27-32

The apostolic church had a disciplined witness. It was disciplined in giving, in sharing, and in suffering. To appreciate more fully the latter, it would be helpful to be reminded of the former. For this we will need to review a couple passages prior to this account of imprisonment of the apostles.

One of the striking characteristics of the apostolic church that Luke lifts up is the sharing of resources among the believers, such that "there was not a needy person among them" (Acts 4:34). In principle, this first congregation "had everything in common" (Acts 4:32). In a very practical way, their experience with Jesus placed them all on the same playing field. It is in light of this that the disposition of one's personal possessions was so important (see also Acts 2:43-47).

Enter Ananias and Sapphira (Acts 5:1-11). Their story is told in sharp contrast to the spirit of the congregation. The consequences of their actions are most sobering. It would not stretch the imagination too far to see a parallel here with the first covenant people of God. When they murmured against God's ways in the wilderness, they too were judged. Ananias and Sapphira were not content with how the Spirit of God was organizing the apostolic church in terms of its shared generosity. Wanting to keep more for themselves, they conspired to rebel against the work of God. Like the people in the wilderness who were judged by earthquake (Numbers 16:1-40; Korah's rebellion) or by snake bite (Numbers 21:4-9; murmurings in the wilderness), this anti-stewardship couple was judged in a most dramatic fashion.

Is it any wonder that the apostles were so bold in their witness, even in the face of imprisonment? When they experienced the power of the Spirit of God bonding them together in common through generous sharing of resources, caring for each other's needs, and miracles of healing for "the sick and those afflicted with unclean spirits" (Acts 5:16), they were made all the more confident in their defense of the faith before the religious authorities. "We must obey God rather than men" (5:29).

This present imprisonment is not the first time Peter and John had been arrested and placed in custody. Nor would it be their last. Yet, this did not deter them. As Peter explained, what God had done through Jesus in raising him from the dead and in providing forgiveness of sins was far too important and powerful to be suppressed by human fears or jealousies. Peter ends his response with a reference to obedience (5:32). The role of the witness is to give testimony dutifully. Peter and the other apostles had been privileged to see and hear Jesus, before his crucifixion and after his resurrection. They were privy to the most intimate revelation of God in the world from the beginning of time. There was no way they would shirk their responsibility to testify to the one who was "leader and Savior" (5:31).

Jesus, as leader into resurrection life (Acts 3:15), would be made perfect through his suffering (Hebrews 2:10). Those who would be obedient to him should expect no less a life of suffering from the same world that rejected him.

After Gamaliel counsels caution to the council (Acts 5:33-39), the disciples are beaten in chastisement (a foretaste of suffering still to come!) and admonished not to speak in the name of Jesus again. In a response that only those who are thoroughly convinced of the truth can understand, the apostles rejoice in their sufferings (Acts 5:41; see also, Romans 5:3-5 and 2 Corinthians 4:7-12), as they continue to proclaim the name of Jesus.

Revelation 1:4-8
It is very likely that this visionary book was written during the reign of Domitian (81-96 AD). As emperor, he took emperor worship very seriously, calling himself "savior" and "lord" and having statues erected all over the empire, not just in his honor, but also for his worship. This put the Christian believer in dire straights. For there was "no other name under heaven given among men by which we must be saved" (Acts 3:12). What were Christians to do when confronted with the choice of worshiping Caesar and prospering as a good citizen of Rome or of worshiping only God through Jesus and not bowing down to Caesar and therefore risk losing freedom, home, employment, family, and life itself?

When the churches in Asia Minor were confronted with this situation, John stepped forward and shared his vision in order that the church may be guided by the one true light and not be misguided into the dark alleys of fear, doubt, and disbelief. From the *get-go*, John reminds his readers that Jesus is "the ruler of kings on earth" (1:5). Caesar may seem to be all-powerful and everywhere present throughout the empire, but it is God who is the beginning and end of life itself (the alpha and omega — the first and last letters of the Greek alphabet). This is Jesus, crucified and now risen. His resurrection is a singular event. He is the "first-born from the dead" (1:5). To follow and obey him will get the believer farther down the road of life than conceding anything to Caesar, even if suffering is part of the journey. To be faithful witnesses to the one who is called "the faithful witness" (1:5) would be the greatest honor, even if martyrdom would result. Seeing how God the Father rewarded Jesus' faithfulness sends an encouraging message to those who would strive to be faithful even unto death. In truth, Jesus promises "the crown of life" (Revelation 2:10; how ironic that the first Christian martyr was named Stephen, whose name means "crown") to those who are so obedient. Paul would argue in his letter to the Romans, "If we have been united with him in a death like his, we shall certainly be united with him in a resurrection like his" (Romans 6:5).

With this confidence, the Christian can feel safe even in the midst of persecution, like books being held in place by bookends, like all the letters of the alphabet contained between the first and the last. God brackets our lives, such that there is nothing outside the grasp of God. Come what may, the believer is God's! Though the devil may have his day, God will have his way! This is the spiritual truth that gives the believer strength and comfort in trying times.

John 20:19-31

The gospel writer John is really the kindest to his readers in terms of the ending of his account of Jesus' life. Matthew, true to his teaching purposes, leaves the reader in the middle of a conversation. Jesus gives the Great Commission to his disciples; then, period. No further comments, no response from the disciples, no resolve as to where Jesus goes from here. Luke is a bit more gracious on this matter; he includes the ascension and reports that the disciples rejoiced by worshiping God daily. Mark messes with our minds and leaves the point of his sermon a mystery! "Figure it out for yourselves," he seems to say. "I'm just going to leave you hanging with the disciples who were totally discombobulated by the events that occurred." Those who were unhappy with Mark's seeming lack of closure added another softer ending that combines what Luke and Matthew did (Mark 16:9-20). John is extremely reader-friendly in his closing. He tells us exactly why he wrote the gospel (20:30-31). The epilogue is like the denouement after the climax in a novel and simply trails off with a personal authentication of the testimony and an offhand remark about how much Jesus really did beyond the scope of the gospel record.

Jesus' appearance to the ten apostles on Easter evening has the purpose of comforting and settling them with the truth of his resurrection and then giving them a commission. "Peace be with you. As the Father has sent me, even so I send you" (20:21). What Matthew does with a well-structured Great Commission (Matthew 28:13-20; statement of authority, purpose of the commission, method of discipling, and assurance), John expresses with a modeling metaphor. Just as Jesus was sent by the Father to the world, so the disciples are sent by Jesus into the world. With the Holy Spirit, they are empowered to forgive sins or to retain sins. Remembering the synoptic story of the healed paralytic (Matthew 9:1-8; Mark 2:1-12; Luke 5:17-26), this was tantamount to giving the disciples the voice of God in the course of human discourse: Blasphemy to some but a treasure in earthen vessels for others.

Because it was considered blasphemy by the religious leaders of the Jews, the disciples had cause to fear them. It was prudent for them to be behind closed doors. Fortunately, Jesus knew where to find his timid band of followers. He knew what they needed. When Thomas finally encountered the risen Jesus, he acknowledged him, "My Lord and my God!" (20:38). One can almost hear the confidence echoing through the centuries to us today. It certainly resounded in the streets, courts, and prisons of that day. Those who had been behind shut doors, once they witnessed Jesus risen from the dead, set their fears aside and boldly witnessed to him, despite what consequences lay in store. The same apostles who were huddled together on the first day of the week were on the streets, at Solomon's portico, and in the temple proclaiming the name of Jesus as Messiah for all the morrows of their lives.

Application

More and more the Western church is awakening to the persecutions against the body of Christ that have and are taking place around the world. The resurrection may have glorified Jesus' body, but his church is still suffering the crucifixion in many corners of the world. From the Middle East to China to Sudan, the news reports malicious actions taken by those in power against Christian minorities. What disciplines can be entered into by those who wish to make a difference for peace and justice on behalf of sisters and brothers in Christ?

In the spirit of Peter who stood before the authorities on behalf of the gospel and the apostolic community, we can discipline ourselves to prayer (Acts 2:42). Like a seatbelt, we can fasten our spiritual brothers and sisters to God with our prayers. Prayer can also arouse our own spirits to become involved in the answer to our prayers. Material support can be provided by the wealthy Western congregations for those who have less and are more vulnerable to the oppression of local authorities. Congregations can be inspired to reach out in physical ways to provide what is lacking in other fellowships that are enduring persecution. Moral and political support can also be garnered through education and advocacy on behalf to those whose voice is muffled by sobs and tears. For example, Amnesty International (www.amnestyusa.

org) and Voice of America (www.voanews.com) provide avenues for education and advocacy. In our age of communication, ignorance is no longer an excuse. Neither is inconvenience, since we can access so much and reach out so far from the comfort of our own home computer.

Suffering does not just come at the hands of those who persecute Christians. There are many other sources of suffering in the Christian's daily life: bad health (physical and mental), work stress, job loss, broken relationships, criminal decisions, accidents, intrusive and abusive people, self-doubts. Congregations also can suffer as a body from complainers and dissenters, poor leadership (lay and clergy), demographic and economic changes in the neighborhood, strategic deaths or transfers of key people, catastrophic weather that destroys the facility or kills many members. Yet, in the midst of all these possibilities, Jesus stands with us and for us, championing our cause with a tenacity that will not be thwarted by "things present, nor things to come" (Romans 8:38). Having this knowledge, believing this to be true is what gives the disciple of any age in any age "the peace of God, which passes all understanding" (Philippians 4:7). It even allows the disciple the strange response of rejoicing in the midst of suffering or shortly thereafter, as the Psalmist writes, "Weeping may tarry for the night, but joy comes with the morning" (Psalm 30:5).

In the spirit of *Shema* (Deuteronomy 6:4-9), Christians are to carry with them the confession of Jesus — in the words of no-longer-doubting Thomas, "My Lord and my God!" However, in our age of conciliation and compromise, we often capitulate the heart of our creed for the sake of better human relationships and at the sake of the truth. We become overwhelmed by a new age homogeneity that filters out distinctions and contradictions to reduce truth to what we can hold in common.

Here are some of the ways this is expressed in the general public square: "Well, whatever you believe that gets you by, that's what's important." Or, "I don't care what you believe as long as you believe in something." Or, "We're all going to the same place; it's just that some of us get there by a different route." Or, "There's only one God who loves us as we are, so it's okay that we understand God in our own way that makes sense to us." Or, "We're really not all that different; anyway, who's to say just who is right or wrong about this or that?"

These statements reflect our neopagan culture, which has moved beyond the Christendom of the West since the fourth-century AD to the close of the last century. "We're not in Kansas anymore, Toto!" More than ever before, Christians need to be clear about their faith: Jesus alone is the Messiah through whom alone is life that is eternal. John had no doubts about this and made it clear in his gospel. Christians today need to have this clarity of John and the boldness of Peter in professing the faith publicly so that others may believe and find the life in his name.

A complacent Western church must listen to the witness of the third-world Christians and also Christians who are suffering persecutions in so many lands around the globe. They understand what it means to witness to the truth, especially in the face of suffering. Yet, because they believe Jesus to be the Christ, the Son of God, risen from the dead, they also experience the joy that comes fresh every morning, like the songbird in the tree at sunrise.

The hope of the believer is that no person is so lost or no society is so dead that the love of God through Jesus cannot rise to reveal sin that can be forgiven, grief that can be comforted, fear that can be overcome, anxiety that can be relieved, evil that can be transformed. Such hope is possible for anyone who will dare to put one's finger into the wounds of Jesus, whose sacrificial death was requited on that sacred Sunday morning.

Easter 3
Acts 9:1-6 (7-20)
Revelation 5:11-14
John 21:1-19
Mark Molldrem

Finding ourselves in being found in Jesus

Socrates' famous dictum, "Know thyself," has been passed down through the ages in philosophy classes and psychology classes as instructors and students struggle with the perennial human question, "Who am I?" A couple of the fundamental keys we have in answering that question are family, name, friends, and work. Our first experience in identity is reflected through our up-bringing. We learn who we are by the intimate circle of people around us at the kitchen table, in the bathroom, and under the covers. As we learn our name, it becomes a most important handle with which to get a hold of ourselves; though what it says about our identity other than a label by which others call us, we are hard pressed to say — until we get into the meaning of names and hope the origin and signification of our name at least catches our fancy. When we are old enough to form a cadre of friends, we begin to learn so much about ourselves, as we play our thoughts, emotions, and behaviors against these others who have come into our lives like walking mirrors. Then, too, how we express ourselves through our work becomes an identifier for who we understand ourselves to be, although this is fraught with the dangers of relying too much on external factors to come to grips with an intensely internal personal dynamic.

The Bible directs us to "know the Lord" (see Jeremiah 31:34) and promises us that, as we do, we will know ourselves and ultimately learn the deepest meaning to our lives. This was Paul's experience. He learned his true identity only after his encounter with the risen Jesus. Not only do we learn who we are when we "consider Jesus" (Hebrews 3:1), we also discover what we are to do with our lives. Peter found this out after he ate breakfast with the risen Jesus.

One's fingerprints, Social Security number, driver's license, iris scan, or DNA test will reveal something about identity — who am I? But, it is only in one's encounter with the risen Jesus that we understand the meaning of this *who* that I am and the *what* that I am to do with my life.

Acts 9:1-6 (7-20)

When we first meet Paul, Luke refers to him in his Hebrew nomenclature and describes him as young and consenting to Stephen's death (Acts 7:58; 8:1). Acting as a kind of "coat check," he has so much to learn! At the time, he thinks he has a good idea of who he is. His later comments about his pedigree (Philippians 3:4-6) confirm a rather high opinion of himself. With his identity *intact*, he proceeds on his mission in life — to eradicate the sect of the way. Saul ravages the Christian church (Acts 8:3, imperfect tense indicating a continuing act of destruction and ruination, such that one translator, not erroneously, put deliberate intent into the sense of Saul's actions: "Saul *attempted to destroy* the church").

Our text begins with a more poetic, though not necessarily euphemistic, description of Saul's activity. He is described as "breathing heavily" (9:1) against the faithful in terms of threats (Acts 26:11) and actually following through on his threats (Acts 26:10). Saul is acting with zeal. He has a passion, fueled with a deep sense as to who he himself is. Perhaps the depth of his passion for persecution is revealed reflectively in his converse passion for proclaiming the faith at great risk to himself and also great pain (see 2 Corinthians 11:21b-29). The murderer of the faithful becomes a missionary to and for the faithful, regardless of the cost to himself. This is a radical turn around that is occasioned by his meeting the risen Jesus. How fascinating it would be to know more of the anecdotal moments of Christian encounter and internal dialog that preceded this monumental event and laid the seed for such a fruitful development in his story!

It is interesting to note that on the road to Damascus there is no condemnation of Saul by Jesus. He simply identifies himself and gives instructions for Saul. Reminiscent of Samuel in the temple, Saul responds by doing what is required of him. He goes into Damascus and waits for Ananias to restore his sight. Ananias, reminiscent of Moses' hesitancy to go into the court of Pharaoh, follows the instructions of his vision. Saul's sight is restored after three days. In preparation, Saul had undergone a complete fast (three days) and had sat in darkness. It is only in his own darkness that Saul will finally see the true light, as John writes, "The light shines in the darkness and the darkness has not overcome it" (John 1:5).

When all is said and done, Saul receives three visions. The first is the one of the risen Jesus on the road to Damascus. The second is about Ananias coming in to call on him. The third is when the scales fall from his eyes and he sees that Jesus is indeed the Christ, "the Son of God" (Acts 9:20, 22). God's work with Saul has been complete and thorough. These visions changed Saul. The first encouraged him to continue to his original destination but with a different agenda now. The second prepared him to be beholding to a disciple of the way, giving him a different paradigm with which to view these previous objects of his scorn. This would be the beginning of a new love in Saul's heart that would find expression in such letters as Philippians, Thessalonians, Timothy, and Philemon. The third led him into a new career. He was baptized and began preaching the name of Jesus, rather than persecuting the name of Jesus.

We can only begin to imagine the consternation of the Jews. They thought they knew and understood Saul. His reputation had preceded him. But, identities have a way of changing to their true character when the risen Jesus is involved. Saul came to know himself so much better, so much fuller, and so much deeper after he met the risen Jesus on the road to Damascus. His life took on a new trajectory, as he was inspired by seeing Jesus for who he truly is — the crucified and risen one. In light of this, he discovered himself, who he had been and who he was destined to be (1 Corinthians 15:9-11).

Revelation 5:11-14

These few verses are the concluding descriptor of the heavenly worship that is reported in chapters 4 and 5 of Revelation. After introducing himself as the seer and Jesus as the seen in chapter 1, and after sounding the seven messages to the seven churches (No batch email here! Each a personal word!), John is transported to the heavenly throne room through an open door. *Worship should always be an open door through which the glory of God is manifest!*

God is seated on the throne, surrounded by majestic color. Surrounding the throne are 24 thrones on which the elders are seated. There are also four sleepless, living creatures, who "never cease to sing, 'Holy, holy, holy, is the Lord God Almighty' " (Revelation 4:8). The 24 elders take their cues from them and join in a heavenly chorus of praise. Looking carefully, one can see a lamb in the midst of this wonderful scene — at once slain, yet very much alive and worthy to take the judgment scroll from the hand of God. The praise of the elders turns now to the lamb, whose exploits on earth are rehearsed with a melody from Calvary (Revelation 5:9).

This is the context in which the angels appear and join the song of praise to the lamb, who continues to be the center of attention in this sound-bite of heavenly worship. To the lamb is ascribed a plentitude of benediction: to the lamb belong power, wealth, wisdom, might, honor, glory, and blessing. There is a mouthful! No wonder it took "myriads of myriads and thousands of thousands" to get it all expressed! Even the creatures of earth chime in with concurring verse.

There is a totality of worship pictured here. Heaven and earth resound with it. The creatures from above and below cannot keep silent. At the heart of the worship, coursing with truth and life-giving joy, is the acknowledgment of Jesus, who is worthy of such adoration because of his work on the cross. He was slain and his blood was shed (like the sacrificial lambs of Old Testament times), so that a people could be ransomed from sin and death, given identity as citizens of God (kingdom) and purpose to serve God (priests). See Revelation 5:10.

With such a vision of heaven and earth united in adoration of Jesus, the worshiper can withstand the judgment of God, which will be unleashed from his hands as he breaks open the seals on the scroll. Thank God that the judgment scroll is held by such hands, for it was those same hands that were pierced out of mercy for the fallen! Not unlike Job, then, the believer will hold fast in faith, even when threatened to be trampled under the thundering hooves of the four horsemen and all that is to follow.

John 21:1-19

The post-resurrection appearances of Jesus are important in the gospel account to verify the nature of the resurrection itself. The mere physicality of the descriptions is a blatant clue informing the reader how to perceive this portion of the narrative. Rather than psychologizing or mythologizing the resurrection, John takes care to construct the story with tangible elements, so as to convince the reader/would-be believer that Jesus truly overcame death bodily. Indeed, Paul talks about a dramatic new creation in Christ (2 Corinthians 5:17; see also Romans 6:5 and Hebrews 10:20). His claims for new life are grounded in the radical nature of the resurrection.

Like a second ending to revisit this phenomenal event before letting it go with the final stroke of the pen, John reports the seaside experience. Previous to the fishing and breakfast escapade on the beach, Jesus had appeared to Mary Magdalene by the tomb and to the disciples twice in Jerusalem (John 20). Now, seven of the disciples have a spicy encounter with Jesus, seasoned with angling advice, a shared breakfast, and conversation about demonstrating love.

We find the disciples no longer huddled together behind closed doors for fear but rather out and about under the sun, moon, and stars. Maybe they were trying to get back into the routine of their lives before their three years with Jesus. Maybe they were simply hungry. Maybe they were still waiting around for guidance as to what to do with all that they had experienced — like John's version of a Pentecost event. Men do not wait well, so they get busy doing what they do best — before football, baseball, basketball, and racquetball were invented. They go fishing!

It is curious that in the boat at 100 yards off shore, the disciple John could identify the man on the beach as Jesus. It was not that his eyesight was better than 20/20. He was able to read the signs. The catch of fish upon his instruction pointed to the man as Jesus himself. Of course, Peter was all too ready to believe that. Remember, he had seen Jesus in the closed room twice already. So, he eagerly and whimsically threw himself into the sea to arrive first on the shore to greet Jesus. The others came in their laden boat. Who knows what the purpose is for mentioning that exactly 153 fish were caught, other than being a simple way of underscoring the record, the material content of all who are involved, the risen Jesus included. He is, after all, the one who invited the disciples to prepare their fish on a fire that he apparently had already started.

Perhaps at a distance it is easier to believe things. One can simply make up one's mind just what is to be imagined and accepted and then simply assert that it is so; offer a few proofs and not worry too much about the details. Hence, the confidence at 100 yards. But, when eye-to-eye in the very matrix of the stuff of life, it is harder to come to claims other than the material description of what simply is verifiable in a scientific, pragmatic way. Hence, the odd comment that once on shore, shoulder to shoulder with Jesus "none of the disciples dared ask him, 'Who are you?'" (21:12). As if they had some doubt somewhere in the recesses of their common sense brains; really, now, when was the last time the Romans let a condemned, crucified individual who had been placed in a sealed tomb slip through their hands?

However, in the shared meal (just like with the disciples who were on their way to Emmaus), Jesus is revealed as risen. The meal becomes the occasion for the disciples to have their eyes opened wider to the grand reality of the resurrection of the crucified one. John does not hesitate to tag this as "the third time Jesus was revealed to the disciples after he was raised from the dead" (21:14).

Having been so identified, Jesus turns to Peter for a lesson in consequences. If he loves Jesus, then he will serve his bidding. Once we have clear who Jesus is, our identity is also shaped and our purpose is exposed. We are "fishers of men" or followers of Jesus or disciples or Christians or believers in the way. The descriptors are many. The point is that our identity is locked up in his identity. This is why the New Testament writers so often exhort the Christian to imitate Christ, live worthy of the gospel, do as Jesus would do, be an ambassador for him, and find gain in him. This being the case, our purpose becomes clear. We are to serve him. This is expressed by Jesus' threefold questioning of Peter about his love. If he loves Jesus, then he will feed his sheep. This is a metaphor for caring for the church, the believers, any who would claim Jesus as Lord and Savior and those who need to claim him as Lord and Savior.

It would be hard to miss the parallel here from the foot washing lesson in the upper room on the Thursday before his trial. He clearly said that he gave them an example to follow. Foot washing is a sign of servanthood, which is the quality that best characterizes the followers of Jesus. They are to be servants one of another, as well as servants to the needs of all of God's hurting creation. Now, on the beach, the lesson is the same, although it comes through the aroma and flavor of grilled fish. Just as Jesus provided his disciples with breakfast, so too are they to provide for the needs of others in any and all ways through which the love of God may shine and be manifest in tangible ways.

Application

The two most defining questions for humans to answer are *Who am I?* and *What am I to do?* Christians find the answers to these questions in the encounter with Jesus, crucified and risen. Just as Saul was confronted with himself when he met the Lord on the road to Damascus, so are we exposed to the presence of the one who is "the image of the invisible God" (Colossians 1:15). Pursued by the risen Jesus, Saul discovered himself to be the very one who was persecuting the Savior of the world, as he attacked his body, the church, in the world.

Fortunately, Jesus had other plans for Saul and led him in a new way, so that he himself could be a proclaimer of the way. Saul would be known to the world as Paul, the author of such identity quotes as "Wretched man that I am. Who will deliver me from this body of death? Thanks be to God through Jesus Christ our Lord" (Romans 7:24) and "Whether we live or whether we die, we are the Lord's" (Romans 14:8b). He also had a clear sense of his purpose, as expressed in 2 Corinthians 5:20, "We are ambassadors for Christ, God making his appeal through us." Also, "Of this gospel I was made a minister... to preach to the Gentiles the unsearchable riches of Christ" (Ephesians 3:7-8).

With these two fundamental questions answered, the where and the how of life are secondarily important. It is telling to observe that Saul continued on his way to Damascus. In a similar way, Christians today should keep alert to where they are actually living and working, rather than dream about far off places or even flock to different locales than the one God has already put them in. God did not change Saul's geography radically that day. He simply led Saul to do things radically different in the very place he was going, because of his encounter with the risen Savior. So, too, Christians today need to discover how to see the mission field in their own backyard. This is especially true as our nation moves deeper into being a post-Christian society with post-modern sensitivities that make us a field ripe unto harvest.

One of the great challenges the church faces today is proclaiming the relevance of Jesus in a relative world. Deconstructionist temptations abound to sap the essence out of the gospel. The unique, final, universal, efficacious, and sufficient quality of Jesus' life, death, and resurrection stand over against all tendencies to relegate him to the ranks of the many prophets who populate history, or to recognize him as important only insofar as the Christian community mythologizes his story toward parochial and selective ends pertinent but to its own perspective, or to judge him simply as a misguided religionist in what would be better as a religionless world. The hymn of Revelation echoes the sense of what C.S. Lewis meant when he wrote in *Mere Christianity* that Jesus either was who he said he was, namely the Son of God, or he is no better off than a man who thinks of himself as a poached egg — or worse, he is the very devil from hell!

There is a T-shirt with this written on it: "Hey, Doood! If you are going to take up space on this congested li'l planet, then shouldn't you at least have a point?!" As Peter learned his point to "Feed my sheep," we learn that we are to serve the Lord in ways that make use of our talents, interests, opportunities, and resources. Then our lives have a point! Faith in Jesus is acted out in tangible, practical ways that serve our neighbor by proclaiming the gospel of Jesus clearly and boldly and by caring for the many needs of the neighbor. In this way we are the voice, hands, and feet of our Lord in the world today — an expression and extension of his resurrected body.

Easter 4
Acts 9:36-43
Revelation 7:9-17
John 10:22-30
Mark Molldrem

How can the dead testify?

We have an affair with death that ranges from fascination to revulsion. Consider the telling analysis of Jessica Mitford's *The American Way of Death Revisited* (which first came out in 1963 and was updated in 1998), the psychological plumbing of Elizabeth Kübler-Ross' *On Death and Dying*, the emergent attentiveness in the West to *The Tibetan Book of the Dead*. Perhaps Woody Allen captured the pop cultural attitude best when he said, "I do not want to attain immortality through my work; I want to attain it by not dying."

The season of Easter gives us pause to reflect upon the universal destiny of life as we know it — death — juxtaposed to the proffered reality of new life in Jesus Christ not only for earthly time but also for eternal existence. Tabitha, Peter, John, white-robed martyrs, and angels give us something to ponder as we hear Jesus say about the sheep who hear the good shepherd's voice and follow, "I give them eternal life, and they shall never perish" (John 10:28).

Acts 9:36-43

Tabitha was a good Christian woman, "full of good works and acts of charity" (9:36). Yet, she got sick and died. In a religious worldview that saw things in a balance, there must have been many questions raised. Evil is to be punished and good is to be rewarded. This is the balance that makes sense with a moral God at the helm of the universe. Psalm 1 testifies to it. Job's friends argue for it. We can only speculate as to the kinds of questions that may have raced through the minds of her Christian friends, as to why such a good Christian woman would be afflicted so and the Christian community hurt by her loss.

One thing we know for sure is that they sent for Peter, presumably for his pastoral presence and comfort in their time of grief. Or, could they have been looking for something else, something more dynamic, something explosive? After all, Peter had been in neighboring Lydda where he had healed Aeneas, a man bedridden for eight years with paralysis (Acts 9:32-35). Perhaps he could do something miraculous on behalf of Tabitha. Had not his Master — and hers — raised Lazarus from the dead? Did not the Master say that they would do signs even more wonderful than that (John 5:12-14)? Death is an unwelcome guest — or should one say intruder? What lengths will one go to repel the thief that steals the precious gift of life from God?

When Peter comes, he finds no fleet-footed gazelle, but a death-bagged trophy ready for mounting on the wall of the slain. This does not deter him. In prayer, he faces death itself, like Ursula LeGuin's Festin in *The Word of Unbinding*, and counters its powers with a command from a new day: "Rise!" Unable to withstand, death cowers and releases its prey. The gazelle is afoot again.

Earlier in Acts Peter proclaims the name in which he performs such a sign of God's powerful presence in the world: "In the name of Jesus Christ of Nazareth" (Acts 3:6). This invocation was pronounced over a lame man, who responds by walking. It may be that to avoid any appearance of magical incantations, the disciples, like Peter, are not always cited with a formula response to people in need. Each situation of God's signature seems to have its own character and depends on the act itself to testify to the living presence of Jesus, rather than a pre-set order of chosen words or even ritual actions.

Worthy of note is the role the miracles play in the narrative. They serve as vehicles to convey people from the spectator curb into the flow of traffic that turns to the Lord, believes in the Lord, and moves to the destination of faith. The residents of Lydda were transported in this way; so, too, were the residents of Joppa (Acts 9:35, 42). Notice also that their belief was not "in Peter," but "in the Lord." Peter was but the instrument the risen Lord used to extend his will into the life of Tabitha and the witnesses of such deeds.

Revelation 7:9-17

Just before the seventh seal becomes the seven trumpets, breaking an interlude of heavenly silence, there is a brief conversation between the seer of Revelation and one of the elders. The topic of conversation is a great multitude, "standing before the throne of God and before the lamb" (7:9). They are the witnesses from "the great tribulation" (7:14), which was most likely the persecution of Christians under the reign of Domitian in the later part of the first century.

Domitian was big into emperor worship, referring to himself as "savior," "lord," and "god." Despite the egomania involved in such claims, the practice of emperor worship served a political function of unifying the empire under the symbol of Caesar, while allowing the worship of any other number of regional gods in addition. Yet, the Christians owed their primary allegiance to God, before whom there could be no other in heart or in stone. For refusing to take the oath of allegiance to Caesar and rendering the required offering at his image, the Christians were persecuted even unto death. Whether this persecution was throughout the entire empire or regionally focused in Asia Minor is not entirely clear. What seems to be evident is that the book of Revelation is addressed specifically to the churches in southwest Asia Minor for whom the persecution was real.

The multitude gathered is an innumerable, inclusive lot. There are no human boundaries that can exclude one from belonging to the faithful (7:9). This band of believers stands, palms in hand, with ready praise to God, like the crowd on Palm Sunday greeted Jesus as he entered Jerusalem. They acclaim, despite their tribulation, that salvation (not just in a psychological "wholeness" sense or a physical "well-being" sense, but in the eschatological sense of God's ultimate, inevitable, effective, and final victory over evil and death itself) belongs to God, the one who indeed reigns above and over and beyond anything Caesar can imagine. To this the angels agree with a resounding "Amen," while affirming the multitude's acclaim, launches them into a refrain of their own, ascribing wondrous attributes to God "for ever and ever" (literally, "into the ages of ages"). In this brief sound-bite, we hear those from heaven and those from earth join together in antiphonal chorus. The multitude has passed through death to life to join in celestial hymnody. Their witness cannot be silenced by any act of Caesar; from on high their testimony will resound to encourage those still below to be faithful.

As is true with so much of the book of Revelation, there is reliance on Old Testament texts for the substance of message as well as the imagery of expression. For example, the hymn "Salvation belongs to our God" (7:10) can be seen as a direct quote of Psalm 3:8. Isaiah 4:5-6 provides vivid imagery of God's sheltering presence, which Revelation 7:15 evokes. Who could read Revelation 7:16-17 and not hear an echo of Isaiah 25:8 and 49:10? What the Old Testament expressed in timely yet timeless words, the New Testament sets forth as fulfilled in the revelation of Jesus Christ, who has come and will come — the lamb, whose blood has been shed in time and for all time.

John 10:22-30

How can the dead testify? Taking the gospel of John as a sermon on faith in Jesus, crucified and risen, we can hear Jesus tell the Jews who were questioning him that indeed he will testify to his identity even from the grave. "The works that I do in my Father's name, they bear witness to me" (10:25). His greatest work was to die for the sins of the people and effect atonement with God. "As Moses lifted up the serpent in the wilderness, so must the Son of Man be lifted up, that whoever believes in him may have eternal life"

(John 3:15). From the grave, he would cry out to the world (through the preached word!), "See how much I love you? See to what length I will go to have you back where you belong? I will go into your darkest corner, death itself, to assure you that there is nowhere that my hand cannot hold you fast."

It was during the Feast of Dedication that this encounter is set. That is telling, when one remembers the Abomination of Desolation inflicted upon the people during the wretched reign of Antioches Epiphanes in the second-century BC. The nature of the work that Jesus would do for the people would be an act of deliverance. As the Maccabbees delivered the people from the foreign overlords, God would deliver his people from their fiercest enemies: sin and death. As Judas Maccabeus recaptured the Holy City and cleansed the temple from the defilement of Antioches (sacrificing a pig on the altar), Jesus would reclaim the hearts of God's people and wash them pure from sin through the power of forgiveness so that death could not snatch ("take away forcefully") them away from God's intentions. One could read this reference in a predestinarian way, or one could read it with the heart of a pastoral counselor, assuring the believer that in faith one can have the confidence that whatever happens, one is ultimately in the care of God. There is a realism here that can admit, "We know not what the future holds," while at the same time adhere to the certainty, "but we know who holds the future."

When Jesus said, "I and the Father are one" (10:30), a line was drawn in the sand. On the one side, there would be those who heard blasphemy. No human can claim oneness with the almighty! Such an assertion must be silenced, by death if necessary. On the other side, there would be those with ears to hear who would discern the very voice of God trumpeting a remarkable development in the self-revelation of the almighty. Jesus talks about how the love of God is like that of a good shepherd who is willing to lay down his life for the sheep (John 10:11-15). In that act of self-giving, self-sacrificing love, a quality of life is transferred to the believer. This quality of life can only be described as life eternal. It is a quality of life that has dimensions beyond the three we experience spatially in the flesh. Jesus begins to define what this "beyond" means by describing its non-perishing attribute. It is not that one will not die in the sense of all living organisms who come to the end of their life's energy either through accident or natural decline. It is that one will not be lost to God. The image of not being snatched from God's hand contains within it the sense of safety and protection, of endurance and valuation due to the simple fact that God holds that life in a fourth and fifth (?) dimension beyond our current comprehension. The raising of Lazarus, described in the next chapter (John 11), is but a foreshadowing of what the resurrection of the dead will be, for Lazarus will surely die again and like the rest of us will have to wait until the final day when the dead will be raised imperishable. We will need to look to Jesus' resurrection to begin to get a glimpse of what that may mean for us. Here we need to return to the Easter and post-Easter narratives along with Paul's insights in 1 Corinthians 15.

One of the verities of the Christian faith is that as we follow the Good Shepherd in life and in death, we shall be safe. This is the essential message of the two visual images in this text: the first being one of the sheep who follow Jesus and the second being in the Father's hand from which no one will snatch the believer.

Application

Prayer can work miracles. When Peter prayed, he accessed the very power of the risen Lord Jesus and was able to apply that power for the benefit of Tabitha. This is a strong witness to the effectiveness of prayer. We do not know of how many other situations there may have been for Peter and the disciples when they prayed and gained no specific response as dramatic as the raising of Tabitha or the healing of Aeneas. We would certainly be able to identify with them in *this* regard, for all the apparently unanswered prayers we offer over our sick and dying and dead.

How do we understand this? Do we have to extrapolate a theory of dispensation? Or do we chastise the potential recipient or benefactor for lack of faith to receive or convey the miracle? Or do we look for other ways in which God is actively bringing life to the "dying and dead," allegorizing our experience into wisdom or truth propositions? In light of the resurrection of our Lord and Savior, we remain uneasy with the status quo of life as it seems to be lived. After all, God is able to work wonders. Whether God will do so in some demonstrative way in our lives or in the lives of those for whom we care remains to be seen. In faith, we pray and wait and hope. Perhaps that in itself is the miracle and the sign to the world that God is indeed to be taken seriously. This praying, waiting, and hoping is also the posture that prepares us to receive our living Lord rightly when he does show his mercies and when he will come again.

Until he comes again, our world will continue to be a bloody place. A movie in which a group of young people are placed on an island was released in Japan. Only one will be able to come off the island — the one left alive, the survivor. The game plan in everyone's mind is simply to kill before being killed. It is *Lord of the Flies* revisited with a vengeance! Will Freddie Kruger become an "also ran" in the Hall of Flame into which such incendiary movies, depicting the baseness and depravity of human spirit, will be relegated? Blood, whether splashed across the big screen or onto the streets, makes quite a mess. It is a sign of the tragedy of human existence where there is so much suffering and death.

What the world needs is less hurt and more hope! That is precisely what God gives the world in Jesus. He takes our human hurts upon himself — the wounded, bloodied lamb — and offers us a vision of God and ourselves that transcends the reality we have come to think as normal. It transcends it by allowing us to see the majesty of God (a la the seer of Revelation) expressed best through the lamb. Because of what the lamb has done for us, it is true that all "blessing and glory and wisdom and thanksgiving and honor and power and might" (7:12) properly belong to God. We can lay no claim on these attributes, try as we may to create a *new world order*. It is only when we finally learn to live beyond our self, beyond our community, beyond our world, serving God (7:15) and his purposes in the world, that we will penultimately find shelter in the maddening pace from day to day until that final day, when we will ultimately find our eternal rest by those "springs of living water" (7:17).

Reflect on the question that was asked of Jesus: "How long will you keep us in suspense?" (10:24). We love suspense. It will lure us to pay big bucks to go to the theater. It will keep us watching the serial soaps in the afternoon or evening hour after hour, week after week, to see what will develop. Yet we do not like too much suspense, especially when it comes to important matters, like who will be president of the United States. Suspense is really only enjoyable when we have resolve. Until then, it can feel like we are bursting (sometimes painfully), wanting to know how it will all turn out. Jesus' questioners wanted a resolution to the suspense. However, the word (God's answer) works slowly and mysteriously. The "plainly" that they wanted for the communication was complex and cumbersome; the word was wrapped up in humanity and in one-on-one caring and in words tumbling down a mountainside in parables and hard sayings reinterpreting the Law of Moses and in gasps of a dying Master alone on a cross.

Part of the mystery in the working of the word is that any questioner needs to hear in order to believe but also needs to belong in order to hear. How important it is to belong to a Christian congregation in order to be in a position to be exposed regularly to the word through worship, Bible study, fellowship, and service! *And* how important for every congregation to be alert to the questions and problems of daily life that drive people to seek the deep and abiding answers that God's word provides. Yet, in the end, faith itself, knowing oneself to be a sheep of the Good Shepherd, is a gift. It is not a "logical conclusion" at the end of a set of questions and answers. It is more like the experience of being *held*, which an infant knows to the marrow when cradled by the loving parent. This is a foretaste of that quality of eternal life in which believers will know themselves to be secure in the embrace of God for temporal life and through momentary death and into an imperishable eternity.

Easter 5
Acts 11:1-18
Revelation 21:1-6
John 13:31-35
David Kalas

All things new and improved

We don't much care for new things being forced on us, but we do like to have new things offered to us.

When something new is forced upon us, we have a kind of gag reflex that rejects the new and unfamiliar thing as an unwelcome change. We like to be able to chew on something before we have to swallow it. (We recognize and indulge this in ourselves, even though we often resent it in our congregations.)

When something new is offered to us, on the other hand, we are naturally drawn to it. Even if we had not previously felt dissatisfied with our "old" version, the offer of something new makes the old seem somehow inferior. Of course, in our age of continual upgrades of computer software and hardware, we are encouraged to believe that our old version is, indeed, inferior.

As consumers, we are particularly fond of "new." The word "new" has been married for so long to the word "improved" in our culture that we have come to assume that they always go together. And often they do.

Even beyond our consumerism, we're grateful for the freshness and hope that come with a new season, a new semester, a new year. We find that a new coat of paint surprisingly rejuvenates a room or a house. Some of us feel inwardly renewed by having a new haircut or by wearing new clothes. We like the fresh start of a new job or of life in a new community. And we often wish that we could create that appealing new and clean feeling in some of our old, continuing responsibilities and relationships.

God offers something new. Indeed, in the end, God offers everything new. New and decidedly improved. And that's good news for us — good news for us to hear, and good news for us to proclaim.

Acts 11:1-18

Marketing experts have made a science of determining how many different times — and, for that matter, in how many different ways — a consumer needs to hear a message in order for it to make an impact. But before Madison Avenue was trying to get through to us, God was trying to get through to us. And it seems that God, too, must communicate his message at multiple times and in various ways before we get it.

In the rooftop episode preceding this passage, Peter was a hard sell for the message that God was trying to convey to him. Then, in this passage, the same truth that broke through to Peter finally dawned on Peter's critics. That truth was that God wanted to include the Gentiles because salvation through faith in Christ was available for them too.

Ironically, before the Gentiles could be converted to Christ, Christ's own followers needed something of a conversion. They had to change their thinking, their paradigm, before the gospel could go out into the Gentile world. It's an unnerving thought that — then or now — God's work is delayed because of God's own people. Surely he expects opposition to his work from a sinful world. What a tragedy, though, when opposition comes from his own workers.

God desired to do his work among the Gentiles, but the early church was initially reticent. They were stuck in an old understanding — perhaps even an old misunderstanding — that prohibited the Jews from much contact with the Gentiles. Even the very term used in this passage — Gentiles — reflects the fundamental us/them mentality of the early Jewish Christians.

It's not as though this rooftop revelation to Peter was a new directive from God and the early church just didn't get the memo. Quite the contrary, God had indicated again and again his desire to include the nations (which is literally the meaning of the Hebrew term, *gowy*, from which comes the Yiddish terms *goy* or *goyim* for Gentiles).

Back in Genesis, God chose the family of Abraham to be his own special people. But that choice was embracing, not excluding. God's expressed desire was not merely to bless that family, but through that chosen family "all the families of the earth" (Genesis 12:3) and "all the nations of the earth" (Genesis 18:18) would be blessed.

The Psalms prophesy that "all the nations" will one day worship God (Psalm 22:2; 86:9), and the Psalmist calls on the faithful to proclaim the goodness of God among the nations and all peoples (96:3), and all the nations themselves are called on to praise the Lord (117:1).

God's global good will is made still clearer in the words and works of the Old Testament prophets. God's expressed plan for Jerusalem was not merely to be the holy city for his people only, but for all people, all nations (e.g., Jeremiah 3:17; Micah 4:1-2), and the temple, too, was to be "a house of prayer for all peoples" (Isaiah 56:7). Jerusalem, God's people, and God's servant are all variously given the assignment of being a light and guide to the nations (e.g., Isaiah 49:6; 60:3), and that with the purpose "that my salvation may reach to the end of the earth" (Isaiah 49:6).

Isn't it interesting that Peter himself took some convincing on this point? Back on the Day of Pentecost, Peter had quoted the prophet Joel to explain the work of God, including the promise that God would pour out his Spirit "on all flesh." Still, what Peter understood in theory on the Day of Pentecost was hard to accept as reality in the house of Cornelius.

For the crowds in Jerusalem on the Day of Pentecost, the manifestation of the Spirit was not self-evident proof enough, and so Peter had to validate what was going on by citing scripture (the Joel prophecy). Meanwhile, for the early church in this episode, their own scriptures were not enough to make them understand that God's good plan included the Gentiles. They needed to see (or to hear that Peter had seen) the manifestation of the Spirit there in Cornelius' house.

Revelation 21:1-6

The way the Bible starts makes sense to us: "In the beginning." That's a good, logical place to start. We have our notions of where or how any particular thing is supposed to start. The introduction and preface lay the groundwork at the beginning of the book, not at the end. The overture precedes and anticipates the rest of the performance. The syllabus is handed out on the first day of class, not the last.

Here, in the penultimate chapter of the Bible, however, we are surprised to discover what sounds like an introduction, an overture. Right where we expect to find an ending, we find instead a new beginning.

What a strange time to start something new: at the end. What author writes an introduction at the end of the book? What coach implements a new game plan as the game clock ticks down to zero? Yet here we are introduced to an entire array of newness. There's a new heaven — was there something wrong with the old one? — and a new earth, as well, complete with a new Jerusalem.

The newness God promises is not merely new surroundings. A dysfunctional family, after all, can move into a new house, but the new surroundings do not make their patterns of relating new. So God's promised newness is not merely new environs but new everything.

The new arrangement includes the beautiful image that God's dwelling will no longer be far off, but "with them." Surely scripture affirms God's presence with his people throughout but still there was always a recognition that his throne and his dwelling were off in heaven. No more. This is new.

Likewise, we find here that lovely image of comfort, which so many of us have quoted in hospital rooms and funeral homes along the way. "He will wipe every tear from their eyes." Some gospel songs have rejoiced in the prospect that there will be no more tears, no more crying in that day ("mourning and crying and pain will be no more"). But the promise here is one step sweeter than that. The testimony is not merely that tears will be gone, but specifically God will wipe them away. It is a personal and tender act of comforting by God, and it is an embodiment of his making things new. God is not a sleight of hand magician who waves a magic wand and says "Abracadabra" to make tears go away. Rather he is a loving parent who makes the tears go away by wiping them away himself.

The final specific piece of newness mentioned in this passage is the absence of death. "Death will be no more." Death, in scripture, is a more comprehensive thing than the mere cessation of brain and organ functions. From the day that Adam and Eve ate the fatal fruit but kept on walking and living, we discovered that death is something deeper and more pervasive than just the end point on a person's time line. We as Christians should be particularly aware of this truth, since we also understand that life is something more than just the continuance of brain and organ functions (see, for example, John 3:16; 6:47-51; 11:25-26).

Taken all together, this passage is a great affirmation of the goodness of God's original creation. What is promised and portrayed here is not new in the sense of being different. If I go to a restaurant where I always order the same thing and one day say, "I think I'll try something new," then I mean that I will order something different. What God promises here, however, is not new-different, but new-renewed. It's not something different from or other than heaven and earth and Jerusalem, but rather a new heaven, new earth, new Jerusalem. God's desire to dwell among his people is certainly nothing new for Emmanuel. And the promise of a painless, tearless, and deathless reality is a return to the way God originally created and intended it to be.

John 13:31-35

Present your people with this statement by Jesus, but don't tell them where it comes in the gospel or in the story: "Now the Son of Man has been glorified, and God has been glorified in him." Ask your people when they suppose Jesus said those words and not many are likely to place it at this point in the story.

Perhaps as Jesus enters Jerusalem on Palm Sunday, amid that ancient ticker tape parade, we might imagine Jesus saying, "Now the Son of Man has been glorified." Or when the crowd is eager to crown him king following the feeding of the 5,000, or at his transfiguration, or at the empty tomb.

There are a number of good, natural choices, but John 13 is not one of them. Just a few minutes earlier, Jesus was crouched down at his disciples' feet, his hands in the dirty wash water, performing a servant's function. And, just moments before he makes his "glorified" statement, he has watched one of his chosen twelve disappear into the night to betray him.

Now the Son of Man has been glorified? I'm sorry, but what did I miss?

It seems apparent that Jesus defines "glorified" differently than we do. Jesus does not use this word in any of the synoptic gospels, but it is something of a theme in the gospel of John. Jesus talks about glorification on three occasions (8:54; 11:4; 12:23, 28) prior to John's extended Last Supper scene. And in the dialogues, monologues, and prayer that make up that Last Supper section of John, Jesus makes repeated reference to glorification (13:31-32; 14:13; 15:8; 16:14; 17:1, 4-5, 10).

The theme and theology of glory in the gospel of John deserve more attention than can be given here. For preaching purposes, however, it is worth noting that "glorify" is evidently not something a person can do for himself. As I cannot tickle myself, someone else has to do it, so too I cannot glorify myself. Jesus says as much in 8:54, and he demonstrates it in his later references. His aim is not to glorify himself but to glorify the Father (e.g., 13:31; 14:13; 15:8; 17:4), he is glorified by the Father (13:32; 16:14; 17:1; 17:5), and both the Father and Son are potentially glorified by Jesus' followers (15:8; 17:10).

Jesus addresses those with him as "little children." Our common association with that phrase and Jesus, of course, is his "let the little children come to me" statement in the synoptics (Matthew 19:14; Mark 10:14; Luke 18:16). The Greek word (*paidion*) used there, however, is not the same as what appears (*teknion*) in this passage. Both are translated "little children" in the NRSV, although *teknion* never actually is used in reference to children in its several New Testament appearances. In addition to this one instance in the gospel of John — the only time Jesus uses the term — Paul uses it as a term of parental endearment and concern with the Galatians (4:19), and it is found seven different times in the five chapter epistles of 1 John.

So in the larger scope of the Last Supper scene in John, Jesus identifies his relationship to his disciples as teacher, lord, master, and model of servitude (13:12-17), as the vine to their branches (15:1-10), and as a friend (15:12-15). Here, in his use of *teknion*, Jesus suggests a kind of tender parental concern for his followers.

The tender term precedes the hard (and, to the disciples, bewildering) news that "I am with you only a little longer" and "where I am going, you cannot come." Both of those unhappy statements, however, are ameliorated later, as Jesus promises to send the Spirit in his absence (16:7), as well as to return for them so that they can be where he is (14:1-3).

Finally, Jesus concludes this section with a "new commandment," though at first blush the commandment to love does not seem new at all (see, for example, Luke 10:27 and Leviticus 19:18). What's new about this commandment, however, is its standard for love (see Alternate Application below).

Application

Call it "Covenant (Version 2.0)." The original covenants with the Old Testament people of God involved almost exclusively one group of people — the descendants of Abraham, Isaac, and Jacob. They were marked by the circumcision-sign of the covenant, and they carried in their Ark the terms of their covenant. Now, however, the God who had for centuries promised that a new covenant was coming (see, for example, Jeremiah 31:31) had put the product on the shelf. Characterized by the mercy of its maker, this covenant was extended to all people. They would be marked by his Spirit, and the terms of the covenant would be written on their hearts. That's surely new and improved.

Call it "Command (Version 2.0)." Centuries before the query prompted the parable of the good Samaritan (see Luke 10:25-37) or the disciples sat around the Passover meal with Jesus, God instructed his people on how to love one another: "as yourself" (Leviticus 19:18). But now, after extended and concentrated time of knowing and being with Jesus, and on the eve of his "greater love has no man" act, Jesus issues a new version of the love command: not to love "as you love yourself," but rather "as I have loved you." That's surely new and improved.

Finally, call it "Creation (Version 2.0)." The God who made heaven and earth makes a new heaven and a new earth. The God who made everything good in the beginning makes everything good again. And the God who made everything makes everything new: new and improved.

An Alternative Application

John 13:31-35. A common unit of measure in Bible times was the cubit. Those of us who grew up reading the King James or Revised Standard Versions will remember the familiar description of Noah's ark being so many cubits high, so many wide, and so many long. Likewise, later, with the story of Solomon's temple.

When we translate into contemporary measurements, we generally approximate a cubit as eighteen inches, for it was reckoned as the distance from a man's elbow to the tip of his middle finger. Of course, that makes the cubit a varying measure. I have a gentleman in my congregation who is 7' 2" tall. His cubit is longer than most.

If I asked all the folks in my church to break out their rulers, tape measures, and yardsticks to measure the altar rail at the front of our church, I daresay that they would all come up with the same figure. If, however, I asked all the folks in my church to measure our altar rail in cubits, then we would end up with very different figures. How many cubits long a thing is depends upon whose cubit you're using.

At the Last Supper scene in the gospel of John, Jesus told his disciples that the time had come to use a new cubit.

The issue at hand is the measurement of love. The standard human measurement had been a flawed and fluctuating one — I will love you the way that you love me. Then Jesus, reiterating the standard of the Old Testament law, commended a higher measure — I will love you the way I love myself. The demand was significantly higher, though the measure was still flawed and imprecise.

On the night before he was crucified, Jesus raised the bar once more. "Just as I have loved you, you also should love one another." Now I will not merely love you the way that you love me, for I will love you even if you hate me. Now I will not merely love you the way that I love myself, for I will love you at the expense of myself. Now I will love you the way that Jesus loved me. Now we are using his cubit.

Easter 6
Acts 16:9-15
Revelation 21:10, 22—22:5
John 14:23-29
David Kalas

Guess who's at the door

It's a picture of God that we see again and again throughout the pages of scripture.

We see it in the familiar story of the shepherd who leaves the 99 in order to pursue the one lost lamb. Again, a few verses later, we see it in the father running to meet his prodigal son. We see it also in the cherished portrait of Jesus standing at the door and knocking. And we see it most dramatically in the Bethlehem stable. It is a picture of a God who comes to us.

It is not a rare thing. Indeed, it so prevalent a pattern in scripture that we might not even notice it!

In the beginning, the Lord comes walking in the Garden of Eden. And, in the wake of Cain's failure, the Lord comes to counsel him. He comes to visit Abraham with good news. He comes to the rescue of the Hebrews in slavery. He comes in an awesome display at Sinai in Moses' day and at the temple in Solomon's day. He comes to meet Paul on the road to Damascus. And he promises to come to us again.

Even though our gospel lection predicts Jesus' departure, still there remains a dramatic promise of his coming. Indeed, perhaps the most surprising and dramatic coming of all.

Acts 16:9-15

We are reminded all along of the variety of means by which God communicates with people. Here, we read that "Paul had a vision," and he and his companions understood it as direction from God. Elsewhere, God's word is brought by angels, by prophets, by preachers, and even by a donkey. He gives dreams and the interpretation of dreams. He inspires otherworldly utterances, as well as the interpretation of those utterances. He writes on walls, thunders from mountains, and remains the still, small voice.

In this particular instance, it seems that God is giving direction to his missionaries. On this, Paul's second missionary journey, the team has focused their attention in Asia Minor, which was Paul's boyhood home, as well as the region where he spent most of his first missionary journey. Then comes this vision of a man from Macedonia, across the Aegean Sea from Asia Minor.

That Paul's vision came during the night serves as an interesting metaphor. During his waking hours when his eyes were open, it seems, the apostle was not seeing much beyond the confines of the immediate mission field there in Asia Minor. So the Lord took the occasion of Paul's sleep to expand the horizons of his vision and work. There were other souls to be reached — souls on the other side of the Aegean — and that vision in the night prompted a whole new move in Paul's missionary work.

The crossing of the Aegean was, in Neil Armstrong's famous phrase, "one small step for man." It was a more significant step for the church, however, as Paul's missionary effort entered Europe, the Greek peninsula, and moved a step closer to Rome itself.

The book of Acts itself also takes a significant step at this point. Suddenly, the narrator steps on stage and becomes one of the characters in the story. Everything up until this point has been written in the third person, but in 16:10 the language abruptly shifts to first-person, plural. "We" becomes the operative word for the next several verses as Luke himself becomes part of the team. Neither Luke here, nor Paul elsewhere, elaborates on how the two met or on Luke's participation in Paul's itinerary. Based on the pronouns used, it seems to have been very brief at this stage, though we know from later references that Luke became a more constant companion of Paul near the end.

On the other side of the Aegean, we see no evidence of missionary activity in Neapolis. Instead, the action moves almost immediately to Philippi. Luke reports that the group went "where we supposed there was a place of prayer" on the sabbath day. This move reflects Paul's pattern of going first to the Jews in any given place to preach the gospel to them. That they were forced to look for "a place of prayer," however, suggests that there weren't enough Jews in Philippi to establish or maintain a synagogue. The place of prayer was the alternative, informal meeting place in the absence of an official synagogue.

Interestingly, it appears that only women were gathered in that makeshift congregation on that sabbath day.

Among the four gospel writers, Luke is known as the one who is most attentive to the role of women in the story. Likewise, here in the book of Acts, the women are the ones who are holding the fort in Philippi. Lydia is often thought of as the first Christian convert on European soil. It is Lydia's hospitality that supports Paul and his companions during the time in Philippi, which is reminiscent of the women who provided for Jesus during his ministry (see, for example, Matthew 27:55). It was a woman whose liberation from her demon-possession is the hinge on which the rest of the story in Philippi turns.

Luke identifies Lydia here as "a worshiper of God," just as he does Titius Justus later (Acts 18:7). An almost identical reference is also made to Cornelius earlier (Acts 10:2, 22). The strong implication is that Lydia was a Gentile who had come to worship the God of the Jews. She has already demonstrated, therefore, an open and receptive spirit: open to hear something that she hadn't heard before, and to receive that new truth into her life. So she, like Cornelius before, completes her journey: first to the worship of the Father and then to the salvation in his Son.

Luke reports that Lydia "and her household were baptized." Later in Paul's eventful stay in Philippi, Luke tells us that the jailer "and his entire family were baptized." It is, in both instances, a beautiful image. Rather than the convert living his or her newfound faith in isolation and living in a divided household, we see the entire household coming to Christ. Like the Samaritan woman whose contact with Christ led her entire village to believe in him (John 4:39-42), Lydia and the jailer did not merely respond to the gospel themselves; they brought their households with them.

Finally, the episode concludes with a kind of metaphor for the relationship between faith and works. Lydia opens her home to Paul and his companions and in the end it seems that her home becomes the gathering place for all of the new believers there in Philippi (see Acts 16:40). Her household is not only baptized, representing their faith, but her home is also opened to others in hospitality, representing good works.

Revelation 21:10, 22—22:5

The city that wants to attract tourists will put together promotional materials boasting all that the city has. The recreation, the culture, and the entertainment; shopping and dining; convenience and cleanliness: these are the types of things that a city might claim to have and to offer.

Near the end of the book of Revelation, John offers a very different sort of promotion of the city he has in mind. His subject is "the holy city Jerusalem."

We are introduced to Jerusalem early and often in scripture, but King David is the man who really puts it on the map. He conquers it, makes it his capital, and then effectively makes it God's capital by moving the Ark of the Covenant there. A generation later, Solomon cements it as God's dwelling place, building the glorious temple there.

As the years pass, Jerusalem becomes a city like no other. Not that it is the biggest or the highest or the wealthiest (except, perhaps, in the gilded days of Solomon). Rather, it gains an ethos as the center of God's activity. The accumulated testimony of the prophets is that his glory, his throne, and his eternal purpose are there. All peoples and nations will come to worship the Lord who dwells in Zion. And while the northern kingdom was allowed to slip away between history's cracks, David's throne in Jerusalem will always have one of his descendants on it. One day, some particular son of David will reign there in uncommon strength, justice, peace, and security forever.

I saw a map once from the sixteenth century that depicted the world as a kind of three-petal flower. The one petal, stretching from the center to the northwest, was labeled "Europe." A second petal, growing down from the center to the south, was labeled "Africa." The third petal, reaching out from the center to the northeast, was labeled "Asia." And in the middle of the flower, the center of the world: Jerusalem.

A modern cartographer would not endorse such a map of the world, but a theologian might. Scripture surely paints a picture in which Jerusalem emerges as the center of the world. Here in our passage, a new Jerusalem is depicted as the perfect culmination of God's will for the world.

John's promotion of the city is an unconventional one. Rather than boasting about what the city has, he makes a point of identifying what it does not have.

The city has no temple (21:22). At first blush, that might seem a negative thing. In contrast to the quaint little towns where there was a church on every corner, this city might seem like a godless place with no temple at all. But, no; quite the opposite.

John also suggests that the city has no sun or moon (21:23) or lamps (22:5). Who would want to go to such a dark and dreary place? Our culture is drawn to the bright lights and neon of Broadway, South Beach, or Vegas. But what sort of low-watt city is this? It is, it seems, the most radiant spot in the universe, "for the glory of God is its light."

The city has no nightlife on the one hand (22:5), but neither does it ever shut down (21:25). And, for would-be residents, see the quality of life implied by what is missing there: "nothing unclean," no one "who practices abomination or falsehood," and "nothing accursed."

Ask a broken and discouraged person what they would change about their circumstances, and chances are that they will speak in terms of what things they'd like to be rid of. No more pain in their bodies. No more fighting in their marriages. No more violence in their homes. No more lies, no more alcohol, no more strife. On and on the list goes, and you could add to it from the parishioners you've counseled.

For the weary inhabitants of a fallen world, John's list of what will not be part of the new Jerusalem is very good news, indeed. The news gets better still, for the vision is not just a glimpse of what's missing but also an assurance of what's there. The passage is laced with one great, recurring promise: the glorious presence of God and of the lamb.

John 14:23-29

Our selected gospel lection comes from the midst of John's Last Supper scene. The synoptics' accounts of this event are comparatively short, while John shares with us a great deal more dialogue and monologue (and even a bit more action in the form of the foot washing) than his counterparts. Several of the prominent themes from John's Last Supper section are represented here in this excerpt from it.

Love is a central theme of the Johannine literature in general. John's gospel, after all, is the one that offers the great "for God so loved" summary of the good news. It also includes the new love commandment (John 13:34) and the author's self-identification as "the disciple whom (Jesus) loved" (see, for example, John 19:26). Jesus tells his disciples that love is the ultimate evidence that they belong to him (John 13:35). Meanwhile, one cannot read John's first epistle without being struck by the central role of love. It is the essence of God's nature (4:8b), the proof of our relationship to him (3:10; 4:20-21), and the practical living out of that relationship (3:16-18).

It is within that larger thematic context, then, that we meet this particular passage. Here the causal relationship presented is between love and obedience. "Those who love me will keep my word," Jesus says.

That relationship is not a two-way street. Obeying God does not automatically lead to loving God, as many a grim legalist has demonstrated. Loving the Lord ought to manifest itself naturally in keeping his word. If it does not, the professed love is likely to be shallow or altogether counterfeit.

A second significant theme, in this selection and in its larger context, is the glimpse we are given of the Trinity. This is a real gift of the fourth gospel.

Of course, Jesus does not present us with a systematic theology on the three persons of the Trinity. But then, he shouldn't. The Father and the Spirit are not objects of study for Jesus; they are his loved ones. Rather than a philosophical discourse, we are given a peek into a loving relationship.

While Jesus speaks a very great deal about the Father throughout the gospels, this Last Supper scene from John's gospel is our best opportunity to hear him speak about the Father and the Spirit. We discover several themes that are also explicit in this particular excerpt.

One: the theme of sending. The Father sent the Son, and the Father and/or the Son will send the Spirit. (Similarly, it should be noted that the Son also sends the disciples.)

Two: there is a pattern of the members of the Trinity focusing attention on one another, glorifying one another, and even arguably serving one another; while the focus is never on themselves. While this pattern is more explicitly fleshed out in the larger context, it is surely indicated here by the Spirit's purpose being to remind the disciples of everything Jesus had said (v. 26) and by Jesus' deference to the Father (v. 28).

Three: there is the theme of a certain relationship between the disciples and the Trinity. Jesus' followers are not merely on the outside looking in but rather there is a more intimate connection (or opportunity). Elsewhere, Jesus' prayer is that the unity of the disciples would be like the unity of the Trinity. Also, as we mentioned above, the disciples become a kind of extension of the Trinity as they are the next ones being sent. Here in our passage, there is the marvelous promise from the Trinity to Christ's followers: "We will come to them and make our home with them."

Four: finally, a theme that is significant in John's Last Supper scene — and well represented in this excerpt from it — is the prospect of Jesus going away.

It's hard to know for sure the state of mind of Jesus' disciples on this occasion. On the one hand, he had spoken plainly to them on several occasions about what would happen to him in Jerusalem. On the other hand, how could they possibly be expected to understand such things in advance of them happening? I can tell my five-year-old daughter about some elements of life that will confront her when she goes off to college, but I should not expect her to grasp my words and their meaning at this stage of the game.

Now his departure is very much at hand, whether the disciples grasp it or not. Yet, in both this passage and this larger section of John, Jesus portrays his going away as a positive thing. It is best for him, and it is best for them.

Application

That God should come to us at all is itself remarkable. He should have turned his back on us and walked away back in the Garden of Eden. And again and again since then. Instead, he comes to us. Like a concerned shepherd, like a forgiving father, as a baby referred to as Emmanuel, he comes to us.

Now, in the lections from John and Revelation, we are presented with two more remarkable images of his coming.

First, there is the personal, individual coming. The NRSV translates the whole promise as plural — "those who love me" — in order to be inclusive. In the original Greek, however, it is expressed in the singular. So the New King James Version reads, "If anyone loves me, he will keep my word; and my Father will love him, and we will come to him and make our home with him" (John 14:23 NKJV).

It is an astonishingly intimate image. That the Father should send his Son into the world because he so loves the world is surprising, but at least it is the "big picture." Here, however, it is unimaginably personal: the triune God will come to and dwell with me. You. Anyone who loves him and keeps his word.

In the Revelation passage, we see the other astonishing truth of his coming. While Caesar is famous for saying, "I came, I saw, I conquered," the Lord has said a more dramatic thing. He promises to come, and then he promises to stay. Central to the picture of the new Jerusalem is the abiding presence and glory of God. He dwells there with his people. So this God does not just come to see, to visit, or to conquer. He comes to stay.

An Alternative Application
Acts 16:9-15. "Faith of Our Mothers, Living Still." While we don't know anything specifically about Lydia as a mother — including whether she even was a mother — her example may be a good one.

First, we have good reason to infer that she was an exceedingly capable woman, apparently running her own business. One senses that she may have embodied the strong and able woman described in Proverbs 31.

Second, we see that she was a devout woman. In the absence of any synagogue to support her in her adopted faith, still she was there at the place of prayer with other devout women.

Finally, as we noted above, Lydia's conversion was not a solitary event. Conversion never should be, of course. It is not much of a rock if it doesn't make any ripple. But Lydia's conversion was accompanied by good works. In an act that makes her an especially appropriate hero for this day, we see that Lydia set a pace of conversion and belief for her entire household.

Ascension of Our Lord
Acts 1:1-11
Ephesians 1:15-23
Luke 24:44-53
Mark Molldrem

Jesus rules!

In golf, Tiger rules. In tennis, Venus. Depending upon which teen you talk with, any teen idol rules. In America, the people rule, despite what some political cynics or party technocrats say. For Christians wherever, Jesus rules!

One might think that such a theme would more appropriately be served on Christ the King Sunday. That is at the end of the Pentecost season, six months away. The festival day of the Ascension is just as appropriate to lift up the reality of the lordship of Jesus. Viewed from the perspective of the church calendar, this day effectively closes out the "season of Christ," celebrating his position in the divine economy as it culminates his work on earth. (Christ the King Sunday closes out the "season of the church" by accenting the role of Christ in relationship to the church and the cosmos.)

An underlying question that begs our sincere attention is this: What has gained ascendency in our lives today, threatening to replace Jesus in our hearts?

Acts 1:1-11

Everybody loves a sequel, especially if the first part was so good! Sometimes the follow-up story, however, leaves one wanting; but not in this case. Luke knows a good market when he sees it. Two thousand years of history have proven him right. "In the first book, O Theophilus...." Luke penned his gospel of the acts of Jesus, not just because everybody was doing it, but to give "an orderly account" (Luke 1:3); and, not just for the sake of the truth, but "that you may know the truth" (Luke 1:4) about Jesus — the you referring to any Theophilus, lover of God, who may be reading the book. The knowing does not mean intellectual abstraction about God but personal attachment to God.

Now, with the return of Jesus apparently delayed (see 1:11) and so many great things happening before his very eyes, Luke does not want the acts of the apostles to be misunderstood or forgotten. So, he takes pen in hand once again and constructs a narrative that could just as easily be titled "The Acts of the Holy Spirit." It is designed to make sense to anyone who is already familiar with the story of Jesus; yet, it is told in such a way that even those unfamiliar with Jesus are introduced to him through the sermons and personal testimonies laced throughout the account. Many are brought to faith through the faithful witness of the disciples, who are empowered by the Holy Spirit. The church grows, demonstrating in its daily life what believers do while they are waiting for their Lord to return.

Structurally, these introductory verses in Acts are linked to the closing verses in Luke. Luke's account of the commissioning of the disciples as witnesses (Luke 24:44-49) is recapped in Acts 1:1-5. Then, the ascension, related briefly in Luke 24:50-53, is expanded upon in Acts 1:6-11. How the disciples got out of the temple, where they were "continually... blessing God" (Luke 24:53), is what the book of Acts is all about, beginning with the Pentecost experience and spreading out into the streets of Jerusalem, onto the roads into Asia Minor, and across the waters to Rome.

Consistent with his propensity to locate his narrative in verifiable history with public figures, Luke uses the term proof 1:3 to refer to the post-resurrection appearances of Jesus. This word carries a different sense than (witness), in that a witness or testimony would emphasize the person's perspective on the subject, whereas "proof" conveys the sense of credible evidence on its own merits. A witness would say, "Jesus is the risen Savior of the world." A proof would say, "Jesus walked on the path toward Emmaus at 6:00 p.m. Sunday after Passover." Both may refer to the same event but express it differently, one focusing on the meaning and the other on the matter of the experience. In Acts, Luke does not specify the details of these proofs, although in his gospel narrative he recounts the details of the travelers on the road to Emmaus (Luke 24:13-43). Paul delineates several appearances of Jesus after the resurrection in 1 Corinthians 15:3-11; John, in John 20:11-29 and 21:1-23.

Luke passes over the specifics with a reference to the forty days between the resurrection and the ascension, which is his primary focus in transition in these introductory verses. Just as the forty years of wandering in the wilderness was a complete time to judge the people for their faithlessness (Numbers 14:26-35) and just as the forty days of temptation in the wilderness (Matthew 4:1-11; Luke 4:1-13) was a complete time to evidence Jesus' faithfulness, so too is the forty days of post-resurrection life together a complete time to convince the disciples that Jesus is indeed the risen Savior of the world to whom they will witness with the rest of their lives. (Three other significant spans of forty worth remembering, as recorded in scripture, are Genesis 7:1-5, the forty days of rain producing the flood, revealing God's judgment upon the earth; Exodus 24:12-18 and Deuteronomy 9:9-11, the forty days that Moses spent on the mountain receiving the revelation of God through the law; and Jonah 4:3, the forty days given to Nineveh to repent.)

Ephesians 1:15-23

"Paul... by the will of God." These are the words that begin the Letter to the Ephesians. These words thrust us right back into the book of Acts where we read of the conversion of Saul (Acts 9). These words expose the authority and power behind the thoughts, words, and actions of this singular man, who could rightly be called the theologian of the church. Though he did not write a systematics like Aquinas, Barth, or Tillich, he wrote in a few preserved letters more to shape the Christian understanding of the gospel at its heart than all the other writers of Christendom.

Because the Ephesians are (Acts 1:11), in Jesus, Paul is thankfully mindful of them in prayer. His intercession is that they may grow "in the knowledge of him" (1:17), which is richer and more immeasurable than the one extremely long sentence (1:15-23) in which he expressed his thoughts. David H. Stern, in his translation, *Jewish New Testament*, does a nice job of cutting up the meat of Paul's writing into chewable portions. (This or another translation that expresses the meaning of the text in "ear-palatable units" would be preferred by lector and worshiper alike over a reading from anything resembling the Revised Standard Version treatment of the text, as good as it is with the Greek.)

Though Paul is indeed grounded historically in the events of Jesus and the early church, he writes conceptually about them. He asks the question, "What does this mean?" In reference to the ascension that Luke recounts, Paul expresses its meaning. Jesus is not only raised from the dead; he is also intentionally and demonstrably placed at the right hand of God, the place of honor, "in the heavenly places" (1:20; spatially separate from earth, so there is no confusion of conflating heaven and earth into one sphere, making any expression of heaven but a metaphor for an enhanced experience of earth's realm). Jesus has a superior rule "far above all rule and authority and power and dominion" (1:21). As he expresses also in Philippians 2:9-11, Jesus' name exceeds all others; no other name can ascend higher than his. The notion of ruling is again visualized by the world as Jesus' footstool (see Psalm 110:1-2; 1 Corinthians 15:24-27). A final image Paul uses to conceptualize the ascended state of Jesus after the resurrection is that of Jesus as the head of the body. The head fills the body with purpose as it guides its function.

When Paul writes of "the knowledge of him," he is not referring to gnostic knowledge or the secrets of the mystery religions prevalent in his day. He is directing his readers to the saving faith that comes from a personal relationship with Jesus. Notice how many times Paul uses the construct "in him" or "in Christ" in the previous verses to today's text. Because Jesus "fills all in all" (see also Colossians 3:11), believers will find their all in him. The knowledge of Jesus, which comes through a faith relationship with him (trusting his work for our welfare, as expressed in Romans 5:6-11, for example), provides the riches that are the inheritance of the saints of God. These riches are gifts like the forgiveness of sins, the strengthening presence of God, and the hope of eternal life. Paul even says that this faith relationship with Jesus is a gift from God, "the immeasurable greatness of his power in us... according to the working of his great might" (1:19). Faith in Jesus is itself a manifestation of God's power in us.

Luke 24:44-53

Is the ending of Luke's gospel nothing more than what denouement is to the climax of a novel? Or is this actually part of the climax that keeps on building beyond the record and beyond the sequel to the beyond of beyond? The analogy of gospel narrative to story is beneficial only to a point, because the story is decidedly different than either a novel, a docudrama, or even "real TV." We are dealing with God's dealings with the world. That is an ever-unfolding event that certainly has its accents in history (creation, call, exodus, exile, restoration, crucifixion, resurrection), but also holds promise of plot yet to be written. Luke understands this. That is why there is the explanation of consequential expectations to the work of Jesus, namely, repentance and forgiveness of sins, preaching and witnessing, waiting for empowerment from God to be about these very things, and worshiping God with joy in the meantime.

Just like he did with the two travelers on the road to Emmaus, Jesus takes time to help his disciples understand how the scriptures are fulfilled in him. The key is to look in those passages that describe the suffering Messiah (for example, Isaiah 50:6, 52:13—53:12; Psalm 22). What this Messiah will effect is nothing less than the forgiveness of sins, which will set right the relationship with God. This message is not just for a chosen few; it is to be spread to the nations. It may begin in Jerusalem, but it is not to end until it has reached the farthest corners of the world. The power to accomplish this communication feat will not come from within a group of highly successful, self-motivated people. The power will come "from on high" (24:49). There will be — there must be — a divine empowerment to accomplish all this.

Just as the disciples learned to trust Jesus through his ministry with them, they would need to trust him when he gave his word about sending "the promise of my Father" (24:49). The disciples would soon learn that one fulfillment spills over into another. The promises of the Messiah were fulfilled in Jesus, who in turn made promises on behalf of his heavenly Father to send the Holy Spirit (refer to Acts 1:4-5). This promise would soon be fulfilled, as recounted in the opening scenes in the Acts of the Apostles (Acts 2).

Luke concludes his gospel narrative in the same spirit with which he began it: with great joy! The angels announced the mood at the birth of Jesus (Luke 2:10), and the disciples retained the mood after the crucifixion, resurrection, and ascension (24:52). This joy, no doubt, filled each day in delightful ways as they moved in and out of their routines. But one fact stands out in Luke's description of the joyful fellowship of those whose lives had been touched by Jesus. They were "in the temple" worshiping (24:53). The disciples expressed their faith in worshipful acts that had a public and corporate dimension to them. When Jesus addressed them with directions on what to do after he ascended, he spoke to them as a body. The plural form of address is used, both in the imperative verb and the pronoun. Thus, when the Holy Spirit did come upon them, "they were all together in one place" (Acts 1:2).

Application

In our post-modern world, meaning is elusive. The age of absolute faith is past. The age of absolute science is past. The age of absolute history is past. Everything is revised and considered revisable. In our efforts to make sense of an ever-changing sketch, we seek after a line of meaning to connect the dots. If the God who is God does not provide the connections of meaning for one, something else will — whether that be Satanism, occultism, Wicca, amorphous new age spirituality, astrology, voodoo, communism, nationalism, capitalism, or nihilism, to mention a few possibilities.

Jesus presented himself alive to the disciples after his death on the cross, "speaking of the kingdom of God" (1:3). Christians today are to announce to our present world, "Jesus rules!" He is the ascended one, who claims power and authority over the world. He empowers his disciples, then and now, to witness to the meaning of life in his name. Jerusalem was the epicenter at that time, but now the whole world has become the stage on which this pronouncement is to be made. It begins in each particular locality where the church exists and expands in ever-enlarging circles. The empowerment for this to happen comes from God through the Holy Spirit, as the church is emboldened to give witness to the "witness" that is our privilege to believe and steward.

We are living in a time of anarchy of opinion. It is the result of a mindless democratization of values, which leaves citizens in a morass when it comes to making intelligent decisions. Ted Koppel makes this pithy comment in his book *Off Camera: Private Thoughts Made Public*: "The spirit of cultural diversity and political correctness is turning sour. We are in danger, in our efforts to be fair, of acceding to some wrongheaded positions, simply because they are held by someone in a minority group." The practical difficulty of such a situation reveals itself for Christian parents who cannot discern proper family commitments in their weekly schedule. They try to pack it all in and crowd out Jesus, who is to be their "all and in all" (Colossians 3:11). Worship and Christian education (whether Sunday school or confirmation or adult classes) become optional, "skippable," because of other events that "we just need to attend."

The sense of priorities that are determined by the criterion that Jesus is Lord, Jesus rules, must be reclaimed by Christians who are living next to neighbors for whom this is a foreign notion. One of the ways we can publicly witness to our faith is by being certain places at certain times with certain attitudes and behaviors that can speak louder than words. A touchy example of this would be the Christian family who chooses worship and Christian fellowship on a Sunday morning over golf, soccer, hockey, or company. A sticky example of this would be the Christian in a board meeting shaping company policy, not by the bottom line necessarily, but by what is just and equitable for the employees or customers, even if the stockholders have to "bite the bullet" this time. The Third Commandment about the sabbath has as its assumption that Jesus is Lord of the sabbath, and that his lordship extends into every day because of it. In our day, it will probably be more prickly to preach about these things than to preach about being saved by grace. Now, there's a sad commentary on the state of our hearts.

Referring to the state of our hearts, we can ask ourselves if, despite the prosperity of the past years, there is a prosperity of joy in our lives. When we skim across the headlines of our nation and world, observing the continued and growing need for peace, security, quality education, relief from poverty, and the exploitation of children, we must admit that human hearts are easily distracted from the one thing needful — to have and to hold a living relationship with the Lord of life. Sin is the root cause of all that is wrong in our world. The crisis of our human culture is spiritual. Economic policies, educational methods, military posturing, welfare reforms, and legislative initiatives can only go so far in advancing the human agenda. Until there is total surrender to the will of God, there will always be the need for preaching and witnessing.

With the growth of metropolitan areas, which are attracting the population of the world into teeming centers of humanity, the instruction of Jesus takes on a new meaning today: stay in the city. A slogan that has been part of the Evangelical Lutheran Church in America's ministry has been put on promotional buttons and reads: In the City for Good. As Christians work together in the places where humanity is at its thickest, there is strong potential for the Holy Spirit to visit the enterprise "with power from on high." Our troubled cities will benefit from such a concerted effort by the body of Christ, which will discover Christ filling all with himself wherever the heart's eye is focused on him.

Easter 7
Acts 16:16-34
Revelation 22:12-14, 16-17, 20-21
John 17:20-26
Craig MacCreary

Locked in a room with open doors

Years ago, Ernest Campbell, former preaching minister at New York's Riverside Church, titled a volume of sermons *Locked in a Room with Open Doors.* There is hardly a year goes by when I am not drawn to the sermon from which the title of the book was drawn. In the sermon, Campbell covers the many things that hold us back from going through the doors that God has opened for us — the fear of the new, worry, fear of the unknown. The assumption is that we ought to be able to go through the doors that are open to us and that we should deal with what is holding us back. Campbell's point is that while God has opened doors for us there is something that restrains us.

Life often does feel like that. Often when I sit down to my computer I experience this. There always seems to be at least one more program or feature that I need to able to take full benefit of all that I already have. I always seem to be one more download away from bliss or total security. A full life is only an upgrade away. Often some dialogue box will come up with some reason why I cannot fulfill my heart's desire — locked in a room with open doors! I am locked in: at least until I open the door of my computer store and go in to buy the needed update to my computer that will make all upgrades possible. I cringe at the introduction of the latest Microsoft operating system as I ponder what might be withheld from me as a result of failing to buy into all the new possibilities.

The assumption behind Campbell's words, written long before the massive introduction of computers and the internet, is that no one should stay put if they can avoid it. Given the times of social upheaval and challenge in which he was writing, it was clear that one should march through any opening for increased justice and diminished oppression. On this score, Campbell was clearly right. However, in our time there is a case for those who do not go through all the doors that are opened to increased consumption and waste. Staying put and sticking with what you have may be as faithful a response as moving through all the doors that may be open to us.

Each of these texts make a case for remaining where we are without yielding to the temptation of dashing off in all the directions that might be open to us.

What saves the jailor in the Acts text is that Paul and Silas do not exit through the doors that are open to them. Indeed, their witness moves the jailor to open the door to a conversation about salvation. Staying in place has its merits. The heart of the message of the book of Revelation is in a sense, "Stay put, stay on message, and stay at it for Jesus is coming." Of course, the author is living in exile so there was not much alternative to staying put. The situation of the church today might not be all that different from the situation of John of Patmos. How do we stay at it and stay as a presence in the culture when the culture is less likely to affirm or even understand what we are about as a people of faith?

Despite Jesus' plea in the lesson from John that all his people be one, the ecumenical movement has fallen on hard times. It seems, in many ways, we have rushed through a door and crossed a threshold where churches have an increasingly hard time naming or even believing in a fundamental unity. Does Generation X see the same Jesus in the religious life of baby boomers? Can a megachurch member understand the faith life of those congregations with fewer than fifty in attendance on a Sunday morning? Have we crossed a threshold where we find lack of understanding and appreciation for the "varieties of religious presence" in our communities? One might even ask what kind of unity Jesus would pray for amongst Christians, Jews, Muslims, and other faiths. Have we crossed a threshold where we find it hard to hear and speak with one another?

The lectionary this Sunday invites us to consider whether some of the thresholds we have crossed have left us further from or closer to Jesus' intentions.

Acts 16:16-34

Certainly, there is no doubt that in this text Paul opens a door for the demon-possessed slave girl. Of course, in the process, he opens a can of worms, as well. However, it is not uncommon to find that a healing poses some serious challenges. Many families have grown dependent upon having a sick member whose illness the family has grown reliant upon to divert and distract them.

The late Edwin Friedman, family therapist, told stories of his mentor, Murray Bowen, who found that the visit of family members to mentally ill relatives often made their sick relatives worse. He found that from time to time when one member of a family got better another member would manifest the symptoms of the same sickness. It seemed that a family needed at least one sick member to talk about, to blame for their problems, and to divert from doing the hard work of developing healthy patterns amongst themselves. Opening the door almost always opens up challenges in one form or another. It is hardly surprising that the reaction of the slave girl's handlers is less than enthusiastic.

How did Paul come to be such a font of blessing in this situation? We would like to think that this came about as a result of Paul's well-meaning, thoughtful, and faithful understanding. That is not the case. "Paul, very much annoyed, turned and said to the spirit, 'I order you in the name of Jesus Christ to come out of her.' And it came out that very hour." The movement of the Spirit here does not wait for Paul to summon up the appropriate emotional correctness or theological soundness. This seems less than satisfactory.

Sometimes a simple reversal of the equation brings some insight. In this case, annoyance becomes the occasion for opening some doors, which is often a lot better than annoyance being the cause of doors closing. My computer gives anger, frustration, exasperation, and infuriation, as synonyms for annoyance. When things get to that point options for better days begin to close. Certainly, as Paul is portrayed in scripture he is capable of annoyance and all its potential synonyms. Things that are normally negative, beyond the positive of merely venting, are turned into a positive when directed at the demonic. The reader wonders why it took several days for Paul to get to the place where he could lay down the order to the demon to come out of the girl. Was he afraid of being misunderstood showing an interest in the future of a slave girl? Certainly, doors remain closed when our fears of being misunderstood so overwhelm us that we do not say what needs to be said. Perhaps he had to sort through just who he was angry at.

Do we find it easier to be annoyed with people? Are we trying to fix them when we should be using our emotional energy to create an environment in which the demonic can just pour out of them? It is easier to wallow in being annoyed, feeling sorry for ourselves, and blaming God for putting all those frustrating people in our path? It is certainly a lot easier than directing our energies toward casting out the demonic. How often have we stood in the way of what could be done to open doors? It took Paul a while of staying put before he could open any doors.

The net result of what did happen is that Paul and Silas found some doors opening to them, only they were behind jailhouse doors. Knowing that Paul is a Roman citizen, it seems strange that Paul does not play the citizenship card to stay out of jail.

It seems that the plan here is about these doors being open to the ministry of Paul and Silas. Prison is open to them and open to what God is doing. The Lukan author makes it clear that the prisoners were listening to them singing and praying. The faith gains credibility in this scene precisely because the privilege card is not played. Indeed the book of Acts is the story of a church that gains credibility with the least and the most vulnerable. Paul will play his citizenship card but not to get out of jail. He will play the card to get to the magistrates so that they apologize to Paul and back off.

This must have been quite a sight for Paul's fellow prisoners and surely lifted his credibility in their sight. Acts reminds us that Peter the first, the original disciple, stayed with Simon the tanner when he was in Joppa. Of course a tanner was a filthy occupation that was on the low end of the career tract in the ancient world. One wonders if the current churches, mega and mainline, see their plans as measuring faith development in terms of credibility with the least. Have we crossed a threshold that separates many of us from the original plan?

Of course, there is the miraculous earthquake that throws open all the doors and releases the prisoners from their chains. It is a different story for the jailor whose career and life are on the line if all the prisoners escape. Paul and Silas choose to stay put in jail locked in before open doors. One can easily make the case for rushing through the open doors. Certainly this miraculous escape mechanism would be quite an impressive tale to be told in the ancient world.

If Christianity is to be about a magic faith moving from one miracle to the next then dashing through those open doors would be the thing to do. But Paul and Silas are held back by the ethical and moral dimension of the faith. I am reminded of Mahatma Gandhi who refused to hurt the British war effort in World War I because he enjoyed the benefits of living under the British Empire and therefore he had a responsibility for its defense. There are some thresholds that should not be crossed because in the long run they violate what we should be about. Sometimes we should be locked in a room with open doors.

Revelation 22:12-14, 16-17, 20-21

"Blessed are those who wash their robes, so that they will have the right to the tree of life and may enter the city by the gates." This is the promise of the book of Revelation — those who have had their robes washed can enter into the "Holy City, the New Jerusalem" God is bringing about. Revelation 21:25 makes very clear that those who long to enter the gates to this new order of things find that these portals are never closed.

Nevertheless, I don't know a pastor of any theological orientation for whom it feels that way. In every typology of churches there is always the classification that names congregations as mules, cats, or some other creature that is hard to corral and heard. A random sampling of most pastors tends to show that a disproportionate number of them have wound up serving these churches. I know the feeling, yet a caveat is in order here. There is great danger in identifying our pet projects and ideas as the portal through which folks must pass in order to enter the kingdom. We run the risk of being every bit as much a gatekeeper as some of our less progressive and more recalcitrant members. However, the doors are never closed to what kind of wisdom and learning God might bring out of our journey with people who just cannot seem to bring themselves to look at life through our lens.

Revelation makes clear that if there is a block to entering the New Jerusalem, it is internal rather than external. It seems that in our age we have plenty to come clean about if we are to enter the new order of things. The outer garment in which we have wrapped our faith needs a good soak in cleansing water. I bristle at those who see in the cross primarily a vengeful God sacrificing his only son in an orgy of blood sacrifice. My faith is not wrapped up in such an interpretation. Yet, the text says there is a blessing in immersing one's robe in some cleansing. I need to be immersed into the world of those who bring to the cross the experience of being abused.

This passage suggests that a clean, refreshed feeling is a precursor to entering through the gates that are never shut. Often in church we take that to mean primarily a cleansing of our sins. But we can be so dirtied in church that we feel so unclean as to be inhibited from marching right through the open gate. If you are a parent of a child and you are holding down two jobs, insufficiently parented because your parents were holding down two jobs, and you are dealing with a child pumped up on food additives — you don't need to be shamed for your lack of skill in handling your child when they become a nuisance. How do we leave people refreshed enough that they can enter through the gate that leads to the New Jerusalem? Many parents have an accumulation of blood, sweat, and tears trying to fight the good fight with their children.

"The Spirit and the bride say, 'Come.' And let everyone who hears say, 'Come.' And let everyone who is thirsty come. Let anyone who wishes take the water of life as a gift." While that is what the spirit and the bride say, we often have devised ways that say, "come but see footnote at bottom of the page." "Please come as long as you are very much like us and do not tip the balance of our comfort zone." We need to come clean as to how, even despite our best intentions, we have become frenetic gatekeepers of gates that do not need keeping for they are always open.

John 17:20-26

Do you feel yourself freezing up and going into shut down mode when you hear this kind of language? One can certainly feel doors closing when we hear much of the language of the gospel of John. This gospel invites us with such language as John 3:16 and puts us off with language that seems to suggest that Jesus is the only avenue to gain access to heaven because he is "the way the truth and the life." I approach this gospel in anticipation and dread for it seems to have been the source of as many doors closing as hearts opening.

Yet, Jesus' prayer is his petition that all will be able to see his glory. In his narration of Jesus' life, John makes clear that this prayer has been answered in church experience. In the first chapter he tells us that "the word has become flesh and lived among us and we have beheld his glory." Of course, in the gospel the glory can only be apprehended in light of the cross. Yet, it seems that there are certain events that illumine the meaning of the cross just as the cross illumines their meaning. In the opening chapter of the gospel John the Baptist, on seeing Jesus, proclaims, "Here is the lamb of God who takes away the sin of the world." Whatever else we may say of the cross it clearly must be about taking away the sin of the world, not adding to it. Any understanding of the cross that adds to the sin of the world cannot be legitimate.

The medieval crusaders' understanding of the cross as something in the name of which one must do battle is far from the glory that takes away the sin of the world. Neither can one simply find affirmation of the cross in the notion that the glory of the cross is in just taking it. There is no taking of abuse that can appeal to the cross as something glorious. This seems to be the fundamental error of the Mel Gibson movie, *The Passion of the Christ*. The ability to take it and be able to come back for more seems to run through many of his movies. Perhaps there is a glory in that but not the glory of the cross.

Jesus' prayer is for the fundamental unity of the church to be found in its comprehension of Jesus' glory. Clearly, in the gospel that glory focuses on the cross, yet that understanding must arise out of a correlation between the cross and the events of Jesus' life. When that happens, doors open to the taking away of the sin of the world.

Application

Ernest Campbell, in his sermon, "Locked in a Room with Open Doors," gives a laundry list of what the locks are in people's lives as they face the opportunities that surround them: worry, hatred, fear of the new. "The enemies are not all out there. Some are on the inside. It is so easy to fall into the habit of blaming our unrealized selves on outside forces. The mood of the day might well be caught up in a paraphrase of one of Shakespeare's better known lines, 'The fault, dear Brutus, is not in ourselves, but in our systems that we are miserable.' " Yet, what is on the inside also pushes us to needless activity.

What prompts feverish actions and all-too-frenetic activity on my part is: a mentor pastor that I do not want to let down, plain old-fashioned guilt, the inability to handle silence, and general anxiety as to what is coming next. These texts challenge me to consider whether in the next phase of my life I should yield to my drives or consider that it is God's plan for me to stay put, whether in my frenzied activity I have become a gatekeeper, and whether I seek to justify my theology more by action than reflection.

An Alternative Application
Revelation 22:12-14, 16-17, 20-21. One approach that I have found helpful is to consider my own history with a text. I often ask myself whether I have crossed any thresholds in reflecting on a text through the years. Increasingly, I find myself pondering the questions I find myself asking of a text. Years ago, I would not have asked the question of whether a text helped to break or add to cycles of violence. As one who does believe very much that the rule of God is about justice, I have found myself asking, "Where is the shadow side of this kind of preaching?"

Increasingly, I find that I ponder how the text will impact on other faith traditions and how doors to new meaning might be opened through that conversation. These texts measure my pilgrimage in terms of prisoners released, people free to enter the New Jerusalem, and the glory that Jesus intends for his people.

Pentecost Day
Acts 2:1-21
Romans 8:14-17
John 14:8-17 (25-27)
David Kalas

The day the Spirit moved in

Things change in a house when someone new moves in. Whether it is the birth of a baby, the arrival of an exchange student, the advent of a foster child, or the coming of an elderly parent needing care, things change in the house when someone new moves in.

Some of the changes that come are anticipated and welcome. We look forward to the fun and lovely patterns of life that will come with the new arrival. Other changes, however, are not anticipated — perhaps not even expected — and consequently those changes may not be welcome.

It's no different when God moves in. Things change. We'd be doomed if they didn't! But while some of the changes that come with his arrival are anticipated and welcome, some others are not.

We might say that Pentecost was an occasion when God moved in in a new and special way. The coming of the Holy Spirit changed things demonstrably in the church, just as his arrival and presence changes things demonstrably in an individual life.

We may find that people's comfort level decreases as we talk through the Trinity. A generic reference to "God" is widely accepted and embraced. Many different people may mean many different things by "god," but the word and the concept are easily accessible. Once you start talking about Jesus, however, there's a considerable drop off. Jesus is a more polarizing figure. Not all the folks who feel comfortable with talk about God are ready to get on board with Jesus. When the conversation turns to the Holy Spirit, even a lot of the folks who are willing to talk about Jesus — perhaps even a lot of the folks in our churches — begin to clam up. The Holy Spirit seems more mysterious and more threatening. He is not as easily relegated to heaven as the Father and not as easily relegated to history as the Son. The Holy Spirit is God "moved in," and we may rejoice in the results or we may be uncomfortable with them. Either way, though, the Spirit is here.

Acts 2:1-21

"They were all together in one place." After this day, that could never be said again of Christ's church. Not, at least, until the fulfillment of all things. At the beginning of this day, they were all together — all the believers, the followers, the disciples — in one city, in one room. By the end of this day, the believers were possibly heading and spreading to almost every place, "from every nation under heaven," from Mesopotamia to Rome.

It has often been said that the Acts of the Apostles might better be called the Acts of the Holy Spirit, for surely the Spirit is the driving force. He is promised in chapter 1, he comes on the Day of Pentecost in chapter 2, and he is the one who guides and empowers the work of the apostles and the church from that day forward.

The account of Pentecost features a handful of different images commonly associated with the Holy Spirit. Those images are revelatory, and we might use them to help our people gain a greater comfort level with the subject of the Holy Spirit.

First, there is the "rush of a violent wind." In Greek, as in Hebrew, the words for "wind," "breath," and "spirit" are largely interchangeable. It's not merely a case of homonymity (as with "lead" in English, for example). Rather, it is an instance of a single concept with several layers. It adds insight and depth to the image of God breathing his breath into Adam (Genesis 2:7) and makes for an illustration of the Spirit in Jesus' encounter with Nicodemus (see John 3:8).

Next, there is fire. In this instance, a manifestation of the Spirit is tongues of fire, but throughout the pages of scripture the presence (Deuteronomy 5:4), guidance (Psalm 78:14), refining (Zechariah 13:9), character (Deuteronomy 4:24), and judgment (Isaiah 66:15) of God are represented by fire. In addition to the imagery found in scripture, we have also come to associate fire with the Spirit in our hymnody. Samuel Longfellow's hymn, "Holy Spirit, Truth Divine," prays, "Holy Spirit, love divine, glow within this heart of mine; kindle every high desire; perish self in thy pure fire." Likewise, Henry Tweedy sang, "O Spirit of the living God, thou light and fire divine...."

Perhaps the most amusing association with the Spirit on the Day of Pentecost was wine. The behavior of the Spirit-filled apostles led a few observers to think that they were drunk. While their conclusion was not correct, it was insightful. Paul himself implies some similarity between being filled with wine and being filled with the Spirit (Ephesians 5:18). The image is further reinforced in Peter's citing of Joel's prophecy that the Lord would "pour out" his Spirit (v. 18). The picturesque language suggests a kind of liquid abundance, as well as a new understanding of what it could mean to live "under the influence."

The two key validations of the Spirit's presence and work in his people are signs and scripture. "Signs" and "portents" (v. 19) are said to accompany the Spirit's work, which in this instance means the many tongues. And throughout the New Testament, signs and wonders give evidence of the Spirit's presence and power (Romans 15:19; Hebrews 2:4).

Signs, however, are not enough. They can be deceptive (see Matthew 24:24), and so the other validation is also required. Peter's reassurance to the marveling Pentecost crowd was that the signs taking place before their eyes had been foretold in scripture. Seeing the signs of God was not enough; they had to square with the word of God.

Romans 8:14-17

What line delineates between the people of God and the rest of the world? For some folks in ancient days, it was the line between circumcised and uncircumcised. For some folks today, perhaps it is baptism, church membership, or adherence to a certain doctrine or creed.

In the three lections for this week, the demarcation of the people of God seems to be the Spirit of God. The gift of the Spirit to the people of Cornelius' house became the persuasive proof for Peter and the early church (see Acts 11:15-18). Jesus said that his followers would receive the Spirit "whom the world cannot receive" (John 14:17). And here, in Paul's letter to the Romans, the apostle claims that "all who are led by the Spirit of God are children of God."

We may be uneasy with this delineation, for it seems a little out of our control. (We may have that in common with the Jewish Christians in the early church who were reluctant to welcome Gentiles.) Things like baptism, membership, and beliefs seem to be our choice. The Spirit, however, does not flow at our direction, but moves independently, like the wind (John 3:8).

The greater importance of what Paul says in our selected epistle lection for this week, however, is not how the Spirit delineates between different people, but rather how the Spirit delineates within an individual person. The delineation is between past and present, between old and new.

The apostle Paul presents us with a "before and after" portrait of ourselves. The "before" picture is that of a slave who cowers in fear. He is insecure in his role and in his relationship to his master. The slave is property, with a set (and limited) value. The "after" picture, by contrast, is that of a confident son. He is not property, but progeny. And while he, too, has been bought, his value is inestimable (see 1 Corinthians 6:19-20). He is utterly secure in his role and in his relationship with the God he knows as "Abba! Father!"

John 14:8-17 (25-27)

This selected passage might just as well be used on Trinity Sunday as Pentecost Sunday, for it presents us with much fodder for a study of the of the three persons of God. The Son is at the center of the episode, but the passage offers us great insight into the relationship among the members of the Trinity.

While the traditional Christology of the Nicene Creed affirms that Jesus is co-equal with the Father, his earthly posture is one of submission to the Father. Jesus' remarks here about the Father and the Spirit reveal a complex interrelationship and interdependence. The Son will ask the Father, and the Father will send the Spirit (v. 16), but the Father will send the Spirit in the Son's name, and the Spirit will remind them of what the Son said (v. 26).

Philip's request at the beginning of the passage is met by some disappointment from Jesus. "Have I been with you all this time, Philip, and you still do not know me?" Of course, we ought not judge Philip too harshly, for it's apparent in other passages that many or all of the disciples had been with Jesus for so long without knowing or understanding who he was (e.g., Matthew 28:17; Luke 24:25-27, 36-45).

The commendable thing about Philip, meanwhile, is that he has learned this much from Jesus: God is Father. Philip's expressed request was not to be shown "God," but specifically to be shown "the Father." So while Philip had not yet grasped the nature of the Trinity, he had begun at least to understand the nature of God.

Jesus' surprising answer, meanwhile, was that Philip had already seen the Father. Such is the inexplicable mystery of the Trinity: Jesus spoke of the Father in the third person and to the Father in the second person, yet still claimed that "whoever has seen me has seen the Father."

The beauty of the portrait of the Trinity here is that they do everything with and for one another: "I do not speak on my own"; "the Father may be glorified in the Son"; "I will ask the Father"; "he will give you another Advocate"; "the Father will send in my name"; and "the Holy Spirit... will... remind you of all that I have said to you." In total contrast to the self-seeking and self-serving that characterize the devil and fallen humanity, the persons of the Trinity are always serving and glorifying one another. That mysterious loving oneness is a model for marriage, as well as for the fellowship of believers, who are also meant to experience God's oneness (c.f., John 17:22-23).

Finally, the oneness of the Trinity is not a closed system. The three persons of God do not revolve around each other to the exclusion of everyone and everything else. Rather, we are the beneficiaries of God's readiness to share of himself (e.g., John 14:12-13, 16-17, 26), and we are graciously invited into that loving oneness of God (John 17:23).

Application

While Christmas and Easter enjoy almost unanimous celebration by Christians throughout our world, Pentecost receives a more uneven treatment. For some churches, they wouldn't know that Pentecost was a date on the church calendar if their pastor didn't tell them and many of their pastors don't tell them. Other congregations, by contrast, might be surprised — even offended — to discover that an observance of Pentecost was limited to just one single day in the year.

Different folks apply the story of Pentecost in different ways. For some, it is like the Crucifixion and Resurrection — a one-time event in history that has a once-and-for-all impact. For others, the event of Pentecost is viewed more like baptism — a one-time event in an individual's life, but not a once-and-for-all event in history. For others still, Pentecost is understood like other blessings from God (e.g., healing) — not merely limited to a single occasion but offered continually throughout a person's life.

Whatever your view or your congregation's understanding, we can take all three passages for this week together and agree at least on this: Whenever and wherever the Spirit moves in, things change.

The change manifested in the church in Acts 2 (and beyond) has several component parts.

First, the apostles come pouring out of the house where they were sitting and into the streets, proclaiming in every language the things of God. And that became the new posture of the church. No longer was it a "sit in one place all together" group. Now it had become a "pour out into the streets" group, proclaiming the good news throughout the world.

Second, we see a boldness in the apostolic church from this day forward. Peter, who just a few weeks before cowered at the suggestion that he might be associated with Jesus (e.g., Mark 14:66-72), now declared the name of Jesus in the streets. Two chapters later, he stood before the same group of leaders who had orchestrated Jesus' arrest and crucifixion, but he was unflinching and unwavering.

Finally, the Spirit's move into the church in Acts 2 was also manifested in signs and wonders. Page after page of the book of Acts reports the miracles and marvels that surrounded the work of the apostles.

Meanwhile, the Acts lection offers a glimpse into what happened to the church when the Spirit moved in, the John and Romans passages speak to us of what happens when the Spirit moves into an individual life. According to Christ's promise, the Spirit "will teach you everything" (John 14:26), as well as remind us of all that Jesus taught. According to Paul, it is this Spirit that confirms the change that has occurred in our relationship with God. Now that the Spirit has moved in, we have a new way of relating to God and a new understanding of ourselves, not as fearful slaves but as children who are joyfully confident in their Father's love.

Alternative Applications

Acts 2:1-21; John 14:8-17 (25-27). Pentecost is the holiday that comes after waiting. It is the celebration that comes only after some time passes.

Pentecost, as suggested even by the name (which refers to fifty days), required something of a countdown. The Old Testament law prescribed that the Israelites should "begin to count seven weeks from the time the sickle is first put to the standing grain" (Deuteronomy 16:9). Those seven sabbaths, plus the day after the seventh sabbath, represented the fifty days between the offering of first fruits, and this Pentecost (or Festival of Weeks) holiday. That was when the real harvest began.

The New Testament event we know as Pentecost was also a function of waiting. While Matthew's account of Jesus' ascension implies an immediate implementation of the Great Commission (Matthew 28:16-20), Luke's account features a specific instruction to wait (Acts 1:4-11). The global mission of Christ's followers remains in force, but Luke's record of Jesus' final instructions includes a prerequisite for that mission: to wait for the Holy Spirit and power (Acts 1:4-5, 8).

Jesus said that John baptized with water but that soon the disciples would be baptized with the Holy Spirit. So, it is that the first fruits are not the same thing as the full fruition. And Pentecost was the occasion when Christ's followers began the harvest in earnest.

Acts 2:1-21. When folks saw and heard the apostles on Pentecost, some assumed that the apostles must have been drunk. That was their limited way of explaining the apostles' appearance and behavior.

What do the folks who see and hear us assume? How do they explain our appearance and behavior?

It may be, of course, that there is nothing to explain. If we seem to be just essentially like everyone else, then that may be more an indictment of us than the Pentecost presumption that the apostles were drunk.

I wonder, too, if many of Christ's followers through the ages — perhaps including some of us — could never be mistaken for drunk simply because we seem irrepressibly sober.

I don't drink and so I am out of my league here, but I think I know what I would do if I wanted to keep a bit of a buzz on. I would start with a drink first thing in the morning. I would make sure always to have something with me — a bottle, a flask — so that I could imbibe continually throughout the day. A drink or two would accompany my lunch and my dinner. I would seek opportunities to get together with like-minded friends to get drunk together. And I would be sure to have a nightcap before bed.

That would be my approach if I wanted to live under the influence of alcohol. Perhaps it also serves as a model for how I might live under the influence of the Spirit. And then it might be my privilege, too, to be misunderstood by the people around me, just like those Spirit-filled forefathers in Jerusalem.

John 14:8-17 (25-27). I believe that Jesus' relationship with his twelve disciples serves as a model for his relationship with us. As we see him with them in the pages of scripture, we get a glimpse of how he deals with us — calling, correcting, teaching, reassuring, empowering, sending forth, and so on.

One of the components of Jesus' relationship with his original twelve disciples was the questions he would ask them. One penetrating question I believe he still asks many of us today is the one posed to Philip in this passage: "Have I been with you all this time and still you do not know me?"

The question has a thousand variations. Has this person been in church for so long without ever making a personal decision for Christ? Has this man believed for so long in the historical figure without knowing the living Lord? Has this woman cherished his teachings and example for so long without knowing his salvation? Has this preacher served him for so long without fully knowing his power or his presence?

Jesus seems surprised that Philip could have followed and seen and heard for those several years without coming to recognize fully who Jesus was. We might do well to ask ourselves and one another this Sunday if Jesus might be equally surprised and disappointed by us after "so long."

Holy Trinity Sunday
Proverbs 8:1-4, 22-31
Romans 5:1-5
John 16:12-15
Mark Molldrem

One God: Father, Son, and Holy Spirit

Christians are "stewards of the mysteries of God" (1 Corinthians 4:1). One of those mysteries is the self-revealed identity of God as Trinity. Christians themselves have had to struggle to understand what the Trinity means. The history of church theology is rife with heated conversations plumbing the depths of human insight on this subject. From Irenaeus in the second century to Augustine in the fifth century, the church forged basic formulas and commentaries that have since then shaped Christian thought on the matter. (It was in 381 at the council of Constantinople that the Trinitarian formula of the one God existing co-equally in three persons was first formally adopted. All three of the Ecumenical Creeds — Apostles', Nicene, and Athanasian — express this.) The Trinity has been a stumbling block for non-Christian faith systems to grasp what Christians in fact believe, let alone become convinced that Christianity contains the essential wisdom that perceives God's disclosure in the world.

The danger in the culture of the West, of which we are the heirs, is that there is an unholy trinity that strives to usurp the affections of the would-be faithful. Power, possession, and pleasure lure the hearts of all who search for God down deadly, blind alleys. Momentary satisfactions replace the deeper contentment in the truth. The eyes of our heart are not enlightened by an enduring relationship with the God who is; rather, the eyes of our heart are merely delighted by passing fancies that fail to fill the empty hole that is left by squandered efforts.

The texts assigned for this festival day celebrating the Trinity invite us to explore more deeply the nature of God's self-revelation, so that we may better understand the God who is and may better give an account of the gift of faith that is within us.

Proverbs 8:1-4, 22-31

Proverbs is typical of the wisdom genre that comprises a portion of the Old Testament literature. It does not rank equally with the law and the prophets or even the histories; but, it is valued nevertheless. It makes clear repeatedly that wisdom is to be found in the fear of the Lord. It describes the ways of the righteous and it gives practical insights on daily living and relationships. Truth be told, Proverbs 8:1-21 would have been a better pericope for this Sunday. But, since it has not been assigned as such, attention will be paid to those verses that have been assigned. Let the preacher be encouraged to explore verses 5-21 for added insights and images that can be used effectively in drawing out more fully the content of this discussion.

Just as Mexico markets itself in attractive ads in the first person ("I am ancient... I have many stories to tell"), the writer of Proverbs knows how to grab our attention, even when talking about something as ethereal as wisdom. Wisdom is personified as one standing by the gate, calling out to those who pass by, getting them to turn their heads and take heed to what is being said. Interestingly, wisdom, a word of the feminine gender, is described as being created by God (8:22), being brought forth (8:24) at the beginning of the generating acts of God. Wisdom is not God, but is beside God, like a *master workman or as a little child* (8:30). Wisdom neither stands as God nor in the place of God but *before him* (8:30), expressing mirth in the acts of God manifested throughout the creation (8:31). With this in mind, it makes no sense at all to elevate Wisdom (Sophia) to the role of recipient of our prayers or adoration, as some contemporary worship planners do.

Wisdom is part of the created order. Just like the sculpted body points to the heavenly sculptor and just like the painted sunset points to the heavenly artist, so too does wisdom point to the one who does all things well. The litany of creation is Wisdom's affirmation of the thoroughness of God's design (for example, 8:29) and a way to give glory to God, the originator of it all. This is part of Job's wisdom insight, that all things belong to God and are held in his hand (Job 1:21). Therefore, come what may, glory and honor are to be given to God. This is an expression of "the fear of the Lord" and finds its proper posture kneeling in ashes on a dung heap, repenting.

Since Wisdom is part of the established order, it is an immanent expression of God the Father, Creator of heaven and earth. Paul appeals to this aspect of God's self-disclosure in Romans 1:20-21 and again in Acts 17:22-28. So does Peter in Acts 10:34-35. What can be known of God is by necessity accessible to humanity in terms of awareness; the experience of God in the world makes sense to the other experiences of human existence. Proverbs 8:17 comments on this, giving positive encouragement to those who diligently seek the Lord: Lover and beloved will be united; seeker and the sought will be brought together.

This having been said, it must be admitted that sin clouds our understanding and even our ability to receive the truth; so, more of God's activity in self-disclosure needs to be forthcoming. It is not that there is something faulty with God's efforts to make himself known to us and beloved by us; it is that the fullness of God begs further expression and this, in fact, proves itself capable of penetrating the barriers that sin erects between us and God.

Romans 5:1-5

Don't miss the mighty "therefore" (5:1) that Paul uses to make a bridge between what he has already spelled out (especially in Romans 3:21—4:25) and what is to follow (especially Romans 5-8)! This is important because there is a decision that needs to be made in how one preaches this text. Is it proclamation or invitation? It all depends on what ancient manuscripts you accept as most authoritative. Arguments can be made on both sides in terms of the number of supporting manuscripts and in terms of the precedence of alternative traditions. However, when one looks at the context and the entire theology of Paul, the weight of the argument shifts to accepting in 5:1 (over the alternative reading), as presented in the Nestle-Aland and also Westcott-Hort text.

The key rests in the conjunction "therefore," as well as in the construction of (functioning like a gerund in English, "being justified"). Paul has made the case so far in his letter that justification is a gift of God's grace through the work of Jesus on the cross (Romans 3:21-26). *Therefore*, "we have peace with God" (5:1). This is declaratory; it is not an invitation into what might be. If Paul wrote this letter as email, he would have CAPITALIZED everything to emphasize his point! (Note: not in anger, but in joy, as he soon states!) Paul is proclaiming a new state of affairs, described in the present tense. It is a *fait accompli*, accented by his use of the perfect form of the verb "have" (5:2).

Paul acknowledges the work of Jesus as establishing the ground on which the believer can gracefully stand. He then applies the wisdom of faith to the hard realities of the believer's life, characterized by suffering. Suffering bears fruit: endurance, character, and hope (5:3-4). These are blessings from God (the Father), which reward the faithful witness who suffers for the name of Jesus. The practical result is a hope that does not disappoint, because it is confirmed by the Holy Spirit, which is present as a gift from God. This hope sets one's vision on the glory of God that is coming and will be shared with the believers in Jesus. It is not unlike the marathon runner who visualizes the tape at the finish line, an image that keeps drawing the runner step by step closer to the desired goal of finishing the race as the victor.

Using the Trinitarian formula, one could express the message of this passage in this way: The believer's relationship with God the heavenly Father is now one of peace because of the justifying work of Jesus on the cross, a work imparted by the Holy Spirit, giving one strength and confidence for all circumstances in life.

John 16:12-15

Nestled in the midst of Jesus' farewell to his disciples (John 16 and 17) after the Passover supper on Thursday night of Holy Week, Jesus speaks of the dynamic expression of God as Father, Son, and Holy Spirit. As the Son, he announces that he is heir to all that is the Father's. He also states that the Holy Spirit will take what is the Son's and declare it to the disciples. Through Jesus, the disciples will experience the fullness of God: himself as the Son, the Father who sent him, and the Holy Spirit who will be sent by him.

Jesus is the essential revelation of God, but he is not the complete revelation of God. Remember, he admitted that he did not know the hour of the day of the Lord (Mark 13:32); nor, was he able to impart to the disciples all that he wanted to. It would be necessary for the Holy Spirit to come and continue the self-revelation of God and lead those who believe into fuller communion with God, their creator and redeemer and sanctifier.

The Holy Spirit has a specific function in the divine economy. He is to apply the truth of Jesus to the lives of the disciples and all those who would come after them in faith. The Holy Spirit would specifically be about the business of giving witness to Jesus. "He will glorify me" (16:14). There certainly are many truths in the world worth knowing, just as there are many aspects of wisdom that the human mind is capable of grasping. But, the truth that the Holy Spirit is concerned with, just as the wisdom that biblical Wisdom is concerned with, is that which relates particularly to the Godhead and one's relationship to God in living faith.

These few verses in John's gospel are similar to other texts in the New Testament that are rendered with a Trinitarian formulation. Look, for example, at Matthew 28:19; John 16:1-11; Acts 1:1-5; Ephesians 1:3-14; Colossians 1:1-8; and 1 Thessalonians 1:1-10. The scripture writers knew that to speak about the fullness of God, they would need to speak of the Father, the Son, and the Holy Spirit. Anything short of that would diminish our experience and understanding of the one God, who reveals himself in these dynamic co-eternal and co-equal persons.

Application

Whether American politics can rise above its ground level of power, pragmatism remains to be seen. Perhaps it never can but hope rests eternal with every new election and the rising of a new generation into the fray. Of late, it cannot be said that we have leaders who exemplify wisdom and character in their statesmanship. Maybe such qualities are recognized only in retrospect and are granted only by a narrowed focus of memory. It remains true, however, that there is a general groundswell calling for rising above trivial pursuits of partisan politics and attaining to what would truly be advantageous for the common good of the many. For this to occur, wisdom will need to be sought after. It will be found ultimately and truly in God and it will be received by men and women only as a gift from God.

If Wisdom stands at the gate and calls out for adherents, then those who would be blessed by her instruction would best be found in petition on their knees. As Wisdom herself acknowledges the greatness of God and rejoices before God, then those who would be wise must learn the humility of receiving wisdom as a gift from God. To prepare with humility, one can engage the discipline of prayer and the focus on *the other* (as Dietrich Bonhoeffer taught us). For wisdom of which the Bible speaks does not serve self-aggrandizement but rather the lifting up and the building up of *the other*. Here the true intentionality of politics finds its expression. Here the Christian can heartily engage in the business of politics on every level — in the neighborhood, at school, within city management, for county and state and national government, and as an international advocate on issues that eventually affect all of us. In our ever-shrinking and more complex world, wisdom is a gift to be sought for the well-being of the community, more so than for individual decisions pertaining to one's own life exclusively (if even this were possible!). As one former president said, "Ask not what your country can do for you; ask what you can do for your country." As another president has said, "I ask you to seek a common good beyond your comfort."

God the Father, as creator, is the source of this wisdom and the one to whom such petitions are directed. When we pray in the Lord's Prayer to our heavenly Father, we ask that his will be done on earth as in heaven. This will of God is the wisdom for which we seek. To perceive God's will in any situation will give wisdom for one's response and consequential decisions and actions.

When Jesus was asked in John 6:28, "What must we do, to be doing the works of God?" he could just as easily have been asked about doing the will of God or living according to the wisdom of God. The response would have been the same at any rate: *believe in the Lord Jesus, whom the Father has sent into the world* (John 6:29). This is the central affirmation that has drawn Roman Catholics and Lutherans around the world together in new ways recently, manifested by the signing of the *Document on the Doctrine of Justification* (fall 1999) and celebrated together by Catholic and Lutheran siblings in Christ around the world.

How comforting a word to hear that peace is already the character of our relationship with God because of the work already accomplished by Jesus on the cross. It is "a done deal"! Now, we can simply rest in it and cease our striving to earn God's favor. We already *are* standing in the grace of God; *this* is the ground of our hope, our confidence about the future quality of our existence, whether delimited by time or by eternity.

This allows us, with Paul, to view the up-side of suffering. It becomes the opportunity to develop and manifest endurance and character and hope, giving glory to Jesus — the one who suffered the most for us. It would be helpful here to read the sequence of Paul's writing not in a linear fashion but in a circular one. There is a dynamic relationship between suffering, endurance, character, and hope. It is not so much that one leads reasonably and sequentially into the others. There is a creative tension between all of these qualities of Christian life that feed into and feed from the others. It has been said, "Sports does not build character; it reveals it." In one sense that is true; but in another sense it is true that sports builds the character it longs to show. So too, suffering can at times produce endurance, which in turn builds character, which is fertile ground for hope; but, it is also true that the confidence of hope generates and strengthens a new character that enables one to endure the harshest of realities. If one can picture such a "wheel of fortune," the cross of Christ would be its axle.

The Christian can have the confidence that God is faithful in the self-revelation of the divine economy. What is the Father's belongs to the Son, which in turn is passed on by the Holy Spirit to those who believe. Unlike the telephone relay game which ends up with a message that is totally foreign to the original, what the Holy Spirit imparts to longing hearts is the essential truth that arises from the very heart of the Father and is passed to the Son. This is why Jesus can refer to "the Spirit of truth" (16:13) and Paul can pray that the disciples receive "a spirit of wisdom and of revelation in the knowledge of him" (Ephesians 1:17).

Christians are encouraged to pray daily to be led by the Holy Spirit. Our confidence, based upon the promises of scripture, is that the Holy Spirit is working to bring us into the full knowledge of the truth (see Ephesians 1:17-18). This truth is more than wisdom; it is more than information about Jesus; it is more than the perception of where the Holy Spirit is indeed working. It is a truth that centers itself in a living, growing relationship between the believer and Jesus the Messiah. It is a truth that blossoms into "the fear of the Lord" (Proverbs 9:10), inspired by the work of the Holy Spirit who unwraps, like a gift, a fuller experience of God in the world, including one's own individual life.

Proper 4 / Pentecost 2 / Ordinary Time 9
1 Kings 18:20-21 (22-29) 30-39
Galatians 1:1-12
Luke 7:1-10
Wayne Brouwer

The united colors of faith

The Italian-based clothing company Benetton Group has captured worldwide attention with its global ad campaigns simply titled "The United Colors of Benetton." Using gripping images and striking hues, the billboards portray people in real-life settings (rather than coiffed and posed models in a studio) wearing textiles produced under their brand. The implication is that no one size fits all, and that among the many varieties of cultures and experiences, Benetton engages and adapts.

This is a fitting analogy for the expressions of faith in today's lectionary passages. Elijah calls Israel to return to faith in Yahweh after the powerful showdown with the Baal minions of Ahab and Jezebel on Mount Carmel. Paul wrestles for the soul of the Galatian congregations who have quickly transformed saving faith into a Christianized version of works righteousness. And Jesus marvels at the trust of a man who commands others but now bows in submission. The many colors of faith, displayed in every congregation of God's people.

1 Kings 18:20-21 (22-29) 30-39

When the grand kingdom of David and Solomon became divided, its theological mission as witness to the nations was compromised. Yet the perspective of kings is that the northern tribes (now "Israel") and the southern portion (now "Judah") were never truly separated. Throughout the rest of these narratives the political fortunes of both territories were equally considered. Furthermore, the kings of both realms were similarly judged by the prophetic author as either following in the ways of David and Solomon (thus seeking to fulfill the destiny intended by Yahweh) or compounding the covenant-breaking of those who caused the nation to stray from its divine calling and mission. This is most obvious in the harsh assessments given at the time of the northern kingdom's destruction by the Assyrians (2 Kings 17).

In this connection it is interesting to note the emerging and changing role of the public "prophets." Moses and Joshua each had a unique and on-going relational interchange with Yahweh that made their leadership positions virtually unassailable (cf. Numbers 12, 16-17). After the nation was settled in Canaan, such clear, regular, and unequivocal communication with Yahweh appears to have been muted. During the times of Eli, we are told, "the word of the Lord was rare; there were not many visions" (1 Samuel 3:1). That is why, when Yahweh began speaking directly with Samuel, the Israelites were ready to follow him (1 Samuel 3:19-21). This seems to be the beginning of a national recognition of the status of prophets as part of the necessary social fabric.

When Samuel's leadership was challenged because the people wanted a king (1 Samuel 8), it caused the first subtle separation of church and state. Samuel was a priest by adoption and worked within the parameters of the cultic shrine. But the kings were clearly outside of the Levitical priesthood or its extended family. Prophets at first began to bridge the connection and then later sparred with the kings as the sovereignty role of Yahweh was increasingly forgotten.

This tension is clearly seen in the dominant stories of Elijah and Elisha who battled with the rulers of the northern kingdom in 1 Kings 17—2 Kings 8. Elijah was given the weapons of the curses of the Sinai covenant to bring Ahab and Jezebel to their knees (1 Kings 17:1). He wielded divine power in public displays of combat (1 Kings 18). He was authorized to determine and appoint the leaders of nations (1 Kings

19). When Ahab and Jezebel presumed that they could displace God-fearing Israelites from their divinely determined inheritance in the land (1 Kings 21), Elijah confronted the pair with stern prophecies that they instead would be removed.

Today's lectionary passage is at the heart of this conflict. The question of "who is the true king in Israel?" is tied to religious worship. Indeed, as David and Solomon knew, human regents can never usurp the divine right of Yahweh to claim Israel's royal allegiance. It is precisely because Ahab has become a charlatan intruder, multiplying his crimes against the true king of the nation by marrying Jezebel and allowing her to rewrite the religious agenda of the realm, that Elijah moves in to reassert the rights of Yahweh. The issue on Mount Carmel is not really about which God or gods can perform magic tricks on command, but who will own Israel's heart. Jezebel has coupled herself to Ahab and manipulates the religion of Baal to coerce their citizens into zombie-like subservience. Elijah wishes no one to worship him but seeks rather to break the spell of the wicked witch so Israel can return to its full human potential as the people of Yahweh. This is seen in the rousing final cry of those gathered: "Yahweh, he is God! Yahweh, he is God!"

While today's passage does not take into account the return of the rains after three years of drought, it would be good to mention this context for the Mount Carmel showdown. The Sinai covenant that shaped Israel's identity, bound her to Yahweh. It also included the "Blessings and Curses" section (Exodus 23:20-33, and expanded in Leviticus 26) that warned Israel about the consequences of turning away from Yahweh. Specifically identified among the curses was drought. When Israel, under the magnetic warping of Jezebel's weird ways, left Yahweh, it was not Elijah but Yahweh who brought the drought, hoping for Israel to remember and return. Now that Israel has resoundingly made again a declaration of faith in Yahweh, the rains will return.

Galatians 1:1-12

During a prayer meeting in the church of Antioch, probably in early 48 AD, the gathered group received a very strong divine message that their primary leadership team was supposed to be sent on a missionary journey (Acts 13:1-3). We do not have details about how the plans were laid, but it is reasonable to suppose that they arranged a trip into familiar territory. Cyprus was Barnabas' home turf, and it may well be that after they blitzed across that island they intended to travel back to Antioch along the Pamphylian coast, stopping briefly in Tarsus along the way.

Indeed, they traveled the length of Cyprus, preaching along the way and then boarded boats for the mainland. But at the seaport of Perga, John Mark left them and "returned to Jerusalem" (Acts 13:13). Also, it seems that Paul might have gotten sick at that point in their travels. What the illness was, is not certain, but when he later wrote to those he and Barnabas met in the highlands of central Asia Minor, he reminded them that "it was because of an illness that I first preached the gospel to you" (Galatians 4:13). A further clue to these events is found in Paul's later cryptic testimony that something was wrong with his eyes (Galatians 4:15). Since the Pamphylian coastline is marshy and mosquito-ridden, it might have been malaria that laid Paul low. That would explain why the team went immediately up into the highlands, rather than continuing along the shore.

In Pisidian Antioch Paul preached a historical review of God's work in the synagogue, leading finally to a message about Jesus being the messiah. A week later "almost the whole city" came out, for this new gospel was creating quite a stir. While many believed, jealous Jews incited a riot that forced Paul and Barnabas out of the synagogue. They spent the next days in the marketplace, speaking to Gentiles as well as Jews. But the animosity was building and soon the travelers were forced from the city (Acts 13:14-31).

Down the road, at a smaller town named Iconium, Paul and Barnabas again preached in the Jewish synagogue to good response. Like before, growing Jewish resentment caused them to turn to the Gentiles. Soon a plot against them was discovered, and they moved on again (Acts 14:1-7).

At Lystra the pair encountered a crippled man just outside of town. He was begging for alms, but Paul raised him up healed. This caused a serious commotion and the entire population turned out to worship Paul and Barnabas as Hermes and Zeus, key leaders among the Greek gods. When Paul convinced them that he and his companions were only human, worship turned to disgust, and enemies who had dogged their heels from Antioch turned the crowds against them. They were stoned and left for dead. Fortunately some sympathetic care providers nurtured back the almost extinguished sparks of life in them, and after a short while of secretive recovery, they moved on again (Acts 14:8-20).

Traveling briefly to nearby Derbe (Acts 14:21), the team preached about Jesus and then wended their way home. They stopped briefly in each highland community where they had recently spent a few days or weeks, appointing elders in the new Christian congregations (Acts 14: 22-25). Returning to Syrian Antioch, they brought a report of their mission journey to their home congregation (Acts 14:26-28).

That's when the trouble started (Acts 15; Galatians 2). Reports of Gentile converts to Christianity sizzled toward Jerusalem. Peter came up to Antioch to celebrate this exciting mission work, but others with less enthusiasm were soon sent by James (the brother of Jesus and leader of the Jerusalem congregation) to ensure that all was happening in an appropriate manner. These representatives announced that Gentiles had to become Jews in belief and practice before they could become part of the Christian church. After all, Jesus was Jewish, and was being acclaimed as the Messiah foretold by Israel's prophets.

These ambassadors of the Jerusalem church instituted separated meal and communion practices, making it clear that only those who were ceremonially pure could take positions of leadership in the community. Much to Paul's surprise, even Peter allied himself with those advocating these discriminating practices. Paul, of course, was anything but timid and accosted Peter publicly, creating even stronger polarization among the congregations on these matters.

The disease of Jewish superiority spread to the churches of Paul's and Barnabas' recent mission journey and threatened to split the infant Christian community before it had even an opportunity to get started. In response, Paul dashed off a letter to the churches of "Galatia," the Roman district through which they had traveled on their mission trek.

In the first part of this passionate letter (Galatians 1-2), Paul reviewed his personal journey to an understanding of freedom in Christ and lamented the recent developments that had seemingly stolen away this freedom from many of them. Next (Galatians 3-4) Paul went into a lengthy Jewish rabbinic argument about how Abraham was counted as "righteous" in his relationship with God already before he entered into the rituals of circumcision. Paul concluded that neither circumcision nor any other ceremonial expression was absolutely necessary for a meaningful relationship with God, and that Jesus' recent teachings, death, and resurrection only reaffirmed and expanded this truth. In fact, said Paul, the "law" (that is, the ceremonial dimensions of the Sinai covenant) was like a teacher who was no longer needed after a child became fully mature. Using a rabbinic allegory, Paul pointed Hagar and her son Ishmael as representations of Abraham's "slave" side of the family, regulated by the social codes from Mount Sinai. Sarah and her son Isaac, on the other hand, were symbols of Abraham's "free" side of the family and lived out of the delight that was expressed through ecstatic worship in Jerusalem. In the final portion of his letter (Galatians 5-6), Paul used very strong language to urge the expression of true freedom in Christ. This is found in neither the legalism of ritual religious regimens that bind and burden, nor in licentiousness that turns us evil and ugly. Rather, true Christian freedom is experienced when we no longer consider ourselves under external demands that have no important ends in themselves, but when we voluntarily give ourselves as slaves to God and others out of love. In this context there can be no division between "Jewish Christians" and "Gentile Christians," for the church of Jesus Christ has become the new "Israel of God" (Galatians 6:16).

It is in this context that today's harsh words from Paul emerge. They are aimed at recent converts who were already deeply religious when they came to trust in Jesus as Messiah and Savior. But in their passion to do the right things and be good for God, they began quickly to focus on what they could bring to the table and forgot the grace that saved them.

Luke 7:1-10

John Calvin said that there were two aspects to faith: *assentia* and *fiducia*. The first we often translate as "assent." It is in this dimension of faith that we acknowledge that something exists. *Assentia* is knowing something factually or knowing about someone only from a distance.

Calvin's second aspect of faith might well be termed "trust." It is a heart engagement, involving us personally in an emotional attachment with whatever we might have previously acknowledged only intellectually.

Take a chair, for instance. *Assentia* is our willingness to say that it could hold the person daring to sit on it. *Fiducia*, on the other hand, is the act of sitting on that chair ourselves, trusting its sturdiness to hold our bulk. Both are elements of faith. Both are important. But until the latter is added to the former, faith remains inert, distant, intellectual, impersonal.

The story in today's gospel reading offers strong incentive for us to get beyond talking about God and getting on with the business of engaging God as an active partner in our lives. Faith talk means little if we demand and coerce (like the good ruler knew he could do with his underlings) while never giving ourselves over to the necessary trust factor. This is the marvel that Jesus announces to others. Even God's historic people seem addicted to *assentia* without a lot of show of *fiducia*.

Dr. E. Stanley Jones told of an incident from his missionary days that illustrates James' point. A young girl was tired of things at home, said Jones. She longed for the freedom of the streets and the excitement of the nightlife. She ran away to a large city. It wasn't long before she fell under the spell of a pimp and was degraded into a prostitute.

The girl's mother was beside herself with anxiety. It was true that things hadn't been going right between them, but a mother's love is restless and protective, and she had to find her daughter again. She remembered the child who sat on her lap, and the daughter who whispered in her ear and needed somehow to renew their bond of trust.

Yet how should she begin the search? All she had heard were rumors about daughter, thirdhand reports that she was now wasting her body in the red-light district. The mother went to the city and simply began to walk, hoping to stumble across someone who might know her daughter. Up one street and down the next she trudged, talking to anyone who would listen, hoping for a clue to follow.

But to no avail. Her daughter didn't want to be found: shame, rebellion, spite. Who can say what reasons mingle in our deceptive minds?

Eventually the quest tired even the mother. But before she returned home, she did one more thing. She carried a photograph that had been taken several years before, a picture of the two of them, mother and daughter, at a happier moment in both their lives. She got the photograph enlarged and made dozens of copies. Then she scattered those pictures around the area, hoping that one would catch her daughter's eye.

On each photo she penned these five words: **Come home! I love you!**

One day the girl did see. She began to remember what love was all about. A holy restless gripped her soul, battering her resentment until she had to call her mother. The next day she was home.

Never once did the daughter stop *assenting* to the fact that she had a mother. But it wasn't until her mother's love called out the *trust* of her heart that she believed in all that "home" and "mother" and "love" could mean to her personally.

If Jesus were to take a picture of your faith today, like he did with the ruler in today's lectionary reading, how much depth would it show?

Application

Stories of conversion are not enough to sustain faith or to explore the wonder of life in the Promised Land of God's kingdom. Faith needs to grow. Horizons need to expand. Insights need to connect and skills of service need to be put to use. Most of all, dependence on God needs to multiply.

Growth in the Christian faith happens in several directions at once. As we move on from our first profession of faith we all need to increase our knowledge of the teachings of the Bible and the insights of the church's theology. Second, we need to develop our ability to understand our spiritual gifts and passions in order to take our place in the Christ-service of his body, the church. Third, we need to learn the vocabulary of faith so that we can communicate intelligently to others of the things God is doing inside of us and the vision he has for the world and eternity. Fourth, we need constantly to groom our understanding of the meaning and character of relationships so that we can live as supportive social beings. Fifth, we need to foster the intuitive dimension of our personalities in order to catch the wind of the Spirit and sail the seas of grace. Sixth, we need to strengthen our wills to be able to keep us compassionately strong through times of great stress and upheaval. Seventh, we need to deepen love as we practice care, living as God's signs of new life. These are among the many colors of faith.

The old hymn says, "Change and decay in all around I see." The changing face of life creates a kind of mist in which we can wander aimlessly or become silly in our self-importance. Yet there is also a lot of health in the changes that take place among people who are always growing. The only time we truly stop changing is when we die. More than that, the only time we truly grow well is when we grow in trust.

An Alternative Application

Luke 7:1-10. Even Charles Darwin was impressed by Christian faith that breathed through responsible Christian living, like that of the ruler in today's gospel reading. Darwin had disowned the Christianity of his childhood and was sailing for five years around South America in search of confirmation to his theories of natural selection and evolutionary development. When he stopped for a while at Tierra del Fuego he found a community that defied his prescriptions for normal human development. Under the teaching and ministry of a man named Thomas Bridges the whole society was being transformed into something better than it used to be.

The power in Thomas Bridges' leadership came from his own story. He was abandoned as a baby on the banks of the Thames in London, England. Passers-by heard his feeble cries and rescued him barely alive. It happened on St. Thomas' Day near several bridges over the river, so they called him Thomas Bridges. The family that raised him as their own gave him confidence in the love of Jesus. Though abandoned by his mother, he learned the power of faith that lives through deeds of those who care.

That is why he became a missionary of Jesus Christ and the reason his words, coupled with actions, rang with power. Even Charles Darwin, as he was becoming an atheist, supported Thomas Bridges financially for the rest of his life. Here was faith that made a difference and that was something the world needed more than another scientific theory.

Such faith is a marvel and a great example, as Jesus noted in response to the ruler's simple expressions. Assent wed to trust makes a profound declaration of faith, then *and* now.

Proper 5 / Pentecost 3 / ORDINARY TIME 10
1 Kings 17:8-16 (17-24)
Galatians 1:11-24
Luke 7:11-17
David Kalas

Distinguishing features

When our people hear these three passages read during our worship services this Sunday, they will see the immediate connection between the Old Testament and gospel readings. In both instances, a poor widow loses a son to death. And, in both instances, the man of God restores the young man to life.

The two stories are beautiful.

We begin by recognizing the unspeakable sadness of a parent losing a child. Certain kinds of grief and loss we expect in life, but not this. Even in our marriage vows we recognize the death that will part us. But no parent figures to outlive their child.

The sadness is doubled in the case of these women, for they are both widows. They have already experienced loss inasmuch as their husbands have died. This is grief upon grief for these poor women.

They are, almost certainly, poor women. The grief of death is further complicated by the economic reality for widows in that time and place. We will explore that issue in more detail below, but suffice it to say that these women shared the prospect of being destitute in the wake of losing their sons.

Finally, there is this tragic detail: The deceased sons are the only sons. One child surely does not replace another. Still, there is comfort for a grieving parent in the child or children that remain. But these two women have no such comfort.

Against that backdrop of tremendous sadness, God does his gracious and powerful work. This is the very recipe of the Bible's most beautiful stories: God's lovely work against the backdrop of human sadness. It is there in Israel's miraculous deliverance from slavery and in each of Jesus' healings. It is given voice in the comforting message of Isaiah 40 and seen in the gracious timing of Christ's saving death (Romans 5:8).

So, while we are presented this week with two conspicuously similar stories, those similarities are not the whole story. There is a larger pattern of God's work to be seen and to be celebrated.

1 Kings 17:8-16 (17-24)

Elijah arrives on the Bible's stage without introduction. He appears suddenly here in 1 Kings 17, with no reference to his calling as his prophet, his family background, or his personal biography. We are simply told that he is from Tishbe in Gilead. The exact identity and location of Tishbe is uncertain. Gilead, meanwhile, was the hilly, trans-Jordan region between the Sea of Galilee to the north and the Dead Sea in the south.

Next thing we know, this unidentified Tishbite has an audience with Ahab, the notorious king of Israel. His message is no-nonsense and bold: a chastening drought is on Israel's horizon, and Elijah controls the spigot.

It's an astonishing claim for some nobody from nowhere to make to a king. After all, in a world of thrones and monarchs, it is the king's word that holds sway. He is the one who speaks and makes things happen. Yet Ahab is powerless in this circumstance. His royal edicts make no difference to the sun and clouds. Instead, nature will respond only to Elijah's word.

In preparation for the drought, God makes provisions for his prophet. Specifically, we see two forms of providence: by natural means (the birds and the brook) and by human means (the poor widow). In either case, of course, Elijah's ultimate reliance was on God, yet it is always instructive for us to see the variety of ways by which God accomplishes his provident care and purpose. It is also noteworthy that Elijah's first source from God eventually dried up. The need exceeded that particular resource, though it did not exhaust the provider.

On the national stage, where the story began, we know that the drought eventually led to a confrontation with the king and a showdown with the doomed representatives of Baal on Mount Carmel. But our passage does not return to that broader, national focus. Instead, we move deeper into the personal story of the particular widow whom God used to provide for Elijah. (Or was it that God used Elijah to provide for the widow?)

That personal story turns tragic when the widow's son dies. The medical cause of death is vague, but "medical" isn't where the mother's mind turns anyway. Her response — "What have you against me, O man of God? You have come to me to bring my sin to remembrance, and to cause the death of my son!" — is poignantly true to life. Even in our sophisticated medical age, still our instinct in the face of tragic death is to seek spiritual answers or to assume spiritual causes. The doctor can explain that the child died of leukemia, but we still want the Omnipotent to answer for why the child contracted leukemia in the first place. And so we shake our fists at God for allowing — indeed, perhaps for causing — such calamity.

Interestingly, the prophet of God does not disabuse the woman of her paradigm. He does not take her aside and explain that what she's feeling is perfectly natural, while assuring her that God does not deliberately kill children. Instead, he echoed the very same complaint in prayer: "O Lord my God, have you brought calamity even upon the widow with whom I am staying, by killing her son?"

Scripture does not confirm Elijah's paradigm of cause-and-effect. On the contrary, it simply says that the son "became ill" and that "his illness was so severe that there was no breath left in him." Yet God does answer Elijah's request for the boy's life to be restored.

The miraculous resuscitation seems to be a combination of intercession and ancient CPR. In the end, the boy came back to life, and he is returned to his grieving mother. Interestingly, it is because of this event that she believes Elijah is a "man of God," though she had already witnessed miracles through Elijah (vv. 15-16) and had previously referred to him as a man of God (v. 18). Evidently whatever doubts had been raised by her son's death were put to rest when her son was raised.

Galatians 1:11-24

Unlike our lections from 1 Kings and Luke, this passage is not a story. Still, there is a story behind it. In order for our people to grasp the meaning of the passage, they will need to have an appreciation for the background story. That context has three elements: geographical, personal, and theological.

Geographically, we need simply to observe that Galatia was a region, not a city. While the epistles to the Romans, Corinthians, Philippians, and Thessalonians were all written to the believers in certain cities, Galatia was an entire province in Asia Minor (what we could call modern-day Turkey), where Paul spent many of his missionary miles.

That leads us to the personal context. The Christians in much of Galatia were personally known to Paul. He was the evangelist who had brought them the gospel of Jesus. He had led them to Christ, founded their churches, and maintained a personal sense of spiritual responsibility for them. The letter from which our selected lection comes, therefore, is personal correspondence.

Finally, the theological context is perhaps the most important layer of all. The Galatians have been infiltrated by a group sometimes referred to as "Judaizers." These Jewish Christians evidently taught that in order to be a Christian, a person must still observe certain requirements of the Old Testament law (e.g., circumcision of the males). This was not an entirely implausible argument within its original setting. Inasmuch as the Jews understood that the law was the full expression of the will of God, as well as the terms of his covenant with his people, it seemed to many earnest Jewish Christians to discount or cast aside any requirements of the law. Can we imagine some new wave of God's work that would nullify the Sermon on the Mount?

Some of the believers in Galatia apparently had acquiesced to the Judaizers' paradigm, and so the apostle Paul wrote to correct them. A reading of the larger letter reveals that his correction was candid (1:6; 3:1), impassioned (1:8-9), and sometimes even sarcastic (3:5; 5:11-12).

Because Paul perceived the Galatians as having turned to a different gospel (1:6), it was his endeavor to reassert the true gospel that he had previously proclaimed. To that end, he needed to establish two things: 1) the authority of that gospel; and 2) the credibility of its messenger.

As to the authority of the gospel, Paul's primary argument is that the gospel he had proclaimed was from God and not from human beings. We see here the recurring theme: "not of human origin," "I did not receive it from a human source, nor was I taught it," "I did not confer with any human being, nor did I go up to Jerusalem to those who were already apostles before me," "I did not see any other apostle except James the Lord's brother," and "I was still unknown by sight to the churches of Judea that are in Christ." Instead, he insists that he "received it through a revelation of Jesus Christ."

The distinction reminds us of Jesus' response to Peter's recognition that he was the Christ: "Flesh and blood has not revealed this to you, but my Father in heaven" (Matthew 16:17). It is an epistemological issue, and Paul is making the grand claim that his source of knowledge and truth was neither mortal nor traditional, but divine.

Meanwhile, this gospel of divine origin still had a human advocate, and so Paul felt the need also to establish his credibility as a messenger. Accordingly, he reminded the Galatians about his own history — his "earlier life in Judaism." We remember that his opponents in this controversy, the Judaizers, were perceived as zealous for God's law. And so Paul sought to establish the credentials of his own zeal, lest he be misunderstood as a rogue who was unserious about the law of God. His resume includes "advanc(ing) in Judaism beyond many," as well as being "far more zealous for the traditions of my ancestors." Also, the regrettable fact that he "violently persecute(ed) the church of God and was trying to destroy it" is considered a mark in his favor within this context.

The argument is reminiscent of portions of 2 Corinthians, in which Paul is similarly combating certain teachings and teachers in that church. In order to defeat the influence of the so-called "super-apostles" (2 Corinthians 11:5), Paul asserts his own spiritual credentials, even though he finds the exercise distasteful (2 Corinthians 11:21).

Having established the authority of the gospel he preached, as well as his credentials as the preacher, Paul is ready to proceed with the rest of his letter, correcting the Galatians and reminding them of the truth of the good news.

Luke 7:11-17

The town of Nain was another of the villages in the northern region of Galilee, the region where Jesus spent so much of his ministry. This episode is the only reference to Nain in all of scripture. Unlike some other Galilean sites — e.g., Capernaum, Nazareth, Bethsaida, Magdala — we don't have any other accounts of Jesus' activity in Nain and so this event is its sole claim to fame.

Luke reports that as Jesus was just arriving on the outskirts of Nain, he came upon a kind of funeral procession. We don't know any details about the deceased — name, age, cause of death — except his survivors. He was his mother's only son, and now she was a widow.

That brief detail is enough to tell us a great deal. It tells us that this woman had already known grief and loss in her life. It tells us that, within that ancient context, she was now in a desperate situation. The

Bible's concern for widows (e.g., Deuteronomy 14:28-29, 26:13; James 1:27) and their frequent pairing with orphans (e.g., Deuteronomy 16:11; Job 22:9; Psalm 68:5; Lamentations 5:3) speak to the condition of a widow. She had no husband to support her. Absent an adult son; therefore, she was likely to become destitute (cf. Mark 12:41-44; 1 Timothy 5:3-4).

This weeping woman in the funeral process outside of Nain, therefore, was utterly bereft: emotionally crushed by the loss of loved ones, as well as financially in danger with a most uncertain future.

Luke reports that Jesus "had compassion" for the grieving widow is a significant statement. The underlying Greek word occurs just twelve times in the New Testament, and it is always accompanied by action. This is no empty sentiment, not pity that is all heart but no hands. This compassion results in practical assistance. Furthermore, we note that, in eight of those twelve occurrences, the word is applied to Jesus. In three of the remaining four instances, it is a word used by Jesus in order to describe a character in one of his parables — the forgiving master (Matthew 18:27), the good Samaritan (Luke 10:33), and the prodigal's father (Luke 15:20). The last remaining occurrence is when the father of a troubled son asks Jesus to have compassion on him (Mark 9:22), which he does.

After encouraging the poor woman not to weep (which we will discuss more below), Jesus stepped forward and touched the stand on which the coffin was evidently being carried. That stopped the procession, which suggests a terribly awkward moment.

In our day, we are accustomed to all traffic stopping for a funeral procession so that the sad parade can travel uninterrupted to the graveside. Can you imagine a car deliberately swerving in front of the hearse to bring the procession to a halt? Or as the pall bearers carry the coffin down the aisle of the church, can we imagine a person coming in and blocking their path?

Jesus stopped the funeral procession, which is its own sort of beautiful picture. Then he spoke to the corpse: "Young man, I say to you, rise!" It is a moment reminiscent of at least two other episodes in Jesus' ministry (Mark 5:41; John 11:43). And the scene brings to mind the truths elegantly expressed by Charles Wesley: "He speaks, and listening to his voice, new life the dead receive; the mournful, broken hearts rejoice, the humble poor believe."

The dead young man came back to life. The spectators, predictably, responded with mixed emotions. They were frightened and awed, and they were also filled with wonder and praise. And, as you might expect, the word about Jesus spread quickly.

Application

We have observed stories from two of our three lections that bear a striking resemblance to one another. The resuscitation of one young man by Elijah in 1 Kings and the raising of another young man by Jesus in Luke are closely connected in several obvious ways. But the important similarities go beyond the mere details of plot.

Perhaps you have known some individuals along the way who remind you very much of their parents. You know that the resemblance can take two forms. On the one hand, there is the simple matter of physical resemblance: same eyes or frame, same hair color or voice.

Beyond that superficial similarity, however, there are deeper matters: traits of style and personality that make others say, "You certainly are your father's son" or some such. It's one thing for a girl to have her mother's nose; it's quite another for her to have her mother's spirit.

Herein lays the real issue for the miracles that fill our three lections this week. The raising of two widows' sons is only the superficial resemblance. But see also the providential care of God for Elijah by way of the ravens and a brook. Then, when that provision seems to give way, it leads to the generosity of God sustaining three people — Elijah, the widow, and her son — instead of just the one. Finally, there is the testimony of the apostle Paul in the excerpt from Galatians: the story of the man who was completely turned around by Jesus Christ, transformed from persecutor of the church to its chief evangelist.

Beneath the surface, then, we see these two magnificent characteristics of God's work. First, he sees the needs of people and intervenes to bless. Second, he is capable of not just increasing what is good or decreasing what is bad; but, rather, he can completely turn around any circumstance, taking what is an extreme bad and turning it into an extreme good. From want to abundance, from persecutor to evangelist, from death to life: He is the God of total conversions. This is his distinguishing feature.

An Alternative Application
Luke 7:11-17. "Such a Thing to Say." Coming from anyone but Jesus, the words would seem embarrassingly inappropriate. Who says to a grieving woman, on the occasion of her son's funeral, "Do not weep"? On the contrary, we think ourselves good pastors and good friends when we give opportunity and permission for a mourning person to cry. Yet this is our Lord's unthinkable greeting to a bereaved mother: "Do not weep."

Of course, this is not the stunting and unhealthy command of an adult who is fed up with his child's tears. This is not an irritated, "Stop your crying!" But rather this is the comforting word from the one who knows that there will soon be no reason to cry.

Still, it's interesting that Jesus bothers to say it. After all, couldn't he simply have raised the young man to life while his mother wept? Surely she would have stopped weeping then!

Yet that's not the pattern. We recall that he told grieving Jairus not to fear (Luke 8:50) and the mourners outside Jairus' house not to weep (8:52) even before he had raised the little girl to life. We remember that the angels were surprised by Mary's weeping outside the empty tomb (John 20:13), even though she did not yet know that Jesus had been raised.

Coming from anyone but Jesus, the words would seem embarrassingly inappropriate. Of course, coming from anyone but Jesus, a lot of things he said would be an embarrassment of one sort or another. His audacity to forgive (Mark 2:1-7), his claim to fulfill prophecy (Luke 4:16-21), and his identification with God (John 14:6-9) are all startling examples. He presumed to speak authoritatively to demons (Luke 4:33-35) and to nature (Matthew 8:26), and he claimed for himself an apocalyptic exaltation and authority (Matthew 26:64; Mark 13:26; John 1:51).

In the end, you see, the final issue is not what is said, but who is saying it. Coming from anyone else, his words would be lunacy. Coming from him, they are truth, wisdom, beauty, and power. Our response, therefore, is not, "Such a thing to say!" but "Such a man who says it!" And so we don't resist but rejoice when we hear him tell us not to weep, not to worry, and not to fear.

Proper 6 / Pentecost 4 / Ordinary Time 11
1 Kings 21:1-10 (11-14) 15-21a
Galatians 2:15-21
Luke 7:36—8:3
David Kalas

Preaching to the choir

We preachers are sometimes confused about our audience.

Sometimes we preach like frustrated columnists, as though our high calling is to change public opinion about current events. Or we preach as though we had the president or governor or congress in our congregation, proclaiming what we believe they need to hear, even though they are not there.

One preacher may have such a heart for lost souls of Generation X that she preaches for them, forgetting that her actual congregation is made up mostly of members over fifty years old who have been in church their whole lives. While another preacher may be so recently steeped in the world of seminarians that he preaches to a congregation bewildered by his frequent and familiar references to the Deuteronomist, the Q document, Athanasius, and the eschaton.

The most famous example of a preacher being confused about his audience, of course, is the idiomatic practice of "preaching to the choir." This is an easy thing to do. We preach what the people who are not in attendance need to hear, leaving the faithful to sit and listen to what they already know and live.

But this Sunday may be just the occasion to preach to the choir. This week's lections may feature precisely the truths that the choir needs to hear.

1 Kings 21:1-10 (11-14) 15-21a

The conventional wisdom in real estate is that the three most important factors for any piece of property are location, location, and location. That old saw proves to be unhappily true for poor Naboth. The Old Testament writer introduces us to him with this concise summary: "Naboth the Jezreelite had a vineyard in Jezreel, beside the palace of King Ahab of Samaria."

Naboth's location is marked in terms of two coordinates: "in Jezreel" and "beside the palace of King Ahab." Since he is identified as a Jezreelite, the first coordinate seems appropriate. Naboth is where he belongs. He is at home. We discover later, his vineyard is family land — his "ancestral inheritance."

One might naturally suppose that living in the king's neighborhood would be advantageous. Is there any property in the land more valuable? More secure?

On the other hand, many of us have experienced to one degree or another, the pain and difficulty that comes from having a bad neighbor. And if the bad neighbor is also king, the pain and difficulty is magnified that much more!

Naboth's neighbor, King Ahab, wants to obtain Naboth's land. Apparently it was a nice piece of property, and being just outside Ahab's door and window, the king no doubt saw it every day.

It is the things right under our noses that we are most likely to covet. Not that I don't crave things that are far off; but the good things right next door are the ones I see constantly, and so they are most likely to become an obsession. Perhaps that's why the commandment specifies "anything that belongs to your neighbor" (Exodus 20:17).

Having been denied the opportunity to purchase Naboth's property, Ahab goes home unhappy. Jezebel detects that Ahab is glum, and she inquires about the cause. Being a no-nonsense person, Jezebel is not one to wallow. If something is not to her liking, she will take action to correct it, like here, in the case of Naboth's vineyard.

While Ahab had broken the tenth commandment by coveting what belonged to his neighbor, Jezebel climbed up the list a notch, arranging for false witnesses against that neighbor (see Exodus 20:16; also Proverbs 3:29). And, in almost no time, Jezebel has solved the problem — eliminated it, really — and Ahab is free to take possession of the vineyard.

That's where Elijah finds him.

It is a poignant business for the man of God to find you at the very scene of the crime. Nathan famously confronted David, but not as he was in bed with Bathsheba. This prophet-king confrontation is more reminiscent of the condemnation of Jeroboam at the site of his newly constructed altar (1 Kings 13:1-6).

At first blush, Ahab's greeting to Elijah sounds just like good banter. We discover that a constant tension exists between these two men, with their different allegiances, and so the angry salutation fits the hostile relationship.

This king-and-prophet combo reminds me a bit of Herod and John the Baptist in the New Testament. The king is mixed: equal parts disapproval of the prophet and fear of the prophet. He is antagonistic to the man and his message, and yet reluctant to exercise his sovereignty against the man of God. The wife of the king in each case, however, has no such compunctions.

The way that Ahab addresses Elijah is more than just repartee, however. It is symptomatic and revealing. For what terrible thing does it say about Ahab that he regards the prophet — the courier from God — as his enemy? Call him "my critic," "my challenger," or "my nagging conscience." But "my enemy"? What a terrible, tragic thing to conclude: that the one who bears no weapon other than God's word is your enemy.

Galatians 2:15-21

I live on the south side of a little town in Wisconsin called Whitewater. I have a number of friends who live on the north side of town. I suppose that it would be accurate for me to say to them, "I live closer to Miami than you," but somehow I don't think that they would envy me my shorter walk to the beach.

It is true that I am closer to Miami. It is also true, however, that my friends on the north side of town and I are both very far away. Indeed, in the big scheme of things, we are almost equally far away. None of us is going to put on our swimsuits and sandals and walk to the beach from here. Both of us — north side of town and south — will have to drive or fly in order to get there.

In a high school science class, I once learned about "significant numbers." A tenth of a mile is a significant number when measuring how far it is from my house to my church. But a tenth of a mile is no longer a significant number when measuring how far it is from the earth to the sun, or from one galaxy to another.

Technically, I am closer to Palm Beach than my friends on the north side of town. But I am not significantly closer.

So, too, with the Jews and the Gentiles in this matter of salvation.

As the chosen people of God — recipients of his law and his covenants — the Jews were arguably closer to God than the "Gentile sinners." And yet the advantage was not significant, for the Jews and the Gentiles alike need the same long-distance transport in order to be saved. The Jews' proximity is not such that they are somehow within "walking distance" from God. They must be "justified... through faith in Jesus Christ," just like the "Gentile sinners."

Meanwhile, the role of Christ's death in our salvation is at issue here in an interesting way.

Some Christians tend to ignore Christ's death altogether, thinking that any soteriology that requires his death is a bit primitive. They emphasize, instead, the example of his life. Others have sought to make Christ's death relevant for something other than salvation (an example of human injustice, of unjust suffering, of heroic martyrdom, and the like). Meanwhile, most Christians through the ages have understood that Christ's death was salvific, though the specific paradigms have been somewhat varied.

In this passage, meanwhile, Paul presents us with a truth about Christ's suffering and death that is seldom affirmed in American Christendom. Paul claims that he had been "crucified with Christ" (v. 19).

We are accustomed to the gospel that says he died for us. We may not be so conversant, however, in the gospel that says we died with him. My picture of the cross on Good Friday shows him, not me. But this passage from Galatians may make this Sunday a good opportunity to expand my picture — and my congregation's picture, as well.

The great resulting truth to affirm, of course, is that "it is no longer I who live, but it is Christ who lives in me" (v. 20). Here is a part of the gospel that seems to have been left out of the diet of so many of our churches. We are naturally I-centered, and we have let the gospel and the Christian life become I-centered as well. Perhaps a great many matters of morality, personal priorities, and sense of purpose would be clarified if we awakened to the notion that it is no longer I who live, but Christ who lives in me.

Finally, I am conscious that Paul's final line in this week's passage is a provocative one that so many church folks need to hear and understand.

In my years of local church ministry, I have so often encountered a "good Christian" mentality that, in its own subtle way, exalts the law over the grace of God. These are the folks (and I expect you've met them too) who earnestly believe that their eternal reward in heaven is secured by the good life they've lived. Or they make that same affirmation on behalf of a friend and loved one who has recently died. "Well, you know, Bill wasn't a very religious person, but he was about the nicest person you'd ever care to meet."

The mentality does not wrestle with the rigors and specifics of God's whole law. Rather, some homespun revision of the law has been developed to identify what is a "good person," and it is that goodness — rather than God's goodness — that guarantees one's salvation. It's a common heresy, and Paul follows it through to its logical and startling conclusion: "then Christ died for nothing."

Luke 7:36—8:3

One of the hallmarks of Luke's gospel is the prominence of women in the story. From Mary and Elizabeth at the beginning of the gospel to the women who first bear witness to the resurrection at the end, women play a large role in Luke's account of Jesus. And this week's gospel lection is yet another example of that pattern.

In the main story of the selected passage, it is a woman who emerges as the unexpected paragon. We'll return to her story in a moment. Then, as a bookend to the passage, we meet several other exemplary women. Luke mentions "the twelve" — a kind of impersonal reference to the disciples — and then he goes on to call by name some women who were also part of Jesus' faithful contingent. There is Mary Magdalene, whom we know well. There is also Joanna and Susanna, plus "many others." These women are not merely tagging along with the men. Decidedly not. Rather, these women, it seems, are the ones whose significant generosity and resources provide for the needs of the entire group.

The real star of this passage, however, is the anonymous woman who anointed Jesus while he was in the home of Simon the Pharisee.

While Luke does not tell us her name, he does tell us one significant thing about her: She "was a sinner." No details, just a label, and the rest is left to our imaginations.

In the context of that culture, this unnamed woman and the named Pharisee were at opposite ends of the spectrum. Sinner and Pharisee. Righteous and unrighteous, with Jesus in between. The tableau is a powerful image as the two opposite characters are, for a moment, on either side of the Lord. The woman is prostrate, weeping at Jesus' feet. Simon is likely more elevated, probably face-to-face with Jesus as they reclined to eat. Yet, as in Jesus' parable (Luke 18:9-14), it is the humble and undeserving character who is truly right with God in the end.

Simon assumes that Jesus' status as a true prophet is at stake in this episode. After all, if he truly were a prophet, Simon reasons, he would know the kind of person with whom he was dealing.

Of course, Jesus did know. He knew the kind of woman who was touching and anointing him, and he also knew the kind of man who was hosting him. The woman's life and heart were not the only ones transparent to Jesus there at that table.

Jesus turns the tables on the scene and on Simon. Simon thinks that the issue is who is more sinful and by that measure he comes out on top. But Jesus recasts the issue, asking who is more loving, and on that scale Simon is found wanting.

The paradigm shift is typical. It resonates with the God who "does not see as mortals see; they look on the outward appearance, but the Lord looks on the heart" (1 Samuel 16:7). It is reminiscent of the God who surprises the self-satisfied religious people of the eighth century BC (Isaiah 1:11-17; Amos 5:21-24). It is consistent with the teacher who exalted the Samaritan over the priest and the Levite (Luke 10:30-37), the tax collector over the Pharisee (Luke 18:9-14), and the one lost sheep above the 99 in the fold (Luke 15:4-7).

Simon reckoned that if Jesus knew who this woman was, he wouldn't let her touch him, but Simon had it backward. When Jesus is in our midst, the question is not whether he recognizes us; the real issue is whether we recognize him. That was a part of his point to the woman at the well (John 4:10), and that was certainly at the heart of the matter when he prayed for the forgiveness of his tormentors (Luke 23:34).

It is at this point that a surprising hero emerges from the scene. While conventional wisdom of that day would have put the white hat on the Pharisee and the black hat on the sinful woman, she is the one who comes out on top. For she seems really to recognize Jesus and to honor him appropriately, while Simon had missed it. The Lord himself was in Simon's home, but Simon's inadequate response shows that he didn't recognize the Lord.

Finally, it may be worth noting that the woman offers a picture of love that we may easily lose sight of. Because our conventional picture of Jesus is as the one who touches us, who heals us, who blesses us, we may have an underdeveloped picture of us touching him, of us blessing or caring for him. It is a picture implicit in Jesus' teaching about the sheep and the goats (Matthew 25:31-46). It is a picture tenderly portrayed in Mel Gibson's *The Passion of the Christ* in the characters of Mary, Simon, and Veronica along the Via Dolorosa. It is an image captured marvelously in Christina Rossetti's Christmas song, "In the Bleak Midwinter" — "Angels and archangels may have gathered there, / Cherubim and seraphim thronged the air; / But His mother only, in her maiden bliss, / Worshipped the beloved with a kiss." And it is a picture offered us by this woman who, by what she did for Jesus, "has shown great love."

Application

Let us say that "the choir" represents a certain sort of people. They are faithful and reliable. They attend and they assist. You can count on them to be there, doing their part, week in and week out. They are the quintessential good church folks.

So when you're preaching to the choir, what should you preach? What does the choir — the good church folks — need to hear? Well, for starters, it is worth pointing out that the choir probably needs to hear the same things as the preachers. When we talk to them, we are talking also to ourselves. They and we may need to hear two of the passages that we are assigned this week.

First, those of us who are so habitually and commendably law-abiding need to hear again that we are not justified by the law. In a manifestly bad world, it's easy to feel satisfied with our goodness. So we benefit from Paul's reminder that we are saved by God's goodness, not our own.

Then there is the other hazard of our human goodness. Not only that we may "nullify the grace of God" by some self-reliance, but also that we may be shallow in our love. This was the surprising fault of Simon.

Our natural ally in the gospel lection may be Simon the Pharisee. We are not much attracted to him, and we have inherited a very negative view of Pharisees. But the hard fact remains that he is the one most like "the choir." He is faithful, good, and religious. But he had not been forgiven much. Or at least he didn't recognize that he had. That is the natural plight of the good person, and so it may be our liability too.

Preaching to the choir, therefore, may include the sober reminder that "the one to whom little is forgiven, loves little."

An Alternative Application
Luke 7:36—8:3. "The Trouble with Jesus' Hosts." What an inconvenient place to have to find Jesus.

This woman, "who was a sinner," was apparently eager to find Jesus. She wanted, it seems, to express to him her love, her gratitude, perhaps even her worship. We don't know the details of her story leading up to this moment. Perhaps they would be unnecessarily salacious. It is sufficient to know that Luke the narrator and Simon the Pharisee readily identify her as "a sinner."

We gather from the assorted accounts found in the four gospels that multitudes of people sought out Jesus. We see crowds pressing in on him personally, crowding the house where he stays, chasing the boat that he rides. And so we imagine the excitement certain individuals must have felt when they learned that Jesus was nearby.

This woman was one of those individuals. She learned that Jesus was in the neighborhood. She wanted to go to him. But then came the unhappy specifics of the situation: She "learned that he was eating in the Pharisee's house."

What kind of courage did it take for her to go there? To presume into the private space of Simon's home? To pass through the door into a place where she was neither one of the family members who belonged there nor one of the guests invited to be there? To go in and be noticed — pointed at, whispered about? To go where she knew she would meet with disapproval, condemnation, and perhaps even outright rejection?

What kind of courage does it take for a sinner to find Jesus among the religious and righteous crowd? More courage, I suspect, than many other folks of that day had. More courage than many folks have today, as well: people who are understandably too afraid, too ashamed, and too guilty to come find Jesus in our churches. What an inconvenient place to have to find Jesus.

Proper 7 / Pentecost 5 / ORDINARY Time 12
1 Kings 19:1-4 (5-7) 8-15a
Galatians 3:23-29
Luke 8:26-39
Mark Molldrem

Searching for truth in all the wrong places

Gods and goddesses are plentiful these days, luring adherents into strange expressions of faith. Lam Sai-wing is a very up-scale jewelry salesman, who boasts the world's most expensive bathroom. It cost him $4.9 million to appoint his toilet facility with solid gold furnishings, jewels on the ceiling and two 24-carat commodes as the center of attraction. This extravagance is Lam's way of giving testimony to his fortune, which he claims hit the stratosphere after he worshiped the goddess of mercy, Kuan Yin, at one of her temples on the Kowloon Peninsula in China. Today, he has a pure gold, nine-foot statue of the goddess on his property. (By the way, patrons to Lam's store may use the luxurious facility, but only if they purchase at least $138 US of merchandise.)

Where in the world does one go to find truth? Can it be discovered just about anywhere? Are the rewards of truth finding worth the effort? Just what are those rewards? The Christian church throughout the centuries has charted a course for finding the truth and celebrating the reward, which is more than the pot of gold at the end of the rainbow. The course is mapped out in the Bible, especially the New Testament, where the Holy Spirit leads believers to find the treasure of life in relationship to Jesus. The journey is certainly an adventure, sometimes fraught with dangers, especially from those who value other objects they consider the real treasure. The journey requires faith as the passport to reach the destination of true life with the true God.

1 Kings 19:1-4 (5-7) 8-15a

It was a bad day for Baal. He not only lost the contest on Mount Carmel but also his priesthood (1 Kings 18:17-40). When Jezebel got word of this, she vowed to eliminate Elijah. Elijah fled, like so many of God's people do when their adversaries challenge them. Adam took off in the garden after having a fruit snack. Moses left Egypt after dispatching an Egyptian for beating up a Hebrew. David hid in the cave of Adullam when Saul was in a fury. Jonah headed west instead of traveling east to Nineveh as instructed. Peter went private instead of going public when it came to his faith in the temple courtyard.

Like all these flight-fancy followers of God, Elijah is found by the Hound of Heaven and strengthened for the task at hand. God does not give up on his people, especially when he has plans for them. It is most interesting to see how God manifests himself to Elijah. There is the display of wind, earthquake, and fire that accompanies the Holy One, the almighty of heaven and earth. Nature herself pays tribute to the Lord with awesome spectacles for an awe-inspiring God. Yet, notice that God is not pleased to disclose himself to Elijah in these phenomena. God could have, of course, but God had a higher purpose in mind than simply to stun Elijah with his magnificence. Because God wanted more than wonder and worship, God selected to wait until he could simply speak with Elijah. Communication in relationship is what God sought. For Elijah to understand what was on the mind of God, words were necessary, not just spectacular displays of power, however they might "blow you over," "shake you to the bone," or "bake your biscuit."

It is in "a still small voice" that God reveals his purpose for Elijah. It would be advisable to extend the pericope beyond verse 15a to verse 19a. The reason for this is fourfold. First, the authority of God over the political rulers is reaffirmed, because Elijah will be anointing the successors not only for Israel, but also for Syria. Second, God assures Elijah that his work will continue in his successor, Elisha, whom he is also to anoint. Third, God jolts Elijah out of his self-pity by informing him that he is not the only true believer left; there will be 7,000 other faithful followers of Yahweh! This is the powerful stuff of purpose and promise that catapults Elijah out of his cave of hiding to re-enter the dangers of real life where the likes of Jezebel await him. Verses 15b to 18 provide the meat upon which Elijah could chew to find strength and courage to get on with his duties as prophet of God. Fourth, Elijah demonstrates his faith in God's word by leaving the cave. "So he departed from there" (1 Kings 19:19a).

Galatians 3:23-29

Gentiles who are *in Christ* (3:26) are legitimate heirs of the promise given to Abraham and reaffirmed through his progeny (see Galatians 3:6-9). The Law, as custodian, was more than a code of conduct to identify God's people among the nations. The Law was *Torah*; it was life with wholeness, because it was lived *coram Deo*. The Law was given by God with love, so that the people would know how to express their thankfulness to God for their deliverance from Egypt. It points to God as the source of salvation, and so prefigures Christ, who would come to fulfill the Law (Matthew 5:17). He said of himself, "I am... the life" (John 11:25; also John 14:6). The gospel writer John affirms this in his opening sentences: "In him was life" (John 1:4). It is as if Jesus were saying, "Follow me and live *coram Deo*. Believe in me and live *coram Deo*, for you are seeing the Father in me. As I now live in you by faith, you will know life." The custodian, the law, now turns the keys of the kingdom over to the master of the house, Jesus.

Faith is referred to five times in these few verses of pericope. Another word for faith is trust. Paul is defining faith by its object, Jesus. Faith means to trust Jesus, to put one's entire stock in what he accomplished in his ministry and passion and resurrection for us. Elsewhere Paul explains that faith is a gift from God that receives the grace of God that saves the sinner (Ephesians 2:8-10). Just as Abraham believed God when he made promises — and this was reckoned to him as his righteousness — so too are Christians today like Abraham, as they put their trust in Jesus' accomplishments on their behalf.

Throughout the scripture, faith is understood as a dynamic relationship between God and man that has the qualities of assent, affection, and action. First, there are truths that can be attested to when one says, "I have faith in Jesus." For example, he is the Son of God, the promised Messiah, the crucified Savior of the world who rose from the dead. Doctrine explores these truths and seeks to express them coherently and consistently. The three ecumenical creeds summarize the body of truth to which Christians give their assent, in contrast to other faith systems such as Buddhism, Islam, Baha'i, Shintoism, and Taoism.

Second, the relationship between Jesus and the follower is to be a living one, filled with love. Jesus asked Peter, "Do you love me?" To confess belief in Jesus involves not only the mind, but also the heart. Our affection is directed to Jesus who, as the hymn describes, is the "lover of my soul." The mystics of the Christian tradition have expressed this dynamic throughout the centuries (for example, Catherine of Siena, Meister Eckhart, and John of the Cross).

Third, faith invites and demands action. The believer does not just think the truth, nor just feel a joyous bonding with the truth-giver; the believer also follows the way of the truth in a multitude of daily behaviors that give muscle to the confessions of one's mind and the affections of one's heart. There are disciplines that demonstrate one's allegiance; for example, tithing, prayer, fasting, chastity, and service.

Woven throughout these three aspects of faith is the Pauline thread that ties one to Jesus Christ as the only worthy object of faith. Jesus validates our faith as a saving grace and guarantees our inheritance of all the promises of God, which find their yes in him (2 Corinthians 1:20), promises such as the forgiveness of sins, deliverance from death and the devil, and life everlasting. How can gold compare with these treasures?

Luke 8:26-39

If you like bacon, you may not appreciate this pericope. But, if you were a faithful Jew, following the tradition of the elders and observing all the kosher regulations, you would be quite taken by the events that transpired on the far side of the Sea of Galilee, with the exception of some discomfort that Jesus was going out of his way to minister to Gentiles. Luke has no discomfort in placing this story in a section of his gospel account that emphasizes Jesus' ministry in Galilee and to the Jews. It complements his inclusion of the healing of the centurion's slave, together with it anticipating the gospel going out to all the world, especially through the ministry of Paul, who later traveled through this same area on his way to Arabia and back (Galatians 1:17).

Culturally for a Jew, there was no loss literally to demonize pigs and drive them into the sea. For any Jew this would make perfect sense. What would strike the Jew's attention, however, would be the compassion Jesus showed for the man possessed by a demon (demons, for his name was Legion). The Messiah was concerned with the welfare of all God's human creatures, Jew and *goyim* alike. Plus, the Gentile man, once released from the demon's grip, proclaimed the praise of Jesus "throughout the whole city" (8:39). This nameless man was the first Gentile evangelical, according to Luke. He responded to the magnanimous gift of release from bondage that Jesus had given him. He would put to shame Jesus' own countrymen, who should have been even more eager to proclaim that the Messiah had indeed come to God's people, but who instead called for his death.

Notice how the demon recognized Jesus and asked not to be tormented by him (8:28), for Jesus had commanded the demon to come out of the man. To come out of the shadows of the man's skin and broken psyche, the demon would have to stand (crawl, cower, kneel, slink) in the presence of Jesus, the Light of the world (to borrow from John 1:4 and 8:12). This would indeed be torment for a creature of the dark. This is reminiscent of C.S. Lewis' *The Great Divorce*, wherein the travelers from hell on excursion to heaven experience the pleasures of the redeemed as pain, e.g., the tender grass underfoot was hard as diamonds and felt like walking over "wrinkled rock"; space was enormous, "which made the solar system itself seem an indoor affair," and filled with a strange mixture of freedom and danger; the travelers upon disembarking the omnibus were revealed as phantoms: "Now that they were in the light, they were transparent... man-shaped stains on the brightness of that air" — "the light, like solid blocks... thundering upon [exposed heads]." It was a bad day for demons.

For a resident of Gergesa (modern Kursi, a village on the shore; or Gadara, six miles southeast of the lake; or Gerasa, located 33 miles southeast; there is some debate as to which area is being referred to), questions would be raised about the wholesale loss of an entire herd of pigs, which could feed the people for many months. Perhaps it would become like a Gentile parable, raising the question of treasure (Matthew 13:45-46) and where the heart is (Luke 12:32-34), what in the end is of more infinite worth (Matthew 6:33) and what one should really be concerned about (Luke 12:4-5). In other contexts, Jesus would talk about the worth of a sparrow and the lily of the field to lift up the value of an individual person. Could it be that Jesus would not even think twice about sacrificing an entire herd of pigs in order to save one soul? Again, we see what a high value God places on any human who is in need and who needs to experience the wonder of God's love through Jesus!

Still, the people rejected him out of fear and asked him to leave their country (8:34-39). The reception of the Son of God does not seem to go any better outside Jerusalem than inside, with those who should be glad to be included in the salvation of the world than with those who should have recognized the salvation of the world when it arrived!

Application

In our increasingly secularized world, many Christians will find it harder to witness of their faith. It will feel like foreign territory for them to "go public," let alone say something that challenges the status quo of cultural expectations or allowances. In most of our churches it is probably more true that we are not in flight for fear of our lives, like Elijah, as a consequence of our taking a prophetic stance on a public issue. We are just quiet, hoping no one will really take note of us, unless they want to "join the church," of course.

The *still small voice* speaks to us, "What on earth are you doing for heaven's sake?" What *are* we doing in all the locations where the people of God find themselves? We may be fearful to speak a countercultural word. We may be at a loss as what to say exactly. We may be embarrassed that we have remained in our caves for so long. And, so, the *still small voice* speaks to us also, and we need to hear its thunder!

Take heart. God has not given up on us. Just like he pursued Elijah, God will dog us faithfully until we become faithful to the mission that he has planned for us. Twice God graciously encouraged Elijah to eat what was set before him. What God provided was sufficient and also enduring. Elijah "went in the strength of that food forty days and forty nights" (19:8). So can we, when we feast upon the word of God (both in print and in the bread and wine). It will not be easy to speak and embody God's word in the world today, but we are called to do so nonetheless. Paul himself experienced this with his thorn in the flesh (2 Corinthians 12:7-10). With him, we too can realize the sufficiency of God's grace to bring us through any challenging opportunity to witness to Jesus and carry on the tradition of the early disciples from that Pentecost day.

There will be obstacles that would thwart us from doing this, contemporary expressions of the law (in the Pauline sense) that would bind us from being free in Christ. Consider the "unholy trinity" of our culture: individualism, relativism, and pluralism, to which growing allegiance is given from every quarter. Individualism tempts us to put our trust in self as the final arbiter of truth and what is right. Relativism tempts us to affirm everyone's right to view the world from their own particular perch, authenticity and justification to be found therein. Pluralism tempts us to acknowledge many forms of equally valid realities, which may be contradictory to one another, but nonetheless seem to have some foothold on the terrain of truth. All three — fool's gold at best!

When we are baptized into Christ, we surrender the claims of the self (the Old Adam and the Old Eve) to the claim of God on our lives. We are called to perceive the world through the given revelation from God as the absolute standard to which all truth is subject, "having the eyes of your hearts enlightened" (Ephesians 1:18) by the gospel of Jesus. He alone is "the way, the truth, and the life" (John 14:6), at whose name "every knee should bow, in heaven and on earth and under the earth, and every tongue confess that Jesus Christ is Lord" (Philippians 2:10). Here is the true treasure of the church, which it has to share with the world, even if it seems at times like casting pearls before swine.

What do we make of demon possession these days? Ironically, in our post-modern culture, the door of credulity is open to consider such a phenomena. Not too many year's ago psychiatrists would have treated the poor Gerasene as a nudist necrophiliac, prescribing a change of scenery and some behavior modification along with a line of credit at JCPenney. The populace, however, has become more willing to accept the strange and unexplainable in terms of "other-worldliness," as dramatized, for example, on *The X-Files*, *Dark Angel*, *The Sixth Sense*, or *End of Days*.

More tangible and to the point of our everyday life is the possession of the human spirit by the consumer demon. A brief drive through any new subdivision with homes sporting three-door garages will give ample evidence of its powerful presence. Houses, having the floor space of two to three times a more common dwelling and costing five to ten times the building price of a Habitat home, more than dot the landscape. The loss of a herd of pigs is a signal sent to all who put their pride in possessions, their security in what they own (or what owns them!). Jesus reminds us, "One thing is needful" (Luke 10:42). Similar words were spoken to the rich young ruler who sought advice on going to heaven (Matthew 19:16-22). Amidst all that seeks our attention, that competes for our passions, that desires to seize our souls, we need to hear the call of Jesus, "Follow me." He has the power to cast out the demon of self-centeredness, which is self-destruction, and cast a new light on the path of life that gives one a thrilling new future of self-sacrificing service to the glory of God.

The Gerasene returned home, "proclaiming throughout the whole city how much Jesus had done for him" (8:39). What an apt description for the life of the Christian, for the witness of a congregation — to be at home in our homes (familial and spiritual) sharing our experiences of life with Christ. The season of Pentecost is an opportunity for Christians and their congregations to take stock as to how they are doing just that.

Proper 8 / Pentecost 6 / Ordinary Time 13
2 Kings 2:1-2, 6-14
Galatians 5:1, 13-25
Luke 9:51-62
Timothy Cargal

A share of the Spirit

"Be careful what you wish for, because you just might get it." Now there is a bit of sage advice that has a multitude of applications. I thought of it recently when I was watching the video of the film *Bruce Almighty.* I am generally not a big fan of "Divine comedies," even though I am certain God must have a sense of humor (the evidence is just too overwhelming). But this one struck me as far better than most and worthy of some serious reflection.

The story is about Bruce Nolan (played by Jim Carrey), a local news reporter for a station in Buffalo, New York. He is denied a promotion to anchor that he was certain he deserved and was going to get. He launches into a tirade against God for the lousy job God is doing of taking care of his life and expresses complete confidence that he himself could do God's job better. The next day, he has a meeting with God (played by Morgan Freeman), who bestows the full range of divine powers upon Bruce and then leaves on vacation.

Once Bruce realizes these powers are real, he immediately begins to use them for his personal enjoyment, enrichment, and even revenge. But as the prayer requests of even just the residents of Buffalo begin to pile up, God meets with Bruce once again to point out that doing God's job requires attending to far more than just one's personal desires. Being God comes with not only power but responsibilities.

The film raises a number of religious and theological issues in generally sensitive and constructive ways. (For instance, when Bruce asks God during one of their check-in sessions how he can make someone love him without violating their free will, God responds, "Welcome to my world; let me know when you figure that one out.") But within the context of the scripture lessons for Proper 8, it is the question of why anyone would desire godlike powers and what one would do with such powers if they were available that comes most to the fore.

2 Kings 2:1-2, 6-14

You have to wonder if Elijah didn't feel a bit like the God character in *Bruce Almighty* as he traveled with Elisha toward his rendezvous with that "chariot of fire" on the other side of the Jordan River. Having parted the waters of the river by striking it with his cloak, Elijah had then essentially asked Elisha what wish he could fulfill for him as a parting gesture. Elisha knew what he wanted; "Please let me inherit a double share of your spirit." Elijah was taken aback. "You have asked a hard thing," he responded, "yet if you see me as I am being taken from you, it will be granted to you."

Well, Elisha did see Elijah taken up into God's presence, and he picked up Elijah's mantle that had fallen to the ground. He returned to the banks of the Jordan, struck the waters with the mantle, and in a test of what he hoped were his new abilities demanded, "Where is the Lord, the God of Elijah?" (not unlike Bruce parting "the red soup" in a diner). The waters parted just as they had before, and as the other prophets saw Elisha approaching they declared, "The spirit of Elijah rests on Elisha." Difficult as it may have seemed, Elisha's wish had been fulfilled.

But wait a minute. That was just too easy. Elisha only had to watch something most of us would gladly pay good money to see and to pick up a cloth shawl to have his wish fulfilled. How come Elijah had insisted he had "asked a hard thing"? Was it really the difficulty of fulfilling the wish that Elijah had considered "hard," or was the "hard" part something else altogether?

Let's go back and look at the details of this story again. We need to start by making sure we understand who all the characters in this story are. This story is not just about Elijah and Elisha; it is also about "the company of the prophets." This "company" was a training guild, a kind of informal school where one could learn to be a prophet much like one could apprentice to become an artisan or to learn a building trade. The Hebrew expression would more literally be translated as "the sons of the prophets," and the recognized prophet to whom they discipled themselves — in this case, Elijah — was their "father." Thus, upon seeing the chariot of fire Elisha exclaimed, "Father, father! The chariots of Israel and its horsemen!" he was calling out to Elijah, the leader of the prophetic guild in which he was apprenticed.

Now this familial language of "fathers" and "sons" within these prophetic associations plays a key role in this story. Listen again to Elisha's wish: "Please let me inherit a double share of your spirit." The "father" of the guild is about to be taken away, and so Elisha is now concerned about how the inheritance is to be divvied up among the "sons." Thus, his request for a "double share" is not about having *twice* as much of the Spirit as Elijah. Rather, what he is asking for is the "birthright," the legal principle in that society that the firstborn son was to receive two of the equally divided shares of the father's property as compared to his younger brothers' single share each.

It is not quite the whole truth to then characterize his wish, as some commentators have, as requesting only a fraction rather than twice as much of the spirit that Elijah had. What is more important than the relative quantities of spirit divided among the members of the prophetic guild is that along with the "double share" of the birthright comes the authority of being the next "father" over the "sons of the prophets." The "hard thing" to which Elijah referred in responding to Elisha's wish was not the difficulty of fulfilling the wish, but the responsibility Elisha would need to live it out. Sometimes the very things we wish for are not the answer but rather the source of our difficulties and struggles.

Galatians 5:1, 13-25

What is one to make of Paul's seemingly self-contradictory statement that those who have been "called to freedom" must nevertheless "through love become slaves to one another" (v. 13)? Aren't "freedom" and "slavery" by their very definitions mutually exclusive categories?

Inherent in Paul's understanding is the conviction that there is no such thing as absolute freedom. We tend to think of freedom as a kind of right, or indeed a power, that enables us to act in accord with our own desires. It is hardly incidental in this regard that so much of our ethical and philosophical discussions of freedom deal with the issue of "free will." Freedom is the opposite of constraint; it is being released from the control of another's will or needs. We think of freedom primarily in terms of "freedom from" something.

Paul does not discount this "freedom from" dimension; that is why he can say, "Christ has set us free" (v. 1). But Paul would remind us that there is a second dimension or aspect of our freedom, what we might call "freedom to" and that Paul speaks about in terms of how we "use [our] freedom" (v. 13). He draws the distinction between the different uses of freedom as to whether they are characterized by "self-indulgence" or "love" expressed as obligation toward others. So strong should our sense of obligation nevertheless remain in our exercise of freedom that Paul can describe the freedom to act with love as "becom[ing] slaves to one another." Freedom does not equate with antinomianism, freedom from the very notion of an external law or constraint itself. Freedom contains within itself the "freedom to" fulfill the wisdom of God's gracious instruction to humanity ("the whole law," v. 14) about how to live in community.

It is indeed possible for these two dimensions of freedom — "freedom from" external obligation and "freedom to" act for not only ourselves but others — to fall into conflict with each other. Those who see freedom as only a means to self-indulgence have confused it with "the desires of the flesh" (v. 16). To give yourself over to such desires in fact is an abdication of freedom because "the desires of the flesh" will "prevent you from doing what you want" because you will be enslaved to the "law" of the flesh rather than bound by the "whole law" of God in which "you are led by the Spirit" (v. 18).

Paul would argue that seeing freedom only in terms of "freedom from" obligation to anything other than one's self results in self-indulgence and a long list of vices (vv. 19-21). These attitudes and actions not only devour others in their attempt to satisfy themselves, but ultimately consume those who engage in them as well (v. 15). But those who properly conceive of freedom as not only "from" but also "to" others produce the virtues of the "fruit of the Spirit" (vv. 22-23).

Luke 9:51-62

The exasperation Jesus seems to feel toward his disciples in the gospel lesson is almost palpable. Within the span of these twelve verses, the evangelist reports that Jesus "rebuked" his own disciples and rebuffed the responses of three different would-be disciples. What might be missed by reading this passage in the isolation of the lectionary is that the evangelist has carefully placed each of these vignettes at the outset of a major transition in the narrative structure of the gospel. The reason for Jesus' apparent exasperation is that the first phase of his ministry has drawn to a close and still neither his inner circle nor those who might yet be drawn in to join his ministry seem to be able to conceive its ultimate purposes and costs.

The evangelist's comment in verse 51 about the approach of time when Jesus would be "taken up" and his consequent determination "to go to Jerusalem" is not made in passing. It is in Jerusalem that Jesus' ministry will find its culmination in his passion, resurrection, and ascension. This journey to Jerusalem will provide the structure for Luke's account down through 19:27, where the final Passion Week will commence with Jesus' "Triumphal Entry" into the city (19:28-46). All along the way, Jesus will continue to instruct his disciples.

In the first of these vignettes, Jesus and his entourage are denied hospitality by a Samaritan village precisely because they are on their way to Jerusalem. Clearly the root of this snub is the centuries-old feud between the Samaritans and the Jews regarding the proper site for sacrificial worship of the God of Israel (cf. John 4:19-26). For James and John this slight should be punished by calling "fire to come down from heaven [to] consume them" (v. 54). No doubt they believed this was the purpose of Jesus' journey to Jerusalem itself, to bring down the fiery judgment of God upon all God's perceived enemies. Jesus' rebuke is aimed not just at an egregious overreaction to an ethnically motivated slight, but at the notion his ministry is in the first instance about destroying rather than redeeming those who alienate themselves from God.

Bringing reconciliation rather than destruction to those who oppose you is costly business, as Jesus' responses to the would-be disciples make clear. It can mean foregoing even one's own legitimate needs in order to commit one's self to ministry for others (vv. 57-58). It places demands on our lives that at times conflict with the normal obligations of society, even from within our own families (vv. 59-60). It requires that we commit ourselves completely to the cause of God's reign of justice without looking back to what we may have left behind (vv. 61-62). All of these things Jesus had done as "he set his face to go to Jerusalem," and those who would truly follow him must do the same.

Application

The transformative moment of the film *Bruce Almighty* comes when Bruce finally recognizes that the only proper use of those divine powers is to meet the genuine needs of others rather than his own or even their personal desires. Foremost among those needs is for one to know the love that God has for us, to have someone in our lives who, as Bruce expresses it to God, will love and see us through God's eyes.

It is a moment that Paul himself could have scripted, for no sooner had he announced to the Galatians that "Christ has set us free" from bondage to our sin than he immediately warned us all "not [to] use [our] freedom as an opportunity for self-indulgence." Could such "self-indulgence" have been what motivated Elisha to strike the Jordan and to demand, "Where is the Lord, the God of Elijah?" Had he wanted the "double share" of Elijah's spirit in order to assume the "birthright" of leadership over the prophetic band or to indulge his own sense of self-importance at being able to conjure such miracles as Elijah had performed? Was he driven by compassion and love for his fellow "sons of the prophets," not wanting them left wandering and hopeless without a "father" to lead and instruct them? Or was he driven by "enmity, strife, jealousy, anger, quarrels, dissensions, factions, envy," lest some other of his once colleagues should rise up to be the new leader over him. Why do we seek Christ's freedom and God's blessings — to use those freedoms and blessings to love our neighbors as ourselves or to satisfy our own desires even if at the expense of others? "If you bite and devour one another," Paul warns, "take care that you are not consumed by one another."

Perhaps had Elisha really understood the "hard thing" that he had asked of Elijah — had he recognized that the "double share" of Elijah's spirit was to enable him to serve the prophets and the people as a "slave" rather than to lord power over them — perhaps then he would not have sought miraculous power to keep his own feet dry as the first proof that his wish had been fulfilled. It is our sinful nature that seeks to put our own desires ahead of all else. Indeed, when the God character in *Bruce Almighty* asks Bruce why he has not been dealing with that backlog of prayers, he confesses that there were some perceived injustices in his own life that he wanted to redress first. "By contrast," as Paul wrote, "the fruit of the Spirit is love, joy, peace, patience, kindness, generosity, faithfulness, gentleness, and self-control" (Galatians 5:22). These qualities of life are directed toward the needs of others. These attributes are the proof that "the spirit of Elijah rests upon" us.

We don't really need the ability to invoke miraculous power to deal with the mundane details or common problems we face in our daily lives. What we really need, like Bruce Nolan and those young men in ancient Israel's prophetic guild, is to be in relationships that sustain and nurture us. What we really need is the freedom to find ourselves in service to others. The good news is that it is not a "hard thing" for God to fulfill our longing for a "double share" of the Spirit that can produce the fruit of love, joy, peace, patience, kindness, generosity, faithfulness, gentleness, and self-control that enable us to understand, serve, and be in relationship with one another.

It is not a "hard thing" for God to give us a "double share of the spirit," yet it is as Elijah knew, and Elisha and Bruce Nolan came to understand, an important responsibility for all those who receive this gift. God gives us the Spirit not for our own benefit, but in order that we might benefit others as agents of divine grace. A tremendous responsibility, yes, but never a drudgery. May we all fulfill Paul's challenge: "If we live by the Spirit, let us also be guided by the Spirit."

Alternative Applications
Galatians 5:1, 13-25. This lectionary reading invites us to explore the meanings of freedom at not only the personal level but at the level of societies and nations as well. What does it mean for the United States and other democracies to "promote freedom" around the world? Are we just promoting "freedom from" the tyrannies of dictators and a "freedom to" fulfill our personal desires, or do we make it clear that there is no absolute freedom apart from a continuing obligation for others? If other societies see our notion of freedom as promoting lawlessness, have we ourselves forgotten the necessary correlation between rights and responsibilities that are essential to genuine freedom?

2 Kings 2:1-2, 6-14; Luke 9:51-62. There are several parallels between the Elijah and Elisha stories and particular details in the gospel lesson. Maybe James and John saw themselves as being in the same league with Elijah in their ability to call fire down from heaven, and maybe a desire for such ability initially motivated Elisha's wish for a "double share" of Elijah's spirit. Elisha's own call to follow Elijah had involved plows and a reluctant severing of family ties (cf. 1 Kings 19:19-21). In the end, however, both Elisha and Jesus' disciples came to recognize the responsibility for others that lies at the heart of God's call on our lives. In what ways might our own failings to recognize the implications of God's call be exasperating to God? What can we learn from the purposes and costs of Jesus' ministry that can help us to live out our own calls?

Proper 9 / Pentecost 7 / Ordinary Time 14
2 Kings 5:1-14
Galatians 6:(1-6) 7-16
Luke 10:1-11, 16-20
David Kalas

What must I do?

The Philippian jailor does not appear in any of our selected readings for this Sunday, but his fundamental question reverberates through our texts. "What must I do to be saved?" he asked Paul and Silas (Acts 16:30). It is an elemental question and our selected passages can help us elucidate the answer.

What do I need to do? This is the pragmatic question of the would-be home buyer sitting with the loan officer in the bank. It is the poignant question of the husband who wants to make things right with his wife. It is the desperate question that the patient asks the doctor in the wake of some positive test result, some unfavorable diagnosis.

"What must I do?"

As soon as we understand the high stakes involved in a given situation, this is the question we ask. As long as we are happily ignorant, we may skate along without any sense of urgency or responsibility. But once we recognize the scope and the gravity of the situation — whether financial, academic, relational, or medical — we want to know what must be done. What we must do.

That was Naaman's circumstance. He had a severe medical need, and he wanted to know what, if anything, could be done. As an accomplished man, a man of action, he stood ready and willing to do whatever he needed to do in order to find a cure. Still, he was unprepared for the answer that came down.

For the Christians in Galatia, the circumstance was not a medical one, but a spiritual one. It was the jailor's question. It was the central issue of what we must do in order to be saved — in order to be justified, to be reconciled, to be made right with God. They had heard the answer to that question from Paul. Since he was last there, however, they had heard divergent answers from other preachers. Plausible answers, it seemed to them. Paul wrote to remind them of the right answer — God's answer — to the great question.

In the end, we discover that the answer — to Naaman, to the Galatians, and to the people in our pews — is fundamentally the same. And that is the good news we are privileged to proclaim this week.

2 Kings 5:1-14

In just one verse, the biblical author tells us all we need to know about Naaman. He was a "commander," "a great man," "in high favor" with the Aramean king, a "mighty warrior." And he was a leper. Up until that final detail, his portrait was unblemished. But that one detail clouds every other thing.

Our modern idiom says, "If you have your health, you have everything." Well, Naaman didn't have his health. He had everything else, it seems. He was accomplished, high-ranking, famous, honored, strong, brave, and probably rather wealthy.

For all of his other achievements, however, here was an enemy that Naaman could not defeat. His skill, his strength, his strategy, and his sword were all useless in this personal battle. He was a man accustomed to winning — if not, after all, he would likely be either demoted or dead — and yet he had no strategy for victory here, no plan of attack for beating leprosy.

Then there came a ray of hope from a surprising source. A servant girl in Naaman's house — human loot from one of his many military campaigns — knew of a way that he could be healed. There was a prophet in Samaria who could cure Naaman of his leprosy.

As a military man, Naaman was probably accustomed to using intelligence gained from indigenous sources. Perhaps this young girl was on to something. And so, with a rich reward and a letter from the Aramean king in hand, Naaman set off for neighboring Israel to find healing.

Like the Magi of the Christmas story, Naaman went at first to the wrong address. Like them, he went first to the local king: a testament to our human reflex toward worldly power, importance, and resources. But the Israelite king was as unable to cure Naaman's leprosy as the Aramean king was. He took offense at the provocative assignment, until Elisha, the prophet, sent word that the incurable patient could be referred to him.

Naaman's entourage was forwarded to the home of the man of God. We do not know Elisha's address or neighborhood, but we might reasonably assume that it was a humble abode. There is certainly nothing in Elisha's biography, or in what we know more broadly about the prophets, to suggest that he would have been well-to-do. So we are presented with a picture of contrasts when Naaman arrives at Elisha's door.

Naaman frequented the palace in Aram, yet now he knocked on the door of a commoner in Israel. Naaman knew what it was to lay siege to great walled cities, yet now he came as a petitioner to the door of a mud house. Naaman carried with him a reward whose sum likely exceeded the entire net worth of Elisha and his household.

A military man might look at life in terms of rank. He gives orders to those under him. He takes orders from those above him. In Naaman's case, virtually everyone was below him; it may be that he took orders only from the king himself. As he stood outside Elisha's door, he may have been pondering their relative rank.

What piece is worth more: a bishop or a rook? Who ranks higher: the commander of the Aramean army, or an anonymous prophet from Israel? In the worldly realm, there's no question that Naaman wielded more power and authority. Perhaps in some other realm, however, this reputed man of God held sway.

Perhaps Naaman reconciled himself to an exercise of mutual respect — peers who salute simultaneously. He would honor and reward the prophet, in keeping with the great favor that the prophet would do him. And the prophet, meanwhile, would make an appropriate fuss over the visiting dignitary, bowing appreciatively before both the rank and the reward.

Instead, however, the prophet's servant appeared at the door to pass along to the commander an instruction: "Go, wash in the Jordan seven times, and your flesh shall be restored and you shall be clean."

Naaman was indignant. This was not at all the sort of treatment to which he was accustomed. Forget the mutual respect: nothing around him was of comparable rank. The flea-bitten prophet and his servant were not worthy of him. The muddy Jordan was not worthy of him. The undignified assignment was not worthy of him. He turned on his heel to leave when one of his own servants stopped and exhorted him.

That servant's exhortation becomes the turning point in the story and in Naaman's life. The substance of that exhortation is what you and I get to preach, as we will explore.

Galatians 6:(1-6) 7-16

Circumcision is not easy pulpit material for most of our churches.

In my situation, I am very fortunate to have a director of Christian education and a director of music who work hard to create a service that has thematic integrity. So the children's sermon and the choir's anthem are designed and selected each Sunday to echo the theme of the sermon. I would hate to tell either of them that I will be preaching about circumcision this Sunday.

Still, circumcision is central to the larger context of Paul's letter to the Galatians, and it is operative in our selected text, as well. Indeed, the word for circumcision (in several forms) appears five different times in our lection.

The Galatians had fallen under the influence of the so-called Judaizers, who preached an amended gospel. Paul was profoundly disappointed by how easily swayed the Galatian Christians were by such heresy. So he wrote a letter that is, even at its trough, emphatic, and rises to sarcasm, harsh critique, impatience, and anger.

For the Judaizers, the central issues were likely God's law and his everlasting covenant with the Old Testament people of Israel. Paul saw their conclusions, however, to be at odds with what he understood about faith, salvation, and life in the Spirit.

In Galatians, as elsewhere, we see that Paul operates with a spirit-versus-flesh paradigm. Now when a modern reader thinks about the works and the desires of the flesh, the associations are with standard fare physical appetites. But for Paul, even a dependence upon the circumcision of the old covenant is a way of catering to the flesh. And he believes that "what the flesh desires is opposed to the Spirit, and what the Spirit desires is opposed to the flesh; for these are opposed to each other" (Galatians 5:17).

Paul uses an agricultural metaphor to illustrate the choice we face as human beings. We may "sow to [our] own flesh" or "sow to the Spirit." As in the case of ordinary sowing, there is a predictable harvest. A farmer knows going in that by sowing corn he will harvest corn in the end. Likewise, we should be as matter-of-fact about our sowing in life. Sowing to the flesh, according to Paul, reaps corruption, while sowing to the Spirit reaps eternal life.

Paul's presentation is a refreshing one to folks who are weary of notions that eternal life is being tied to human merit or a capricious god. Paul offers an orderly picture: simple cause-and-effect.

The apostle also uses the natural image of sowing and reaping to offer an encouraging word. "Let us not grow weary in doing what is right," he writes, "for we will reap at harvest time, if we do not give up."

How often have I seen in my pastoral work — and how often have you seen in yours — people who have needed to hear precisely this word? I have sat with profoundly disappointed spouses, discouraged parents, sick patients, and from time to time I have looked in the mirror at a disheartened pastor and preacher. These folks are all weary in their own ways, and they are on the verge of giving up. But Paul says, "no" — an encouraging "no."

I have counseled people who have said that they could endure almost anything — for a time. And they could keep on going in their present circumstance if only they had some assurance of a light at the end of the tunnel.

Well, Paul offers just such an assurance: We reap what we sow. There is a natural order, and God is faithful. In the face of all the disappointment and despair, therefore, we cling to the predictability of the harvest — "if we do not give up."

Luke 10:1-11, 16-20

Ask your people this question: "Who are the people who are not in church?"

Some of them may think immediately of individual names. They think of regular attenders who happen to be out of town, or certain folks they haven't seen in a while, or perhaps some close friends or family members who simply won't come to church.

Other people in your congregation will not think of specific individuals, but rather entire groups: inactive members, high school kids, young adults, or perhaps the great general category of "the unchurched."

After you have given your people a moment to cogitate on the question for themselves, you can suggest what might be Jesus' answer: workers.

At first blush, it will seem to be a great insult, of course, to suggest that your church lacks workers. You and I know very well how hard working some of those folks in our pews are. And not just hard working in the other areas of their lives, but hard working in the church, as well, faithful, loyal, tireless workers.

Still, I think that is the gist of how Jesus would answer the question.

For the uncommitted, inactive, and unchurched not to be in church is no great surprise. They are simply playing their part. They are the harvest, and they are precisely where they ought to be: out in the mission field! And those folks are not lacking, according to Jesus. It's the workers. That's who is missing. Those are the people who aren't in church.

Or perhaps they are in church, but where they should be is out in the fields.

Jesus sends out his disciples to be workers in that field. And he doesn't airbrush, for them, the picture of their assignment: "I am sending you out like lambs into the midst of wolves."

In one moment, we are workers going into the fields. In the next moment, though, we are helpless lambs walking into a lair. What gives? Why the sudden — and significant — change in imagery? Because workers-in-the-harvest describes our mission. But lambs-among-wolves describes our experience.

That's an important distinction to make. For we are not called to victimhood; martyrdom is not our mission. Our purpose is not to risk our lives, but rather our purpose is to bring in the harvest. That mission may meet with hostility, and Jesus prepares his followers for that contingency.

Jesus' matter-of-fact instructions to his disciples are refreshing reading in our day. Culturally, we are so afraid of offending anyone that we think their offense is an indictment of our message. Not so. It is the foreseeable response of a certain percentage of the hearers. Remarkably, Jesus does not seem to fret overly much about those who reject the word. No apologies necessary; just shake off the dust against them.

When the disciples returned from their short-term mission, they were giddy with excitement. But their excitement may have been misplaced. It was not the salvation of souls that had them so thrilled; rather, it was the submissiveness of demons.

So it goes. So often there is a discrepancy between the objects of human fascination and the things that are truly important. The disciples had misunderstood what was truly exciting, truly thrilling. They were more taken by their relationship to the enemy than they were with their relationship with the Lord; more fascinated by power than by love and grace.

That preoccupation did not die with Peter, et al. In every generation, and still today, it is easy for the followers of Jesus to become distracted by the peripheral. But Jesus calls our attention back to this centrality: "Rejoice that your names are written in heaven."

Application

"What must I do?"

Naaman must have asked that of the doctors back in Aram. And that question must have been near the forefront of his mind as he and his entourage traveled down to Samaria and to Elisha's house.

Naaman's servant knew the import of the question, for he appealed to its possible answers. "If the prophet had commanded you to do something difficult, would you not have done it?"

We know the answer. If the prophet had required of Naaman some great, heroic feat in order to achieve his own healing, this proud and accomplished man would have set right to work. We are reminded of Saul's sinister requirement that David present him with the foreskins of a hundred Philistines as the bride price to marry Saul's daughter. The ambitious David both achieved and doubled the requirement. Surely Naaman would have done the same.

Similarly, if the prophet had made Naaman's healing an expensive affair, wouldn't the commander have willingly paid the price? After all, his life was at stake. What wouldn't he have done? What wouldn't he have spent?

When the word came back, however, that what he had to do was a simple and humble thing, Naaman balked. There was no personal achievement involved in this business of bathing in the Jordan. No purchase. No pride.

The Galatians, too, were caught up in an exaggerated notion that they had to do something to earn their salvation by legalistic works. But Paul reminded them that there was no boasting in the flesh involved in salvation. No, only the simplicity and humility of the cross of Christ.

Still today, there are folks in our midst who, like Naaman and the Galatians, would find God's good news far more palatable if it involved some room for personal achievement. Perhaps they are proud, and so they want salvation to be a product of their own righteousness. Perhaps they are guilty, so they feel they need to earn it. Perhaps they are legalists, and they feel compelled to comply. Perhaps they are pragmatists, and they find a free gift incomprehensible.

Whatever the case, some servant or apostle or preacher needs, again and again, to come along and say, "If you had to do a difficult thing to be saved, you would do it. So why not a simple and humble thing? Believe on the Lord Jesus, and you will be saved."

An Alternative Application
2 Kings 5:1-14. "Out of the Mouths of Servants." It's hard to read the story of Naaman without being struck by the contrasts between the human beings involved. Three particular characters sit in positions of importance and power by human standards: the king of Aram, the king of Israel, and, to a slightly lesser degree, Naaman himself. Two monarchs and a high-ranking military commander represent considerable earthly power.

In the face of Naaman's physical malady, however, these three men are powerless. Naaman clearly needs to go to someone for help. The best that his lord can provide is a letter of introduction, and Israel's king is dumbfounded by the whole affair.

Meanwhile, we meet three other players — people who can't compare to the rank and influence of the first three. There is the little servant girl in Naaman's household. She is young, helpless, and something of a victim. Yet she — unlike the previous three characters — knows where to turn in the time of need.

Shortly after, we meet the Israelite prophet. He has no crown on his head or stripes on his sleeve. Yet he is clearly in touch with a power that dwarfs all of the kings' and commander's resources.

Then there is the unnamed servant of Naaman: The one who talks him out of his rage and into the river. He sees and reasons clearly when Naaman does not.

The two sovereigns and the soldier are basically powerless in this story. Instead, it is the three other individuals, comparatively insignificant by worldly standards, who are the agents of power. We are reminded by Paul that "God chose what is foolish in the world to shame the wise; God chose what is weak in the world to shame the strong; God chose what is low and despised in the world, things that are not, to reduce to nothing things that are, so that no one might boast in the presence of God" (1 Corinthians 1:27-29).

Proper 10 / Pentecost 8 / Ordinary Time 15
Amos 7:7-17
Colossians 1:1-14
Luke 10:25-37
Mark Molldrem

Living forward in the present

"I felt almost guilty thinking too much of heaven." That is what David Burton, a Southern Baptist turned Catholic told a writer for *Time* in 1997. Burton, brought up to think of eternal life as the ultimate reward for living a Christian life, was surprised to encounter some religious leaders in his new church who didn't want to talk about heaven. Believing that most of us just don't have the knack of living righteously without the "carrot" of eternal life dangled in front of us, Burton found himself saying about good works: "Let's do this so we can go to heaven." Almost at once, someone in his new surroundings would say, "No, no, no. Let's do it because we *should* do good."

Burton found himself thinking that heaven was "too much like an ace in the hole, that it was sort of like cheating" he said, to hold eternal life out as a motivator for holy living (*Time*, March 24, 1997, p. 72).

Odd as it may seem to us religious types, a lot of people today aren't much moved one way or the other by talk of an afterlife, no matter whether it's for judgment or reward. But we cannot go far, especially in the New Testament, without considering the power of eternal life in calling believers to righteous living in their present, earthbound circumstances.

The three pericopes for today offer a fine opportunity to talk with your people about eternal matters. Amos, though living in a time that had no firm concept of afterlife, nonetheless spoke words of damning judgment with final consequences. Paul, writing to the Colossians, praised them "for the hope laid up for [them] in heaven" (Colossians 1:5). And Jesus, with his story of the good Samaritan, provided a memorable answer to the question, "What must I do to inherit eternal life?" (Luke 10:25).

Amos 7:7-17

It is unfortunate that Amos is among those who are referred to as "minor" prophets in the Old Testament. Of course, they are "minor" only because their writings are shorter; not that their message is any less important. Amos, as his name suggests, bears the burden of God's people in his heart and proclaims on his lips God's word to them. It is a word of judgment that "all the sinners of my people shall die by the sword" (Amos 9:10). There is only a brief glimpse of restoration given at the very end of his prophecy. Although, it only takes a little light to dispel darkness, in Amos' world there is a lot of darkness to dispel.

Called from his peasant upbringing as a herdsman and dresser of sycamore trees, Amos takes on the powers of the nations and the king of Israel. Coming from Tekoa, six miles southeast of Bethlehem, Amos locates his pulpit in Bethel, the religious center of the northern kingdom. The time is mid-eighth century BC during the reign of Jeroboam II (c. 786-746), a generation before Isaiah arises as prophet in the southern kingdom. Amos utters God's judgment against the surrounding nations (chs. 1-2) and then specifically against Israel (chs. 3-6). He rails against apostasy, greed, immorality, and oppression. His herald cry is: "Let justice roll down like waters, and righteousness like an ever-flowing stream" (Amos 5:24).

The plumb line vision (7:7-17) is third among five visions that conclude his written record. Although the judgment described in two visions is mercifully set aside (the plague of locust and the devouring fire; Amos 7:1-6), the plumb line remains in the midst of the people. There will be no averting this word from the Lord. Destruction will come. The religious places will "be made desolate... be laid waste" (7:9). The political fortunes of Jeroboam will go by way of the sword. What an ironic use of the plumb line! It is intended to aid in building straight and true. It's message here is that the judgment is true and will come straight upon the nation with God's exacting precision.

Amaziah, seeking to protect his turf at Bethel, rebuts with the same kind of wide-eyed optimism that Jeremiah had to face 150 years later (Jeremiah 7:4). Amos is not deterred. He is not a professional prophet with transferable credentials. He must obey the direction of God and simply do what God put in his hands to do where God instructed him to do it. The plumb line therefore also falls on Amaziah with a personal word of judgment (7:17).

Colossians 1:1-14

Even though writing from prison (Colossians 4:3, 18), Paul sets a positive tone for this letter. He is gratified to see that the gospel is "bearing fruit and growing" not only in Colossae but also in the whole world (1:6; granted, "the whole world" was a tad bit smaller to Paul than it is to us). Epaphras was the sower of the gospel among the Colossians. Paul may never have visited this congregation in person, though he passed through the area on his third missionary journey. He is content to let this letter and the prayer with which it is sent connect him to the Christian fellowship growing there.

Paul gives thanks for the cruciform life of the Colossians. They believe in Jesus as the Messiah, which can be represented by the vertical beam of the cross, signifying the relationship between the human and the divine. They also have love for all the saints, which can be represented by the horizontal beam of the cross, signifying our human relationship with one another. Paul's own suffering counts as nothing compared to the life of faith and love growing in Colossae. The gospel is pre-eminent.

Paul's prayer (1:9-10) is a great blueprint for the prayers of pastors for their flock, parents for their children, and Christians for their friends. First, he prays that the Colossians will know God's will. This involves more than just mental cognition of what God's will is. In his *Small Catechism*, Martin Luther spells this out in commentary on the Third Petition of the Lord's Prayer: "God's good and gracious will comes about without our prayer, but we ask in this prayer that it may also come about in and among us."

This brings Paul to the second prayer request, that the Colossians "lead a life worthy of the Lord" (1:10). This will certainly be done, when God's will is worked out in daily life — the decisions made, the actions performed, and the words used.

As this becomes the character of life, Paul's third request will be fulfilled that the Colossians will increase in the knowledge of the Lord. This growth, like bearing fruit from a mature plant, will manifest the very intent of the will of God, namely, to be active existentially in the life of the believer, bringing about the desired responses in word and deed. Thus, it becomes ethical knowledge, not esoteric knowledge, and abounds more and more in the life of the believer, like a light on a rheostat switch being turned on brighter and brighter (see 2 Corinthians 3:18).

And thus there is "the hope laid up in heaven" for the Christian from Colossae (Colossians 1:5).

Luke 10:25-37

The good Samaritan story is such common knowledge that President Bush could allude to it in his inaugural address and expect to be understood: "When we see that wounded traveler on the road to Jericho, we will not pass to the other side," the new chief executive said. What is not so well remembered is the question that brought about the story. The question is not so much the one about the neighbor, though that is the immediate question. Rather the question to which the story and Jesus' other words respond, is the one about inheriting eternal life. Jesus pushes the impertinent lawyer to answer the question himself. It is written in the law that one should love God (Deuteronomy 6:4-5) and love their neighbor (Leviticus 19:18). The lawyer, as well as any good Jew of the day, would know that.

"What must I do to demonstrate that I have the quality of life that is valued by God?" This recasts the focus of the question toward the here and now of life. It would be easy to talk about eternal life as a kind of "never-never land," off in the sky somewhere, at which one will arrive after this life has run its course. But Jesus keeps the focus on this gritty earth, telling a story that enables one to conclude that the love of God and the love of neighbor are characteristic of the eternal life that one hopes to gain. When we behave as the Samaritan demonstrates, we have some grounds for saying we have inherited eternal life. It surely comes to us as a gift (Romans 6:23b), and that gift finds expression in how we actually love in our daily life. That's why it's important to ask, "Who is my neighbor?"

The neighbor is the one in need; the neighborly one is whoever provides for the need.

Mercy is characteristic of neighborly love. Notice how the Samaritan went out of his way *to* the wounded man, rather than out of his way to pass by *on the other side*, as the priest and Levite did. This is not just a physical matter but also a cultural one. For Jews and Samaritans did not have much to do with one another, due to a long-standing history of animosity fueled by jealousy and judgmentalism (see John 4:1-42). It is a quality of mercy to set aside preconceived notions, however justified one may feel about them, to enable one to respond to another's need. Notice also how the Samaritan was generous and self-sacrificing, offering two-day's wage initially to care for the man at an inn, based on need and not on the deservedness of the individual. Again, a quality of mercy.

Application

Our era had been tagged as the Communication Age. The church has a communication to give to our nation and to the world, just as Amos had for his day. It is an echo of the judgment that Amos rendered audible and visible through the words and images with which he communicated "the word of the Lord" (7:16). In our age, of course, there are enough problems — wrongdoings, hatreds, broken promises — to keep a regiment of Amoses busy issuing divine judgment. Thus, the church today sometimes needs to bring out the plumb line and raise a prophetic voice — locally, nationally, and globally.

Because of the revelation of Jesus Christ, Paul remained hopeful, even under the hand of persecution and rejection, of the hope laid up for eternal life that would be manifest in his present age as well, with Christ being all and in all (Colossians 3:11). Therefore, his prayer for the Colossians can become our prayer for one another today. This prayer will help us focus on what is truly important in life — the rule of God in our hearts and in the cosmos. To increase in the knowledge of God means the transformation of the self away from this age only, but to color this age with the hues of eternity.

This is the way to live, "because of the hope laid up for you in heaven" (Colossians 1:5). To live in the present in a way that anticipates the future reality of God's rule over all affirms the importance of the present, however fleeting and however partial. "Already now we can live in the power of the future; already now we can shape our lives in accordance with God and his future kingdom," is the way Eberhard Arnold expressed it in a 1923 lecture. His contribution to the welfare of Christian community was to stress that Jesus was serious in his call to radical discipleship. "This is why the church exists: to dare to start *now* with this future, perfect world of God's kingdom." (See *Salt and Light*, a collection of writings and talks by Eberhard Arnold.)

This last comment was made to his brothers and sisters in Christ of the Rhon Bruderhof facing oppressive measures from the Nazi regime (1933). Soon this community of radical Christian idealists would be raided by the Gestapo. They would have to whisk their children off to Switzerland for safety. In the face of this, they felt compelled, in the words of Emmy Arnold, "to continue to live for the witness entrusted to us and to speak out... and so we continued to build" (*A Joyful Pilgrimage*).

What a benediction verse 11 contains for those who are sick, struggling, dying, doubtful, fearful, or tired. Because Christians are the heirs of grace, we can thank God at all times, for God will strengthen us with the gifts necessary for daily life. Paul learned this through all his trials and was able to report God's salutary word to him, "My grace is sufficient for you" (2 Corinthians 12:9). These similar words to the Colossians are very encouraging to Christians today. They point them forward through trials because God's strength for endurance will be present. They can proceed with confidence, for joy will be their reward as they exercise patience, knowing they can thank God in all things (see also Romans 8:28-30 and Philippians 4:4-7).

The hope laid up for us in heaven, as Paul writes, has the power to shape our lives on earth in the here and now. The good Samaritan is to be every Christian, not striving to "inherit eternal life" through works of righteousness; but, rather, manifesting the already-inherited gift of eternal life through righteous acts of mercy in the name of Jesus, who commands his followers "Go and do likewise" (Luke 10:37). He commands us already as disciples. We are heirs of grace and now called upon, in Paul's words, to "work out your own salvation in fear and trembling; for God is at work in you, both to will and to work for his good pleasure" (Philippians 2:12-13).

Proper 11 / Pentecost 9 / Ordinary Time 16
Amos 8:1-12
Colossians 1:15-28
Luke 10:38-42
Mark Molldrem

After the handshake and the hug

The master brought his disciples into a darkened room with one instruction: "Find the truth." One disciple came upon a table and declared that the truth is flat and square. Another touched the wall and said, "The truth is hard and wide." A third disciple stumbled upon a ball and concluded that the truth was round and bounces. The fourth disciple simply stood in the middle of the room, not impressed with the other statements. He thought and thought, until finally concluding, "The truth is empty." Finally, the master lit a candle, visually revealing the objects and space that gave rise to the various comments and announced, "The truth is that you have all been in the dark."

Amos, Paul, and Jesus each have something to say about perceiving the essential nature of their given situations. As we listen to them, it will be like a candle lit in a dark room, illuminating our reality for clarity in thought and action.

Amos 8:1-12

With another text from Amos this week, we return to the eighth century BC. If God is going to "never again pass by" (8:2), it would be well and good to understand why. Perhaps in that knowledge there may be found courage for endurance unto the other side of silence.

In his fourth vision, Amos sees a basket of summer fruit. It is one basket representing one fate for the nation. This is in contrast to Jeremiah's two baskets (Jeremiah 24:1-10), one that represents the future of the exiled remnant and the other that represents the lack of future for those who will perish in Jerusalem and Egypt. Israel, i.e., the northern kingdom, has reached the end of its story. Assyria will write the final chapter. The summer fruit has been picked. It is rotting now under the hot sun, never to see autumn.

Judgment will come upon the people because of their oppression of the poor (8:4), their cheating, and their greed (8:5). There is more interest for the sabbath to be over for the sake of gain, than for the sabbath to come and linger for the sake of rest and refreshment. God will not overlook any of this impertinent behavior, just like one cannot help but notice the floodwaters of the Nile. As the waters outside the banks devastate the land, so shall devastation result from the flood of disobedience, drowning the people in their sin. Instead of songs of victory, praise, and thanksgiving in the temple, there shall be lamentation.

Amos visualizes the people in sackcloth and baldness as signs of their wretchedness before the Lord. Whereas Pharaoh mourned for his firstborn son on the day of deliverance generations ago, this generation will enter into mourning as "for an only son" (8:10). When the hearts of God's people are hardened, they too shall know "a bitter day" (8:10).

More penetrating than these images of judgment, is the absence of God that Amos declares (8:11-12). How dreadful for a people who have been blessed by the word of the Lord from their founding days (whether one marks that in Ur or at the foot of Sinai)! The promise will not be repeated; the Torah will not awaken any ear or stir any heart. The people will be left in silence, because they will not be able to find the word of the Lord, as during a famine when no grain can be harvested (8:11). Here is God's wrath at its most horrible expression, for it means that those left in silence will perish! If it is true that mortals do not live by bread alone, but by every word that proceeds from the mouth of God (Deuteronomy 8:3), what else but death could result from the silence of God?

This death is applied to the up-and-coming generation, those "fair virgins" and "young men" who will, in fact, "faint for thirst... fall, and never rise again" (8:13-14). The gods they sought out in their darkness, whether in the shrines of Samaria (see 2 Kings 17:30) or in the calf idol at Dan (1 Kings 12:28-29) or the powers that be in Beer-sheba, will prove impotent. The one, true God will stand by in silence and grieve the people of his making, who now reply to him with mocking, substituting hands-on deities for the inscrutable deity of cosmos and history.

Colossians 1:15-28

When Paul was in Athens (Acts 17:16-34), he found himself in an idol-laden city among philosophers of several stripes who loved to chat about anything new in the world of ideas. When pressed by these talking-heads, Paul seized the opportunity to present the gospel of Jesus in the Areopagus, a public setting where kings had once been advised by councils. Paul connected with his audience in a most unusual way. He did not address them on what they thought they knew, whether they were Epicurean or Stoic philosophers or religious believers. He started with what they did not know, drawing attention to the altar "to an unknown god."

In Colossians, Paul fleshes out the Christology upon which his very knowledge of God (the unknown, unless God chooses to reveal himself to the world, 1:25-27) is based and upon which his confidence in the resurrection rests. These descriptors of Christ can be better understood against the background of gnostic thought that pervaded so much thinking at the time. Although there are always variations from person to person and between schools of thought within a general outlook, basically, the Gnostics relied on "insight" rather than "revelation." Knowledge of God was attained by taking one's self as the starting point.

Typical of gnostic cosmology is a multi-storied universe, filled with emanations upon emanations from God, proceeding from pure spirituality to more material substance. Tertullian (160-220 AD) in *Adversus Valentinianos 7*, characterized the gnostic universe as an apartment building, "with room piled on room, and assigned to each god by just as many stairways as there were heresies: the universe has been turned into rooms for rent!" Though gnosticism surely had pre-Christian roots, it infected Christian tradition with heretical notions that reduced the status of Christ in salvation history and spiritualized the resurrection. (For a more complete understanding of gnosticism and the role it played in the formation of early church doctrine and structure, see Elaine Pagels' *The Gnostic Gospels*.)

Paul claims that Christ is the very image of the invisible God, not a distant emanation from God. Christ is the firstborn of all creation (1:15). This is not meant in terms of a temporal sequence. It emphasizes that Christ stands above and beyond creation in an essential way, such that he is superior to it. This term refers not so much to his relationship to creation, as it does to his relationship to God. For Paul goes on to describe how all things were created "in him... through him and for him" (1:16). All things hold together in Christ, who is "before all things" (1:17). All these prepositions work together to elevate Christ above the creation, as God the creator is above the creation. Jesus Christ is neither a *lesser god*, nor is he *mere mortal*; he is the fullness of God (1:19; see also John 1:14).

His work is "to reconcile... all things" to God by means of his sacrificial death, "making peace by the blood of his cross" (1:20). This is a work external to humanity and becomes a revelation to humanity for the sake of salvation. It is a work done by God through Jesus Christ. One cannot attain to it through mere insight. It is a gift from the very Son of God (see Colossians 1:3), the mystery of God's heart unwrapped for the whole world to see.

This is the very reason that Jesus Christ is also the head of the church. This is not just a titular distinction, but one in fact, dynamically lived out in time because he is firstborn from the dead (1:18). His preeminence is established by the singular event of the resurrection.

This is the faith in which Paul urges the Colossians to remain "stable and steadfast" (1:23; see also Ephesians 4:14; Galatians 1:6-7; Revelation 2:10). He offers his own sufferings as a sign for the Colossians to take him seriously, an authentic witness to the gospel of Jesus, into whom all disciples are to grow in maturity.

Luke 10:38-42

It is true that in John 11—12:11 we learn of a more intimate relationship between Jesus and the Mary-Martha-Lazarus family. Yet, in Luke we are treated to a scene in which Mary teaches us a very important lesson in life: *one thing is needful* and that is to listen to Jesus (10:39, 42).

The same family word is used regarding Martha receiving Jesus into her house and regarding the reception of the seventy in the outlying villages (Luke 10:8 and Luke 10:38). In this receiving there is implied an openness to hear the message of Jesus. Mary embodies what this means when she literally sits at Jesus' feet to listen to him.

Jesus sees in Mary a person who has chosen the one thing needful. This is highlighted by Martha's busyness in serving daily bread in contrast to Mary's choice to receive the Bread of Life. This is "the good portion" that will endure beyond the mold of daily bread. The preposition under or beneath attached to the verb "to receive" not only prefigures Mary's posture with Jesus, but also the depth of her devotion. Unfortunately, Martha "was distracted with much serving" (10:40) and gained only anxiety for her efforts, rather than "the good portion."

Jesus can look on an entire crowd and have compassion on them all (Matthew 9:36); yet, for Martha, he can dismiss her anxiety and not lift a hand to help her, but rather lift up Mary as an example to redirect her attentions. That would necessitate a choice for Martha. If John 12:1-11 is a different perspective on the same scene, we still have Jesus lifting up the importance of attention and devotion around him. A choice still has to be made, whether between the poor and an extravagant offering to Jesus, or between feeding others and being fed by the supplier of all.

Application

Imagine Amos' prophecy applying to us today. It is really not too hard to imagine. There is a growing disparity between the rich and the poor in America, with some suggesting that the middle class is becoming smaller and smaller. (Compound this with the dramatic difference between quality of life in first-world nations and third-world nations.) One out of five children in America, the wealthiest and most powerful nation on earth, live in poverty. Every day in most every newspaper there are reports of greed and graft from armed robbery to embezzlement to stock fraud. Court TV shows are filled with claims of deceit, broken promises, and meanness — and we find this entertaining!

Further imagine what it would mean to have the judgment of God fall upon us now. What would we grieve? The loss of our pensions? Our church buildings? Our national identity under the perception of manifest destiny? Would it ever dawn on any one of us to reel at the loss of our salvation? Does anyone dread the silence of God, or do we think that with the radio, television, and internet so available that we are bound to hear something important along the way? Or even more scary: Do we think that as long as our churches are paid for and the appointments kept clean and in place that we are guaranteed God will remain in our midst?

Look carefully at Amos 8:13-14, although they are not part of the assigned lectionary. They should be. It is very unpleasant to hear these words that cast the future into severe doubt. Dare we consider that the next generation may not rise up, but rather fall? *En mass* they have already fallen for just about anything and everything that is not holy. Granted they are on a spiritual quest, but they have ventured into the fields of pluralism and relativism so as to avoid having to be decisive. They only have to select one among many possibilities, any of which could suit their purpose. They do not perceive the choice as singular and a matter of life or death. The only thing that will be sacrificed on the altars of our own making will be ourselves. Such a sacrifice is not strong enough to bond us to God.

The "shifting from the hope of the gospel" that Paul fears may have already taken place today. So much of the language of Christians today has lost it Christo-centric heart. From self-professing Christians when talking about other faith systems, one hears such expressions as: "We all believe the same thing; we are all going to the same place; there's only one God." This seems to be the core of the faith of so many these days, especially in an effort to be conciliatory and inclusive. The result for Christians is a watered-down religiosity that does not shape one's life distinctively but more-or-less sets a mood of spirituality. This mood links one's daily endeavors to factors other than one's specific relationship with the living God or his mediator, Jesus Christ.

John Dart, once news editor of the *Christian Century*, wrote an article for the January-February 2001 issue of *Sojourners* magazine in which he observed that, whereas in the past, religious coverage was conducted on a denomination vs. denomination model, in the future it will pit believer (whether Christian, Muslim, Jew, Mormon, New Age, Hindu, and so on) vs. non-believer (atheist, agnostic, secularist, areligious). He also projects that "if religious literacy continues to slide [in the media]... religious nuances might seem irrelevant when all one needs to know is if a group's members are believers or non-believers."

The "divine office" (Colossians 1:25) from which pastors work is a gift, through which the pastor makes the word known so that the believer can be presented mature in Christ (Colossians 1:28). This is the goal of Christian ministry. Parishioners must, therefore, hear over and over again that Christ is pre-eminent by virtue of his work and his relationship to the Father. Paul writes of a veil that is over our eyes preventing us from seeing God clearly, a veil that can only be lifted through Christ (2 Corinthians 3:14). In worship, the veil is lifted through liturgy, word, and sacrament.

A question every congregation should ask itself is whether it is so focused on people and programs that it neglects the person of Christ. We say we do these things in the name of Christ (hospitality and focus groups and fellowship events, and so on); yet, how easy it is to engage in these activities and not mention the name of Christ. We become a distracted Martha, rather than a needful Mary. We must never forget that the purpose for ourselves and those we would evangelize is to sit at the feet of Jesus, to choose the good portion, which cannot be taken away from us when the handshake and hug are over, the discussion ended or the program folded.

Proper 12 / Pentecost 10 / Ordinary Time 17
Hosea 1:2-10
Colossians 2:6-15 (16-19)
Luke 11:1-13
Mark Molldrem

Fullness by any other name...

"The whole experience was dirty, draining, and depressing." That's how George Stephanopoulos, in his book *All Too Human*, described one period in the run for the Clinton presidency. In the book, Stephanopoulos tells the story of his political education, which, to a point, was also a spiritual education. With ambition and vanity, George quickly rose in the ranks of those who served President Clinton. He became the president's senior advisor and basked in the fame and the fury of that position. Then he discovered that this lifestyle did not provide him with the fullness of life that he wanted. He admits in this painfully honest and revealing book that he failed to heed the advice of his father, who, after reminding him of the myth of Icarus, said to him upon Clinton's election to the White House, "Be careful. Keep your balance."

How do we keep balance in our furious world? How do we maintain an even keel amid siren sounds promising fulfillment and satisfaction in this pursuit or that acquisition? Let's listen to what Hosea and Paul have to tell us from what they witness in the course of human events. They will direct our attention to how God is acting in the world, an attention that will ultimately be focused on the cross of Christ. From Christ Jesus we will hear today some important words about prayer, which is God's gift to keep us in the balance between heaven and earth, God's rule and our temptations.

By the way, I am using the word "fullness" a good bit in this discussion. Admittedly, it's one of those churchy words that people don't use often in everyday speech. (If you doubt that, just go to an internet search engine, type in "fullness" and see how many religious and how few secular sites come up!) But if you look up "full" in a dictionary, there are plenty of connections to life. If you choose to speak about fullness using that term, you might want to remind your hearers of some of those associations.

Hosea 1:2-10

The prophecy of Hosea, along with that of his contemporary Amos, sealed the fate of the northern kingdom. "The days of Jeroboam" (Hosea 1:1) would be among the last days of Israel. God, through the hands of the Assyrians, would see to that. Before the close of the eighth century BC, Hosea's harsh words against the house of Jehu would be fulfilled: not pitied and not my people will be the name by which Israel will be remembered. There was a dreadful price to be paid for the religious apostasy that characterized the nation. Rather than relying on God as their fortress and their might, the leadership crafted political alliances with the Assyrians and the Egyptians. They permitted and even promoted Baal worship in concession to local culture. Immorality was rampant, as the priests filled their personal coffers with gain.

Onto this scene strides Hosea (whose name means "salvation," related to the root word for Joshua) with a word of judgment. In contrast to Amos' visions (for example, the plumb line and the basket of fruit), Hosea lives out a personal parable through which he speaks volumes to the nation. Hosea is instructed by the Lord to take a wife — and not just any wife, but Gomer, a woman unfaithful in relationships. In his marriage, Hosea would be mirroring God's relationship to his people. Just as Gomer practiced harlotry, so too had the people of Israel practiced harlotry, even though they had been married to the Lord (1:2). Gomer's three children by Hosea are named prophetically as types of the people of Israel.

First born is Jezreel, named to recall the sins of Ahab and Jezebel (2 Kings 9:7-10), the latter whose flesh would be eaten by the dogs of Jezreel. What is sobering about this judgment is that God judges the very ones whom he had used for his judgment earlier (see 2 Kings 9:30—10:36). No one escapes the wrath of God, not even those whom he raises up to execute his wrath. The house of Jehu will be brought down, just like the house of Ahab was brought down, by the hand of the Lord in judgment for its sins.

Second born is Not Pitied. God will no longer offer his mercy to the people who have proven so rebellious. Judah, however, will still be favored to carry out God's purposes. Instead, through Judah, the promises made to God's people will be fulfilled. They shall inherit the moniker "Sons of the living God" (1:10).

Third born is Not My People. Not only will God remove his favor from the people, but also his identity. They will no longer be known as the people of God, for they will be no more. When God removes his presence from the people (symbolized by his removing his name from them), their presence on the landscape of time disappears. After the Assyrian rampage through the countryside under Sargon II, the rod of God's anger (Isaiah 10:5), was completed in 721 BC, that is exactly what happened.

Colossians 2:6-15 (16-19)

Apparently, Paul has not visited this congregation (Colossians 2:1-5). Epaphras was the seed-planter of faith and Paul is confident in and appreciative of the work that he did (Colossians 1:7-8). Paul does, however, want to affirm and encourage the Colossians in their faith (Colossians 2:2, 5).

In these few verses of our pericope, Paul provides a synopsis of the faith in terms of the incarnation, crucifixion, and resurrection of Jesus the Christ. To say that "the whole fullness of deity dwells bodily" in him (2:9) is to strike down the gnostic notion that Christ is a demigod, a distant emanation from the one, true God. Placing the prepositional phrase "in him" at the beginning of the sentence is Paul's way of emphasizing that precisely in Jesus God has incarnated his presence and love for humanity (see also John 1:14). We get the real McCoy in Jesus, not a hand-me-down! This underscores the sufficiency and the superiority of Jesus when it comes to the knowledge of God amid competing truth claims of various philosophies and human traditions, which Paul decries as "empty enticements" (2:8). The writer to the Hebrews argues this same point, only within the context of the sacrifice system of the first covenant (Hebrews 8-10 especially).

Verses 13-14 make wonderful declarations about our sins and the cross of Christ. It is similar to what Paul writes in Romans 5:6-11. Our sins are our death. God takes the initiative to cancel "the bond which stood against us with its legal demands" (2:14; see also Romans 3:26 and 6:23a). The indictment is nailed to the cross with our sins in the body of Jesus, so that we may be free of their curse. This is what forgiveness means, what grace is all about (2:13).

Just as Christians are buried with Christ into death in baptism, so too in that same baptism are they raised to new life, fullness of life in him (2:10). Because Jesus is raised from the dead, he is the head of all rule and authority and can provide us with that which we could not attain to ourselves, namely a growth that is from God (2:19). Paul goes on to describe this growth later in his letter (Colossians 3:12f), as he applies the grace of God to the various situations and conditions of human life together.

As Christians are rooted in what Christ has done, making them alive to God, they can be built up into a fullness of life that also comes from God. This fullness of life is not necessarily manifest in ascetic disciplines or ritual practices (2:16-18), but in a growth into Christ-likeness, represented by Paul's expression to hold fast to the head (2:19). In the second half of this letter, Paul details what this means in terms of the character of daily Christian life.

Luke 11:1-13

One cannot read the gospels without noticing that Jesus was often in prayer. Whether that be in a lonely place apart, in the upper room, in Gethsemane, or on the cross, Jesus was certainly a man of prayer. It is not strange, then, that the disciples would approach him and ask him to teach them to pray. It was common custom for a rabbi to give a special prayer to his disciples, so that they too could use prayer to voice their heart to God. The disciples saw John the Baptist giving his disciples such a prayer, and this band of devotees wanted one from Jesus, their rabbi.

In response, Jesus encouraged them not only to pray, but he also gave them precious words to use in their prayers. Whether they used their Lord's prayer before or after their individual prayers, or in place of them all together, they would be praying for the essentials of the godly life. First, their petitions would honor God and seek God's rule in their lives and on earth above all else. Second, their petitions would focus on essential human needs for life — namely, personal well-being, well-being in human relationships, and well-being in relationship with God.

One of the interesting words used in Luke's version of the Lord's Prayer is the conjunction which, in this instance means, "for, the ground or reason being...." The petition to forgive us our sins is offered, strangely enough, grounded on the observation that Christians in fact forgive those who are in some way indebted to them (11:4). The way this should be understood is not as an argument with God based on works righteousness: "God, you must forgive our sins, based on the fact that we ourselves have already forgiven others." That would go against the basic understanding throughout the New Testament that forgiveness is a free, unmerited gift from God. Instead, think of it as a human touch-point that provides assurance that God is indeed a forgiving God; for, if we can be forgiving, then certainly God, who is above and beyond us, can be forgiving. We are, after all, created in God's image.

It is interesting that Matthew's version of the Lord's Prayer uses the adverb in this petition to express the relative manner in which God should forgive our sins — as we forgive those who sin against us. Jesus' explanation in Matthew 6:14-15 (see also Matthew 18:21-35) confirms this nuance of meaning. In contrast, Luke's recording of Jesus' reflections on a father's treatment of a son's request (Luke 11:11-13) validates the intentional use of the word meaning "for, the ground or reason being" is an expression of the reasoning by which we may approach God expectantly with our requests.

This is further drawn out in Luke by Jesus' little story of importunity (11:5-8). It's odd, don't you think, that friendship is not the basis for response to a request; rather, audacity and obtrusiveness is (11:8). Jesus again lifts up this angle on prayer in Luke 18:1-8. The point is simply not to lose heart; be persistent and keep knocking on heaven's door. That is the privilege of prayer. God invites us to come before him like an insistent child will approach daddy ("abba" — the Aramaic expression for the Greek Pater, which lacks the formalism of the traditional and liturgically oriented formulation found in Matthew's version of the Lord's Prayer as "Our Father in heaven ...").

Application

How many Jews going through the Holocaust and those living in its aftermath have considered themselves Not Pitied and Not My People? Berish, the innkeeper in Elie Wiesel's *The Trial of God*, declares, "God is merciless, don't you know that?" He states, what the people of the northern kingdom in the eighth century BC could have uttered anachronistically, "Purim is over. For good." (Purim is the feast celebrating the deliverance of the Hebrew people from the plotting of Haman, recorded in the book of Esther, possibly written in the fourth or fifth century BC.)

Yet, there is a promise in God's word of judgment: "In the place where it was said to them, 'You are not my people,' it shall be said to them, 'Sons of the living God' " (Hosea 1:10). Though six million indeed perished in the Holocaust, yet as a people the Jews survived. Again, from *The Trial of God*, in a terse exchange Sam, a stranger, says, "Blessed be the Lord for his miracles." To which Mendel, the eldest and wisest of the ensemble, replies, "A whole community was massacred, and you talk of miracles?" Sam rebuts, "A Jew survived, and you ignore them?"

How can we speak of fullness of life in the midst of such tragedy? It certainly is not easy and only comes after much struggle; but it is possible, because God's promises persist. Just as God provided a promise in the midst of his judgment upon Israel, so too there are promises in any and every situation where we may find ourselves. Fullness of life, after all, is not found in our own satisfaction, but in satisfying God's will in our lives. Note how survivors of cancer, whether patients or bereaved loved ones, grow beyond their grief when they become involved in advocating education or funding research in the field. Note how some prisoners, upon release from incarceration, join the battle for prison reform. The faithful not only look for practical responses like these to hard-knock situations; they also search for a deeper understanding of the mysteries of God and how to communicate them to a world that puts God on trial. The faithful will still find fullness of life in the midst of tragedies, as they continue to praise God and love God — in spite of themselves and for the sake of the neighbor who is struggling to find God's true nature.

In his book *Why Christian?* which he describes as "for people on the edges," Douglas John Hall strives to provide a convincing, Christian response for people who are looking for resolution to their spiritual longings, whether they are on the edges of faith or on the edges of the Christian tradition or on the edges of the church. This apologetic work attempts to make clear connections between Christian belief and the human situation.

This is so needful in our day and age when spiritual energy is strong, but, more times than not, misdirected. The Zeitgeist has endorsed the spiritual journey and consecrated by the powers of individualism, relativism, and pluralism, it is considered to be self-defined and self-directed. Paul, in Colossians, helps guide the quest to find its fullness "in him," that is, in Jesus Christ. Over and over again, the reader of this letter is directed to Jesus in order to find the fullness of life (in him) that is the longing of every human heart.

There may be some discussion just how to translate the last prepositional phrase in verse 15, whether it should read "in him" or "in it" (that is, the cross). This simply points to the obvious, so that to find Jesus one must look to the cross. To look to the cross is to see just where Jesus does his work on our behalf. To see the cross is to see how God shows his love for us and to what extent God will go to claim us as his forgiven and accepted beloved. It is as the beloved that the believer grows into the fullness of life that God intends.

What better way to grow into the fullness of life that God intends for his beloved than to pray? Today, what we learn about prayer from Jesus is that prayer is offered to God's glory; it is asking for needs, not wants; it is concerned about right relationship with God as well as one's neighbor. Ultimately, prayer is communication with God that there be communion with God (Luke 11:13) — that we have God, like a log absorbs fire into its very being until it changes its wood fiber composition into heat and light. In this way the log becomes more than itself; transformed into fullness of life. In the same way, Christians become more than themselves as they let God's Holy Spirit burn within them to will and to work his good pleasure.

Proper 13 / Pentecost 11 / Ordinary Time 18
Hosea 11:1-11
Colossians 3:1-11
Luke 12:13-21
Mark Molldrem

"Up" is not the only heavenly direction

Annual meetings, whether for a business corporation, a nonprofit agency, or a local congregation, usually yield official resolutions. These documents outline a concern that is then addressed with a "Therefore, be it resolved...." The resolution calls for a course of action to respond appropriately to the situation. Some of these actions involve signing up, turning on, moving out, focusing in, rising above, getting beneath, hunkering down, pushing through, facing off, aiming toward and away from — potentially heavenly directions all.

The Bible is God's record of resolutions in dealing with humanity. Although there are many different instances throughout the Bible when God expressed his resolve regarding a specific situation, the essential resolve of God is to love his entire creation, reaching out and drawing in. God's resolve to love shapes our resolve to love not only God, but also one another.

Hosea 11:1-11

One of the most beloved images of God in the Bible is that of a parent. Jesus prays to his heavenly Father. Paul often refers to God as Father (for example, Colossians 1:3 and 1 Thessalonians 3:11-13). Deuteronomy compares God to a mother eagle hovering over her young (Deuteronomy 32:11). And Hosea speaks God's word to the people in terms of the parent-child relationship: "When Israel was a child, I loved him, and out of Egypt I called my son" (11:1).

Despite this love, the family relationship was strained, like all earthly families are, with rebellion. Just as teenage youth tune out their parents, the people of Israel would not listen to the voice of God. They went after what intrigued them at the time (11:2). There is a line in the hymn "Borning Cry" by John Ylvisaker, which expresses this well: "in a blaze of light you wandered off to find where demons dwell."

Just like children can take their parents' care for granted, not even noticing all that is being done for them out of love, so too the people of God in Hosea's time were oblivious to the many ways God provided for them. Being taught to walk righteously, being healed, supported and fed, the people had every reason to be grateful to God but they were not. Instead, they "wandered off." They listened to the siren sounds of other gods, distracted by subtle, sweet lies.

For this there would be discipline, a hard love resolved to purge the sin, yet save the sinners (11:8-9). Verse 8 alludes to the war of kings (Genesis 14:1-12) as an example of what God does not want to have happen. Just as Abram provided deliverance then, God would restore his children to their family inheritance after the discipline. It is true that the northern kingdom, as such, was obliterated, never to resurface on the map of history. However, Judah was the salvaged remnant. Of course, the Gentile Christians were later grafted onto the tree of God's pleasant planting, as the New Israel, the church, inheriting the promises of God through the Messiah who had come and in whom they believed (Romans 11:17-24).

Note the anguish of God in being true to his holiness as well as his compassion. His holiness calls for judgment, such as that regarding his rebellious people: "They are appointed to the yoke, and none shall remove it" (11:7). The Assyrian conquest was decisive, as the archaeological and historical records reveal. Still, God's compassion calls for a word of hope (11:11), which was indeed extended to Judah (Assyria's intrusions were thwarted short of the total devastation that the northern kingdom was subject to) and by further extension, to the New Israel, the church.

God's resolve to love even his rebellious children would bring him to express his righteousness through Jesus the Christ, who would endure the wrath of sin for our sake and release his compassion of forgiveness, which would open the way for life abundant and life eternal.

Colossians 3:1-11

One of the ways we structure our language is through directional metaphors. "Wake *up*." "He *sank* into a coma." Spatial orientations such as up, above, and over carry with them a more positive, desirable connotation than down, under, and low. It is better to have one's health at its *peak*, than to *drop* dead. It is better to *come in* than to *wander off*, as the people of Hosea's day did. So, it is no accident that Paul would use such an expression as "seek the things that are *above*" (3:1). He, then, goes on to use a different image of clothing — "put off... put on" — to talk about the character of the Christian life (the quality of which Hosea would have loved to see in his day and for his people!).

The resurrection of Jesus and our participation in it introduces us into the superior life, the stronger life, the godly life. Paul describes the character of that life in 3:12f. In our text for today, he identifies those things that are antithetical to such a life. It reads like a dirty laundry list: fornication, covetousness, malice, slander, foul talk — to mention just a few. The list is suggestive, not exclusive. Such clothing is not becoming for a Christian. It is to be *put off*, not in the sense of a time-delay ("Don't put off till tomorrow what you can do today"), but in the spatial sense of putting away from one that which should not be near, neither to the body nor to the soul.

Paul's premise is that Jesus has been raised from the dead and that *that* resurrection has the power to change the life of the believer. "If then you have been raised with Christ" is not a quandary; it is an appeal to reason. Paul takes believers in Christ Jesus and walks them into the next step with Jesus. The life that was lived *for us* will now shape the life that will be lived *for him*.

One can imagine Paul leading a tour through the Christian home, as it were. He has already shown us the washroom (Colossians 2:12; baptism). Now, he is showing us the laundry room where our Christian apparel is made presentable. In this matter of dress, we are all subject to the same standards, for Christ is "all and in all" (3:11). By the power of his new resurrected nature, he gives believers a new nature that is continually being shaped in his likeness (3:10).

Luke 12:13-21

Jesus talks a lot about money and its relationship to spirituality. He takes a coin and distinguishes what belongs to Caesar and what belongs to God. A widow's mite impresses him more than the apparent generosity of the wealthy. A field with buried treasure gives him occasion to talk about the value of the kingdom of God. When profit motivates the provisions for offerings in the temple, he gets quite physical in his outrage. It should come as no surprise that someone would ask him to settle a matter of inheritance. Jesus knew the tradition of Deborah (Judges 4:4-5) and Solomon (1 Kings 3:16-28) and might have been tempted to take pride that he should be considered worthy of judging a matter of such importance. This was not a trick question, like so many of those by the Pharisees and scribes. This was a genuine request to arbitrate a very sticky issue.

Jesus goes to the heart of the matter: covetousness. To what extent will one go to get what one considers a right belonging? That one would come to the Lord to resolve the matter is a good first step. But one must be ready to take the step in the direction Jesus indicates. Despite Jesus' protests to the contrary, he *is* the appointed judge in all matters of sin. Covetousness is a sin that strikes at the heart of commandments nine and ten. Covetousness will easily come between the bonds of family, certainly between friends, and without mercy between strangers. Jesus answers the request with a parable that points the hearer to seek the things that are above. That means, one will only discover true wealth and the inheritance that endures when one becomes rich toward God.

To be rich toward God ultimately leads one into a lifestyle of generosity. The wisdom imparted to those who value "things above" is that this is the only way to find peace, satisfaction, and contentment among things down below.

Application

There is a weakness in every human-divine analogy. It can never be a 100% correlation. The analogy of parenting is no exception. We would be sorely mistaken if we thought that God must act like the best concept of parenthood we have.

In teaching positive discipline these days, it is common to hear about "lap talks" for toddlers, "time-outs" for preschoolers, and "revoked privileges" for grade-schoolers. There is a progression of dealing with errant children in order to redirect them to the proper behavior. Of course, it gets more difficult the older and the bigger the children get. Ask the parent of any teenager or young adult who still lives at home. It is understood that there is a limit to the extent to which parents can go in disciplining their children. Spanking has become a "no-no" in our abuse-sensitive age. And grosser forms of restraint, severe corporal chastisement, and even threat of death are outright illegal — for human parents.

We would be remiss if we subjected God to such standards from below. God, from above, is free to exercise his divine right to deal with his creation in any manner so chosen, for God is God. Jesus warned his disciples to fear him who could (not necessarily *would*, but could!) not only kill the body but also cast it into hell (Luke 12:4-7). He was not talking about the devil here. God is not subject to our human standards or expectations. From the beginning God was entirely and eternally free to do what God chooses to do! The wonder of God's self-revelation through Jesus is that God has clearly chosen the sovereignty of compassion over the sovereignty of holiness as the essential core of divine being. God's holiness is still present and will also find expression; yet, when we look at the larger picture of unfolding history, we see the unmistakable stamp of compassion upon his creation and upon his people.

When we hear such words as Hosea's today, we should frame them in a personal, existential context so that they address us now. Otherwise it is too easy to take an objective and distant view that focuses on a historical, political, and social analysis of God's word and misses the dynamic, ever-present urgency for every new day. When we examine our own lives in light of God's word (even as addressed to his people in the eighth century BC), where do we experience ourselves educated, healed, loved, supported, fed — touched by the compassion of God? Where do we experience ourselves yoked and chastised, judged by the holiness of God?

Not only our personal lives, but also our collective cultural life, need to be attentive to God's word. As a dramatic comparison regarding the changing standards of our society, compare the early television sitcoms of the '50s, when spouses could not sleep in the same bed, to the sitcoms of today when couples on first dates are going to bed together... when Elvis' hips could not be shown on the screen to when sexual intercourse is displayed. In this and many other ways, it could be said that behavioral expectations are much lower. Some may talk about how good it is that there is a growing tolerance for what is acceptable behavior, given the variety of human predilections. Others would say that we have become a more crass, rude, and value-vacant society.

Christians need to ask constantly the question, "What do I wear today?" The answer has public consequences. The "clothes" that we put on will reveal to the world how Christ is "all and in all" in us. What behavior, what personal expressions will embody the new nature that is consistent with Christ-likeness?

How can we best love our community, our culture, our nation? Christian congregations around the country can be like a public address system, interlinked and blaring out for all to hear: There is a better way to live, and together we must set our minds on things that are far *above* our current standards of morality. Imagine what it would be like if the church actually spoke forth the character of the redeemed life and embodied it not just as a congregation of people but also as individuals scattered throughout the community.

The Christian call (see Philippians 3:14) is to rise above what may pass as acceptable human standards and live by virtue of the standards that Christ sets for us and commands us to imitate, as he does in John 15:12f. Ethics is not an optional addendum to the Christian faith, but a critical and necessary expression of it. How Christians live their lives is an expression of Christ in them. When Paul says, "Christ is all and in all," he is expressing the power of the risen Christ to change the believer inside and out. He himself experienced this and reflected upon it over and over (Acts 26:4-13; Romans 7:7-25; Galatians 1:11-17; Philippians 3:4-11).

Many wealthy Christians are involved in a group called Responsible Wealth. Its purpose is to advocate tax fairness, a living wage, and also initiate responsibility-oriented shareholder resolutions. Made up of people who are in the top 5% of income earners in America, Responsible Wealth is resolved to love the society into a more equitable system that will benefit others, even at the expense of some of their own advantages. (See *Sojourners* magazine, January-February 2001, "What's Right With This Picture?") These folks take seriously Jesus' words that warn against covetousness.

In our consumer culture with its aptitude for acquisition, it is necessary to discover how to value earning power in a free market economy and how to discern the godly purpose for which it is to be used — which is not the self, but to meet the needs of others and thereby serve and glorify God. One's true treasure does not become the abundance of possessions or the ability to acquire them, but the kingdom of God, the rule of God in all aspects of one's life (Matthew 6:33, 13:44-46; Luke 10:25-37).

In this way, one becomes rich *toward* God, the most heaven-bound of directions.

Proper 14 / Pentecost 12 / Ordinary Time 19
Isaiah 1:1, 10-20
Hebrews 11:1-3, 8-16
Luke 12:32-40
Mark Molldrem

The goodness that roared

In the study of the martial arts, the student learns the difference between the good, the higher good, and the superior good. If one seeks to do something that will benefit another and that very act will also reap a reward for the doer of the deed, then that person is said to perform the good (even though there may be an ulterior motive attached to it). If, however, one desires to assist another person without any personal regard to whether or not such an act will be of personal advantage, then that person is said to perform the higher good.

It is when one can act unconsciously in a way that simply benefits another person, because that is the way one is, it can be said the individual has performed the superior good. Sang Kee Paik, a master student of the San-Sang system of oriental martial art, writes, "A black belt always carries with him his power capability. He must always carry with him his ethic of superior good... He must develop his ethic so that his ethic perseveres over any and all circumstances, no matter how difficult his situation may be."

Today, the scriptures exhort us to learn to do good, whether during a time of judgment, persecution, or simply waiting for the Lord's return. Beyond even the superior good, one might think of it as the heavenly good, for it is done out of obedience to the command of God and to God's glory.

Isaiah 1:1, 10-20

Not a whole lot was going right for God's people in the eighth century BC. By the last quarter of the century, the northern kingdom was absorbed into the Assyrian Empire. The southern kingdom, Judah, with its capital at Jerusalem was under siege. At first, Israel and Syria where nipping at the borders; then, Assyria assumed the rod of God's wrath against a rebellious and ungrateful people (Isaiah 1:2-9). This century was a watershed in the history of God's people in the north and in the south. It marked the beginning of the end of their identities as autonomous states (until the period of the Maccabees, 165 BC until the Roman conquest). The north disappeared altogether; the remnant of the south continued to be just that, only a remnant, never to attain again to the ideal of the davidic kingdom, an ideal fulfilled in the coming of the Messiah, Jesus of Nazareth.

Throughout the history of God's people there has been a dual call to worship God rightly and to serve his purposes faithfully. When the worship life of the people became tainted with syncretism from indigenous cults, the prophets rose up to sound the alarm, not just because idolatry had infiltrated the true worship of Yahweh (Isaiah's name means "Yahweh is salvation"), but also because the people had lost sight of the connection between worship of Yahweh and serving his purposes in daily life.

Hence, the definition of what is good, not in terms of proper worship practices, but in terms of proper habits in daily life. To be the people of God is not just to use the correct name of God. It is not simply to worship in the prescribed manner handed down from the time of Moses, and do so only in the places that are dedicated solely to God without any piggybacking from local deities. To be the people of God means to behave according to the will of God in relationship to one's neighbor: "seek justice, correct oppression; defend the fatherless, plead for the widow" (1:17). In short, to learn to do good. Not so much sacrifice as sacrificial living is what God desires. Micah, a contemporary of Isaiah, understood this also (Micah 6:8).

Concomitant with this call to more heavenly good is the offer of forgiveness for those who will repent and obey the word of the Lord (1:18-19). Like a spectrum analysis, Isaiah describes how completely God will forgive — as complete as changing the color chart. (Micah 7:18-19 and Psalm 103:11-12 use a dizzying spatial distinction to express the extent of God's forgiveness.)

In addition to forgiveness, when there is compliance to God's will, there are attendant rewards for the righteous. "You shall eat the good of the land" (1:19). These are bold words to speak in the midst of the civil chaos that was occurring at the time. No wonder the writer to the Hebrews lifts the prophets up as worthy examples of faith, trusting in the promises of God even when events unfolding would decry them (Hebrews 11:32-38).

Hebrews 11:1-3, 8-16

A church under fire needs encouragement. This is what the letter of Hebrews is all about. It was written to a church during a time of persecution. It was not a persecution to the death (Hebrews 12:4), yet it was severe enough (Hebrews 10:32-34) to warrant concern about the strength of faith to endure. To address this, the writer of this missive takes on the task of apologetics. He claims the all-sufficiency of Christ as superior to (fulfillment of) the Old Covenant (Hebrews 8:1—10:18). Based on this affirmation, the Christian community hears an encouraging word — to persevere (Hebrews 2:1-4).

In Hebrews 11, the writer provides example after example of those who lived by faith, not seeing the promise fulfilled in their day, but still holding on to the hope that it instilled in their hearts. So, the Christian community can hold on through the time of trial, even when they do not hold the fulfillment of the promise in their hands. In the next chapter, the letter develops the example of Jesus, who endured so much suffering and leads the believer forward through it. Then, comes a wonderful exhortation to "buck up" and let the world see just what Christians are capable of doing when hard pressed: "Therefore lift your drooping hands and strengthen your weak knees" (Hebrews 12:12).

Our pericope, focused on the example of Abraham and Sarah, defines the nature of faith. It is an assurance and a conviction (11:1).

The conviction is that the eyes of faith perceive a reality that is beyond the reason of mind or the immediacy of experience. This is the basis of Paul's comments in Romans 8:18-25, where he is convinced that there is a future glory that contextualizes all current suffering. It is this conviction that gives one wholeness (salvation) in the very midst of brokenness (see Romans 5:3-5 and 1 Corinthians 4:7-10).

The assurance is that what is perceived is indeed real (beyond what reason and experience can attest to with logical or scientific proofs) and can be trusted. The object of faith is foundational for taking any action. Thus, Abram was assured of his inheritance and acted upon that assurance by leaving his home and embarking to a new land — sight unseen. Though he in fact did see the land eventually, the true fulfillment of the promise was yet beyond him, embodied in the holy city, Jerusalem, in one respect and in Jesus Christ in another.

Luke 12:32-40

Little flock, indeed! What significance in number was the small Christian sect compared to the numerous adherents of Judaism? What insignificance in number were the followers of the way compared to the population of the Roman Empire! "Little flock" is an appropriate salutation. Because it is a collective noun, the imperative mood of the noun is in the second person singular, giving the reading as if addressed to each individual, thus personalizing the entreaty (12:32). Since the verb is in the middle voice, it emphasizes the subject's participation in the outcome of the action indicated.

"Be not afraid," Jesus says, to each lamb of the flock. The reason is that God's pleasure is to rule in us and over us. We will share the rule of God that ultimately takes in everything. How we can participate in that rule now and live in a state of not being afraid is to "sell your possessions, and give alms" (12:33).

Such actions are not only good for the recipient of the kindness; they are also salutary for the doer of the good. The entreaty invites participation in the very goal sought by acting in a way that manifests confidence rather than fear.

As Jesus goes on to talk about servants waiting for the master, he describes those who live in the present anticipating the future, which shapes their behavior of readiness. So too, living with the confidence of the coming rule of God disarms fear in the present, regardless of how formidable the challenges or crosses appear. Those who do this become the "blessed, happy ones" of God.

The image of girded loins and burning lamps (12:35) is one of preparedness. The servants are to be dressed for work, not donned in leisure clothing, casually waiting for the master to return. The follow-up parable/explanation (Luke 12:41-48) makes this clear. The flame from the lamps will provide the light to see what needs to be done. It just may be that there is plenty of time to tend to the tasks at hand, because the master may not return until the second or third watch. Since not even Jesus knew when he would return (Mark 13:32), how could the servants expect to know? Therefore, constant vigilance is necessary.

Application

There is such a mix of public people in the world's spotlight. There are religious celebrities with feet of clay, strong moralists with no religious leanings, amoral individuals who push the envelope of our culture and justice system, immoral people who wink at God, and non-Christian religious folks with profound ethics. Amidst all of these, the average person on the street is looking for a word to guide the community into a better world. Isaiah's call to "cease to do evil, learn to do good" (1:16-17) will resonate with many and can be the basis of a conversation that will focus individuals on the importance of their particular life's opportunities and responsibilities.

Christians can ask of themselves how their personal piety is connected to the practices of daily life. What measure of consistency is there between the hearts and the habits of those who profess allegiance to God? As James reminds us, there is no good worship without good works. It is sobering for anyone at the altar or in the pew to hear these words: "When you spread forth your hands, I will hide my eyes from you" (Isaiah 1:15).

In what ways are our hands "full of blood" (1:15)? In what ways do our lives bear the stains that God decries? If the prayers of the righteous have great power in their effect (James 5:16), what happens to the prayers of those whose lives are flagrantly out of sync with God's purposes? How much more learning do we need before we can recognize any heavenly good shaping our lives with God-pleasing consistency?

George Forell's timeless little book, *Faith Active in Love*, makes the necessary connection between a heart that is alive to God in faith and the hands that are then active in loving deeds for God in the world. We could apply the nature of faith in another way today, if one's audience would warrant attention to this direction. In the ongoing debate between creation and evolution, rather than polarizing positions with either/or rhetoric, it would be helpful to acknowledge the different modes of perception with which faith and science operate. These do not need to be exclusive, but rather complementary. This could avoid the errors of religious scientism on the one hand and the errors of scientific religionism on the other hand.

In yet another direction for faith to be explicated in relationship to the necessity of learning to do good, one could delineate how an envisioned future is both gift from God and something that one must work toward. When churches (or communities) go through a revisioning process to discern the preferred future into which God is calling them, they need to understand that this is first and foremost a gift from God. This is not something that can be earned by merit of the congregation. The future is in God's hands and God will give it to his people when they are ready to receive it. Faith waits expectantly for the future to come, as in the closing remarks of the book of Revelation: "Amen. Come, Lord Jesus!" (Revelation 22:29).

Still, faith is not inert. It does not simply sit around like Estragon and Vladimir waiting for Godot (Samuel Beckett's 1952 tragicomedy *Waiting for Godot*). It is more like Martin Luther, when asked what he would do if he learned that Jesus would be coming tomorrow. His reply, "I would plant a tree in my garden today." Faith calls forth effort that strives toward what the promise holds forth. Abraham necessarily had to leave Ur and travel beyond the horizon, an effort of no small means. He did not earn what was beyond the horizon in the Promised Land. His faith, however, the assurance and the conviction of it, led him to act upon it.

Jurgen Moltmann in *Theology of Hope* makes a similar connection between the promises of God and the commandments of God. The promise points to the goal; the commandments point to the way. He writes, "The promise of the covenant and the injunctions of the covenant have an abiding and guiding significance until the fulfillment... The commandments of the covenant, which point our hopes in the promise to the path of physical obedience, are nothing else but the ethical reverse of the promise itself." One does not earn the promise by observing the law; but, one does observe the law as a way of living in the promise of what is coming. The law, or the learning to do good, is the proleptic embodiment of the future into which God is calling us. The future shapes us in the present through the effort that we put into living in the promise.

There is a definite countercultural current in the Christian lifestyle. In today's consumer ethos, where possession and accumulation are measures of wealth and power, Christians are guided by the words of Jesus to "sell... and give" (Luke 12:33). Because the Christian's true treasure is in the heavenly good, priority consideration is given to what one can live without in order to provide for another's needs. Here is a measure of true wealth that stems from having the right values (see Matthew 6:33 and 13:44-45). Since behavior will follow what is valued (Luke 12:34), it is vital to have right values.

When one's treasure is correct, namely the rule of God in one's life, then there is no fear of loss nor fear of purposelessness nor fear of worthlessness, for the treasures in heaven do not fail.

Proper 15 / Pentecost 13 / Ordinary Time 20
Isaiah 5:1-7
Hebrews 11:29—12:2
Luke 12:49-56
David Kalas

Hall of fame game

Every major professional sport has a hall of fame. So do a lot of more obscure sports. Many college sports boast a hall of fame of their own. Both the rock music industry and the country music industry enshrine their best and brightest stars in halls of fame. Inventors, cowgirls, and robots all have halls of fame, as well.

Being "in" a hall of fame, of course, can mean one of two things. If I say that I am in the such-and-such hall of fame, it can mean that I have been elected to membership in the hall, which is a great honor in that particular field. Or if I say that I am in that hall of fame, I might simply be saying that I am presently walking through the museum-like building that is identified as the hall.

The two meanings are entirely separate, of course. For the accomplished people who are "in" the hall in the first sense are probably very seldom "in" the hall in the second sense. Busts, pictures, jerseys, and memorabilia of the famous members are what I would find in each hall that I visited; I would not find the members themselves.

Let us imagine for a moment that the members were there and that such halls were not merely repositories of mementos and tributes, but that the actual people themselves were there. Then a visit to such a hall would be a heady experience, indeed.

Each summer the National Football League signals the beginning of the preseason with its hall of fame game. It is played in Canton, Ohio, at the site of the Pro Football Hall of Fame. On that weekend, the newly elected class of hall of fame members are honored and installed, and two current NFL teams play one another in an exhibition game as part of the festivities.

Mostly, the stadium in Canton is filled with ordinary fans that day. But suppose it was the members of the hall who were in attendance. What would it be like for a current player or team to play in front of the legends?

Imagine being a player on the field. You look up in the stands and see Johnny Unitas, Jim Brown, and Jim Thorpe — watching you play. Nearby are Sid Luckman, Walter Peyton, and Don Hutson. Face after legendary face: Raymond Berry, Dick Butkus, Chuck Bednarik, and Ray Nitchkie. And, in a special box overlooking the field, you see the imposing figures of George Halas, Tom Landry, Bill Walsh, Paul Brown, and Vince Lombardi.

These are the men to whom the game belonged before you took the field. Indeed, in many cases, before you were born. These are the players and coaches who set records and won championships. Trophies and awards are named after these guys — and now they're watching you play their game.

And so, "since we are surrounded by so great a cloud of witnesses," says the writer of Hebrews, let's play our best and play to win!

Isaiah 5:1-7

In the midst of the most unsavory episode from King David's life and reign, the prophet Nathan comes to him with a story. It is all innocently told in the third person until, at the end, the prophet reveals that

David himself has a role in the story. Here, in the book of the prophet Isaiah, we encounter a story with a similar dramatic shift.

In the first two verses, the audience is introduced to the owner of a vineyard, and they are told his brief story. It is, initially, a scene full of beauty and promise, but it ends with disappointment. Then comes the shift. What seemed to be a detached, third-person account suddenly becomes quite personal. The storyteller-prophet is displaced by the Lord himself. And the fruitless vineyard of the story, the audience discovers, represents them.

For some years now, it has been the popular practice among many preachers to distribute sermon note-taking sheets to their congregations. The sheets offer an outline of the sermon, often including sentences with blanks left to be filled in by the listener. But long before such sheets became fashionable in North American pulpits, the Old Testament prophets employed a variation with dramatic effect.

What Nathan did with David and what Isaiah did with the inhabitants of Jerusalem was to leave a blank on the sermon sheet, only to invite the audience members to fill in their own names on that blank. "Now, friends, do you see that blank line next to 'the vineyard'? Go ahead and write 'Jerusalem' there. Jot down 'Judah.' Or you may simply write, 'Us.'"

We may have a preconceived notion about the typical judgment-prophet's message. We recognize that the bulk of his material is divided under two broad headings: 1) the people's chronic sinfulness; and 2) the coming judgment of God. Both of these subjects are covered and cataloged in some detail.

This Isaiah passage, however, offers a somewhat different take on the people's sinfulness. For the prophet does not itemize their faults. He does not catalog here the details of their injustice, idolatry, greed, and hypocrisy. Instead, in the brief story of the vineyard, the people's failure is not cast in terms of what they were, but rather what they were not. We will explore further this poignant truth below, under the heading "What Might Have Been."

What began as a promise turned into disappointment. And what was disappointing, according to the prophet, would soon be destroyed. "I will tell you what I will do to my vineyard," the Lord says, ominously.

In broad strokes, the pattern of this Old Testament passage may remind us of several New Testament passages. Just as the fruitless vineyard can expect to be ruined, so John the Baptist warned that the fruitless trees will be cut down (Matthew 3:10). Similarly, when Jesus was disappointed by a fig tree that had nothing to offer (probably symbolic of Jerusalem in the larger context), he cursed it, and it withered (Mark 11:12-21). Jesus also told an open-ended parable about a landowner who, upon discovering that a particular tree was not producing as it should, instructed that it be cut down (Luke 13:6-9). So we see this consistent theme of pragmatic judgment: doing away with the worthless tree or vine that is not functioning as it ought.

In the case of the Isaiah prophecy, the proposed judgment has a distinctively painful element. We sense that God does not need to do the vineyard harm directly; he needs only to remove his blessings from it (the wall, the care, the rain), and it will be devastated. We are reminded of David's wisdom, who, upon facing a choice of punishments, reasoned, "Let us fall into the hand of the Lord, for his mercy is great; but let me not fall into human hands" (2 Samuel 24:14). Forebodingly, it seems that the vineyard of Isaiah's day would no longer be in the hand of the Lord and that is perhaps the worst fate of all.

Hebrews 11:29—12:2

By the time we meet up with the author of this famous "faith chapter," he is already 28 verses into his marvelous litany. Having begun with a definition of faith, he has since been inspired to offer examples of it. Indeed, many examples of it! He begins in humanity's second generation, with the exemplary Abel, and works his way forward through the many early heroes of faith.

When we join his survey in verse 29, we discover that he has only made it to the book of Exodus. Even after accelerating a bit, he was only in Joshua by the end of verse 31. It's understandable, therefore, when he stops short of the judges, saying, "Time would fail me to tell of Gideon, Barak, Samson, Jephthah...." The author moves from individual examples to broad categories: men and women who, by faith, "conquered kingdoms, administered justice, obtained promises, shut the mouths of lions, quenched raging fire, escaped the edge of the sword," and on and on.

If I were still working with youth groups, I would present verses 33-35a as a sort of quiz, inviting the kids to give one specific example from scripture of each of the categories identified by the writer. My experience is that adults are not so receptive to such quizzes. Still, it would be a good exercise — for individuals or for small groups — to put names on these descriptions.

Meanwhile, in the midst of verse 35, there is a sudden and unanticipated polar shift. Having heaped up a great pile of blessings and victories, climaxing with a reference to people coming back from the dead, the writer abruptly turns 180-degrees, saying, "Others were tortured... suffered mocking and flogging... stoned to death, sawn in two, killed by the sword... destitute, persecuted, tormented." If reading were driving, we would have suffered whiplash from such a sudden and dramatic turn.

How can the writer move so seamlessly from victories to defeats? How can he shift, without warning or explanation, from tales of success to such images of failure? A quotation of verses 35b-39 should appear in the dictionary under "non-sequitur."

The author does not treat the accounts of destitution and death as being inconsistent with the early accounts of marvels and miracles. He sees a great continuity where we are inclined to see a great diversion. He recognizes a continuous flow where we perceive a watershed.

The linguistic link between the two sections is the word "resurrection." The word represents the climax of what we might call the victory section: "Women received their dead by resurrection." In the very next phrase, the writer repeats the word, but with a very different flavor: "Others were tortured, refusing to accept release, in order to obtain a better resurrection." And so begins the series of grim descriptions that we might call the defeat section.

But the writer of Hebrews would not call it that. He does not regard the accounts of torture, persecution, imprisonment, and martyrdom as defeats. For him, the escalator just keeps going up. There is, you see, "a better resurrection." By extension, there is a better life and reward than what the first group of heroes could experience here in this world. This world, after all, is not worthy of them. And so it is that, one way or another, faith always gains its reward.

Still, when the writer comes to the end of the chapter, we discover that the escalator has yet another floor to go. For all of these heroes of faith, saints and martyrs still "did not receive what was promised." There still remained "something better." And that something better, he suggests, came with the present generation, "so that they would not, apart from us, be made perfect."

Thus the author makes one more effortless, seamless shift. All of the preceding generations of the faithful, having been introduced in a line, are now collapsed into a single unit. They are all together now as an audience. And now it is our time — and our turn — to be faithful.

Luke 12:49-56

You probably receive, as I do, the religious catalogs featuring various bulletin covers and artwork that we can purchase for our churches. When significant holy days and seasons come round, there is a superabundant offering of options, including matching stationery and offering envelopes.

Perhaps the greatest supply of such resources is found during the Advent and Christmas seasons. One of the great recurring themes of the artwork and texts is "peace." The images are peaceful. The angels proclaim, "Peace on earth." One candle in the Advent wreath is designated as "peace," and the baby is heralded as "the prince of peace."

It seems, however, that Jesus did not get the memo.

"Do you think that I have come to bring peace to the earth?" he asks his followers. And with earnestness, hopefulness, and a bit of sentimentality, we eagerly answer, "Yes! That's exactly what we think!"

"No," he answers, "but rather division."

What follows may be a bit surprising for some in our congregations. Perhaps not having read much of the Bible for themselves, they are left with only what they have heard and what they have been told through the years. What they have been told, in so many cases, is that Jesus brings peace.

To address the discrepancy, we might do well to define just what we mean — or what scripture means — by "peace." The predicted "prince of peace" (Isaiah 9:6), on the one hand, may anticipate an eschatological messianic achievement of global peace among peoples and nations. The "peace I give to you" (John 14:27), on the other hand, may refer to a personal experience, an inner peace that is quite independent of the larger context.

In our gospel lection, meanwhile, it seems that Jesus is speaking of neither global peace nor inner peace. Instead, he goes on to reference interpersonal relationships: fathers and son, mothers and daughters, and in-laws.

The divisions that Jesus anticipates — indeed, causes — will not cut along the traditional lines of nations, ethnic groups, or social classes. Rather, the divisions will be close to home and very personal. The "us" and "them" are completely redefined, for "they" are not on the other side of the tracks, or a different color, or across the ocean. No, "they" are at the supper table with "us." It's an astonishing proposition.

I endorse the mostly unquestioned assumption that God would have us be good family members — that Christian husbands and wives, fathers and mothers, and children all bear a certain responsibility before God to play our parts well. That theme can be traced from the Old Testament law through the Proverbs and into the writings of Peter and Paul.

At the same time, however, this passage reminds us of the subordination and redefining of family that we find in Jesus' teachings. He insists that we love him more than the nearest and most natural of our love relationships (Matthew 10:37). He seems to take for granted that discipleship may require the certain abandoning of those relationships (Matthew 19:29). And he reformulates the boundaries and membership of family (Luke 8:19-21).

Application

You and I are called to be faithful, and we call our brothers and sisters, the friends and members of our congregations, to be faithful too.

And what does that faithfulness look like?

It doesn't look like Judah and Jerusalem of Isaiah's day. That generation of God's people had not lived in proper response to God's guidance and care. Their lives were not marked by justice and righteousness. They had not born fruit pleasing to God. Rather, they were a disappointment to him.

So what does faithfulness look like? The writer of Hebrews knows, and he shows us.

In his marvelous chapter on faith, the writer walks us through the snapshots and memorabilia of the faith hall of fame. There we see the inspiring busts of Abel and Abraham. We remember the stories of Moses and Joshua. We see old footage from the era of the judges. And we are reminded of the noble martyrs all along the way, suffering unjustly but staying faithful, even through pain and death.

Perhaps those great heroes of faith come to mind, too, when we read Jesus' teaching. He depicts faithful discipleship as a fierce personal allegiance that has priority over every other love, affection, and ambition. Personal faithfulness to him may create tension and divisions between us and other people, and it may cost us some relationships.

Now we know what faithfulness looks like. And to challenge us on to brave and no-nonsense faithfulness where we are, the writer of Hebrews shows us the stadium. All of those marvelous saints from days gone by — the legendary men and women of faith through the ages — they are "so great a cloud of witnesses." We run the race in front of that audience. When we get winded or wounded; when we are inclined toward discouragement or despair; we look up in the stands, and we remember what faithfulness looks like. Best of all, we look to Jesus and we remember what faithfulness looks like; then we "run with perseverance the race that is set before us."

An Alternative Application
Isaiah 5:1-7. "What Might Have Been." I don't remember many occasions during my growing up years when my parents scolded me. They were low-key parents, and I was a pretty good child. I do remember one occasion, when I was about sixteen years old, I was caught in the midst of a rather significant deception. There was no big scene at the time. And the next time I was in the same room as my mom, it was awkwardly silent. After several tense minutes, she finally was the one to break the silence. She turned to look at me, and she said, without raising her voice, "I'm so disappointed."

So many years later, I still feel the pain of that moment. I don't think she could have said anything more effective or more penetrating to me.

That is the thrust of God's message through Isaiah to the people of Judah and Jerusalem. He was disappointed — so profoundly disappointed. There was such hope and promise at the beginning. He had invested such effort and care, but the people did not produce accordingly.

We see hints of this divine disappointment from the very beginning. In the opening chapters of Genesis, we are introduced to a universe and a garden that are created to be so very good. The man and woman — they were created even better, for they were made in the image of God: "ordained to be transcripts of the Trinity," as Charles Wesley wrote, "creatures capable of God" in his hymn, "Sinners, Turn: Why Will You Die." Yet just a few chapters later, God looks at what has become of his good creation and creatures; he "saw that the wickedness of humankind was great in the earth, and that every inclination of the thoughts of their hearts was only evil continually. And the Lord was sorry that he had made humankind on the earth, and it grieved him to his heart" (Genesis 6:5-6).

The great tragedy of the vineyard — of God's people — is not merely how bad they were, but how good they ought to have been. When a C student brings home a D, the disappointment is not so great because the expectation was not so great. But when a straight-A student brings home a D, it's a stunning disappointment. We expected so much better from him or her.

God expected so much better from his vineyard. And he still does.

Proper 16 / Pentecost 14 / Ordinary Time 21
Jeremiah 1:4-10
Hebrews 12:18-29
Luke 13:10-17
David Kalas

Mixed reactions

The promos for a new movie feature all sorts of glowing quotes from an assortment of reviews. The ads for a political candidate boast the support of important newspapers and individuals. And the over-the-counter product reports the endorsement of "four out of five doctors surveyed."

In fact, of course, not every review of the movie was favorable, not every significant paper and individual backs the candidate in question, and we never get to hear what that fifth doctor thinks.

The point is that very few things enjoy unanimous approval. Most things meet with mixed reactions.

That's fine, of course, for as long as we're dealing with matters of opinion, taste, or preference. The film embraced by one as "deeply moving" is dismissed by another as a "chick flick." One person's music is another one's noise. And what was just right for Papa Bear was too hot for Goldilocks.

When we move out of the realm of opinion and taste, however, mixed reactions can mean trouble. The doctor does not expect a wide variety of responses to the rubber mallet reflex test. The colonel does not permit a wide variety of responses when he gives an order. And the elementary school math teacher does not welcome a variety of responses to the equation "two-plus-two-equals...."

In some arenas of life, mixed reactions are natural and inevitable. In other areas, mixed reactions are surprising and troubling.

Remarkably, God gets mixed reactions.

Ever since Adam and Eve's misadventure in Eden, God has been getting mixed reviews from the human beings he loves so much. His miracles have yielded both converts and skeptics. His commands have prompted both devotion and resistance. His teachings have inspired both adherents and critics. From the assorted soils in Jesus' parable (Matthew 13:18-23) to the Jerusalem crowds of Holy Week (cf. Mark 11:8-10; 15:11-15), the Lord has suffered mixed reactions from the very ones created in his image.

The passages for this Sunday portray a wide range of reactions to God, his word, and his work.

Jeremiah 1:4-10

Here is the call of Jeremiah. It is personal and unique to Jeremiah, on the one hand, and it is absolutely typical of God's call, on the other.

The personal elements of the passage are lovely affirmations of the individualized nature of God's work in our lives. We are not mere numbers or replaceable cogs. Rather, the Lord affirms that he personally formed, knew, consecrated, and appointed Jeremiah. The prophet was not just one in a million called up in a draft. No, his creation and his call were the product of personal one-on-one involvement by God.

That personal quality is characteristic of how God works all through scripture. Though there is the larger theme (and unit) of a covenant people, still God deals with folks individually. We read the accounts of his individual calls in the lives of Noah, Abram, Moses, Gideon, David, Isaiah, Jonah, and on and on. Likewise, in the New Testament, Jesus does not broadcast an invitation to discipleship; he calls the disciples personally. The gospel of John features chapter after chapter of one-on-one encounters between individuals and Jesus. Later, God also calls the apostle Paul in such a personal and individual way that we might even say he was targeted.

God's call on Jeremiah's life was not well received at first. Jeremiah felt quite unqualified for the task he was being given (cf., Moses in Exodus 4:10 and Gideon in Judges 6:14-15), and he may have been right. But our human qualifications are not finally the point when it comes to the work of God. More specifically, *we* are not the point when it comes to the work of God.

God made that fact clear to Jeremiah. The real issue is not Jeremiah but God. See how many first-person, singular verbs God uses in this passage. First, there is the account of all that God has already done (I formed, I knew, I consecrated, I appointed). Then comes the list of what God is presently doing (I send, I command, I am with, I have put my words, I appoint).

Jeremiah has some first-person singular things to say too. Specifically, he says, "I do not know" and "I am only." Give him credit for his humility and perspective, for we do God's work no great favor when we rely too heavily on what we do know and what we are. Jeremiah was not mistaken in what he said about himself. His mistake was in thinking that he was the issue in the first place.

Hebrews 12:18-29

A familiar assignment to high school English students is the compare-and-contrast essay. The approach is also familiar to the reader of Hebrews, for compare-and-contrast is the name of the game in this epistle.

The author and audience of this epistle are less certain than with many of the other New Testament letters — more fodder for the scholars. This much seems evident, at least: the author and the audience were Jewish and intimately familiar with the Hebrew scriptures. Furthermore, the author reveals a strong Greek influence in his heritage or education, for his method of interpreting the scriptures reflects a distinctively Greek perspective.

Beyond those basic assumptions, the rest is guesswork. For myself, I think of the letter to the Hebrews as serving the same function as a French-to-English dictionary might for an American tourist in Paris. The writer of Hebrews takes what is new and unfamiliar — the gospel of Jesus Christ — and translates it in the terms of what is old and native — the Old Testament law and prophets.

The analogy is imperfect, of course, since there is a more derivative and deliberate relationship between the Old and New Testaments than between French and English. Nevertheless, the purpose remains the same: to help people understand what is new and foreign in the light of what is old and native.

The letter to the Hebrews is not useful in this function for most of the people in our pews, however. It is the symbols, stories, and rituals of the Old Testament that are foreign to so many American churchgoers, and so the law and the prophets do not make a helpful point of reference in explaining and understanding the gospel. If anything, we may find ourselves using the letter to the Hebrews in reverse — that is, using the gospel message to help our people gain an understanding and appreciation of the Old Testament.

In our particular passage, the compare-and-contrast approach focuses on the two covenants — the old covenant represented by Mount Sinai and the new covenant represented by Mount Zion. The writer offers dramatic side-by-side pictures. The former comes mostly from Israel's experience at Sinai in Exodus, and it demonstrates the awesome and terrifying context of the old covenant. The latter picture, meanwhile, is not the product of some particular event in scripture but is rather a more fanciful compendium of images designed to illustrate the glory and beauty of the new covenant.

The images associated with the new covenant — what we "come to" — are no less dramatic and awesome than those associated with the old covenant. Both elicit reverence and awe. But the new covenant imagery has a quality of approachability, welcome, and celebration that are plainly absent in the Mount Sinai scene.

The writer of Hebrews is eager to illustrate how superior the new covenant is. The invitation and opportunity are so much better than ancient Israel's relationship with God was or could have been. At the same time, however, the greater intimacy does not mean greater informality. The invitation is to be closer, not less careful.

The subject of a kingdom who stands outside the palace and the one who stands inside the throne room are suitably impressed by the majesty of the place. The latter has the greater privilege, of course, to enjoy a personal audience with the king. At the same time, while there is less distance, there is perhaps greater fear.

The fear should not be mistaken for the uncertainty that comes from serving a capricious God. Quite the contrary: We enjoy a stability ("a kingdom that cannot be shaken") and security ("the sprinkled blood that speaks a better word than the blood of Abel") that bear witness to the steadfast love of God. And so our fear is not insecurity, but "reverence and awe."

Luke 13:10-17

There are two different plot lines at work in this episode. The one is the plot line to which Luke is paying the most attention: Jesus' ministry and the growing antagonism of his opponents. The other plot line is the one that may be most important to the people in our pews: The life story of the woman who was healed.

We don't know anything about the woman except that she had been in her hunched over condition for eighteen years. What is the hope quotient after eighteen years? What level of expectation do we have that some circumstance or condition will get better after living with a thing for so long? While our sense of hopefulness naturally diminishes over time, the plot of this woman's story reminds us that Jesus can step in *at any time* with healing and deliverance.

The narrator attributes the woman's condition to "a spirit." That seems somewhat primitive to the modern mind, but we are willing to overlook it coming from Luke. It is harder to overlook, however, when the same kind of diagnosis comes from Jesus himself ("a daughter of Abraham whom Satan bound for eighteen long years").

We see in the story of the man born blind in John 9 (see vv. 1-3) that Jesus does not automatically concede the contemporary theological interpretations of illness or handicap (or even of tragedy, as in Luke 13:1-5). Yet here in this passage, Jesus affirms that the woman's condition is Satan's doing, she is in bondage, and she ought to be set free. It seems, in our day, like an impolitic way to talk about a handicapping condition. Perhaps we have largely abandoned our heritage of providing healing in favor of providing acceptance and accessibility.

The other plot line is the ongoing story of Jesus' ministry and the evolving resistance to him. This is the fourth episode in Luke's gospel (along with 4:16-30; 4:33-36; and 6:6-11) when Jesus appears in a synagogue, and the third occasion when what he says or does in the synagogue spurs anger and opposition. The controversy here (as in ch. 6) centers around Jesus healing on the sabbath. The uncertain matter is whether the sabbath was really the issue, or whether Jesus was really the issue.

If we are predisposed to be antagonistic toward someone, then we will find fault with almost anything that person does. Perhaps that's why Jesus' opponents here locked themselves into such an untenable position.

On the other hand, if we are slavishly devoted to some principle, our legalism may blind us to a greater good. Perhaps that sabbath-protectionism led to the myopia of Jesus' opponents here and in chapter 6.

We see in verse 15 a distinctive characteristic of Luke's gospel. While all four gospels include people calling Jesus "Lord," Luke is the only one of the synoptics that includes pre-resurrection references to Jesus as "the Lord" in the narration. Even in John's gospel, those narrative references are few before the resurrection (John 6:23; 11:2), while in Luke they are quite common (e.g., Luke 7:13; 10:41; 11:39; 12:42; 17:6; 18:6; 22:61).

Finally, we are presented with a striking contrast between the healed woman and the opponents of Jesus. At the end of the episode, she is erect and praising God. Jesus' opponents, however, are "put to shame." Her condition had changed that day, but theirs had not. Is it possible that it is easier to be set free from Satan's bondage than from that of legalism?

Application

The printed invitation includes these initials at the bottom: R.S.V.P. *Please respond.*

From cover to cover, scripture is full of invitations: invitations from God to humankind. And from the God who calls the hiding couple in Eden, to the good shepherd who calls the lost lamb in the wild, the underlying tone of the invitation is always the same: *Please respond.*

Some folks, like the first of the four soils in Jesus' parable (see Matthew 13:1-9, 18-23), are completely unresponsive. If the parable is to be taken literally, they are a minority. Among the majority who do respond to God, meanwhile, the responses vary widely.

The three selected passages for this Sunday are a study in those varied human responses to God.

The Jeremiah lection features the explicit response of Jeremiah to God's call, as well as an implication about the response of the people to whom Jeremiah is sent ("do not be afraid of them").

The Hebrews passage recalls the wilting, fearful response of Moses and the people at Sinai, as well as that earlier generation's failure to respond obediently to God's human spokesman — "the one who warned them on earth." Meanwhile, the writer of Hebrews exhorts his audience to an appropriate response: "Do not refuse to respond to the one who is speaking" and "Offer to God an acceptable worship with reverence and awe."

Finally, the gospel lection depicts the mixed reactions of the synagogue crowd. Jesus' opponents were "indignant" about his work, while others were "rejoicing at all the wonderful things that he was doing."

An honest and sympathetic look at the people involved in these stories will result in some conclusions that hit pretty close to home.

Many of us understand Jeremiah's resistance to take on some task for God, not because of any disrespect for him and his work, but rather because of our great respect. God and his work deserve better, more qualified servants. Instead of actually responding to God, we inadvertently respond instead to something about ourselves.

The congregation around Sinai, meanwhile, was not the last to stay at a distance from God, fearful and uncertain. Like the recipients of the epistle, many of us may need to be reminded of the profound and awesome invitation of the new covenant, lest we treat it casually or lightly, lest reverence is replaced by nonchalance.

A careful look at the folks gathered in the synagogue may also feel like a look in the mirror. They are, after all, an earnest, religious lot. It was not some obvious vice or wickedness that made them unreceptive to the Lord's work. Rather it was their own well-meaning devotion to their understanding of what it means to obey God.

If we review the record of our own individual lives, we will find that we have given God mixed reactions over the years. And if we review the record of scripture, perhaps it will help us see more clearly how we are responding to him now.

Alternative Applications

Jeremiah 1:4-10. We mentioned earlier the first-person, singular verbs that appear in the Jeremiah passage. One set of verbs identifies what God had already done in Jeremiah's life, and the other set what God was presently doing in Jeremiah's life. Either set would be a useful basis for an expository sermon exploring God's work in our lives.

The first set of verbs affirms the work and purpose of God in our lives from the very start. His work in us and his will for us did not begin just when we started paying attention to him. The newborn does not know or love the parent, and certainly the baby has no plans. But the parent knows and loves the baby, and the parent has so many plans, and so many preparations already in place. So it is with God and us: long before we know or love him, he already knows and loves us, and he has plans for us well before we are interested in knowing what they are.

The second set of verbs affirms the basic paradigm of God's call. The components in verses 7-10 are reminiscent of Jesus' Great Commission to his disciples (Matthew 28:16-20). Many of those elements are also seen in Moses' call experience at the burning bush (Exodus 3:1—4:23). We might explore and understand God's call in our own lives by examining the second set of verbs in this story of Jeremiah's call.

Luke 13:10-17. The wise man said, "Hope deferred makes the heart sick" (Proverbs 13:12a). How sick, then, must this hunched over woman's heart have been?

When it comes to hope, most of us prefer to make a low-risk investment. Not getting our hopes up is both a personal policy and our prudent advice to those dearest to us.

On the other hand, few postures could be so patently unChristian as despair. The man or woman of God should never be without hope.

Perhaps the story of the woman who, after a hopelessly long time, met with healing and deliverance should be a challenge and encouragement to us and our congregations. Perhaps we ought to reacquaint ourselves with the God for whom it's never too late (cf., Luke 8:40-55; John 5:1-9). Perhaps we ought to run the risk of hoping that the situation we had given up for lost can still be touched and restored to wholeness by the Lord.

Proper 17 / Pentecost 15 / Ordinary Time 22
Jeremiah 2:4-13
Hebrews 13:1-8, 15-16
Luke 14:1, 7-14
Timothy Cargal

Etiquette for God's realm

It has happened to me often enough in my ministry that I must conclude that it is a common experience among pastors. You have performed the marriage ceremony and have accepted the family's (usually insistent) invitation to attend the wedding reception, not infrequently because they would like you to say the prayer before the meal or attend to some other formality of the occasion. But formality not being what it used to be, you arrive at the banquet hall to find that not all of the seating has been pre-assigned with place cards. Most of the tables have what might be called "open seating," but the head table and perhaps a few close by do have designated seating for what must be presumed to be honored guests.

No host is directing the wedding guests, so what do you do? Do you assume that since you performed the ceremony and will soon be giving the invocation that there must be a place card somewhere with your name on it, and if not at the head table then certainly one of those nearby? But it would be embarrassing to nonchalantly make your way past each setting only to find that none of the settings had been set aside specifically for you. Besides, the evening would be passed much more pleasantly seated with folks you know from your congregation than with distant relatives who have come for the festivities from equally distant cities. So do you simply head for some much less prominent seating?

Being the pastor, you will immediately recall that Jesus told a parable relating to this very situation. You head for one of those undesignated tables. Better to be asked to join the prime seating than to be perceived as presumptuous (Luke 14:8-10). Proud of both your biblical literacy and your exemplary humility you find a seat on the fringes of the room. Yet as you sit there, you begin to wonder: Was Jesus really saying nothing more in this parable than the advice one might have just as easily found in the manners books by Emily Post or Amy Vanderbilt?

Jeremiah 2:4-13

The lectionary reading from Jeremiah is the second segment of a five-part oracle that spans all of chapter 2. The oracle begins by recalling the covenant fidelity of the Israelites to God using the imagery of a young bride and groom on what might be called their honeymoon (2:1-3). The remaining sections consist of alternating indictments of Israel and Judah's religious (2:4-13, 20-28) and political disloyalty (first with the Assyrians, 2:14-19, and later with the Egyptians, 2:29-37). The overarching structure of the oracle is provided by the use of the *riv* form, a type of "lawsuit" in which God substantiates charges against the people by calling witnesses, cites proof of God's own fidelity to the covenant, challenges the people to defend themselves against the charges, and finally pronounces the verdict and punishment.

Following a summons to hear these charges (2:4), the reading begins with a rhetorical question put to the people as defendants by God as the prosecutor. God asks what it was that the divine had done to provoke their ancestors to reject the covenant with God and to seek "worthless things, and became worthless themselves" (2:5). This charge plays on two meanings of the Hebrew word *hebel*; it is used to mean "idols" (see Jeremiah 8:19) and "something that is worthless" (most famously the "vanity" that is cited some 36 times in Ecclesiastes). Thus by turning away from the worship of God to instead make a covenant with "empty" idols, the people had become worthless themselves. Another wordplay is used when the specific god of these idols, Baal, is identified at 2:8. Baal is the name of a god in the Canaanite pantheon and the common Hebrew word for "husband." The people have left their marriage covenant with God, despite the blessings God had given them in the Exodus from Egypt and settlement in the bountiful land promised to Abraham, and taken on a new husband in Baal even though that meant going "after things that do not profit" (2:6-8).

God has been left literally dumbfounded by this rejection. Even those peoples throughout the Mediterranean basin who worshiped gods that in actuality were non-existent ("even though they are no gods") have nevertheless remained faithful in their loyalty to them (2:10-11). From this action God distills two charges against the people of Judah: "They have forsaken me," a real source of provision for the "living water" on which their lives themselves depend; and they have mistakenly concluded that they could provide for themselves when they "dug out... cracked cisterns that can hold no water" (2:13).

Hebrews 13:1-8, 15-16

The book of Hebrews closes with a number of briefly stated admonitions. The topics to which they refer are wide-ranging and switch rapidly. To the degree that the author makes any attempt to relate them to a common theme, that theme is expressed in the final verses of the lectionary reading. Doing good by sharing of one's self and one's possessions are "sacrifices" that are "pleasing to God," and the offering of such sacrifices is a continual responsibility.

The first set of admonitions (13:1-5) can be construed as specific examples of ways that one can fulfill the opening command to maintain "mutual love." Recognizing a mutuality between persons calls forth "hospitality to strangers" because there will be occasions in which we will all find ourselves to be the stranger. It reminds us that the inhuman conditions in which some people are imprisoned and even tortured is dehumanizing to us all. The mutuality of love within marriage, extending even to sexual relationships (a truly radical notion in the social context originally addressed by this author), must be honored not only between the partners but also by society itself.

Attitudes toward money and possessions are to be established by the recognition that God is the source of all that we have (13:5-6). God's provision is both secure and sufficient. Any affection relative to the material goods necessary for this life is properly directed to the one who supplies them rather than to the goods themselves or the money that is exchanged for them.

The specific "leaders" referred to in 13:7 would appear to be the elders within the religious community (cf. 13:17). They are the ones who "spoke the word of God to you" both by formal instruction and by the conduct of their lives, setting an example of faith for others to imitate. The foremost such leader is, of course, Jesus Christ, whose consistency of example is emphasized by the declaration that he "is the same yesterday and today and forever."

The lectionary skips over the material in 13:9-14. There would appear to be two reasons for this decision. First, this material at a minimum tends toward a "supercessionist" position of followers of Christ as compared to those who have remained within the traditional covenantal relationship of Judaism. It presents the kosher dietary practice as of no benefit, and exalts the "altar" at which this community worships as one at which the Jewish priests "have no right to eat." The irony is that these arguments follow very traditional forms of rabbinic disputation melded with specific Neo-Platonic philosophical speculation. Thus, the second reason for passing over these verses is that a proper understanding of the details in this argument (the significance of being "outside the camp," of "having no lasting city, but looking for the city that is to come," and so on) requires extensive explanation. If the religious and philosophical aspects of this argument are correctly understood, then it can be properly seen as a debate *within* a religious tradition rather than one religion superseding another. Unless the topic of the sermon was itself the relationship between Judaism and Christianity, the intricacies of explanation called for go far beyond what can be developed homiletically as background.

Luke 14:1, 7-14

The gospel lesson recounts two of a series of three parables (14:7-11, 12-14, 15-24) constructed around the behavior of hosts and guests at dinner parties. The evangelist has placed all of these parables in the narrative context of a sabbath meal to which Jesus had been invited (14:1). Whether the occasion prompted the series of parables in the manner that the evangelist presents them, or alternatively the evangelist gathered them together at this point in his narrative because they share a common setting, is of course now impossible to determine (cf. the cluster of parables about lost sheep, coins, and sons in Luke 15). It is also somewhat beside the point. One of the characteristic features of Jesus' parables, as with most successful parables, is that they draw on a common experience of life to explain the uncommon or unknown. Thus, these parables are not ultimately about table manners but about proper decorum for those "who will eat bread in the kingdom of God" (14:15).

The first of the parables is related from the vantage point of the invited guest. Elaborating on what was already well-established advice (cf. Proverbs 25:6-7), Jesus directs guests not to presume that they are among the most prominent persons invited to the meal. It is better to be brought up to a higher station among those who have gathered than to embarrass yourself and your host by being asked to make a place for others who are more honored. One could, of course, employ this bit of conventional wisdom as a way to game the system and seek to draw attention and honor to one's self. Deliberately and publicly taking a place associated with low honor, one could make a most public show of false modesty while being escorted by the host to a more honored position in the sight of the assembled guests. To cut off such Machiavellian schemes, Jesus underscores the moral of the story: "For all who exalt themselves will be humbled, and those who humble themselves will be exalted" (14:11).

The point of the parable is hardly about place settings at dinner parties. It is about the core value of humility within the realm of God. The evangelist has highlighted this purpose by identifying the story as a "parable," and phrasing the moral in the passive voice also subtly reinforces it. This verb form was commonly used to indicate divine agency without explicitly naming God as the one who acts. Thus, to say that some "will be humbled" while others "will be exalted" is to say that God will bring down those who exalt themselves and will honor those who are genuinely humble in deferring to the honor of others.

The second parable takes up the point of view of the host rather than the guests and is thoroughly rooted in the patronage systems of Greco-Roman society. Within those cultures people were able to place others within their debt by feting them as honored guests at public gatherings. If prominent members of the community accepted your invitation, you not only assured yourself a reciprocal invitation from them but also immediately raised your own social standing by their willingness to incur this social debt. Hosting one's peers or social superiors was a means of maintaining or advancing one's own social position.

Jesus advises people to instead host "the poor, the crippled, the lame, and the blind" at their banquets. Since such people in that culture were socially despised and economically disadvantaged and so unable to repay the social debt themselves (14:14b), it is possible to hear in this advice a reversal of the usual customs. But it may be the parable is less about overturning the patronage system than about recognizing the ultimate patron. Since God is the patron of the physically, socially, and economically disadvantaged who are invited as guests in the divine kingdom (as in the third parable of this sequence, 14:21b), then receiving them likewise earns God's favor. Once more the use of the passive voice ("will be blessed," "will be repaid") implies that God does for them what the disadvantaged cannot.

Application

When we are trying to teach the rules of social etiquette and decorum to our children, one of the tried and true principles is to point out patterns that make sense of what can otherwise be a hopelessly confusing hodge-podge of apparently *ad hoc* rules. Thus while we may hope that they will one day be able to immediately discern the difference between a salad fork and a dinner fork, between a soup spoon and a dessert spoon, between a butter knife and a steak knife, we usually begin by pointing out that the proper eating utensils for each course of the meal can be identified simply by working from the outside-in of a correctly arranged place setting. Obviously if they don't eventually learn the distinguishing characteristics of each utensil they will never be able to correctly set the table themselves, but familiarity with the patterns will itself help with learning the particularities.

So it is as well for learning the etiquette of God's realm. There are *similarities* between the world in which we live and the realm perfectly ordered according to God's will, and that is why Jesus was able to use parables as a means of relating our common experience to the all too uncommon expectations of divine justice. There are fundamental principles at work in God's wisdom that provide the basis for all the specific types of behavior that are expected of those "who eat bread in the kingdom of God."

The New Testament lessons for this week help us to identify those principles and patterns. One is the need for mutual love. When we recognize the interdependence we all share with each other, we will recognize our need to deal with others in the ways we would consider just for ourselves. Another is our ultimate dependence upon God. When we have the faith to see God as not only the source of what we have gained in the past but also a sure help for what we will need in the future, we will be able to keep our affections directed at the one with whom we are in relationship rather than on the things that arise from that relationship. Yet another is genuine humility. When we come to understand that the most honorable thing in any of us is that God has accepted the role as our patron, we will be able to acknowledge the respect that is due to everyone as a child of God.

Alternative Applications

Jeremiah 2:4-13. One wonders where the prophet Jeremiah would have come down in the discussion about God in our public lives. Would he have joined those who see the removal of the words "under God" as forsaking our nation's relationship with the God who, in the words of our Declaration of Independence, as Creator "endowed us with certain inalienable rights"? Or would he have agreed with those who remain in covenant with God but would nevertheless accept the removal of the phrase because it has become in some sense meaningless? In other words, is an expression of "ceremonial deism" in public life itself an expression that we, like the people of ancient Judah, have gone "far from [God], and went after worthless things, and became worthless [ourselves]" (Jeremiah 2:5)?

Jeremiah 2:4-13; Hebrews 13:1-8, 15-16. Many modern Christians have divided their lives into two portions. There is the mundane, day-to-day stuff of living that we consider ourselves more than competent to take care of. We do our jobs, tend to our families, and perhaps (time permitting) even contribute to the broader civic good. Then there are the big things that threaten to overwhelm us. Sometimes they are bad things like catastrophic illness, or they may even be good things like entering into a new marriage or celebrating the birth of a child. When these things happen, we reach beyond ourselves and turn to God for help. Yet these lessons remind us that we are dependent upon God's help for the mundane stuff as well. Even the things we take for granted are there because God's faithfulness to us is "the same yesterday and today and forever." Maybe it is time to take a break from patting ourselves on the back and to thank God for the "fountain of living water" from which we draw on a daily basis.

Proper 18 / Pentecost 16 / Ordinary Time 23
Jeremiah 18:1-11
Philemon 1-21
Luke 14:25-33
Mark Molldrem

Life with attitude

We live in an ever-coarsening culture. The edgy sounds and razor lyrics of punk and rap music have set a cutting edge to what defines our time. It's a raw look at who we are and what we do as a society. The language now deemed acceptable for general broadcast in the public media has reached new depths of baseness, not just with the words that are permissible to air, but also in the way certain topics are talked about. Dress has become more undress, with fashions flaunting undergarments, as well as slovenliness. Rudeness is justified either as "my rights" or "I'm just being honest with you."

Sadly, this coarseness is part of the ethos that defines America at the beginning of this new millennium. It expresses an attitude that is self-absorbed, angry, and dispirited, playing on the threshold of nihilism. Injected into this malaise today are words from scripture that convey an *attitude*, to be sure, but one that is quite different than what arises naturally from the human heart. These words redirect our focus to a more substantial ground on which to stand, from which a healthier and hopeful attitude can arise for the living of our days.

Jeremiah 18:1-11

Jeremiah would have made a great homiletics professor for the eager preacher, more by example than by erudite lectures on the composition and delivery of sermons. Baruch, his faithful scribe, knew this and recorded for posterity many of Jeremiah's sermons. The first twenty chapters of Jeremiah contain sermons delivered during the reigns of Josiah and Jehoiakim, in the last half of the seventh century BC. Each sermon is introduced in a manner like this: "The word that came to Jeremiah from the Lord" (Jeremiah 1:4, 11; 2:1; 3:6; 7:1; 11:1; 14:1; 16:1; 18:1). Notice in this formula that the Lord is the source of Jeremiah's message. The prophet speaks not on his own authority; nor is his message simply what he thought up while burning the midnight oil.

Good sermons have good illustrations, and Jeremiah's sermon in today's text is no exception. The visual image of a potter toiling over a lump of clay is sufficient for Jeremiah to speak about how God is dealing with his people. Just as a potter can take a misshaped lump of clay that at first did not respond to the potter's design and remake it into something else, so too can God rework his people in new ways, "as it seemed good... to do" (18:4). It is God's prerogative to do with the clay of his creation (the house of Israel) as he chooses.

The relationship between God and his people, the clay, is a dynamic one. The response the people offer to the working of the divine hands will make a difference in how those hands work the unfolding creation. When there is repentance in the clay, God, the potter, will not throw the sample away but will continue to work with it and develop a newer, more satisfying design. If, however, there is evil in the clay — a resistance to the potter having his way in shaping the clay, then the potter will not be able to finish the intended design. The clay will be taken off the wheel, and it will no longer have the opportunity to come to life.

Out of this undesirable result comes the exhortation to repent (18:11). Short of this, there can only be judgment, which will disappoint the potter and leave the clay in despair. This message of Jeremiah does more than lift up the threat of judgment; it emphasizes the invitation of a caring potter that the clay remain responsive and thus on the wheel of life. This does not minimize the seriousness of the judgment; what it does more so is motivate a response of returning to the Lord.

Philemon 1-21

It is understandable, though unfortunate, that Philemon gets only one slot in the lectionary. Perhaps every pastor should determine to preach from this text/story this weekend, because this is the only time we will intentionally see Philemon and Onesimus. They have so much to offer us that it would be a shame to pass them over for any reason.

This is a beautiful story of forgiveness and Christian fellowship at its richest. Onesimus was a slave in the household of Philemon. We do not know the circumstances of why he apparently ran away. We learn that Philemon was a faithful Christian who expressed his love for the Lord and for the Christian community. Apparently, however, Onesimus did not convert to the faith while in Philemon's household.

Somehow, Onesimus ends up with Paul and becomes a Christian. Paul wants to send him back to Philemon. He is concerned, though, about everyone's attitude in this matter. He lifts up Onesimus as a valued servant (not slave; vv. 13 and 16) in the Lord. This he makes clear in his choice of words describing Onesimus. The word for "slave" describes his station in life; the word for "servant" (from which we get the word *deacon* and the *deaconite ministry*) describes his status in the Christian community. Paul affirms Onesimus as "a beloved brother." With this new identity, Paul encourages him to return home to his master, most likely with a refreshed vision for serving the family with an attitude of mission, an attitude that transforms Onesimus' station.

Paul, like a master potter, "works" Philemon to reshape his attitude toward the one he had considered useless up until now. Since Paul found Onesimus true to his name (meaning "useful"), he confidently sends him back to Philemon, who will benefit from his service. In fact, Philemon will discover a new attitude in his own heart, a discovery for which Paul prepares him.

One of the angles from which Paul persuades Philemon is that of debt. He recognizes that Onesimus has cost Philemon some financial loss. Paul is willing to assume the debt and promises to pay it. Then, he deftly reminds Philemon of the debt he himself owes Paul (probably for his salvation in Christ through Paul's witness — what price can be put on that?). Paul does not belabor the point, for it is sharp enough to penetrate immediately.

Underlying all of this is the notion of passing on what one has received. Just as Paul received the saving grace of God through Jesus Christ, he passed it on to those who would hear and receive it in turn, like Philemon. He now calls upon Philemon to extend such grace to Onesimus, especially since both of them claim Jesus as Lord in their lives. Between the lines (especially in vv. 14-16), one can sense a hint of what Paul wrote in Philippians 4:17: "Not that I seek the gift, but I seek the profit that accumulates to your account." Paul recognizes that Philemon will grow in his Christian discipleship by exercising the freedom he has in Christ to welcome Onesimus back into the home with forgiveness and new appreciation.

Some interesting comments can be drawn from the conjecture around the word in verse 9 that the Revised Standard Version translates "ambassador" and the New Revised Standard Version renders "an old man." The latter seems the more authentic, but the former makes good sense, even though its attestation in the manuscripts is minimal. The confusion arises over the difference in spelling between the words by one simple letter. It is easy to understand how a change from one to the other could be made in the tedious copy process of those early centuries.

The word for "ambassador," with the extra letter, would be consistent with other language Paul uses in his letters — for example, 2 Corinthians 5:20 and especially Ephesians 6:20. The authority of his witness as commissioned by the risen Christ Jesus is emphasized here. This puts quite a lot of pressure on Philemon to comply with Paul's appeal.

But the word for "an old man" has greater corroboration among the manuscripts. In that case, Paul would seem to be appealing to the charm of his age, like an elder statesman, who is also in prison. How could Philemon refuse a request from such an individual in those circumstances? This may not carry the theological weight of the former word, but it nonetheless comes across as highly motivational.

Luke 14:25-33

Jesus is no stranger to hyperbole, a figure of speech that uses exaggeration to make a point. (The Greek word from which the hyperbole derives means "to exceed." See Matthew 18:6 for an instance of Jesus' strong use of language; also Luke 23:29-31.) *Hate* is an offensively strong word to use in reference to family ties. Jesus uses it freely when talking about the priorities one is to have in life. What Jesus likely means here is that while there are many important relationships in life, there are none more important than the relationship one has with him.

It may be for our sensitive ears that Matthew 10:37 expresses this same thought in a more palliative way. Reference is made to degrees of love. We can comprehend degrees of love, whereas the terminology of hate makes it sound like we must choose one over the other. John 3:20 expresses this, as light and darkness are set in antipathy and those who choose evil do so because they hate the light. The same Greek word for *hate* is used in the Johanine text and the Lukan text.

It may be helpful to reflect on this pericope in light of Jesus' passion predictions in Luke 9:22-23, 43b-45. Jesus knows his destiny is the cross. He will need to give up everything to reveal the fullness of God's love for the world. Therefore, any who follow him must be willing to walk the same road to Calvary, giving up everything for the sake of attaining what Paul calls "the prize of the heavenly call of God in Christ Jesus" (Philippians 3:14).

It is not that we attain it through our efforts; we embrace what Christ has done *for* us. In so doing, we accept his claim on our life, which is a total claim so that he may give to us his total blessings. Hence, the language of "denying self" that Jesus uses in describing how his disciples must follow him. Part of this denying of self is to relegate all other matters into secondary and tertiary positions, even the icon of family.

Jesus offers two very common images to help his hearers understand the *cost* of being his disciple. When one begins a building project, it is important to know just how much it will cost in order to be able to complete it. Constructing a tower is no small enterprise. Neither is following Jesus! One best be prepared to bear the cost, including denial of self, subjection to the will of God, rejection and even possible martyrdom.

In like manner, when an army is set against another, the combatants must have a complete understanding of their resources to determine if this is a cause that can be won. Battles are a matter of total commitment, for they mean life or death. So does following Jesus! It is a matter of life or death. There really is no middle ground. To side with Jesus, one must be willing to give up everything, like a soldier pledging allegiance to his general and offering his life on the front line for victory.

Application

We say we want warnings before things happen. "Forewarned is forearmed." Especially if there is something for which we may be chastised, we say we desire a warning to allow opportunity to change our ways and avoid the discipline. We get angry at those over us when they just "lower the boom" and don't even give us a second chance with "just a warning this time." However, like the people of Israel, we still "do it" even after the warning. The warning does not seem to work. Jeremiah's potter sermon did not turn the people from their ways. Clay just has a hard time listening, even with ears shaped to hear.

God is compelled by our resistance (like the spoiled clay on the potter's wheel) to deal with us in judgment. Rather than rag on God for "hard times" and ask whiney questions like "Why me?" the right attitude is to embrace the judgment, like Jeremiah had to. Ask the difficult but necessary questions in the midst of God's discipline: "What must I learn from this experience? How can I let God have his way with me better?"

This is a more profound attitude to nurture in life, one that can endure the rough edges of experience with character and courage, because it rests in the promise of God. "At one moment I may declare concerning a nation or a kingdom, that I will pluck up and break down and destroy it, but if that nation, concerning which I have spoken, turns from its evil, I will change my mind about the disaster that I intended to bring on it" (Jeremiah 18:7-8). This can certainly apply to individuals also.

In his letter to Philemon, Paul gives some practical direction for how the "clay" can be pliant, and therefore compliant, in the potter's hands, in God's hands. First, it is important to have a good understanding of self. Paul sees himself as "a prisoner for Christ Jesus" (v. 1; very contextual, given his imprisonment). In other letters he describes himself as a "slave of Christ Jesus" (Romans 1:1; Philippians 1:1; Titus 1:1). Paul does not live for himself or unto himself. He belongs to another. "For to me, living is Christ..." he writes in Philippians 1:21. A vital attitude for Christians to maintain in our very ego-centered culture is one that understands the self first and foremost in the hands of God and subject to the will of God.

Second, having a healthy appreciation of others will go far in balancing the deleterious effects of individualistic tendencies. From the very beginning of his letter, Paul lifts up Philemon as beloved, a fellow worker, a lover of people, a man of faith, an inspiration to others. It would be crass to assert that Paul is simply setting up Philemon to be persuaded to do what Paul wants him to do. He builds up Philemon with genuine appreciation, following his own advice "for building up the body of Christ" (Ephesians 4:12). One of the best ways to keep from turning in upon ourselves (*incurvatus se*) is to focus on the gifts that others bring into relationships and offer for the good of the larger community.

Third, acknowledge, encourage, and work for growth in others, not just for their own benefit, but for what they can then contribute for the benefit of others. Paul grew Onesimus from a slave to a servant, from a domestic to a disciple. This is doing in Christian parlance what the prophets called for in ages past — to beat swords into plowshares and do justice (Micah), to seek good and not evil (Amos). Onesimus became a blessing for Paul and now Paul wants to send him back to Philemon that he may be a blessing to him as well. In this way, the words of the psalmist ring so true: "How very good and pleasant it is when kindred live together in unity!" (Psalm 133:1).

It truly is good and pleasant when people can dwell in unity. Unfortunately, the world does not allow this to happen without a struggle. There are hate groups that recruit followers and train them in violent attitudes and behaviors. Neo-Nazi enclaves exemplify this to the chagrin of humanity. Ethnic communities define themselves over against and at the expense of other communities. The strife in the Middle East in an ongoing illustration of this to the bafflement of world leaders, some of whom have been martyred in the search for peace.

How hard it is for us to give up our wills and subject ourselves to the will of God! Dietrich Bonhoeffer said it well when he described what is necessary for this to happen: "When Christ calls a man to follow him, he bids him come and die." It takes nothing less than that, and that is why the world cannot understand it. In the world and of the world, we seize what we deem important to us, what we can tangibly hold on to — like our possessions and our family. We are oriented to the here and now and are often willing to settle for immediate satisfaction without regard to future blessing. In so doing, we miss the point of Jesus' promise that as we seek the kingdom of God first and foremost, these other good things will be added to our experience in ways that bring joy and satisfaction (Matthew 6:33).

Take, for example, the matter of family. Society has elevated the status of family to the position of demigod. "Family is everything" is a cliché that is repeated everywhere. With such a notion imbedded in our minds, it is no wonder that we have difficulty in comprehending Jesus' words about priorities. He is challenging us with a whole new paradigm for life, which places him as Lord in our life. How can we help young families, for example, live in this paradigm, as they struggle with schedules for their children that include wholesome activities that may conflict with the scheduled activities of the Christian community for worship, education, fellowship, and service? Where do we adapt the church schedule to be responsive to the realities of our culture? Where do we challenge our families to make choices when this cannot so easily be done? Having the right attitude will go a long way in shaping right behavior.

Proper 19 / Pentecost 17 / ORDINARY TIME 24
Jeremiah 4:11-12, 22-28
1 Timothy 1:12-17
Luke 15:1-10
David Kalas

But what if it is broken?

Conventional wisdom says, "If it ain't broke, don't fix it." That's fair advice. But what if it *is* broken? What shall our policy be then?

We make that kind of decision on a regular basis. Some items are so inexpensive or so unimportant to us that we regard them as disposable. If they're broken, we throw them away and replace them. Other items are so valuable to us, however, that we readily invest the time, effort, and money necessary to fix them when they are broken.

Sometimes the choice is not so clear-cut, of course. When the family car is getting old and has a lot of miles on it, and the mechanic says it will cost this much to fix the latest problem, then what should you do? Is it more cost effective to keep putting repair and maintenance money into the car that's already paid off, or is your money better spent on something newer that will require less upkeep?

In the biblical story, we see a God whose creation is broken. It is not his doing, of course, but ours. Indeed, our brokenness seems chronic. The fix is costly beyond estimation. That is the loving, saving choice he made — to remake us rather than to replace us — and at great personal expense.

Our three scripture passages this week bear witness to the brokenness of humanity and to God's costly fix.

Jeremiah was a judgment prophet in the early days of the Babylonian Empire. Like the other judgment prophets, a part of Jeremiah's ministry and message was the identification of the people's sins. In our selected verses from chapter 4, Jeremiah offers a glimpse of the chronic brokenness of humanity — which, in this case, is God's own people.

Our passage from Paul's first letter to Timothy includes a part of Paul's testimony. He articulates the form and depth of his own formerly broken state. Then he bears witness to the gracious and costly "fix" by God that we call salvation.

Finally, the familiar selection from Luke's gospel portrays in story form the beauty of God's approach. The explicit theme is not brokenness but "lostness." God's response to his lost loved ones is to seek, find, and then, rejoice.

The mechanic might tell me that my car isn't worth putting any more money into it, and any impartial observer would have told God that rebellious and fallen humanity was not worth what he intended to invest in us. "You're throwing good grace after bad" might have been the skeptic's counsel.

But love does not count the cost; it just pays the price.

Jeremiah 4:11-12, 22-28

The Old Testament judgment prophets were the bearers of bad news. They did not do much to try to disguise or to soften it. That in itself is something of a lesson to us, for often a fear of confrontation, an instinct toward salesmanship, or a well-meaning pity interferes with our capacity to speak bad news. Jeremiah and his prophetic colleagues, however, did not offer a spoonful of sugar with their medicine. There was bad news for the people, and the people needed to recognize it. "Warning" and "danger" signs do no good if they are in small print.

Here that bad news is represented by "a hot wind" — a provocative image in contrast to the image of a cool breeze. A cool breeze connotes relief and pleasantness for us; a hot wind, therefore, must be a burdensome, destructive thing.

We referenced earlier the chronic brokenness of humanity. God laments it in verse 22, detailing the severity of the problem. He expresses it in three sad observations.

First, God laments that his people "are foolish, they do not know me." Over a century earlier, God had expressed the same kind of bewildered complaint about his people through the prophet Isaiah (1:3). How is it that God's own covenant people should not know him? Throughout their history, he had provided for them, led them, spoken to them, and revealed himself to them. They were uniquely and intimately his, and yet they did not know him. We human beings are surely mystified by the things of God, but he may be even more mystified by us. God's mystery, after all, is due to his vastness and majesty. Our mystery, however, is in our inconsistency and illogic.

Second, God laments that "they are stupid children, they have no understanding." The identification of the people as children carries two great implications. On the one hand, it is no doubt an insult to the pride of the people. They surely did not regard themselves as being like children — particularly like stupid children. It is a harsh criticism to say to an adult, "You're being childish" or "You need to grow up." This was the spirit of God's critique of his own people. On the other hand, we must never lose sight of the beauty in God referring to his people as children. That, after all, is how he always views us. I am an adult with children of my own, and yet my mother still regards me as her child. It is that identification of his people as his children, albeit stupid ones, that moves God's compassion and devotion (see, for example, Hosea 11:1-8).

Third, God laments that "they are skilled in doing evil, but do not know how to do good." This is the great indictment of fallen humanity, and it becomes our own realization about ourselves (see Romans 7:15-19). The question to consider is whether this condition is a matter of degree or a universal state of being. Paul's implication in Romans 7 seems to be that this is a ubiquitous symptom of our "fallenness." On the other hand, one senses in God's words in Jeremiah 4 that he expects better of his people.

Next, the voice of the speaker suddenly changes. After the Lord has expressed what he sees as he looks at his people, Jeremiah then expresses prophetically what he sees as he looks around him. "I looked" is the recurring statement that introduces four descriptions of God's judgment.

The first thing Jeremiah saw was an earth that "was waste and void" and heavens that "had no light." The imagery is reminiscent of Genesis 1, for before God began his creative act there was no light and "the earth was a formless void" (Genesis 1:2). Does the imagery in Jeremiah mean that God's deliberate judgment reverts the universe to its prior, terrible state? Does the imagery suggest that Judah's choice to live without God eventually results in an experience that completely lacks God's gracious influence? Does the state of darkness and void anticipate the saving work of God who will once again bring light and life?

The second thing Jeremiah saw was mountains "quaking" and hills moving "to and fro." It is an eerie sight. I remember flying to the Holy Land some years ago and as our plane passed 35,000 feet over Switzerland, Austria, and Italy, I was awed to see how high above the clouds the mighty mountains of the Alps rose. They seemed to be more a part of the sky than the earth, looking down on the clouds below. I imagine those mighty mountains shaking and quaking, and I have a picture of chaos: Earth is out of control when the largest, most immovable, most stable symbols on earth are quivering.

The third thing Jeremiah saw was "no one at all, and all the birds of the air had fled." There is something peculiarly unnerving about a place that has been completely vacated. That the birds had fled suggests a kind of dread — as though nature itself sensed the terror that was coming and took flight. On the other hand, "there was no one at all" suggests that perhaps the terror had already come. Perhaps the people had not fled and were gone but rather were dead and gone.

Finally, Jeremiah saw that "the fruitful land was a desert, and all its cities were laid in ruins." The prior image was one of desolation. This is an image of devastation. Everything has been ruined, from nature to civilization. We are reminded of Leviticus 26 and the truth that both God's blessings and his curses are thorough. No area of life is untouched by his generosity. Likewise, nothing is shielded from his judgment.

On the tail end of this otherwise unrelenting slideshow of troubles, comes this brief word of hope: "Yet I will not make a full end." How utterly characteristic of God and of his judgments this sounds. In the days of Noah, God did not make a full end but preserved for a fresh start Noah, his family, and two of every kind of animal. In the days of Israel's unfaithfulness at the border of Canaan, God did not make a full end but raised up a new generation to take into the land of his promise. To the people of Jeremiah's day, he promised again not to make a full end. For in the end, his final purpose is not sentencing, but saving.

1 Timothy 1:12-17

In the Jeremiah passage, we saw God's view of the brokenness of his people, and in the end, we also had a glimpse of the mercy that is built into even his judgment, for he does not "make a full end."

In the Luke passage, we see two parables that depict the happy ending of God seeking and saving his people. Both stories are told from the perspective of the "God characters" (i.e., the shepherd of the lost sheep and the woman who lost the coin).

In between the other two lections, in these words from the apostle Paul, we see the other side of the same story. This is the human side: The personal testimony of one who was lost and broken, and who has been sought and saved by God. We do not hear from the people of Judah in the Jeremiah passage. We do not hear from the sheep or the coin in the Luke passage. But we do hear from Paul. He offers the testimonial of all those who have been lost and broken, and who have been the recipients of God's grace.

Paul recalls the specifics of his former condition: He was a blasphemer, a persecutor, a man of violence, and ignorant. Indeed, Paul identifies himself as the "foremost" of sinners. The Greek word translated as "foremost" is *protos*. It is used most often in the New Testament to refer to someone or something that comes first in time or in sequence, which is clearly not what Paul has in mind here. There are a few other uses, however, that lend special insight into Paul's self-identification as the foremost — the *protos* — of sinners.

Jesus told his disciples "whoever wishes to be first among you must be your slave" (Matthew 20:27), and *protos* is the word translated "first." The commandment to love God is cited as the *protos* commandment (Matthew 20:27). The robe that the father of the returning prodigal son calls for is the *protos* robe (Luke 15:22). When Paul calls himself the *protos* of sinners, therefore, he means that he is the blue ribbon, gold-medal sinner.

Lucy once said to Charlie Brown, "Of all the Charlie Browns in the world, you're the Charlie Browniest." Such is the nature of Paul's conclusion about himself. Of all the sinners in the world, he had been the "sinneriest."

This is a little bit of boasting on Paul's part but not boasting about his sinfulness. He is not like the fool who brags about how drunk or wasted he got over the weekend. Rather, Paul is citing his badness as a way of boasting about God's goodness. The magnitude of Paul's sinfulness only serves to bear witness to the magnitude of saving grace.

In this regard, Paul's is a model testimony, for we are rightly struck by the fact that his own testimony is not really about him. Four times in six verses, Paul references Jesus by name. The real headline is not Paul's sin, but the Savior and his love and grace.

Finally, the pattern of the passage is noteworthy, for it begins with thanksgiving and ends with praise. "I am grateful," Paul begins, "to Christ Jesus our Lord." Then, after recalling his sin and God's salvation, his testimony crescendos to a great doxology: "To the king of the ages, immortal, invisible, the only God, be honor and glory, forever and ever. Amen" (1 Timothy 1:17).

If the sheep and the coin could speak, I expect that's what they would say too.

Luke 15:1-10

Luke 15 has often been referred to as the "lost and found chapter" of the Bible. Here we find, in succession, the three great parables of Jesus about someone or something being lost and then found again. First comes the story of the lost sheep, then the lost coin, and then the lost (we call him the prodigal) son.

The three stories escalate in intimacy and value. The lost sheep is just one out of a hundred. The lost coin is one out of just ten. The lost son is, well, a son, and one of only two. Each story ends with the lost item being restored to the proper person, who in turn throws a great celebration.

This whole set of priceless parables, according to Luke, is shared by Jesus in response to some grumbling by the Pharisees and the scribes.

From time to time you get some criticism that assures you that you're doing the right thing. That is surely the nature of what the Pharisees and scribes had to say about Jesus. They thought they were being sharply critical. In fact, however, they were just grouchy evangelists, declaring with a frown the good news about Jesus: "This fellow welcomes sinners and eats with them."

The scribes and Pharisees had the right lyrics. They just didn't realize they were singing them to the wrong tune. They said that Jesus welcomed sinners in the tone that one would say, "This fellow blasphemes God," or "This fellow teaches heresy." Instead, they should have said it with the same tone and expression that one would use to say, "This fellow feeds the hungry," or "This fellow heals the sick." Their critique of Jesus was actually good news.

Jesus responded to their misguided criticism with three stories, two of which are a part of our gospel lesson for this week: the parable of the lost sheep and the parable of the lost coin.

The stories are different, as we observed, in the relative value of the item lost, as well as in the culpability of the item lost. What is identical in the two stories, meanwhile, is the behavior of the "God character." Both the shepherd and the woman devote themselves to finding what has been lost, and both celebrate with others when it has been found.

Such is the heart of God toward his lost loved ones. He does not regard us as disposable — not even one of us. Instead, Christ came "to seek out and to save the lost" (Luke 19:10). Or, as Paul expressed it to Timothy, "The saying is sure and worthy of full acceptance, that Christ Jesus came into the world to save sinners" (1 Timothy 1:15).

Application

What to do with something broken?

Some things are so cheap that there's no point in fixing them, so we simply throw them away. When my shoelace breaks, I buy a new one.

Some things are too difficult to fix, and so we replace those. When I was a little boy, I broke a window or two while playing ball. My dad did not try to gather and reassemble the pieces of broken glass to fix the window; he replaced the window.

Then there are those things that are too costly to fix. It is actually cheaper to replace the item than repair the item, and that's what we do.

See what God does with a broken creation? Surely it would have been less costly to throw us away and create something all new. We don't see any expense to God at the creation; we see a great expense, however, at the cross. Still, he paid the price to fix us.

An Alternative Application

Jeremiah 4:11-12, 22-28. God's emphatic statement — "It is I who speak in judgment against them" — might go unappreciated by the people in our pews. At best, it seems redundant; for the larger context of Jeremiah's message makes it quite obvious that the Lord is speaking judgment against the people. At worst, God's words here may sound bullying or spiteful. In fact, however, there is a great reassurance to be found in this affirmation from God to his threatened people: he is running the show.

The current events of Jeremiah's day were foreboding for Judah and Jerusalem. The Babylonian Empire was a menacing presence, and Judah had little realistic hope of prevailing in any conflict with Babylon. During Jeremiah's lifetime, the Babylonians would conquer Jerusalem, destroy the temple, and take several "shifts" of Jews into exile.

To wonder, in the midst of all the trouble and tragedy, whether God had forgotten his people would have been debilitating to their faith. To think that the gods of Babylon had defeated the God of Israel would have been unbearable. But the Jews faced no such theological crisis, for it was God himself who spoke "in judgment against them."

When I was young, I sometimes objected to my mother's rules and discipline. When I was forced to come home earlier than some friend, I would protest, "His mother doesn't care what time he comes home!" And my mother would answer, "But I do care what time you come home. I do care." That was even her claim in the midst of punishing me: "I only punish you because I care."

That is the nature of the good news hidden in the midst of this judgment message. Judah did not fall to Babylon because God was absent or defeated. Instead, God himself was behind the catastrophe. He declared: "It is I who speak in judgment against them." That means he cares.

Proper 20 / Pentecost 18 / Ordinary Time 25
Jeremiah 8:18—9:1
1 Timothy 2:1-7
Luke 16:1-13
Mark Molldrem

From lamentation to larceny

Our texts today take us over a varied landscape. Any one of them could take the preacher and the congregation in a different direction from the others: Jeremiah to the Wailing Wall, Paul and Timothy to the steps of the capitol, the unrighteous steward to behind-closed-doors dealings.

They all hold together on the theme of how one can intercede with God on behalf of those for whom one cares and shares a common destiny. Jeremiah interceded for "my poor people" (Jeremiah 8:19) with questioning tears. Timothy is urged by Paul to lead the Ephesians in advocating with God on behalf of the civil authorities. Even an unrighteous steward acts as arbiter to avoid small claims court. Finally, of course, Jesus is named the "one mediator between God and humankind" (1 Timothy 2:5) who guarantees the salvation that arises out of the very heart of God.

Jeremiah 8:18—9:1

When God speaks, the prophet speaks. "Thus says the Lord" is the herald cry to perk the ears of those who need to hear. In this text, it appears that we have the words of Jeremiah lamenting the fate of the people. Could it be that when the prophet speaks, God speaks?

Jeremiah has been called "the weeping prophet." He had the uncompromising and unwelcome task of announcing the demise of Judah, the destruction of the temple, and the exile of God's favored ones. Not only was his mouth into his work, but also his heart. In today's text, we see how much his heart is in the prophecy he has been given to deliver. Jeremiah himself shares in the pain of what is happening to the people, whose future will not be in the Promised Land, but in a land of exile. In the statements he has heard and now repeats, we can hear his own questioning and his own dismay: Where is our God? Why have we blatantly disregarded the commands of God? When will we be saved from this catastrophe?

These are questions of lamentation that arise out of a wounded heart. "My heart is sick" (8:18). He would later fill another book with such anguish; but for now, he bears his soul publicly, tear-stained, and dismayed.

Can it be that when we hear the prophet speak, we hear the voice of God? That is to say, do these words from Jeremiah's *angst* express the very turmoil that ravages the heart of the living God, who claims these rebellious children as his own? Are we getting a glimpse into the sorrow of God's wrath, which he exercises in justice but also in pain — God's own pain? What grief God must bear, having to wait with his people for history to clock forward in order to answer the questions raised against heaven: "Is there no balm in Gilead? Is there no physician there?" (8:22). The balm *will* be in Gilead in time, "the fullness of time had come" (Galatians 4:4). The physician *will* stride upon the landscape of a people in need of healing (see Luke 4:23). But until that time arrives, there will be weeping "day and night for the slain of my poor people!" (9:1). Thus says the prophet; thus says the Lord.

1 Timothy 2:1-7

Paul charged Timothy to remain in Ephesus as guardian of the faith (1 Timothy 1:3), for there were some there extrapolating crazy notions. These they were passing on as faithful commentary about Christ's death and resurrection for the salvation of the world. Timothy was to provide oversight for and nurture of the congregation, holding them to the teachings of Paul. We would expect this concern from Paul, who was so clear on the differences between the law and the gospel, between the "myths and... speculations" (1:4) of human minds (see also 2 Peter 1:16) and the revelation of God.

It is refreshing also to receive Paul's very practical concerns for the public life of the Christian community. Complementary to Romans 13:1-7, he expresses his sense of Christian responsibility to engage in prayer for all, especially mentioning those in public office. This is not only a matter of Christian compassion, it is also a matter of Christian citizenship, living "a quiet and peaceable life in all godliness and dignity" (2:2). Our feet need to be grounded below, though our vision is set above.

There is purpose in good citizenship, even beyond a "quiet and peaceable life." That purpose is the same evangelical one that propels the overt preaching of the gospel, namely, that everyone be saved and come to the knowledge of the truth in Jesus Christ (2:4). From the chancel to the curb, the Christian life is to witness to the one, "who gave himself as a ransom for all" (2:6).

Paul's vision for the gospel is quite extensive and inclusive. It is "for all" (2:6 and also expressed in 2:1, 4). In this text for today, he is applying the contemporary notion of *thinking globally and acting locally*, as he advises Timothy to lead the local congregation in Ephesus to pursue the common good in public life in the name of Jesus. For Paul personally, his efforts were to be directed specifically with the Gentiles, wherever they may be. That is why he traveled. His *locus* was the Roman Empire, while Timothy's at this time was Ephesus.

Luke 16:1-13

If we go back to the beginning of chapter 15, we can surmise that the three parables there as well as this parable of the unrighteous steward were spoken to the disciples within earshot of the tax collectors, sinners, and Pharisees. One of the remarkable things about Jesus' teaching is that it is not aimed at a narrow audience, nor is it esoteric in nature such that only a privileged few can truly comprehend what he was talking about. Jesus spoke, for the most part, for all to hear in a way that most could understand, if they had ears to hear.

The theme in Jesus' words for today is stewardship. In the Bible, stewardship means using time-conditioned goods according to timeless values. Jesus applauds the widow who gave so generously (all that she had) out of the abundance of her heart (Luke 21:1-4). Paul applies this principle in one of his best stewardship texts, where he writes, "God is able to provide you with every blessing in abundance [timeless values], so that by always having enough of everything [time-conditioned goods], you may share abundantly in every good work" (2 Corinthians 9:8).

What does Jesus mean when he describes the unrighteous steward as wasting the rich man's goods? Was it that the steward was lax in retrieving what had been loaned to others? Was he foolishly investing the resources in unprofitable ends? Was he stealing from the owner for his own personal gain? Whichever way one may wish to spin this, the steward comes up short in fulfilling his responsibilities to the owner.

It is remarkable that the owner gives the steward the authority to settle matters before he is dismissed. The steward sets out to get back what he can for the owner. He acts like a collection agent, retrieving at least something on outstanding bills, rather than letting them go unsettled. There is advantage in this to the owner, as well as the debtor and also the steward. The owner gets more than he would have gotten if matters were left as is; the debtor satisfies the debt with less than formerly required. The steward comes out of this with a compliment (shrewdness, 1:8) from the owner and with friends on the outside (1:9), where he is now cast.

One of the things to notice about the steward is that he deals with each situation differently. The one who owed oil only had to pay back 50% of the debt. The one who owed wheat, 80%. Do we make of this that the steward had a sense of fairness with the varying circumstances of the debtors? Or, is the steward more concerned to appease the one owing oil, because he will make a better friend after all is said and done? There may be several motivating factors (some even contradictory) in any given act.

What can be made of verse 9? Is Jesus telling us to be wily and get the most use out of "unrighteous mammon" while we can? Or is he speaking tongue-in-cheek about just how far such efforts can really take one? After all, who are these people who can "receive you into the eternal homes"? Are they none other than those who may remember you fondly for a while, and then forget as life takes other directions? Are they those who will pass on your legacy to posterity, until you are but a faded memory at best — as if that is ultimately important?

Jesus finally gets to his point in all of this parable-speak, when he explains how important it is to be faithful in the little things of life as a reflection that one values the truly important things of life. That is to say, one serves God by handling the matters of the world with judicious care, in a way that gives God glory and advances the kingdom, not one's own position. Like the steward, we will get into serious trouble if we try to switch the priorities around and treat the mammon of this world as if it had lasting value.

Application

One of the traditional disciplines that has carried Christians through ages of crises has been meditation on the cross. Peering into the suffering of Christ has the power to shape the soul. Profound mystics in their retreats as well as simple believers in their homes find humility and courage when faced with the suffering of Jesus on the cross. To perceive in some small way the self-giving, self-sacrificing heart of God for his people puts all other human predicaments into a unique perspective. Not that they are diminished or dismissed but they are contextualized into a more grand meaning. They are engulfed by the fullness of God revealed through the life, death, and resurrection of Jesus.

Related to this is the spirit with which so many come to worship these days. Closest to people's heart are such concerns as "How does this relate to my daily life?" "What will I get out of it?" "Will I like what I experience?" "How comfortable do I feel in this setting?" Harder to find is the heart that humbly draws near to God in holy space to present the offerings of praise and adoration, prayer and alms, silence and obedience.

Even when life is collapsing around one, we should bring the hardest of questions before God. It is not necessary to be strong before God; reality actually keeps us rather weak, fragile, sick, and in need of healing from sole to soul. When we can be so honest with ourselves and also transparent before God, we are in a position to receive God's blessing of presence and promise, as expressed in Psalm 23: the deepest, darkest valley need not be cause for fear, for the Lord, like the good shepherd with rod and staff, walks with the vulnerable sheep.

A vital part of the Christian perception of God is that, in Jesus, God assumes the very cries, grief, questions, dismay, and tears of his people, voicing their anguish from the cross, mediating a saving grace through the apparent weakness of the crucifixion itself. Jesus stands in the line of fire between a vulnerable humanity and the enemies of sin and death that would force us out of favor and relationship with God.

Intercessory prayer is a practical application of the intercession Jesus accomplishes for us on behalf of God the Father. Paul writes about this in Romans 8:34 and 2 Corinthians 5:16-21. Jesus is the very expression of God to us and for us. Our intercession on behalf of others is not quite the same as Jesus' role of intercession, because "There is one God" (1 Timothy 2:5). In Jesus, God is not called upon to respond with favor for the sake of the people. In Jesus, God himself is exercising intercession for the ones God loves. Because of this, God does not set up Jesus as a "middleman," similar to the one who is to work out the differences between two contrary parties. Jesus is "God our Savior" (1 Timothy 2:3) who comes to guarantee (the Greek word for "mediator" also carries the sense of "guarantor") that the will of God is characterized by a saving grace that extends to all people. The ransom given by Jesus' life is not a price paid to God to deposit a people into his heavenly account, but is the price God himself paid to buy a people for his own heart.

In contrast to this, when we pray for others, we step forward between those who have our concern and the one who is concerned for them. God's love encompasses all, so we are urged to pray for all leaders in public life, presumably beginning with one's own local officials. Paul becomes an example of this, insofar as he was the apostle to the Gentiles. Just as he stepped outside the box of expectations and expanded his world to include the Gentiles, so is the Christian to step outside the box and reach out with the compassion of Christ to all, whoever they are and wherever they may be. Our prayers will reveal where our hearts are and our prayers will lead us into action in response to the very things for which we ask.

Alternative Applications

In our culture of endless choice, one of the greatest challenges facing the church is to help people keep their priorities in order, so that they can make appropriate decisions in the little things (time-conditioned matters) based upon the big things (timeless values, kingdom goals). In this fall season, with school activities starting and organizations and clubs getting together again after summer vacations, there is tremendous pressure on people for their time, talents, and treasures. Younger and older alike feel this — at school, at work, in volunteer responsibilities, and in ever-increasing recreational opportunities. Individuals and families deal daily with the issue of choosing between so many good options through which to express and enhance themselves. In our increasing secular society, what often happens is that the activities of the church get squeezed out (or at best "squeezed in"). This is symptomatic of how we are becoming more devoted to the pursuit of mammon, rather than God.

Seventy-five years ago, Eberhard Arnold, founder of the Bruderhof communities, raised some serious questions in pre-Nazi Germany that bear hearing today, such as "Are not the state and the organized church, which protect privilege and wealth, diametrically opposed to what is to come: God's new order?" In a lecture delivered in 1923, he offers this challenging description: "Where mammon rules, the possessive will is stronger than the will to community; the struggle to survive by mutual killing is stronger than the urge to love... matter is stronger than spirit, things and circumstances are stronger than God...."

Arnold was neither entranced by socialism nor communism; nor was he captivated by capitalism. He strove to embody an actual fellowship of people organized around the principles of the Sermon on the Mount. His vision was "the new way of communal work and fellowship in things spiritual and material — the voluntary gathering of those who are free of private property and capital." This is a radical view compared to that held by most everyone who is seated in church pews these days. Yet, it calls into question what we are really about in our daily lives and challenges us to look deeper into our confession of sins and how great the love of God must be to still call us his children. Then, we may be inspired to act differently, even if spasmodically, in ways that embody stewardship that is based on kingdom goals (Matthew 6:33), rather than personal ones.

All three of today's texts carry a common theme of citizenship. Jeremiah laments the civil and spiritual disorder that plagues his beloved homeland. Timothy is encouraged to be supportive of those in high places in the community, as a spiritual discipline. Jesus tells a parable about keeping a spiritual perspective on personal affairs. Without that perspective, priorities get skewed and we may fail to handle civil responsibilities appropriately.

Proper 21 / Pentecost 19 / Ordinary Time 26
Jeremiah 32:1-3a, 6-15
1 Timothy 6:6-19
Luke 16:19-31
Mark Molldrem

Blessing the rich man's proceeds

Everybody likes payday. Of course, it's time to pay the bills and set some money aside for a rainy day or retirement; but most enjoyable is putting some of that hard-earned money in the billfold to be used on a whim later in the evening or on the weekend.

Jeremiah, Paul, and Jesus have a very interesting perspective on wealth that may change the way we go to the bank. Through buying a parcel of land, Jeremiah invests in his country when everything was falling apart. Paul urges Timothy and the congregation at Ephesus to be rich in godliness. Jesus tells a parable about material wealth not cutting it, when it comes time for death and the hereafter. The advice each would give us today is to head for the bank with "withdrawal slips" to invest one's assets for the kingdom of God rather than "deposit slips" for one's own benefit.

Jeremiah 32:1-3a, 6-15

Babylon had already trampled the land. Nebuchadnezzer had besieged Jerusalem at the close of the seventh century BC and then again in 598 BC when he plundered the city. Judah was at the mercy of this new empire that had risen over the collapse of the Assyrians (Nineveh was destroyed in 612 BC). When Judah, under the token reign of Zedekiah, revolted against their new overlords, Babylon swept down once again, this time leveling Jerusalem and dismantling the glorious temple built by Solomon. During this time, Jeremiah had been imprisoned and left to starve to death (Jeremiah 37), but King Zedekiah took pity on him and kept him in the court of the guard instead (32:2).

There is no good reason not to include Jeremiah 32:3b-5 in the reading. It provides the reason that Jeremiah was imprisoned in the first place. It also sets in stark contrast Jeremiah's prophecy about the success of the Babylonians against Israel and Jeremiah's action parable of hope, in which he buys the field at Anathoth.

This purchase is a symbol of hope. If "actions speak louder than words," then this transaction demonstrates "loud and clear" that there is cause to hope in the future even in the face of such devastation in the present. Jeremiah took great pains to see that everything was done legally and publicly as a witness to his confidence. The land may be lost to this people, who will be carted off into exile, but the people will not be lost to God. This investment in the land foreshadows the return of the people to again occupy the land that the Lord had promised to Abraham.

What makes this hope so striking is that it is shaped by the same God who in "anger... wrath and... great indignation" (Jeremiah 32:37) is judging the people for unspeakable sins. Not only have they turned their backs on the God of Abraham and Sinai by worshiping Baal, they also turned their children into fodder for the god Moloch, who devoured the little ones in his fiery belly to appease his avaricious appetite for blood. How remarkable that the God of the covenant remains faithful over against his faithless people and holds out for them a hope that will carry them through this time of judgment!

1 Timothy 6:6-19

Paul gives Timothy lots of practical instructions in this letter to help him guide the church at Ephesus. The topics covered include public prayer, the place of women, the office of bishop and deacon, false doctrine, godly living, faithful service, care for widows, and the role of elders and slaves. He accents the importance of what he explains by exhorting Timothy, "Teach and urge these duties" (1 Timothy 6:2c). Then, Paul moves on to his concluding remarks, which form the pericope for today.

Similar to what he wrote in Philippians 4:11, Paul reflects on the basic wisdom of contentment as the companion of godliness (6:6). Since we enter this world naked (literally) and leave it naked (figuratively; "you can't take it with you"), it is best to be concerned with what is truly essential. More than food and clothing (survival minimums), the Christian is to "pursue righteousness..." (6:11). This is the righteousness that comes through faith in Jesus Christ (Romans 1:16-17; Galatians 2:16), to whom Paul offers a doxology (6:15-16). This righteousness means that one's life is understood as existing from, within, under, and toward God.

One stands right with God because one stands in the shadow of the cross of Christ, submitting to the shape of that instrument of certain death and promised life. In the shadow of that cross, there can only be love for the one who gave up his life that we may know the extent of God's love for us. That is why Paul uses cruciform language ("pierced their hearts with many pangs"; 6:10 RSV) when talking about the danger of money-love, seducing one's heart "away from the faith," away from Jesus as one's master.

In a very personal comment to Timothy, Paul commends him to the virtues of the Christian life: "righteousness, godliness, faith, love, endurance, gentleness" (6:11; compare complementary lists in Galatians 5:22-23 and Colossians 3:12f). He charges him to "keep the commandment" (6:14), which is a reference not to any particular commandment among the ten, but to the whole of the divine directive to live according to the will of God — which is love!

Jesus defines it this way when asked about the greatest commandment; it is love for God with one's whole heart and love for the neighbor as for oneself. When in the upper room on the night in which he was betrayed, Jesus bequeaths this commandment to his disciples (John 15:12; the same Greek word for "commandment" is used in these texts cited from 1 Timothy, Matthew, and John).

Paul puts a time reference on this expectation he places on Timothy: "until the manifestation of our Lord Jesus Christ" (6:14). As we learn elsewhere in Paul's letters, he expected the return of Jesus to occur sooner than later (Romans 13:11; 1 Corinthians 7:29). This puts a qualification on how Christians are to live their lives, not pursuing personal wealth and the pride and power and glory that can come with it, but "rich in good deeds" with liberality and generosity (6:18 RSV). In other words, daily life that invests itself in others in many (liberality) intense (generosity) ways "really is life" (6:19). The future is promised us as we stand on a solid foundation; the walls of good works come to rest on the foundation of the grace of God, "who richly provides us with everything for our enjoyment" (6:17).

Luke 16:19-31

The word "Hades" is used only ten times in the New Testament. The synoptic references in Matthew 11:23 and Luke 10:15 refer to Capernaum's fate due to lack of repentance in response to the ministry of Jesus. In Acts 2:27 and 31, Luke cites a psalm and relates it to the resurrection of Jesus, whom Hades could not contain. In Matthew 16:18 and Revelation 1:18, Hades is cast in a subjugated status before Christ. Although Hades gets to ride its day on earth (Revelation 6:8), in the final judgment before God, Hades will be thrown into the lake of fire, an apocalyptic image of final and eternal damnation (Revelation 20:13-14).

In this parable Jesus tells for the Pharisees, a rich man dies and goes to Hades, which is cast as a "place of torment." It is plain why he is there. He was self-absorbed in his earthly life and did not provide for the poor at his gate. This is a parable of simple morality, accentuating the seriousness of how those who have much relate to those who have little. The prophets themselves spoke of these things clearly throughout history. Leviticus 19:18 plainly says to all, "You shall love your neighbor as yourself: I am the Lord." Micah 6:8 describes in no uncertain terms just what God expects: "He has told you, O mortal, what is good; and what does the Lord require of you but to do justice, and to love kindness and to walk humbly with your God?" It does not take someone rising from the dead to convince one of the rightness of such provisions.

If one's heart is hardened to this, repentance will be no easier should someone rise from the dead. One could "fast forward" to Easter morning and the tomorrows beyond, asking the question why the whole world is not converted to egalitarian care, if it were true that "if someone goes to them from the dead, they will repent" (16:30). No! What one sows in this life will have eternal consequences, and it is no secret what the planting should be! It is as distinct as "a great chasm... fixed," so as to distinguish between right and wrong.

In the context of the observation made in Luke 16:14-15, where the Pharisees are noted for their love of money, this parable calls for repentance in the here and now, for after death there will be no chance for recovery. The Pharisees certainly had the resources of blessings at their disposal. When they failed to act with compassion and share with those still in need, they exposed themselves as "an abomination in the sight of God."

Application

One of the fatal features of American culture is the growing gambling industry. The spirit of King Midas broods in our hearts with a "lust for lucre." Paul reminds us that the love of money is the root of all evil. Lotteries and all sorts of ploys are used by states, tribes, and private businesses to seduce us to seek easy wealth by means of frivolous games.

Christians are urged instead to be "rich in good works" (1 Timothy 6:18). True wealth is found in the treasures of kingdom virtues, like righteousness, godliness, faith, love, endurance, gentleness, and so on. Here is where lifestyle will truly reveal one's priorities. It's not that wealth is to be shunned. There are those who know how to make an honest dollar and multiply it by hard work and shrewd investment. If we were all equally poor, we would probably all be equally dead. The wealth of the world has spurred invention, research, and development to advance world civilization to new heights, upon which we can stand and praise and thank God. It is the use of all this wealth that is at issue, whether it is for personal gain or community good. These are not always totally separable but each individual must go to the depth of the soul to search out the core values by which one lives and dies. The good foundation must be laid for the future, which includes eternal life.

This is what Jesus gets at with the story of the rich man and Lazarus. We really do not need to look far to see parallels to this story today. In American cities, many wealthy, gated communities are not far from some of the most poverty-stricken neighborhoods. Vacationers at posh island resorts or third-world getaways can look out over their balconies and the walled enclosure to see people begging in the streets. It is probably the case that those who are reading this column, like the writer, have been privileged to enjoy the proceeds of the rich man. It is also probably the case that there are not too many Lazarus folks in the pews of churches whose pastors, along with the writer, are picking the fruits of this publication.

We cannot necessarily equate the good life with God's benediction upon our lifestyle. If there were but one poor person in the world, we would be called upon "to be rich in good works, generous, and ready to share" (1 Timothy 6:18). How well are we Christians really doing that as individuals, as families, and as congregations?

Allan H. Sager, in his book *Gospel-Centered Spirituality*, describes four spirituality types who listen to the gospel and hear what they are "typed" to hear. These types can be labeled: Societal Regeneration, Theological Renewal, Inner Life, and Personal Renewal. Depending upon one's inclination of mind (knowing God) or of heart (sensing God) and one's response to the mystery of God or to the revealed God, Christians bear a certain type or cast to their spirituality.

With Societal Regeneration types, concerns for justice, peace, and prayer tend toward social action. The Theological Renewal sort want to think correctly about the faith and prayer so as to gain insight. For Inner Life types, the order of the day and night is contemplation, inner peace, and prayer leading to mystical union with God. And those of the Personal Renewal bent seek holiness of life and prayer that leads to experiencing the presence of God. These are not pure types, however, for though we may predominate in one, we may evidence some elements of the others.

What Jesus' parable does for us today is to awaken the Societal Regeneration type that is in each of us, because God calls it out from each of us. (On other Sundays with other texts, there may be other types that need to be awakened and nurtured; but, for today, let us focus on this one, since the texts call us to express ourselves actively, in concrete terms, to embody the word of God.)

It certainly was called out of Millard Fuller, founder of Habitat for Humanity. In his book *The Theology of the Hammer*, he writes, "Putting faith into practice and being relevant is at the very heart of 'the theology of the hammer.'" He goes on to explain how God's love indeed embraced all, but he also observes from scripture that God has "a preferential concern for the poor." Upon this understanding, he set a very lofty and generous goal, which has made his organization wealthy in good deeds: The complete elimination of poverty housing and homelessness.

This is the season of Pentecost, the cycle lifting up the life and ministry of the church, just as the other five seasons of the church year lift up the life and ministry of the Lord of the church. It is time to bear witness in our lifestyle to the very values that God imparts to us. As we mature in Christ (Colossians 1:28), we are equipped, motivated, and empowered to live out the wealth of faith, hope, and love with which the grace of God brings us.

An Alternative Application

You could call this "In Boon and Bane." Flags are burning in the Middle East as Palestinians and Israelis argue over land and governance and independence. The world wonders if there will be any peace in this land of promise. In America, a land where so many promises do come true for so many (read Dan Rather's *The American Dream*), there are families besieged by one catastrophe after another and left wondering how many times can the heart break. Do we have the courage of Jeremiah to still hope in what appears to be a hopeless situation? What field at Anathoth are we willing to invest in as we peer into the future from under storm cloud days?

Jeremiah would have us invest in the promise and power of God, who has shown himself faithful in mighty acts throughout history. To borrow from a Christian hymn penned two-and-a-half millennia later, "When all around my soul gives way, he then is all my hope and stay" (from "My Hope Is Built on Nothing Less").

Venturing deeper into the message of Jeremiah (Jeremiah 32:17ff), we hear him praising God for the great demonstrations of power and compassion that can be recalled from the Exodus event. Courage can be taken when one relies on this one, true God in any and all circumstances, for even when God acts in judgment, there is a word of promise attached. What God decrees comes to pass, both in wrath as well as blessing. The God of exodus and the God of exile are one and the same; he will have his people in boon and bane. Jesus knew this on the cross and committed himself into the hands of God. So too can we all in times of trial find a solid rock on which to stand (Psalm 18).

Proper 22 / Pentecost 20 / Ordinary Time 27
Lamentations 1:1-6
2 Timothy 1:1-14
Luke 17:5-10
David Kalas

System requirements

Before you buy a new piece of software, you check the side of the box where it lists the system requirements. What operating system is assumed? How fast a processor do I need? How much memory? Do I need a CD-ROM drive? Will the program require a certain quality of monitor, a certain card, or a joystick?

Before you buy a new piece of software, you check to see whether or not it will work on your system. Not to check would be foolishness and to buy software that doesn't match your system would be pointless.

Following Christ also comes with its own kind of "system requirements." Jesus spoke several times and in several ways about what is required of a disciple. We have one of those passages before us this week in the excerpt from Luke. When we consider those teachings honestly, we have to admit that the requirements seem to exceed the capacity of our systems. Or, if not the capacity, it at least exceeds the past performance. Jesus' own disciples may have forgotten from time to time the nature of their obligation, and his reminder to them continues to challenge us.

At another level, Paul also gave Timothy a reminder of the system requirements of discipleship. It is a strong word of encouragement and quite different in tone from the selected passage from Lamentations. Paul himself had successfully completed the life Christ called him to live (see 2 Timothy 4:6-7) and from that vantage point he coached young Timothy to that same victory of grace and faithfulness. The author of Lamentations, by contrast, wrote as one whose people had not been faithful. They had not lived according to the requirements, and the result was a terrible crash.

Most of the packaging on a piece of software is devoted to making the sale. In bold and colorful letters and images, all of the features, advantages, and capabilities of the program are listed. The system requirements, meanwhile, are printed small and black on the side.

Jesus himself did not make a splashy pitch for discipleship. It was the requirements and the cost that got the large print from Jesus. This week, the no-nonsense requirements get the large print from us, as well.

Lamentations 1:1-6

In the wake of the several September 11, 2001, terrorist attacks, a few people publicly suggested that the attacks represented the judgment of God upon this nation. Many people regarded that as an offensive interpretation of events. For myself, I thought it was an uninformed interpretation, for what happened in New York City on that tragic day did not have the look of God's judgment. After all, at the end of the day, most of New York City was still standing.

The opening lines from the book of Lamentations paint a picture of a city and a country fresh in the wake of God's judgment. The picture is poignant and tragic, and the level of desolation portrayed is frankly unfamiliar to the citizens of this country.

From the several judgment prophets of the Old Testament, we are familiar with the detailed and threatening descriptions of what *will* become of Jerusalem or Samaria, of Israel or Judah, of Nineveh or

Babylon. That is very much the nature of the judgment prophet's message: to offer a terrifying preview of what is to come on the other side of divine judgment.

In Lamentations, however, the description is no longer a preview. Rather, it is the present reality. God's judgment had passed through like a tornado, and now the author of this lament wanders through the rubble, weeping over all that is ruined and gone.

Walk through a desert or an untamed forest and the absence of people and civilization is a lovely quality and a marvelous experience. Walk through the wreckages of a city, however — a city that once bustled with life and activity — and the absence of people and civilization is haunting. Jerusalem and Judah must have had that "ghost town" look and feel, for all that was left were the ghosts, the thin and pale memories of what used to be.

Even in the context of a happy life, there is something terribly poignant about times and people that are gone. The house and neighborhood where cherished friends or loved ones used to live, school hallways and playgrounds where we spent so many days when we were young, the faded photographs of familiar faces that look so different now — these are all tinged with grief for us, and that comes only with the ordinary passage of time. Imagine, though, if it was not just time that had passed in between, but tragedy. If that house and neighborhood were reduced to debris, if the old school was nothing but charred remains, if the once-happy photos were of people who had since been slaughtered or kidnapped — the grief is almost unthinkable.

Lamentations recalls a time when Judah was filled with life and strength, with vitality and confidence. But that time is gone. Gone, too, are the people who once populated and gave life to the place. They are gone, either because they are dead, or because they were carted off into exile. All that remains, therefore, is grief and suffering.

What shall we make of these grim first verses of Lamentations on this Sunday morning? The passage does not contain a ray of hope, and its only explicit reference to God is a terrifying one: "The Lord has made [Zion] suffer for the multitude of her transgressions." How do we take the poignant and painful lament from a ruined nation from over 2,500 years ago and make it speak to a comfortable American congregation in the middle of the football season?

We might take our cue from Jesus. He was once was presented with two stories of other peoples' ruin and misfortune. He took the stories and brought them close to home for his own audience with exceedingly practical and sober advice: "Unless you repent, you will all perish just as they did" (Luke 13:5).

2 Timothy 1:1-14

Given our theme of "system requirements," it is worth highlighting the "shoulds" and "should nots" of Paul's counsel to Timothy.

There are just two should nots, and they go to the same point. Paul affirms that "God did not give us a spirit of cowardice," and subsequently urges Timothy, "Do not be ashamed, then, of the testimony about our Lord." Cowardly and ashamed — these are the things Timothy must not be.

Such vices may appear harmless in the Christian. They may operate under the guise of being timid, reserved, cautious, or even sensible. But such sensible caution is what drove the third servant to bury his talent in a hole, and his master was not pleased (Matthew 25:14-30).

In contrast to the cowering posture suggested by the two should nots, Paul urges Timothy to a list of strong things. Over against the cowardice that does not come from God, Paul commends these three strong gifts of God: power, love, and self-discipline. Rather than shrinking back in shame, Paul beckons to Timothy to step forward and "join with me."

The three gifts of God listed by Paul are significant terms. In the Greek, *dunamis* is the word we translate power. The word provides a compelling image for us, for it is related to our word "dynamite." Meanwhile, the Greek word Paul uses here for love is the familiar *agape* that is so marvelously explicated in 1 Corinthians 13. Finally, there is *sophronismos*, translated "self-discipline." William Barclay admits that it is "one of these great Greek untranslatable words," but offers this insight into it: "*Sophronismos* is that divinely given self-control that makes a man a great ruler of others because he is first of all the servant of Christ and the master of himself."

We are given more insight into what it means to be a servant of Christ in our gospel lesson. In the meantime, we add these three potent qualities — power, love, and self-discipline — to the "system requirements" of discipleship.

Finally, Paul concludes this section with two imperatives: "hold" and "guard." These are strong terms and picturesque. The would-be man or woman of God cannot afford to be either timid or casual. Rather, he or she must live with a firm and careful grip on the teaching and the treasure of the truth.

When someone appears to be faltering, we say that he is "losing his grip" or that he needs to "get a grip." So it is that, for the Christian to avoid faltering, he must get a firm grip on the truth of the gospel of Christ.

Luke 17:5-10

The apostles' request seems to be an utterly commendable one. They want more faith, and they come to Jesus to get it. It's hard to argue with either their desire or their method.

One wonders, though, how they expected Jesus to respond. Exactly what did they think he was going to do? Could he give them more faith miraculously, like giving sight to the blind? Could he give them more faith didactically, like giving knowledge to a student?

The apostles asked Jesus for increased faith, and he responded by suggesting that even the tiniest faith works great works. The illustration Jesus used is a spectacular one: commanding a tree to be uprooted from the ground and replanted in the sea. Leon Morris observes that the kind of tree Jesus cited was notorious for being firmly rooted, and so "Jesus is not suggesting that his followers occupy themselves with pointless things like transferring a tree into the sea. His concern is with difficulty. He is saying that nothing is impossible to faith."

The pages of scripture are replete with proofs of the principle that nothing is impossible to faith. Surely the disciples were familiar with the stories of Joshua commanding the sun to stand still, David facing Goliath, and Elijah's showdown with the priests and prophets of Baal. Their mistake, however, was apparently a misunderstanding of just where the power to do great things resides.

The disciples assumed that big faith was needed to accomplish big things, and so they wanted their faith increased. Jesus responded, however, that only a mustard-seed-size faith is required to do big things. The final issue is not the bigness of the faith, but rather the bigness of the one in whom our faith is placed.

On the one hand, Jesus' words are a great encouragement to us. Faith is able to do big and impossible things, but the faith itself is not a big and impossible thing. His image of what faith can do is a grand and uncommon picture — a tree transplanted to the sea. His image of the faith itself, however, is an altogether little and common one — a mustard seed.

On the other hand, Jesus' words imply a certain critique of the disciples. They say that they want more faith, but he indicates that they need only a little faith. What did he mean? That they had no faith at all?

Next comes the fascinating transition to what seems to be an entirely different topic. Actually, it doesn't even really qualify as a transition; it's just a sudden shift. Without warning, Jesus moved from talking about faith to talking about servitude. If conversation were a car ride, the disciples would need to be treated for whiplash injuries after the sudden and drastic turn Jesus made.

Of course, that kind of sudden turn is rather characteristic of Jesus. It is something of a pattern in his conversations with people. The Samaritan woman at the well was content to talk about theoretical things, but Jesus suddenly forced the conversation into personal territory (see John 4:7-20). The crowd was naturally concerned with the theological questions of why misfortune and tragedy had befallen the

Galileans slaughtered by Pilate or the victims of Siloam's falling tower, but Jesus turned the emphasis to the people's personal need to repent (Luke 13:1-5).

It may be part of Jesus' tough and wise love that he regularly changes the subject from what we want to talk about to what we need to talk about. While the disciples wanted to talk about big faith, perhaps they needed to talk about humble servitude.

It may be, of course, that the apostles' desire for more faith was not so completely well intentioned. Perhaps they had come to recognize in what Jesus did (e.g., Matthew 17:14-20) and what Jesus said (e.g., Mark 5:34) that faith was the key to miracles and great manifestations of power. Accordingly, they may have wanted faith like a teenager wants the keys to the car — it was exciting, new, and full of possibilities. Perhaps, therefore, it was not the faith that they wanted, but the accompanying power, and that may have been touched with self-importance.

We know that the disciples struggled from time to time with issues of self-importance (see, for example, Luke 9:46-48). We also know from Simon the magician the intoxicating appeal of God-given miraculous power (Acts 8:5-24). It would not be surprising, therefore, for the disciples to crave more faith for somewhat selfish reasons.

One of the compelling characteristics of Jesus' ministry, however, is how selfless his manifestations of power were. He did not use his power or authority to meet his own needs (e.g., Luke 4:1-4) or to save himself (e.g., Matthew 26:51-53). Similarly, though people were clearly impressed by his miracles, he did not work any miracles to prove himself or to spread his reputation (see Matthew 12:38-39; Mark 8:11-12). On the contrary, he often sought to keep his miracles a secret (e.g., Mark 7:36; Luke 5:14, 8:56).

If it was a "self-serving self-importance" that motivated the disciples to ask for more faith, then it is quite natural that Jesus should make the transition that he does. Perhaps he knew the real issue that the disciples needed to understand at that moment was neither miracles nor faith, but selfless servitude. He called upon their own experience with human servants to challenge them to servant-discipleship.

Servants and slaves were a familiar part of the cultural landscape for the first-century Roman Empire. Jesus' disciples, therefore, were no doubt familiar with the life of a servant or a slave. What Jesus said to them here about the lifestyle of a slave was not new or surprising — it was a matter of fact.

The part that was perhaps new and surprising to them — and almost certainly to us — was the equating of the life of a slave with the life of a disciple. The followers of Jesus had already willingly made dramatic sacrifices (see, for example, Luke 18:28-30). But perhaps, in the glare of the spotlight that was on Jesus, the disciples lost sight of the cost of discipleship. Perhaps in the escalating swirl of excitement and speculation about Jesus, this miracle worker with surging momentum and growing support, the disciples needed to be reminded about this basic fact: The job of a slave is to serve his master. He does not live for attention or applause. He does not live for decorations and ticker tape parades. He lives to serve.

Miracles do not require big faith; just a big God. Likewise, the disciple is not called to be big, significant, and important. Rather, the disciple has the privilege of serving the one who is big, significant, and important. The faith we have is in him, and the works we do are for him.

Application

Look at the system requirements for a piece of software and you'll see details of operating systems, processor speed, memory, and such. Look at the requirements for being a man or woman of God, and you discover a daunting list. The shoulds and should-nots of Paul's counsel to Timothy explored above are on the list. Near the very top is this: You must be a servant.

Servants and slaves were commonplace in the New Testament world. You and I, by contrast, live and work in a world of employer and employees, not slaves and masters. We may be somewhat limited, therefore, in our ability to understand this truth of the Christian life.

Of course, the real obstacle to our appreciating and appropriating this truth of discipleship is the "uncrucified" self. Pride does not aspire to serve. Washing feet is not the ego's natural ambition. But an attitude of servitude — "We are worthless slaves; we have done only what we ought to have done!" — is one of the basic system requirements. Try to run the software of discipleship without servitude in place, and the program just won't work right.

The hard message of servant-Christianity is largely unheard in our culture, but it is essential in order for us to understand the relationship — and the life — into which we are invited. After all, we do call him "Lord."

An Alternative Application
2 Timothy 1:1-14. "From Strength to Strength Go On." Strength comes in many forms. On the one hand, there is the strength of the thing that cannot be stopped. On the other hand, there is the strength of the thing that cannot be moved.

Paul urged Timothy to have, and to exercise, both brands of strength. We take his admonition as our own.

On the one hand, we must have the strength that keeps us undeterred from following God's call. Paul encouraged Timothy to be unafraid and unashamed. We know how fear, timidity, embarrassment, and self-consciousness keep us from going full-speed forward in Christ's service. We aspire to that brand of strength that presses on, bold and unstoppable.

On the other hand, faithfulness to God also requires a strength that is immovable, unshakable. Paul challenged Timothy to "hold" and to "guard." The ball is easily knocked away from the player who carries it loosely and lightly. Likewise, if we hold casually what has been entrusted to us, some trial or some temptation will knock it away. We need the strength of a sure grip, fixed and tenacious.

Proper 23 / Pentecost 21 / ORDINARY TIME 28
Jeremiah 29:1, 4-7
2 Timothy 2:8-15
Luke 17:11-19
Craig MacCreary

Christianity, the basic course

A survey of Christian education resources reveals a trend toward an increasing number of programs featuring a back-to-basics theme. No doubt this is the result of realizing that despite all previous attempts, many Christians have something less than a working knowledge of the Christian faith. Perhaps it is because in many corners an academic knowledge that reflects more the need to work through the big questions rather than how to get through the day has derailed us. There is no doubt plenty of blame to go around. As I write this, I do see the anti-intellectual red light flickering on my warning panel. Do we ever get to the big talk without engaging what seems to be carrying on the small talk? Perhaps our longing is for a way to go from one to the other effectively and faithfully. On the other hand, the big questions do come at us fast and furiously with a rapacity that few have experienced. The morning paper, the afternoon blog, and the evening news put global warming, energy depletion, biological science, global terrorism, and economic and business ethics on our plate in ways we have never seen before. I long for the good old days of my youth when it all boiled down to beat the Communists. Scary, yes, but it was a clear enemy who, however treacherous, was still known and had a discernable history.

In the light of change of such global proportions we find ourselves searching for answers of clear biblical proportions that can reassure and guide us. Even the mantra that "it is the economy, stupid" has not reassured us. Despite high levels of prosperity and income, political leaders in Great Britain and the United States find their tenures threatened. Some of us see in other faith traditions the joy and vitality that comes from their answers to the difficult questions and wonder where the vigor in using many of our words lies: salvation, election, and praise. Like the letter writer of Timothy, we long to know that though we seem to be bound up in difficult days, the word of God is unchained.

Each of these texts brings us to a place where we must consider basic words and what we believe are the fundamental building blocks of our faith. What could be more basic than Jeremiah's call to, "Take wives and have sons and daughters; take wives for your sons, and give your daughters in marriage, that they may bear sons and daughters; multiply there, and do not decrease"? Yet, it seems in our day that we are bound up in deep controversy over the meaning of appropriate domestic relationships and what it means to seek the welfare of the city. We seem to be far away from the objective that the letter writer of Timothy envisioned, "Remind them of this, and warn them before God that they are to avoid wrangling over words, which does no good but only ruins those who are listening." If anything, we struggle with the meaning of the most basic words. Classroom, political, and business life often feel like minefields with the potential irruption of political incorrectness every step of the way. Jesus' story, recounted in the gospel lesson, ends on the proclamation that the faith of the Samaritan has made him well. In our day, many have found the faith community a source of abuse and a narrowing of human options. Getting back to basics may be a more difficult ride than many had imagined it would be.

Jeremiah 29:1, 4-7

Jeremiah's prophecy is delivered to those who find themselves living out their life options in exile. This sense of dislocation and disorientation that comes with exile certainly characterizes the experience of many in today's Christian community. Many long for an apocalyptic resolution of the dilemma of living in a world where the power and authority that the faith community once thought it had has slipped away. Others seek the more mundane hopes of participating in the political process to usher in the kingdom. Others take to the hills rather than take action — take on an indifference to the welfare of the city rather than a commitment to its welfare. These seem to be the basic options available to faith communities who have found that they are living in exile.

Jeremiah speaks of another path that God may be calling people of exile to follow. Jeremiah writes an open letter but mentions specifically the leaders of the faith community. "These are the words of the letter that the prophet Jeremiah sent from Jerusalem to the remaining elders among the exiles, and to the priests, the prophets, and all the people, whom Nebuchadnezzar had taken into exile from Jerusalem to Babylon." He gives elders, priests, and prophets a call to embody their usual roles but by "being the change they seek in the world." Gilbert Rendle of the Alban Institute, in the *Leading Change in the Congregation* has written, "Yet as far back as 1960, Thomas Merton published a little book called *Bread for the Wilderness*. The title of the book came from the gospel story in Mark 8 in which Jesus instructed the disciples to feed the great crowd of people who had gathered for three days to listen to him. The disciples asked, 'How can one feed these people with bread here in the wilderness?' Merton's response to that question was this book on the Psalms; which he offered as nourishment for the inner life of faith for those who deal with the mix and the mess of the journey. Merton observed that in truly creative times, which prompt new behaviors and new forms of ministry, what we often need from our God, and what our congregations often need from their leaders, is not a quick map to the final destination, the Promised Land, but 'bread for the wilderness' — sustenance and strategies to help us find our ways."

Jeremiah's letter, in calling to the faith community to enter into the process of building homes, planting gardens, and raising families is calling them to enter into a process where they may find bread for the journey. In the long haul that Jeremiah sees ahead for the exiles, the richest blessing that the faith community may offer to the city is the bread that they do find on the journey.

This poses the question, what bread do we find on the journey in the planting, building, and raising that Jeremiah sees as the task that God is calling the exiles to? The fundamental question is: Have we found bread for the journey? Have we found ways of candor of living with and learning from each other in faith communities that will bless the city? Can we show them a more excellent way as we live out our exile in faithfulness?

Perhaps, once people thought that we could bless the world with a sense of certainty, now in exile our task is to be a blessing by walking faithfully in the midst of uncertainty. The challenge of the faith community is to find bread for the journey in the basic task of life. It is interesting that Jeremiah does not call for more plans, more visions, more ideology, and more theology, but more living, learning, and building wherever that may lead.

Wherever this may lead, we will know when we get there. Basically, this is our situation.

2 Timothy 2:8-15

It is somewhat reassuring to realize that we are not to find ourselves the first to wrangle over words that do no good but only ruin those who are listening. All of us have had the experience of finding ourselves in the words we speak and the words that we hear serving the function more of hiding than revealing the truth that needs to be spoken. Churches get into all kinds of fights that serve the function of avoiding the truth that will move us closer to the kingdom of God. The color of the restroom curtains, length of the pastor's hair, or the volume of the sound system seem safer to talk about than our deepest hungers or greatest fears. The letter writer is saying, "Don't go there." The letter gets down to the basic question of what spoken words get us beyond wrangling to the basic words of our faith.

Verse 11 lays the foundation of the basics of getting beyond wrangling. The saying is sure: "If we have died with him, we will also live with him." The author echoes sentiments here found elsewhere in the Christian scripture, "For if we have been united with him in a death like his, we will certainly be united with him in a resurrection like his" (Romans 6:5) "and I want to know Christ and the power of his resurrection and the sharing of his sufferings by becoming like him in his death" (Philippians 3:10). In John's gospel, Thomas pledges his commitment to die with Jesus. Thomas, who was called the "twin," said to his fellow disciples, "Let us also go, that we may die with him." It remains unclear in John's way of ironically telling the story whether Thomas has the full import of what he is saying. We also have Peter's incredulous response to Jesus' announcement that he is going to Jerusalem to suffer and die.

The basic reality we have do deal with is death, which in the end is not something we can wrangle about for very long. However, asserting this reality into congregational conversations can be difficult. Yet it is the congregation that knows how to go through the death process that is able to speak an authoritative word to me. It is the congregation that cannot let false images die or that lives in the past, or lives for an outside image that is most prone to wrangling in a way that does "no good but only ruins those who are listening."

What commands my attention is the church that does know how to die a death like his so that by doing so it might live as Jesus does. The expectation that confirmation programs or pedagogical styles of the past can be counted on to serve us well, forever, may have to die in order to journey to that place where our children can have faith and our faith have children. Old styles of missionary work where we are always the givers and articulators of faith while others are the passive recipients will need to die in order to make way for our journey to the place where God wants us to be. Old expectations about what a denomination is or membership means will need to be examined to see if they have any signs of life in a new age. My own denomination has shifted its central color scheme from a red, white, and blue denominational seal to a reliance on red and black as the central coloring of the celebration of its fiftieth anniversary. It has been fifty years, not of smooth reincarnations, but deaths along the way of many cherished old loyalties that has made way for the emergence of new life under far different circumstances than anyone would have imagined fifty years ago. I imagine this is the basic reality of most churches and larger church organizations that have endured over time.

As I reflect on the past, the truth emerges that even despite times of unfaithfulness, God has been faithful to us in setting before us challenges that give us an opportunity to grow in wisdom and stature. I suspect when we get down to this basic truth there will be a lot less ruinous wrangling.

Luke 17:11-19

Why does it seem basic in the gospel narrative that the foreigners understand in a way that brings a fuller benefit than is available to those who are insiders? Of course, that is the way an insider might ask the question. However, to put it another way, it is the insider who is more at risk in their faith journey than the outsider. The insider is in the position of saying, "We have never done it that way before." The insider can find themselves shifting from what God can do for them to what they have done — from how great God is to how good they are. The insider can find themselves with a history they believe they have to live up to or live down. The ties that bind insiders can become bars to those on the outside.

The outsider knows that some boundary they, themselves, could not cross has been crossed to bring about their healing. The insider has the opportunity to pull rank in a way that is unavailable to the outsider. The outsider knows they must pool together on the face of what threatens. The Samaritan and the Jews, as outsiders when they have leprosy, pull together in their begging. However, once they are healed, there seems to be a parting of the ways that divides the group. Now it is the Samaritan who remains the outsider by virtue of his ethnicity.

The insider is at risk in a way that the outsider is not. Often the things we value on the inside of church become the things that can prove to be a barrier to the advancement of the kingdom of God. Seniority, unit cohesiveness, and success can cause us to turn inward.

In some ways, this story ought to be titled "The Good Samaritan." What we have here is more than mere gratitude but a crossing of boundaries and recognition of what dangers might be incurred on crossing over from outsider to insider. The Samaritan goes from one who must beg to one who finds himself propelled to center stage. Imagine, in the years to come, how one who has known Jesus and been healed by Jesus would be revered by the community of Jesus. One who was on the margins now finds himself with power and authority of being at the center of attention. Moving from the margins to the center can be every bit as dangerous as moving in the opposite direction. Perhaps it is even more dangerous. A survey of the gospels tends to confirm the treacherousness of this path. Jesus' story of the wicked slave whose own debt was forgiven but who pounces on the one who owed him money makes clear the danger of being one of the insiders who has experienced forgiveness. The parable of the talents suggests that the joy of the center is that those who have much get more leaving others shut out. The good, dutiful, elder son in the story of the prodigal son has done all the things that make him the center of attention, yet he finds that there is no party for him. The gospels portray Peter as one who is at the center of things but he finds himself thinking more like men than like God as he maintains his hold on his role.

The lepers in this story are well on their way to moving from the margins of their society to being the center of conversation and admiration because they were so favored. As they leave, they were made clean. Yet, Christian people are at risk in their cleanliness so that they may make others feel dirty who have not shared in the experience of being cleansed. Watching the lepers walk down the road, we know they are at risk. One instinctively feels that the story is not over yet.

It is not until the Samaritan acts that the action is completed. "Then he said to him, 'Get up and go on your way; your faith has made you well.' " This wellness is described in the story of Zacchaeus as the reason that Jesus has come into the world. The measure of the Samaritan is not that he is at the center of things but wherever he is, he has centered on the activity and work of Jesus.

Application

The texts, each in their own way, take up some basic features of the Christian faith. While in our time many see the need for a return to the basics of doctrine, no doubt a laudatory aim, these texts push us toward a different understanding of what the basics of Christian faith are. Jeremiah lived in a context not unlike our own, in which we live in exile in a culture that is often either indifferent or hostile to the faith community. Jeremiah measures our response not by doctrinal purity but by how well we can bless the society in which we live. Timothy reminds us of the basic fact of the journey is that we die. Of course, we understand this intellectually, but the practical reality of the deaths that we must die along the way as part of the journey often eludes us. Celebrating thirty years of ministry this year, I look back in amazement at the number of deaths along the way that have made me more alive. Good Friday before Easter is basic to the journey of faith. Luke's account of the ten lepers reminds us that it is a basic part of the faith to find ourselves at spiritual risk when we move from the margins to the center. It often makes it difficult to reverse gears and journey the other way.

I get the feeling that these basics are not always fully covered in our faith conversations. However, if we get them right, they will help us cover the ground we need to traverse in our pilgrimage.

An Alternative Application

Luke 17:11-19. Three cheers for the lepers who approached Jesus. They do the dance of approaching yet keeping their distance at the same time. When you are on the margins, you need to learn such a dance.

They call Jesus master, which might seem to be a part of the dance to get Jesus' attention without getting embroiled in too much theological controversy.

However, the lepers are on to something here. The description of Jesus as master is a favorite of Luke's, meaning superintendent or overseer. The word is used in Luke when the disciples' fishing produces no results and when it seems that they are going under in the midst of the wind and the waves. We have many names for Jesus — prophet, priest, king, friend, savior, but overseer?

Perhaps we avoid this name because it takes us in a different direction than we are accustomed. If Jesus is master and overseer then we are workers and laborers. The gospel, then, is about our work orders as well as our salvation. It is about Jesus overseeing our lives. Can there be any part social, political, or economic that does not come under his purview?

Proper 24 / Pentecost 22 / Ordinary Time 29
Jeremiah 31:27-34
2 Timothy 3:14—4:5
Luke 18:1-8
David Kalas

The easiest way to lose

Most televised sporting events now feature some pre-game analysis by the commentators. That analysis usually includes some "keys to victory" segment. The different broadcasts have their own catchy names — sometimes even corporate-sponsored names — for those segments, but they are all essentially the same. Namely, the commentators identify what are the two or three things each team needs to do in order to win the game.

Meanwhile, just as the commentators evaluate beforehand what it takes to win a game, any good coach will analyze and evaluate afterward why his team lost the game. Too many turnovers? Too few rebounds? Chasing balls out of the strike zone? Too many penalties? Missed gap assignments on defense?

Whatever the case, the coach wants to minimize his team's losses, and so he is obliged to evaluate the reasons for those losses. If the coach can identify the two or three things most responsible for his team's losses, he can work to improve those areas of the team's performance and that translates into winning.

Perhaps we, as Christians, should be equally deliberate and purposeful in spiritual matters. Perhaps we should recognize both the wins and losses of our Christian lives and be a bit more analytical about those losses.

Of course, in the world of sports, there is one key to victory that is seldom mentioned in the pre-game analysis. It's a huge key — essential, really — but it's almost never mentioned because it's too obvious. Yet, when it comes to the wins and losses of the Christian life, it may account for a majority of our defeats.

It is the easiest way to lose. Giving up.

It is axiomatic: You can't win if you give up. The sports team can't. The individual athlete can't. The candidate for political office can't. And the Christian can't.

Yet giving up may be the most common cause of defeat in the Christian life. One man gives up in a battle with temptation. This woman gives up in her praying for her disappointing marriage. This teenager gives up in his efforts to share his faith with his unbelieving friend.

In our two New Testament passages this week, we will be encouraged not to give up. And that is a message worth proclaiming — and worth hearing — because any coach, player, or analyst will tell you that you can't win if you don't keep trying.

Jeremiah 31:27-34

I had a friend years ago whose standard greeting was, "What's new?" Not "Hi" or "Hello." Not "How are you?" But "What's new?"

Perhaps I took the greeting too literally, but I found it something of a struggle to respond. If we had seen each other less regularly, it would not have been such a challenge to me. But our schedules were such that we saw each other several times a week, and frankly I didn't have that much newness to report.

Well, the prophet Jeremiah has an answer to that question. In our selected Old Testament lection, Jeremiah is here to tell us exactly what's new.

The newness described in this famous passage might be divided — and preached — in three parts. First, there is a new covenant. Second, there are new people. Third, there is a new reality.

All of the newness is a promise from God: "The days are surely coming, says the Lord." The phrase is characteristic of the prophet Jeremiah, appearing eleven different times in his book (including two times in this passage alone). It is used in Jeremiah to guarantee both coming judgment and future restoration.

Another theme in Jeremiah that recurs here in our passage is God's statement that he has "watched over" and "will watch over" the people. The reader whose memory can go back thirty chapters will recall this theme being introduced at the very beginning of Jeremiah's message. God puts his words in Jeremiah's mouth, and then appoints him "over nations and over kingdoms, to pluck up and to pull down, to destroy and to overthrow, to build and to plant" (Jeremiah 1:10). Then, using a brief and simple vision, God assures Jeremiah, "I am watching over my word to perform it" (Jeremiah 1:12).

That image is revisited here but with a favorable twist. Typical of the judgment prophets, God's message for his people is not exclusively bad news. The near future features judgment, to be sure, but judgment will not be the final word. Just as God had "watched over them" to destroy, so now "I will watch over them to build and to plant, says the Lord."

Meanwhile, "the days are surely coming" and "watching over" are phrases characteristic of the book of Jeremiah, the promise of newness is characteristic of God. He is the one who gives new names (Genesis 32:28), who does new things (Isaiah 43:19), whose mercies are ever new (Lamentations 3:22-23), and who in the end will make all things new (Revelation 21:5).

The first particular of this promised newness is the new covenant. If the promise did not come from God himself, of course, it would have been a blasphemous proposition. After all, the covenant between God and Israel was his initiation and to propose a new covenant would not have been within Israel's scope or authority. So it is God who proposes a new one.

Interestingly, God proposes this new covenant in the context of his people having failed to comply faithfully with the original covenant, like a cuckolded husband suggesting that the couple renew their vows. That's why the other two elements of newness are necessary: new people and a new reality.

The people are new here, not in the sense that God has traded in one group for another, but in the sense that he will make them new. That, at least, is the implication of the new covenant's focus on an inner work by God. While the first covenant was written on stone, this new covenant will be written upon the human heart. Interestingly, the covenant is still expressed in terms of law, but now it is not portrayed as a thing imposed from outside, but rather as a thing that lives within.

That, in turn, suggests a larger new reality. The whole situation will be different, for "no longer shall they teach one another," but rather "they shall all know me."

The first detail is reminiscent of Paul's observations about love in relation to the other gifts of the Spirit. Prophecies, tongues, and knowledge will all come to an end, Paul says, but "love never ends" (1 Corinthians 13:8). Such things as prophecy and teaching are necessarily limited, you see, to a time and place where there is a need for such things but that need will not be eternal. The need for people to "say to each other, 'Know the Lord,' " will not last forever, either.

Instead, "they shall all know me." This newness, obviously, is not an immediate byproduct of what we know as the new covenant of the New Testament. For there remains a need to teach and to encourage one another to know the Lord. Clearly not all people know him. But those days are surely coming and that is good news for us as it was for Jeremiah's generation.

What's new? Virtually everything! A new covenant, a new people, and a whole new reality.

2 Timothy 3:14—4:5

If scripture were music, we would listen for motifs. We'd observe how the composer introduced the motif near the beginning, and then how he wove it through the piece with artistic twists and creative interpretations.

If this New Testament reading were a musical composition, we would recognize immediately the motif Paul introduces with his very first verb: "continue." Therein lies the great recurring theme and message of this counsel to Timothy: continue.

Listen through the passage and hear the composer's variations on that motif. "Continue in what you have learned." "Be persistent." "With the utmost patience." "Always." "Endure." "Carry out." "Fully." These belong together. They are images of perseverance, and Paul is persistent in presenting them.

We remember Joseph's word to Pharaoh about his twin dreams: "The doubling of Pharaoh's dream means that the thing is fixed by God" (Genesis 41:32). So here, the repetition makes the message an emphatic one.

On a time line, we are presented with a kind of relay race image, and Timothy is running a middle leg. The baton — in this case might broadly be called the message — neither begins with him nor ends with him. (We resemble Timothy, in this regard.) He is to continue in what he has learned and believed, bearing in mind "from whom you learned it." So it is that Timothy has been the recipient of a message from someone who ran before him and now he is to pass it along to those who follow him: proclaiming at all times, patiently teaching, and carrying out his ministry fully. This middle leg he runs requires persistence and perseverance.

Another theme — a secondary motif, if you will — is the matter of correction. This is perhaps a lost virtue in American Christianity. We are so much the products of a mind-your-own-business culture, and so fearful of the "holier-than-thou" moniker, that we resist all correction. We resist being corrected, for that seems to us insulting and judgmental. We resist correcting, for that seems unsolicited and intrusive.

Yet, Paul is very concerned about the importance of correction. "All scripture," after all, "is useful" for it. Furthermore, Timothy is called, among other things, to rebuke. The imminent context in which he will fulfill his ministry will be marked by a rejection of sound doctrine and truth in favor of more convenient teachings and myths. In such a setting, correction is necessary — albeit unwelcome.

In our day, our knee-jerk response to correction is one of defiance. It is the ego's reflex: we don't like to be told that we're wrong. The person who never allows himself to be corrected never learns. Set aside the relativism that has poisoned theology, philosophy, and ethics and consider instead virtually any other field of endeavor. Correction is assumed; indeed, welcomed. If I do not accept correction from my math instructor, I shall never calculate properly. If I do not accept correction from the craftsman, I shall never learn the craft. If I do not accept correction from God's word or spokesperson, then I shall be left to wander in some amalgam of incomplete knowledge, unfiltered exposure, and personal opinion. Plus, according to the writer of Proverbs, I shall be on the short end of wisdom (Proverbs 9:8; 12:1).

Luke 18:1-8

The older members of our congregations will remember very dignified portraits of prayer from their younger years. There is the classic painting of praying hands that hung in so many churches. Perhaps a familiar picture of a staid Christ praying in Gethsemane. Or a widespread portrait of an old, bearded man quietly praying at his table over a loaf of bread.

Meanwhile, many of us were also taught to pray with a certain dignity. Whether by tacit example or by explicit instruction, it became clear to us that the posture, the tone, and even the language of prayer should be marked by a certain reserve, a quietness, and above all reverence.

Into the midst of all that orthodoxy and propriety, comes Jesus. Here in our gospel lection, he presents us with a most unsettling picture of prayer. So far removed from those sober and still praying hands; so different from the serene face of Christ in the Garden, Jesus paints us a new picture to hang on the walls of our parlors, hallways, and Sunday school rooms. It is a picture of a woman who will not take no for an answer.

Perhaps her first appearance before this notorious judge was marked by the kind of decorum and deference that we traditionally associate with prayer. Perhaps the first time she appealed her case to him, she did so with a posture and tone that would make her a conventional model for prayer. By the end, she is no portrait of quietness and reserve. Quite the contrary: She has become a conspicuous pest.

Take down the picture of the praying hands and the gentle old man at the table. Replace them with pictures of this woman: knocking at the door, calling out, pressing her face against the windows, refusing to go away. That, according to Jesus, is how we should pray.

While Jesus is not proposing that God resembles the unjust judge, he is confirming that our experience may resemble the woman's experience. For example, we can imagine the discouragement she must have felt when "for a while he refused." We know all about the "while" of an unanswered prayer. We have walked — or shall we say waited — in that woman's shoes.

That is the point at which we may part company from the woman: namely, how we respond to disappointment and refusal. Do we resign ourselves? Walk away from the altar with our tail between our legs? Wave the white flag and surrender hope?

Here is where the woman in Jesus' parable becomes exemplary, if not obnoxious. She does not let delay or disappointment deter her from her destination. Instead, she pursues — indeed, bothers — this judge until he gives her what she seeks.

So it is that Jesus himself encourages us to persevere in prayer, even when that persistence seems to turn prayer into something quite far from our traditionally reverent pictures. So be it. If prayer looks like a bowed head and folded hands, then that's lovely. But prayer can also look like determination, like perseverance, and even like nagging.

Lest we still recoil a bit from such an unorthodox picture of prayer, we may remind ourselves of this truth about nagging in our human relationships. If my wife persists in asking me to complete some project around the house, and I still delay, she may become discouraged. But if she stops pestering me about it, then that suggests she has not only given up on the project; she has also, in that particular matter, given up on me.

I do not want to be the person who gives up on God. So let me knock, pester, and nag — for those are, at their core, acts of faith.

Application

If Moses had given up after that initial, disheartening encounter with Pharaoh, the Hebrews would not have been freed. If the people had given up marching around Jericho after five days, the walls would not have fallen. If the Canaanite woman had given up when she received no response — or a negative one — her daughter would not have been healed. If the apostles in Jerusalem had given up at the first sign of opposition, the church there would have floundered while they cowered. If Paul had given up his missionary efforts as soon as he encountered difficulty, untold numbers of individuals and communities would not have heard the good news.

In short, giving up is the easiest, quickest way to lose. And not giving up is a basic key to victory.

It is worth pondering what losses we have suffered — individually or as a church — simply because we have given up in some of the areas where Paul urged perseverance: in sound doctrine, in the proclamation of the gospel, in patient teaching, in the experience of suffering, or in some particular calling or ministry. Perhaps more sobering still, how many losses have we suffered because we have, unlike the importunate widow, given up in prayer?

This Sunday, we play the part of coaches. Setting aside all the nuances of strategy, all the details of individual plays, we simply remind the team that the single greatest key to victory is, simply, not to give up.

An Alternative Application

2 Timothy 3:14—4:5. "The Neglected Testament." In my years of ministry, I have observed a common and sometimes deeply ingrained prejudice against the Old Testament. In some cases, the dislike is rather innocuous: "It's boring" or "I don't understand it." In other cases, though, the objections are quite insidious, for they undermine our basic affirmations about scripture as canon, as God's word, and as authoritative.

The prejudice displays itself in dismissive remarks, like, "but that's in the *Old* Testament" and in the sloppy hermeneutic that draws a sharp distinction between the revelation of God in the Old Testament and in the New Testament. To assume wholesale differences in God's nature, actions, and will from one Testament to the other is either to suggest that God changed or that one whole section of scripture is unreliable. Either assertion cuts deeply and carelessly into one of the legs on the stool of our faith.

In response to the modern-day Marcionism, and in affirmation of that two thirds of our Bible that we call the Old Testament, we might do well to preach about Paul's remarkable statements in the passage from 2 Timothy.

The key question is this: When the apostle Paul refers to "the sacred writings" and "all scripture," what does he have in mind? Was there, at the time of this letter, any sense yet of a new corpus of writings that he would have referred to so deferentially? Or are these simply references to the writings that were recognized as canonical in first-century Judaism and that we know as the Old Testament?

If we assume the latter, then Paul is saying two things that some contemporary Christians might choke on. First, the Old Testament is "able to instruct you for salvation through faith in Christ Jesus." And, second, the Old Testament is "useful for teaching, for reproof, for correction, and for training in righteousness."

There is nothing in that second affirmation about the Old Testament that would have been anything other than standard orthodoxy for Paul the Pharisee. For him, it was not at all a remarkable thing to say, even though many in our churches might find it hard to say about the Old Testament.

Meanwhile, the first statement — that the Old Testament is sufficient to lead a person to salvation through faith in Christ — may seem oxymoronic to the uninformed, but this is clearly supported elsewhere in the New Testament. It is supported in the ministry of Jesus (Luke 24:25-27, 44-47) and in the preaching of the early church (Acts 17:2-3; 18:24-28).

Preaching the relevance and significance of the Old Testament is not glamorous stuff, but it may be the first step in some of our people recovering and rediscovering the neglected part of their Bible.

Proper 25 / Pentecost 23 / Ordinary Time 30
Joel 2:23-32
2 Timothy 4:6-8, 16-18
Luke 18:9-14
Wayne Brouwer

Keep looking up

In my childhood home, there was a wall plaque, unadorned except for three words: "Keep Looking Up." For us young ones it was a comic command, and we would stumble about with our eyes glued to the ceiling. But for those who have known any kind of adult anguish, there is no other hope or help.

Sir James Simpson, the Scottish physician who discovered the anesthetic properties of chloroform, freed his world from much pain. But his own heart was anguished by the death of a little daughter. When she was buried in a lonely Edinburgh cemetery, Simpson had a single word carved on the headstone: *Nevertheless*. In that small act of devotion he placed his grief in the hands of God. It was his affirmation that he would "keep looking up."

Bertrand Russell once said, "The only adequate way to endure large stresses is to find large consolation." This is the theme for today. Joel helps his community see through the stark tragedy of a locust plague to find divine consolation and anticipation. Paul faces the executioner's blade with confidence of a coronation to come. And the despised tax collector of Jesus' parable reaches for heaven from down on his knees. "Keep looking up!"

Joel 2:23-32

When did Joel live and command attention as the mouthpiece of God? For a prophecy that plays so prominently in biblical theology, we simply don't know. Joel references no king, as do most of the other prophets, causing some to place his dates early in Israel's history (either in the eleventh century, prior to the development of the monarchy, or perhaps in the ninth century at a time when the king was ineffective because of age or other political circumstances) and others to inject him into the post-exilic community (third century) that was trying to find its way after the years of displacement turmoil. Another theory makes Joel a contemporary of Jeremiah, mainly because the first half of Joel's prophecy is stridently apocalyptic with its warnings of impending judgment by way of enemy invaders, a scene that connects well with the Babylonian destruction of Jerusalem in 586 BC.

Unfortunately for the historians among us, the only actual hook on which we can begin to hang a date for this short message is an unusually severe plague of locusts that prompted visions of a looming divine holocaust meted out by some horrible massacring army. But the swarming invasion could have happened during any decade of life in the Middle East, so we are left with a treasury of dating dust. Recent interpreters tend to peg Joel later rather than earlier, primarily because of the words and stylistics of the Hebrew language he uses.

None of this detracts from his powerful message. For one thing, perhaps as much as any and certainly more than most among the prophets, Joel clarifies the meaning of the term "the day of the Lord." This catchphrase and its variations ("that day," "the day of judgment," "the day of Yahweh's visitation," and so on) collectively begin to hold three significant themes as it is rehearsed among the prophets. First, because of the heightened state of wickedness within the covenant community and also among the nations that surround it, Yahweh will have to break decisively into human history as before when battling Egypt for possession of Israel. This time, Yahweh will judge the nations and destroy the rampant evil that has messed up every culture, including that within the societies of Israel and Judah. Second, although the trauma of this visitation will be severe and painful, Yahweh will spare a remnant of the covenant community as a witness to divine grace and as the starter piece in a global renewal effort. This, thirdly, is the culmination of the day of the Lord: the blossoming of the eternal messianic kingdom in which the divine will holds sway again, and life becomes what God intended all along that it should be. All three of these themes — pervasive divine judgment, restoration of a remnant, and ushering in of the marvelous messianic age — are clearly articulated by Joel.

Another brilliant aspect of Joel's timeless message is the manner in which he connects it to current affairs. As Jesus noted when challenged one day by a tragedy in Palestine (Luke 13:1-5), every awful news report is an occasion for spiritual reflection. This Joel does well. He leverages the powerful plague that is devastating the countryside and rides it to new heights of meaning. Although this disaster affects everyone in significant ways, all will soon be traumatized more terribly by a divine judgment that will make this horrible scene seem pastorally idyllic. Joel is a preacher with contemporary significance in his weekly sermon.

Mostly there is the powerful message itself. Joel paints the word of God with lively hues and stark contrasts that call attention to themselves. God will not merely end the nasty locust plight; God will send "autumn rains in righteousness" and "vats will overflow with new wine and oil." God will not only flip a page on the calendar, but instead "will repay you for the years the locusts have eaten," so that "you will have plenty to eat, until you are full," and "you will praise the name of the Lord your God."

If that is not yet enough, Joel sees signs in the heavens, portents among the planets, and the complete refabrication of the warp and woof of the universe. The specific references of verses 28-32 can never be pinned to anything in our realm of experiences, and yet they are accessible at all times and in all circumstances, as Peter would show on Pentecost Sunday when the power of the divine Spirit overwhelmed the crowd in Jerusalem (Acts 2).

How should we preach Joel's message? First, we need to contextualize it by setting it against any locust plagues or other disasters that scream from the headlines of our current newspapers. The message from Yahweh that Joel brings is always lodged in the leading stories that trouble our times. These serve as the powerful mirrors on which the invading judgment of God is momentarily reflected, and we need to make the most of the times because the days are evil.

Second, we need to ride all three dimensions of Joel's understanding of the code term, "the day of the Lord." It is a moment of cataclysmic judgment on our lives and our societies, to be sure, but it is also an episode of gracious care as God notices and succors the lost and the last and the least, the helpless and the homeless, the worn and the wearied. This is a message that reaches into the kitchens of broken homes and puts family members at odds with each other around the same table again for dinner. This is a message that searches the battlefield conflagrations in the wee hours of the morning and binds the wounds of the fallen and rescues the children from collapsing debris. This is a message that probes the psyche of the troubled and marginalized and helps them find healing.

Third, we need to paint this message in bold colors of a present and coming kingdom of God that transforms the ordinary into the extraordinary. Joel uses a few wonderful words to cast a very big vision. We ought to follow suit and give our people a taste of heaven that makes them hunger and thirst after righteousness.

2 Timothy 4:6-8, 16-18

Paul was under arrest again. It had happened many times before (see 2 Corinthians 4), but this time was different. Nero was emperor in Rome, and he had chosen to target the Christian community for the ills of his realm. The church in Rome had felt the scourge of his wrath in a powerful way, becoming the scapegoat for Nero's civic restoration plan begun by an arsonist conflagration. Several years before, the apostle Peter, known widely as the key church leader in the city, had been crucified upside down. Now the empire's prime mover had netted Christianity's dominant evangelist, and his fate was sealed. Paul would die soon, beheaded outside of the capital city in the compassionate execution method reserved for citizens of the empire. Shortly before, in a final gesture of tenderness and testimony, Paul wrote this letter to his protégé installed as senior pastor in the church of Ephesus. Paul was about to die and these would be his final words of encouragement and request.

Even though these verses rehearse painful difficulties Paul has experienced along the way, his closing message is one of powerful trust in the providence of God. This is the echo of a lifetime of faith. Such testimonies are built on the few but near-miraculous signposts of grace that keep us hanging on to religious commitments.

One of the most amazing stories to come out of World War II is told by a chaplain with the US Air Force. A bombing mission in the South Pacific turned into a grueling night of terror for one B-52 crew. The fuel tanks began leaking when hit by enemy fire, and the plane barely managed an emergency landing on the beach of a small island. In the darkness their location was hidden from the Japanese soldiers who held the island but dawn would make them prisoners of war.

"Chaplain," said the flight leader, "you've been telling us for months about the power of prayer. We're out of fuel! We're surrounded by the enemy! If you've ever prayed, pray now!"

While the rest of the crew patched the fuel tanks, the chaplain knelt in the sands to pray. Even when the others knocked off for a couple hours' rest, the chaplain kept to his post. About 2 a.m., a sentry heard something scrape against the sand at the water's edge. A cautious investigation revealed a large metal floating object — a barge — piled high with barrels. Each one contained gasoline — high-octane gasoline — airplane fuel. In a matter of minutes, the crew was roused, the tanks filled, and they were in the air again, bound for home!

Where had the fuel come from? Later investigations told the story. A supply ship captain, surrounded by enemy submarines 600 miles and several weeks away, had set his cargo of aircraft fuel afloat in hopes of saving lives. It landed fifty feet away from the bomber crew *exactly* when they needed it. What an answer to prayer!

"As luck would have it, providence was on my side!" wrote Samuel Butler. A bit more reverent is Paul's statement: "The Lord stood at my side and gave me strength." But what does that mean? Is it a good luck charm? Will it get you out of any scrape, even those of your own foolish doing? Hardly. We know of too many tragedies and cruelties and unrequited injustices even in the Christian community to believe that. A young Christian girl whose sister was sick and whose family was troubled by a long list of difficulties, once wrote to me: "I am angry with God right now... Sometimes I even think our family is cursed. When something goes wrong I think, 'Oh no! *Another* curse!' "

Nor can Paul's trust in God be mere fatalism. The message of the Bible is not compatible with the idea that evil forces are either God's delight or his intent. No one can thank God for providential leading when a drunk driver crushes the body of a child. No one can praise God for providential direction when an airplane crashes or a mine collapses. These are not the things of which providence is made.

Thus it is difficult to read the times we live in or to easily identify the exact way God is moving with power or shaping destinies. The dangers are all too evident when we read the statement signed by 600 German pastors and fourteen theology professors in 1934: "We are thankful to God that he, as Lord of history, has given us Adolf Hitler, our leader and savior from our difficult lot." Such a confession seems demonic now!

In a sense, Paul's testimony is more a confession than a theological treatise. I *believe* God exists. I *know* that God can control the destinies of peoples and nations. I am *confident* that God has a direction, a purpose for this world, and I *want* to be a part of that leading. Even when things go "wrong" (from my own point of view) — even when tragedy strikes — even when no miracles happen — "The Lord will rescue me from every evil attack and will bring me safely to his heavenly kingdom." That's the confession of faith! That's the confidence of trust!

A young schoolteacher named Ray Palmer thought about that one night in 1830. He sat at his desk in the darkness and wrote a little poem to God. It was a prayer of trust, a statement of faith. One day he met Dr. Lowell Mason, a brilliant musician. Looking for verses to set to hymn tunes, Dr. Mason scanned Ray's poetry. It was all quite good but one poem moved him to tears. It was the nighttime prayer. With a melody of simple majesty, Mason published the hymn that spoke with the convictions of Paul. It still grabs hearts. It still brings tears. Its opening line goes like this: My faith looks up to thee!

Luke 18:9-14

A rather distinguished matron of high society felt the need to commission a lavish portrait of herself. But her demands and desires drove her from one artist to the next. None could do it right! Finally she stormed into the studio of still another candidate. As they settled on a fee, she told of her disappointment with others of his profession. "Young man!" she said, "I want you to do me justice!"

By now, the artist was having second thoughts. He looked her up and down and finally let it slip: "Madam," he said, "it's not *justice* you need. It's *mercy*!"

This may well help us think through Jesus' marvelous parable in a fresh way. Who do we think we are? What do we think we need? Why does Jesus take a bad man and make him a model for our prayers?

"Mercy is a beggar's refuge," said George Bernard Shaw, "a man must pay his debts!" That's how we feel when someone hurts us. Can you imagine a rape victim suffering a lifetime of psychological scars while her attacker gets a mild reprimand? Or a family carrying on with the knowledge that the drunk driver who senselessly slaughtered their son didn't even have his license suspended? "It isn't fair!" we shout. A cry for mercy from such trash is a beggar's refuge. We spit on it.

When Austrian Prince Schwarzenberg put down the Hungarian rebellion of 1849, some counselors advised mercy for the captives. "Yes, indeed," he replied, "a good idea; but first we will have a little hanging!" Often our hearts nod in assent.

Even our mercy can be laced with spite. When the first Elizabeth finally came to England's throne after the political and religious wrangling of the sixteenth century, a knight who had formerly despised her came seeking pardon. He threw himself at her feet begging mercy. With a flick of her hand she dismissed him, saying, "Do you not know that we are descended of the lion, whose nature is not to prey upon the mouse or any other such small vermin?"

A royal put-down indeed! But husbands do it to wives and vice versa, neighbors condescendingly do it to each other, church members justify their cases and offer mean-spirited "forgiveness." "Community" becomes a shining ideal that we can't buy with our smoldering bitterness.

In Shakespeare's *The Merchant of Venice*, the main character borrows a great sum of money from Shylock. Due to adverse circumstances, he is unable to pay it back. Shylock demands justice, but seethes with vengeance. And, in a marvelous speech, Portia slices to the heart of human need:

> *The quality of mercy is not strain'd,*
> *It droppeth as the gentle rain from heaven....*
> *Though justice be thy plea, consider this,*
> *That in the course of justice none of us*
> *Should see salvation. We do pray for mercy,*
> *And that same prayer doth teach us all to render*
> *The deeds of mercy.*
> — Act IV, Scene 1

That's the kind of mercy the tax collector mutters about in Jesus' story. The great and good religious leaders stand to strut and pose and behind him all this man feels is the blazing wrath of God. He knows he deserves divine anger. He knows he's not caught in an unfair tragedy of blind circumstances but wrapped up in the fair balances of justice.

Will he stand like a man and pay his debts? No, for in this courtroom there is no limit to the punishment and no door marked "Exit." All that's left is love's second name: mercy! And in the scent of that whisper, life begins again.

Application

Both the epistle and gospel lessons are intensely personal. They could be used to call out experiential reflections on how each person present came to faith and grew in grace. It might even be appropriate, using the 2 Timothy passage, to get people to think about what their obituaries might say and why. Did others catch from them that they indeed spent a life "Looking Up"?

An Alternative Application

Joel 2:23-32; 2 Timothy 4:6-8, 16-18; Luke 18:9-14. There are many great hymns of faith connected to the passages in today's lectionary readings. These could shape segments of a message in which the testimonies of the past might inspire the singing of powerful songs that would renew the personal reflections of those gathered. They deepen their understanding of the journey of faith as they are traveling in pilgrim company.

Reformation Day
Jeremiah 31:31-34
Romans 3:19-28
John 8:31-36
Wayne Brouwer

Forming, deforming, reforming

For many years we drove a small Volvo wagon. It fit the needs of our young family, with its safety features and good cargo space.

When we needed a second car, a friend who deals in used autos and parts found a car he thought I would like. It was a brand new Volvo sedan, available for a used car price.

How could this be, I asked. Here's the story: a young couple ordered a new Volvo sedan to their expressed tastes, including color and interior appointments. Taking delivery of it in late November, the couple was driving it off the dealer's lot during the season's first snowstorm, when a car on the street slid out of control. Twisting and spinning, the street driver spun right onto the dealership lot and smashed into the front end of the young couple's brand new Volvo.

Since the car had not yet left the dealer's lot, the dealer's insurance had to cover the restoration costs. And because the couple had purchased a factory-perfect new vehicle, they demanded not just a restored broken car, but a freshly built sedan. So the insurance company purchased the compromised vehicle and the dealership ordered another one to be built for the couple. The insurance company sold the damaged car to a repair shop, where the front end of the new-but-undrivable sedan was rebuilt. Then my friend, who is connected to that market, bought the car and resold it to me.

When I took possession, my "used" car had 800 miles on it. Was it new? Was it used? Perhaps the best way I could describe it was that my car had been formed, deformed, and reformed.

This idea of restoration is behind each lectionary passage on this Reformation Day. Jeremiah delivers the word of Yahweh declaring that the Sinai Covenant, once formed to give identity and missional purpose to Israel, has been deformed and needs to be reformed so that the best the Creator can offer will blossom again in our world. Paul uses the scare tactic of sin's deformation to urge reformation under God's gracious offer of salvation. And Jesus locks horns, briefly, with the religious leaders of his day in order to point out where true reform can point past the deceptions of deform to the original purposes of humankind as God formed us.

Jeremiah 31:31-34

The theme of the Sinai Covenant is very prominent in Jeremiah's prophecies and central to today's lectionary passage. Most striking is Jeremiah's recognition that this covenant governs Israel's success and its demise, and that one day soon Yahweh will find a way to renew that covenant in a manner that will keep the restored nation more faithful to its identity and true to its mission.

Jeremiah lived almost a century after Isaiah. By his time, Assyria had long ago destroyed Judah's northern neighbor Israel (722 BC). Judah was itself only a tiny community now, limping along with diminishing resources, and constantly tossed around by the bigger nations of its world.

But things were changing rapidly on the international scene. Assyria was being beaten down in 612 BC by its eastern bully province, Babylon. After snapping the backbone of Assyrian forces at Carchemish and wrestling the capital city of Nineveh to the ground, Babylon immediately took over Palestine, the newer name for the old region of Canaan.

Judah was experiencing a rapid turnover of kings, many of whom were puppets of Babylon. Already the country was expected to pay yearly tribute or security bribes to Babylon, and since 606 BC had been forced to turn over some of its promising young men for propaganda retraining exile in the capital of the superpower, in anticipation that they would return to rule Judah as regents of Babylon.

Into these times and circumstances Jeremiah was born. From his earliest thoughts he was aware of Yahweh's special call on his life (1:4-10). This knowledge only made his prophetic ministry more gloomy, for it gave him no out in a game where the deck was stacked against him (chs. 12, 16). So he brooded through his life, deeply introspective. He fulfilled his role as gadfly to most of the kings who reigned during his life, even though it took eminent courage to do so. Although he lived an exemplary life, political officials constantly took offence at his theologically charged political commentaries, and regularly arrested him and treated him badly. Jeremiah was passionately moral, never allowing compromise as a suitable temporary alternative in the shady waters of international relations or the roiling quicksand of fading religious devotion. He remained pastorally sensitive, especially to the poor and oppressed in Jerusalem, weeping in anguish as families boiled sandals and old leather to find a few nutrients during Babylonian sieges, and when he saw mothers willing to cannibalize their dying babies to keep other children alive. Above all, Jeremiah found the grace to be unshakably hopeful, truly believing to the very end that though destruction would raze Jerusalem and the temple, Yahweh would keep covenant promises and one day soon restore the fortunes of this wayward partner in the divine missional enterprise.

Jeremiah's prophecies are not collected in a chronological order. When tracked against the reigns and events of various kings, it becomes clear that chapters 30-31 were received and written during the reign of King Josiah (640-609). These were the days of promising renewal and hope was in the air. Perhaps the covenant relationship with God might be restored and reaffirmed, and there is a sense in which these lines hint in that direction. But deeper still is the acknowledgement that any reformation movements are destined to fail unless they are initiated by God's restorative grace. The "Day of the Lord" belongs to God, not us. But those who are open to the winds of divine grace are aware of the great reformation that happens in God's time.

Romans 3:19-28

At the end of Paul's second mission journey, he traveled to Corinth from Ephesus, either late in 53 or early in 54, and stayed three months with his friend Gaius (Acts 19:1-3; Romans 16:23). When he learned that a good friend (and a leader in the Christian congregation located in Cenchrea, one of Corinth's seaport suburbs) named Phoebe was making a trip to Rome (Romans 16:1), Paul quickly penned what has become the most orderly summary of early Christian theology.

Since Paul had not yet made a visit to Rome, his letter to that congregation was less personal and more rationally organized than was true of most of his other letters. Paul intended this missive to be a working document that the congregation already established in the capital city of the empire would be able to read and discuss together in anticipation of his arrival, which was planned for some months ahead (Romans 1:6-15). Paul's working theme and emphasis was the new expression of the "righteousness of God," which had been recently revealed with power through the coming of Jesus Christ (Romans 1:17).

Because Paul moved directly from a brief statement about the righteousness of God into an extended explication of the wrath of God revealed against wickedness (Romans 1:18), many have interpreted Paul's understanding of God's righteousness as an unattainable standard against which the whole of the human race is measured and fails. Only in the context of this desperate human situation would the grand salvation of Christ then be appreciated and enjoyed.

But more scholars believe that Paul's assertions of the righteousness of God, central to today's lectionary reading, have a positive and missional thrust. In their understanding of what Paul says, it is because of the corruption and sinfulness that is demeaning and destroying humanity that God needed again, as

God did through Israel, to re-assert the divine will. In so doing, God's focus was not on heaping judgment upon humankind, but instead that of drawing people back to the creational goodness God had intended for them. This was, in essence, the same missional purpose that God had planned for Israel during the Old Testament.

This more positive perspective on the righteousness of God fits well with the flow of Paul's message and certainly seems to come to expression in today's transitional pericope. In chapters 1:18—3:20 Paul describes the crippling effect of sin. But once the stage has been set for his readers to realize again the pervasive grip of evil in this world, including within their own divided and deluded hearts, Paul marches Abraham out onto the stage as a model of divine religious reconstruction. God does not wish to be distant from the world, judgmental and vengeful. Instead, as shown to Abraham, God desires an ever-renewing relationship with the people God made. Thus, as exhibited in Abraham's life (Romans 4), God initiates a relationship of favor and grace with us. In fact, according to Paul, this purpose of God is no less spectacular than the divine quest to re-create the world and undoing the effects that the cancer of sin has blighted upon us (Romans 5).

One important idea to keep in mind is that righteousness is not the same as innocence. Innocence is devoid of the knowledge of evil, while righteousness is a deliberate reaction to experienced evil. Thus it is important for Paul to make explicit that righteousness is God's response to evil rather than our attainment. The reformation of a world gone sordid is completely the initiative and accomplishment of God. But in its wake comes the reformation of our lives and societies.

John 8:31-36

Fred Craddock and his wife were on vacation in the Great Smoky Mountains of eastern Tennessee when they stumbled onto an out-of-the-way restaurant called the Black Bear Inn. It proved to be a good place to eat, besides offering the possibility of actually seeing one of those black bears. An entire wall was glass, opening out onto a wild and rugged valley.

As they sat at supper, quietly communing with nature and each other, their solitude was broken by a tall man with a shock of white hair who ambled over. They could see he was well along in years, probably past the fourscore allotted by the Psalmist.

He was hard of hearing as well, since he rudely interrupted their quiet reverie with noisy and nosy questions at least twenty decibels too loud. When he found that Fred taught at a seminary he suddenly had a story to tell about preachers. Without an invitation he pulled up a chair and invaded their space.

Nodding out the great glass window, he said, "I was born back here in these mountains."

But the story was not to be a pretty one. "My mother was not married," he went on, "and the reproach that fell upon her, fell upon me. The children at school had a name for me, and it hurt. It hurt very much."

In fact, he said, "During recess I would go hide in the weeds until the bell rang. At noon hour I took my lunch and went behind a tree to avoid them. And when I went to town with my mamma, all the grownups would stop and stare at us. They'd look at my mamma, and then they'd look at me, and I could see they were trying to guess who my daddy might have been. Painful years, those."

Something big was about to happen. "I guess it was about the seventh or eighth grade," he continued, "when a preacher came to town. He frightened me when he preached, and he attracted me, all at the same time. He was a big man. Thundered when he preached. But he caught me. Every time he preached he caught me with his words.

"I didn't want the people to catch me, though. So I never went to church on time. Waited around outside till they sang the hymn before the sermon. Then I'd sneak in just as he was getting warmed up. When he was finished I'd rush right out. Didn't want to hear the people say, 'What's a boy like you doin' in church?'

"But one morning I got caught. A bunch of women lined up in the aisle, and I couldn't get out. And I got all nervous and cold and sweaty. And I knew somebody was going to see me and say, 'Whatchadoin' here, boy? What's a boy like you doin' in church?'

"And sure enough, suddenly a hand clamped down on my shoulder. Out of the corner of my eye I could see the preacher's face.

" 'Whoa, boy!' he says to me. And he turns me around, and he looks me in the face. And he studies me for a while. And I can just see he's trying to find the family resemblance. And finally he says, 'Well, boy...! I can see it now...! I can see you're a child of... You're a child of... Wait now...'

"And he stared me right in the face. 'Yep!' he says. 'I can see it now! You're a child of... God! There's a striking resemblance!'

"Then that preacher man swatted me on the bottom, and he said, 'Go on, boy! Go claim your family inheritance!' "

The Craddock's were quite taken by the story the old man had to tell. Fred thought there was something familiar about it, so he asked the elderly gent, "Sir, what's your name?"

The man replied, proudly, "Ben Hooper!"

It was then that Fred Craddock remembered his daddy telling him the story of the time the people of Tennessee twice elected an illegitimate bastard boy as governor, and how Ben Hooper had done the state proud.

Ben Hooper had faith. He gained faith when a preacher told him he was child of God. He proved his faith when he carved a future of grace out of a mixed inheritance. This is what Jesus was looking for in the faces of those who surrounded him during the dialogues of today's lectionary passage.

Application

In 1923 Karl Barth was asked to speak on the topic "What Does It Mean to Be Reformed?" at an assembly of the Reformed Churches in Emden, Germany. He said that to be Reformed means to know your history and your community. All Christians are part of the family of God, he observed, but we cannot experience relationships of significance or intimacy with the whole of the Body of Christ, simply because it is too expansive and we are too finite and limited in the scope of our relational abilities.

Just as it is impossible to understand humanity in general until we begin to live with and experience a small collective of humans called family and neighborhood, so we cannot appreciate the whole church of God without nurturing meaningful associations with a particular congregation or denominational culture. It is only through the smaller conglomerate, by learning its language and its habits and its values and its goals, that the meaning and purpose of the larger entity at last becomes manageable and accessible.

You do not understand the body of Christ or the church of God by embracing the whole, said Barth, but you begin to comprehend it through engagement with the community of Christ closest too you. That is why there can never be free-floating Christians or isolated believers. I can never be a child of God all by myself if I am not cognizant of the family of God and interact meaningfully with it. And I cannot interact meaningfully with the whole of God's family apart from deep and profound attachments to that portion of the family that surrounds and nurtures me.

Hence the idea of "reform" or "Reformation" is essentially a historical and cultural acknowledgment of participation in the dynamics of family life. A family grows through changes and alterations that sometimes move it away from its values and identity, and other times restore it to its deepest connections. "Reformation" is always related to "Deformation" that arises out of "Formation." Thus, today's celebration of reform is essentially a means by which to affirm the elasticity that holds the whole of the Body of Christ to its head, and all of God's children in relationship with each other.

Alternative Application
John 8:31-36. During the heated times of the Reformation, when Martin Luther and Ulrich Zwingli were exchanging strong words about biblical interpretations and ecclesiastical practices, Zwingli spent a troubled morning walking the mountain trails of his beloved Switzerland. From a distance he observed two goats making their way in opposite directions on a path barely stitched to the side of a cliff. It was obvious that not even these nimble creatures would be able to negotiate past one another as they met.

Zwingli watched them round a corner and come face-to-face. There was a moment of uncertainty as each feinted a power move at the other. Both goats took several steps backward and set hind legs in a posture of attack. In a surprise twist, however, the goat at the lower level suddenly collapsed onto the narrow ledge until the other goat could walk quickly over its back. Then each danced on.

Zwingli was impressed. Here was strength defined by submission. It allowed two opponents to survive a little crisis in order to get on with the larger dimensions of their lives. Zwingli considered this moment a divine parable and brought it into his next encounter with Luther.

Submission is at the heart of Jesus' short teaching in today's lectionary passage. John Maxwell noted that there are five different levels of authority that a person can attain in life but each is based on an increasing willingness to submit to outside forces or influences.

The first is "position," where people are challenged to respect you for your rank in society. Second, there is the authority of "permission" that happens when you enter a relationship of significance with someone else, and that person allows you to have a say in his affairs. Third comes the authority of "production" in which you are honored for the results you can get. Fourth, there is the authority of "people development" that recognizes the empowerment you have given others. Finally arises the quality of "personhood" where the very character of your life demands respect.

We can all name people who gather one or another of these forms of authority to themselves: a judge, for instance, fits the first; a dating partner, the second; my neighbor across the street did such a good job of bringing up the production in his factory in our town that he was transferred to tackle the development of an even larger plant in another state — that is an example of number three; my uncle who retired as a high school guidance counselor got the accolades of the fourth; and we only have to say names like "Billy Graham" and "Mother Teresa" to explore the last.

Interestingly, the source of all five of these forms of authority exists in our relationship with our parents. A mother has position over us when we are young children. She can abuse that position, as some have, or she can also use it to give us a wholesome sense of ourselves, as many others have.

A father has our permission, early in life, to direct and guide us. We look for support and advice from him. A mother holds over us the authority of production. Before we can tie our shoes or dress ourselves, she is doing things for us we could not begin to handle on our own. So it is with level four — a good parent is able to serve in developing our characters. When we sat around at my grandmother's funeral, some years ago, my dad and all his siblings said the same thing: "Mom always believed in us. She always prayed for us. We wouldn't be the people we are without her care."

In fact, when all these forms of authority are rolled up in a single package it is that fifth form, the one that is particularly hard to earn, which epitomizes the best of what great parenting is about. There is no higher tribute that can be paid a person than to say that he was a father to me, or she was like my own mother. In our brief years of life, as we meander through strange and familiar paths, both untried and yet as ancient as time itself, no one can help us find our truest selves better than a wise and loving parent.

This is the mystery of submission. The best of ourselves rarely comes when we fight it out on our own. Instead, it is brought to life when someone who loves me takes my hand and helps me to reach higher than I thought I could. This is what Jesus is looking for when he talks about lines of parentage.

The ancients always compared our wills to horses. It is a fitting comparison, I think. There is a stallion inside each of us, snorting and restless, and nervously pacing. That energy and strength of character can be thrown about with the destructive power of a mad horse that will not be mastered, or it can be harnessed by a rider and a bit and channeled into speed and purpose and direction.

    Your will is strong. You need it to survive. But you also need it to be brought under submission to a higher power if you would be fully human.

All Saints
Daniel 7:1-3, 15-18
Ephesians 1:11-23
Luke 6:20-31
Craig MacCreary

The twilight zone

Many will remember the television series *Twilight Zone* that aired in the early '60s and in various formats in succeeding years. At the center of the series was always a sudden plot twist that gave a jolt to the characters living in the twilight zone and to the audience that came for their weekly visit to a land beyond normal imagination.

Many of us find ourselves beginning to believe that we have never quite gotten out of the twilight zone. National and world events seem to mimic many of the events foretold in the series including one episode where the earth begins to get hotter and hotter. The capacity to sit at a computer and go online and enter into virtual reality, defying all known time zones, and read newspapers that have not yet hit the streets where they are published makes the twilight zone the next stop on your journey.

Writing about All Saints day after having watched a *Twilight Zone* TV marathon leaves me wondering if the twilight zone is not just a stopover but my permanent residence.

Over the years there were several imitators of the *Twilight Zone*. Most of them were able to capture to some degree the eeriness of the original but none of them were able to capture the moral force of Rod Serling's seminal effort. His agenda was not merely to tantalize the viewer each week with thoughts of how reality might be twisted out of shape into a mysterious plot line.

What was particularly chilling was how the macabre and distorted might break out in the lives of ordinary folks going about their business in familiar contexts. In most of the episodes, we see the principals as people very much like us. Who would ever have thought that they would be candidates to find themselves wresting with the dark side that is about to be revealed in the twilight zone? This was Serling's point — that ordinary people were actually, even in the prosperity and calm of the late '50s and early '60s, living in the twilight of a vulnerable way of life that had not yet risen to the reality of racism, materialism, violence, and dehumanizing technology. Serling was protesting in his own way against the complacency that comes from having other god's before the one, true God. His writing was not the first nor will it be the last to use science fiction to gain a hearing for a message that might otherwise be rejected.

Certainly the apocalyptic writings of scripture such as Daniel are attempting to convey a message that otherwise might not get a hearing. Daniel warns his readers that soon they will be living in the twilight zone of the last of the fallen empires. However, for the saints, the twilight is also the time of daybreak when the cock crows its message that despite our betrayals, denials, faithlessness, and the impending darkness, the Sun (Son) is raised.

The saints are those who live in the context of both of these realities. They live in the context that the powers that be are on shaky grounds to the degree that they diverge from the intentions of God. Secondly, such times are not merely times of the verdict being rendered but of people being empowered by a new reality that is trying to break into the world.

Each of these texts give definition to the term saint as one who sees the fading reality while recognizing the impending dawn and is able to live faithfully in the tension between the two. Most of the people who I would define as saints have a dual capacity to see others as they are and as they might become, an ability to live in the tension between the now and the not yet, and the capacity to stand with the hurting and up to the hurters. "God put this power to work in Christ when he raised him from the dead and seated him at his right hand in the heavenly places, far above all rule and authority and power and dominion, and above every name that is named, not only in this age but also in the age to come" (Ephesians 1:20-21).

Daniel 7:1-3, 15-18

Watching the *Twilight Zone* marathon I quickly became aware of the basic sensitivity that motivated Rod Serling. In the face of fear and stripped of the comforting trappings and services of the empire, normally reasonable people would become an irrational mob. In an episode titled, "Shelter," nuclear war breaks out, and the only shelter available in a respectable neighborhood is the home shelter of a doctor and his family. Of course, the shelter is only big enough for the doctor's family. The neighbors cannot come. The story narrated the breakdown of human decency as neighbor rises against neighbor to save themselves. As Rod Serling says in his closing narration "No moral, no message, no prophetic tract. Just a simple statement of fact. For civilization to survive, the human race must to remain civilized. Tonight's very small exercise in logic from the *Twilight Zone*."

What stands between us and annihilation is the ability to move beyond being a mob to being a community of saints. Sainthood, here, does not mean moral perfection but the ability to recognize that we are all in it together and that we need to tend the garden of the things that make us more alike than different. Choosing to be part of the community of saints over the mob is to acknowledge that the greatest human victories come not from the force of arms but the force of open arms.

Rod Serling's moral compass intrigued and frightened the viewer at the same time. The truth found in the episode where earthlings surrender their responsibilities and sensibilities to travel to a planet hosted by aliens who have promised to "serve man" are shocked when they discover that the book bearing this title is a cookbook. How easily do we become a mob when we believe that all our needs will be met, and we are afraid that we will be left out of the coming good times? One need only think of those who will stand in line or fight in line for the latest Christmas fad or the most recent version of the iPhone. Watching the *Twilight Zone*, I find myself feeling like Daniel, who saw in his "vision by night the four winds of heaven stirring up the great sea, and four great beasts came up out of the sea, different from one another ... As for me, Daniel, my spirit was troubled within me, and the visions of my head terrified me" (Daniel 7:2-3, 15).

It takes a community of saints to help us value ourselves not for what we have but who we are. To value us even at our worst, we need a community that is strong enough and that we trust enough, we can be enough of ourselves that we do not seek status through fads and the getting of things.

One of the themes of Serling's work is the readiness of the mob to seek out a scapegoat for its fears and failures. The episode titled "The Monsters on Main Street" has the residents of a *Leave It To Beaver* street quickly turning on each other in the midst of the sudden loss of all forms of power. They cite each other's eccentricities as clear evidence of guilt. The mob always has a clear profile of the guilty: particularly in the twilight of fear. The saints know that "there is no fear in love, but perfect love casts out fear" (1 John 4:18). The mob thinks that the perfect profile will cast out all fear. The saints proclaim love that seeks to know and be known.

The vision given to Daniel is disturbing in its form and content. However, it is also promising. As the psalmist puts it, "The nations are in an uproar, the kingdoms totter; he utters his voice, the earth melts. The Lord of hosts is with us; the God of Jacob is our refuge" (Psalm 46:6-7). Daniel seems to have gotten over his fear. Though he may, as we do, live in the twilight zone, the community need not surrender to the impulse of the mob for, "As for these four great beasts, four kings shall arise out of the earth. But the holy ones of the Most High shall receive the kingdom and possess the kingdom forever—forever and ever" (Daniel 7:17-18).

Ephesians 1:11-23

The letter writer gives thanks for the faith of the Ephesian community. They persist in living faithfully in the midst of their own twilight zone where life is liminal between the decay of the Roman Empire and the dawn of the present and coming rule of Jesus. Many have criticized the early church for the kinds of compromises it made in the process of trying to get along by going along. We are naturally troubled by passages from the Christian scripture such as this from Romans 13, "Let every person be subject to the governing authorities; for there is no authority except from God, and those authorities that exist have been instituted by God. Therefore whoever resists authority resists what God has appointed, and those who resist will incur judgment" (Romans 13:1-2). For many today it is like living in the twilight zone, giving loyalty and respect to institutions that they feel are corrupt, self-serving, and incapable of giving a straight answer when going to war. Ever since Jesus prayed for his people who were in the world but did not belong to the world, his people have had to struggle with what it is like to live in the twilight of this age and the dawn of the age to come.

For the most part, churches are not likely to win plaudits for living with this struggle. If anything, given the religious tenor of our times, faith communities are likely to be appreciated more for helping people escape or find a respite from this struggle.

Here are six ways of living in this twilight zone.

We are living in an in-between time that requires vigilance to watch our institutions precisely because embodying noble aims is a fragile business. Carl Shurz, a civil war general and former senator, enters into the field of sainthood when he wrote, "Our country right or wrong; if right kept right and if wrong to be set right."

More often than not the real saints are those who have been able to see both how wrong we can be and how right we might be. Winston Churchill wrote in the idiom of his day that. "Man's capacity for injustice makes democracy necessary and our capacity for justice makes it possible." People who faithfully live in the twilight zone of the letter to the Ephesians find themselves saying such things.

Those who live in the twilight zone between the realities of the age that is, and the consummation of the age to come have learned how to pick their battles. In the twilight zone, God is as likely to use our failures to build to his kingdom as our successes. We don't need to win every battle to win the war. Indeed, fighting every battle suggests that the ultimate triumph of the kingdom is more contingent on our efforts than on the hand of God. Living in the twilight zone demands something more of us than picking our fights. It requires us to discern which battle we believe, in God's plan, we are called to wage.

Saints have a prayer life, a communal life, and a biblical literacy that facilitates the discernment process.

Saints know that because they are saints they need not demonize others. They seek to keep the humanity of the other in focus. In the twilight zone, one never knows when the other will be given an opportunity to act like a saint and, given the right circumstance, might do so. It is easier to demonize than to keep one's eyes on this prize. Ephesians reminds us, "That, with the eyes of your heart enlightened, you may know what is the hope to which he has called you" (Ephesians 1:18).

The saints know that if their hope is to have their names written in the book of life, to enter the world to come they need not write anything in concrete in the world that is. The things they most value are always subject to development and growth. The ideals of liberty and justice that founded the United States have grown to eliminate officially sanctioned racism and sexism as well as include the rights of labor and religious minorities. If you live in this twilight zone, you can count on the refinement and development of your most cherished values beyond all human calculation. What is the hope to which he has called you, what are the riches of his glorious inheritance among the saints, and what is the immeasurable greatness of his power for us who believe?

The saints know that the one who has been made "head over all things for the church" (Ephesians 1:22) is the same one who came "not to judge the world, but to save the world" (John 12:47). The task of the church is less to judge than to connect with the world.

None of these will help us avoid the twilight zone. All of them will help us live through the experience of the time between the twilight and the dawn.

Luke 6:20-31

One of the themes of the *Twilight Zone* is that human beings cannot count on an ordinary way of calculating and calibrating their lives. Things do not add up in the way in which we expect. Reality twists and turns beyond human comprehension in ways that leave us vulnerable to having our world turned upside down. As much as I would like to believe that I live in safety beyond the vagaries of the twilight zone this pretty well describes my reality.

I buy a computer with the idea that it will save work time only to discover that the computer has a life of its own that overtakes me. Now I can do more things that have a way of quickly taking up the time that I thought I would gain through better organizing my time. Welcome to the twilight zone. Technology does not save work, it only makes new forms of work. I find myself gaining just enough mastery of the computer to increase the number of times that I am infantilized and reduced to tears by ever-advancing technology. Welcome to the twilight zone.

Part of learning in life is that I should count on having landed immigrant status in the twilight zone. Just about nothing I was told I could count on has stayed in place. I attended a workshop where the leader said organ music sounds to the current generation about like hard rock sounds to most middle-age people — total cacophony. Welcome to the twilight zone.

Something more than *Future Shock* is at work here. As I recall that work by Alvin Toffler, it was a reasoned explanation of the consequences of rapidly advancing technology. It feels like I am in a twilight zone of unforeseen consequences where I can count on very little. In the words of the gospel lesson for All Saints, things become even more unsettling. "Then he looked up at his disciples and said, 'Blessed are you who are poor, for yours is the kingdom of God. Blessed are you who are hungry now, for you will be filled. Blessed are you who weep now, for you will laugh. Blessed are you when people hate you, and when they exclude you, revile you, and defame you on account of the Son of Man. Rejoice on that day and leap for joy, for surely your reward is great in heaven; for that is what their ancestors did to the prophets' " (Luke 6:20-23). Here, again, is one more excursion into the twilight zone. As Frederick Buechner reminds us, this is living by a different set of calculations altogether when you say that those who give get more, you ought to go after the one missing sheep as against the 99 that you have, or the pay off for those who show up late is the same as for those who are the early hired. This confounding of the conventional shorts out my mind once again.

Whenever I have been part of a prolonged electrical blackout, the march of the electrical workers down the street to restore the energy flow looks to me like the saints marching. The saints are the ones who get the energy flowing. The energy flow here has less to do with calculation than with connection to God, each other, and myself. Out of the twilight zone comes a new light that can be cast on things — another example of the way the gospel has of confounding the conventional.

Application

When do you find yourself living in the twilight zone? Certainly, when it can be defined as that place in the shadows between the known and the unknown. However, as I reflect on that, I find myself realizing that I actually never leave the twilight zone. Things have a way of defying my plans, what I count on, and the folks I depend on can often disappoint me. What gets one into ministry is far from what keeps one there. New occasions do teach new duties and time does have the irritating way of eclipsing all my certainties. Clear logic and convincing arguments routinely fail to win the day or even make headway in my home or in my church. Welcome to the twilight zone. This is enough to cause anyone to want to change the channel.

For me, a saint is one who first and foremost knows that in this life, if the light does shine in the darkness, it is nevertheless at best a glimmer. When I was a child, the adults around me were fairly well convinced that Americans had all the light and other Anglo nations were in possession of it to the degree that they sought to follow the American model. It felt like entering the twilight zone when I discovered early on that America may not be the absolute light of the world and that it had a shadow side. It came as a shock to find out that we did not invent the television or the telephone and that Thomas Edison may have been as inventive in some of his financial arrangements as he was in anything else.

Saints know better and anticipate the shadow side of every glorious moment. Saints know that it is not our light but how the light has been refracted through our tragedies, miscues, and blunders that brings any hope into the world. Knowing that it is but a glimmer, saints welcome light from any source. They know enough that they should look to see how their faith commitments and mission appear in the light of others' experience.

On this day, I give thanks for all the saints who have helped me live faithfully in the twilight zone.

Alternative Applications
Luke 6:20-31; Daniel 7:1-3, 15-18. Which came first, the chicken or the egg? Of course this imponderable mystery has kept minds going for years. Does sainthood lead to belonging or does belonging lead to sainthood? Can we believe without belonging or can we belong without believing? I struggle with the reality that of the many of those whom I would call saints in my life I have not a clue as to what their religious background was. Coaches, teachers, some coworkers, who knew what their background was, but clearly in the foreground of their lives was a transparency that revealed a quality of life that invited one to thought and even reverence. Some were found in the church; many would not let themselves be found in church. Many of my saints were from well beyond the safe and familiar religious traditions that I have grown comfortable with. The holy comes at you from many different directions.

The visions of Daniel gave him a serious headache. "As for me, Daniel, my spirit was troubled within me, and the visions of my head terrified me" (Daniel 7:15). The blessings and woes contained in Luke's gospel are troubling if they express what nearness to God is and what distance from God is. There is much to ponder in my experience of sainthood and the scriptures. The route to sainthood has less to do with explaining it than receiving it wherever it shows up as a gift. Being in that number when the saints go marching in will have less to do with explaining it than accepting it.

Proper 26 / Pentecost 24 / Ordinary Time 31
Habakkuk 1:1-4; 2:1-4
2 Thessalonians 1:1-4, 11-12
Luke 19:1-10
Wayne Brouwer

Encouragement

Alan Loy McGinnis told of a woman who was honored by her company for outstanding performance during the just-ended fiscal year. Standing at the podium before hundreds of fellow-workers in a large banqueting hall, she clutched her trophy and wept as she told of the strange route that brought her to this moment of recognition.

A year earlier, this woman's marriage had unraveled, and she was down and out emotionally. She could not give her all to her job and too often she found herself coming up short against deadlines and assignments. She wanted to quit and several times wrote letters of resignation. But her supervisor, Susan, had always encouraged her to wait another day or another week and had pocketed her self-terminations without opening them. Between sobs, the winner breathed words of thanks to Susan and said to her, "You believed in me even when I couldn't believe in myself."

Some of the same is true in the combination of passages for today's homily. Through Habakkuk, God encourages those who give righteousness a good name during times of political and social unrest. Paul writes to encourage new believers who are weathering storms that deny them homes, families, and neighbors. Jesus nods toward Zacchaeus as a shining example of courage in a very misunderstanding world. Perhaps today we can bring some smiles of grace to the faces of discouraged and disheartened pilgrims who find the road to the kingdom by wandering through dark and lonely places.

Habakkuk 1:1-4; 2:1-4

Habakkuk lived in a time of social instability and political crisis. The threat of Assyrian invasion and domination had passed and in its wake came an almost giddy public release of euphoric immorality. For nearly a century, Habakkuk's predecessors had pointed north and warned God's people that Assyria was the tool of divine anger, coming soon to punish this wayward nation. There were bits of relief and breaks of release as other nations (particularly Syria) pushed back hard enough to make the menacing invaders stop and regroup before trying another onslaught. Eventually, even Judah's kinship neighbor, Israel, was felled by the Assyrian axmen, and Sennacharib swamped the south with his troops until the only island left was tiny Jerusalem.

When good king Hezekiah heard the taunts and threats of Sennacharib's boasts, he took the Assyrian general's pompous letter and laid it on the altar of burnt offering in the temple. Through Isaiah, word from heaven came that God would wage the battle and break the stranglehold of this arrogant crew. While the siege captives frittered nervously in disbelief, God miraculously sent the whole Assyrian army packing overnight in a fright that other historians would later describe as a plague. Suddenly, Judah stood free and independent again, splendidly isolated from looming conquest in its mountainous stronghold.

When the religious cries evaporated as the political crisis passed, the new era of peace and prosperity bred social pride and ethical debauchery. Yahweh's deliverance was either forgotten or bandied about as a historical legacy that proved God would always be on the side of this nation. Greed, corruption, and sexual indiscretions rapidly filled the vacuum of external threat. It was then that Habakkuk rose one day to argue with God.

"Why do you allow them to get away with their blatant sinfulness?" Habakkuk demanded. Whether or not he expected a direct and sentient response from Yahweh, we do not know. But this was an instance in which Yahweh took pains clearly and unmistakably to enter into dialogue with a prophetic spokesperson in the community.

"I won't let them get away with it," came the reply from heaven. "See, I'm sending the Babylonians to punish all who think they can live as if I do not matter."

But the cure was worse than the disease, for Habakkuk. "How can you use the Babylonians as a disciplining scourge against us?" he prayed incredulously. "They are even worse than us!"

The conversation continued for a time, with Yahweh more fully explaining the divine plan. Although the Babylonians were indeed a fierce and pagan nation, Yahweh would channel their international aggressions into a military "board of education" to swat some punishing correction into the puffed up little self-important strutter that Judah had become. Babylon itself would then face its own day of reckoning, and the full scales of international, political, and moral justice would be balanced.

Furthermore, according to the word of the Lord in the passage for today, "The righteous will live by his faith." As Yahweh explained to Habakkuk, this meant that those within the faith community of Judah who remembered who they were and *whose* they were would find their religious convictions and their moral faithfulness honored. Although the whole tiny nation would suffer greatly under Babylonian aggression, those who aligned themselves with the covenant that had given birth to the nation and still governed its expected lifestyle would find Yahweh a compassionate and forgiving God.

There are a number of themes that emerge from this brief prophecy, nestled in the times between Assyria's massive threat and Babylon's looming domination. First, there is testimony of absolute confidence in the one who observes the actions and lifestyles of people and nations and keeps sending report cards through cultural critics at every age. It is never wise to ignore those who speak with a prophetic voice of conscience, especially during times of peace and prosperity.

Second, the rise and fall of nations is part of a larger work of God in which unbridled immorality as well as unrestrained aggression will be stopped through international checks and balances. No corrupt regime ought to think it is above either United Nations assessments or divine judgment. There will be an auditing of the record in the end, and it may well come with a steep price.

Third, general godlessness or the failure of religious systems need never dissuade true believers from the rightness of their faith or its expressions. The heroes of history are those who had the fortitude to remain religiously grounded even when their cultures were doing whatever they could to erode places to stand and melt moorings into quicksand. We remember these folks in retrospect as saints, like Martin Niemoller or Mother Teresa or Groen van Prinsterer or Thomas More or Dietrich Bonhoeffer or William Stringfellow.

Fourth, the plan of God is long and comprehensive. It usually spans several generations, making our quick-fix religious solutions out-of-place and ecclesiastically irresponsible. God never promises immediate wealth and personal success if we just do three or four little exercises in holiness. The purposes of God are much broader and we are not asking the right questions if we stop at demanding what God can do for us. The real question, as John F. Kennedy put it to the American people in a slightly different form, is what can we do for the kingdom of God.

2 Thessalonians 1:1-4, 11-12

Paul was on his second mission journey when he stumbled into Thessalonica. He had just come through an eventful time in Philippi where a new Christian congregation had begun out of the most unusual circumstances, organized by the most unlikely people (see Acts 16). Now he was on his way to Corinth (see Acts 18), stopping in a few cities along the way.

Paul's time in Thessalonica didn't last very long — probably somewhere between three weeks and two months. After talking in the Jewish synagogue about Jesus as the promised Messiah, one segment of the congregation became highly perturbed, and Paul and Silas shifted their base of operations to the marketplace in town. Here the primary audience was Gentile, and a number of these people listened with rapt attention and responded with heartfelt conviction to the evangelists' call to repentance and belief. As these non-Jewish converts joined the synagogue believers to form a new Christian community, Paul's and Silas' opponents grew incensed. Not only had these travelers disrupted their synagogue stability by injecting a new twist on the old doctrines that divided the group into differing messianic parties, but now they had assisted in the creation of a religious organization that broke down the fundamental division between Jew and Gentile.

With what appears to be a great amount of rage, these antagonists drove Paul and Silas out of Thessalonica. The itinerant band split into several teams in order to bring the gospel message to a number of different towns but soon they regrouped in Corinth. From there, Paul sent two letters to the Thessalonians, wondering and hoping and praying that they were doing well and addressing at least one critical theological issue from two differing points of view.

These letters are among Paul's earliest pastoral-theological epistolary exhortations, written around the year 50 AD. In our New Testament, only Paul's letter to the Galatians precedes them.

The primary theological issue about which Paul needed to give some further clarity was the return of Jesus. First Thessalonians bubbles with enthusiasm about the way in which the church survived its first few months and became a stable witnessing community in a rather challenging environment. Paul was glad for the testimony brought by Timothy that the congregation was doing well in spite of the forced, quick exodus that prevented Paul and Silas from lingering to explain many ideas about Jesus or the plans of God more fully.

One question that surfaced rather abruptly among the Thessalonian Christians was an uncertainty as to what happened to those who died. Evidently, in the few short weeks since Paul and his team had been ejected from the city, at least one and possibly several new believers had died. Since Paul's preaching had focused on the resurrection as the primary proof endorsing Jesus' claim to be the Messiah, and because the urgency of Paul's evangelistic enterprise was based upon his conviction that Jesus was returning very soon — probably next week, but at the very outside next year — there was some confusion as to what happened to those who believed this good news, but then died before Jesus came back.

In his first letter, Paul gave warm and pastoral encouragement, assuring the grieving families that their loved ones who had died would also share with them the future new and glorious times with Jesus. This would happen because God would instigate a mass resurrection in which the dead would have a similar experience to Jesus' Easter morning reawakening.

Paul's message brought a great deal of comfort, but it also triggered an unforeseen side effect. In light of the dramatic expectation of Jesus' imminent return, many in the Thessalonian congregation set aside their normal social routines and began to meet together in extended worship settings, waiting for Jesus to burst through the door at any moment.

When Paul heard about this, he became more than a little distraught. The good news of salvation through Jesus was meant to energize life, not to make it irrelevant. Those who began to opt out of daily activities and responsibilities in some kind of eschatological frenzy were actually subverting the gospel testimony.

In haste, Paul penned this second letter, praising the group for their earnest and powerful witness but cautioning them quickly to re-engage their routines and obligations. Jesus was coming soon, Paul assured them, but there was likely to be a bit of a wait before that happened. In the intervening month, or perhaps even years, they should remain faithful to their families, friends, and fellows in the social arena who were counting on them for the normal care and support of life.

The verses for today's lectionary reading are marvelously beautiful in their positive affirmation of faithful trust, vibrant witness, and consistent godliness as displayed by this fledgling Christian community situated squarely on the crossroads of society. They were not unusually numerous, terrifically endowed, or powerfully positioned, but they understood the lifestyle implications of the gospel and lived them out in beauty and grace.

These verses cannot be preached so much as used to encourage and inspire. It is a bit like the fellow who met friends at the county fair midway, among the rides and the booths. The couple's young daughter was almost hiding behind a tower of cotton candy on a paper cone. "How can you eat all of that?" the man asked her with an impish twinkle. "You are much too small to get it all inside!"

After a brief hesitation to figure it out, the girl replied, "I guess I'm a lot bigger on the inside than I am on the outside!" That seems to have been Paul's understanding of the Thessalonian Christian, as well. In an alien environment, born out of persecution and conflict, this band of believers gave quick and sure evidence that the power and possibilities of God living within them was much bigger and stronger than anything projected upon them by the limiting perspectives of the world.

Luke 19:1-10

It is easy to jump quickly to conclusions in preaching on the story of Jesus and Zacchaeus. After all, this tale is as commonly known as any of the gospel stories and carries in our minds a great number of preconceptions. Zacchaeus must have been a bad person, most think, because he seems to have been sidelined by the crowds rushing to see Jesus. Moreover, Jesus singles him out for a special visit, likely indicating that he was in greater need of divine transformation than anyone else in town. Furthermore, when the two of them emerge from Zacchaeus' home later in the day, the short one makes promises of financial restoration (seemingly implying that he took fraudulent funds), and the tall one declares the arrival of salvation. All in all, our presumptions seem to add up to a quick perception that Zacchaeus was a bad man, and Jesus rescued him that day.

There are clear hints in the story, as Luke tells it, that point in other directions. First of all, the main character's name means "clean" or "innocent." This might be a foreshadowing of the outcomes of the narrative, but it could also simply be a hint that Zacchaeus was a good man, not a bad man.

Second, the historical developments of occupied Palestine give us every reason to believe that the designation "tax collector" was not a term of derision in the city or region. The Roman government had taken over direct taxation collection responsibilities by this time, and the task that produced Zacchaeus' occupation was more likely the oversight of customs booths for the trade caravans that entered the land at the Jericho portal. Since most occupations were inherited from parents, Zacchaeus probably grew up in a home where his father or grandfather had already developed the business.

Third, Zacchaeus' wealth was probably as much inherited as it was the result of good business activities. For that reason, it is not entirely certain that the man is making a confession of great wickedness when he talks about restoring any funds ill-gotten. He may be making a simple declaration of desire to be fully reliable in business and not blabbing about secret sins of the past.

Fourth, the word usually translated "short" in our Bibles, when referring to Zacchaeus, actually is better interpreted as "young." It is only because the story tells us that Zacchaeus went up a tree to see Jesus that we assume he was short. But it may well be that because of his younger age, he deferred to the older men who crowded around Jesus. In an inventive move, he was agile enough to quickly climb up a tree and get a position that no older men would dared to have taken.

Fifth, although Jesus says, at the conclusion of his visit to Zacchaeus' home, that salvation came today to this dwelling, it need not mean a radical transformation. After all, Jesus is himself the means of salvation. It is likely that Jesus only wanted the people to take note of this outsider among them and treat him with respect. After all, he says that "this man, too, is a son of Abraham," not implying that Zacchaeus had a sudden transformation, but that his neighbors need to respect him for what he truly is and not shove him to the side with their petty prejudices against rich folks.

Finally, Zacchaeus never admits having lived a life of theft and robbery. The present tense of his declaration that he gives half his income to the poor means that this was his already-taking-place-and-continuing practice of life. In other words, instead of ripping off those who came under his business interests, he was more likely to benefit them. He was a generous man, even before Jesus came to town.

All of this seems to imply that the story is told by Luke as an illustration for what Jesus wants to say about himself and what kind of authority he wields on behalf of his Father (see vv. 12-25). In effect, the tale of Zacchaeus, even standing by itself, is as much a call for people to be seen with grace and mercy rather than suspicion and judgment. Not a bad theme on which to preach.

Application

Although they contain rich images, if one wants to be faithful to the intent of the whole message, the passages from Habakkuk are hardest to preach. Both the epistle and gospel passages carry well the theme of encouragement. Dozens of illustrations would bring the message to a great conclusion, but the more personal they can be made, the more lasting impact they will have.

An Alternative Application

Habakkuk 1:1-4; 2:1-4. If you are up for a challenge, get into Habakkuk's times and dialogue and help your congregation wrestle with the problem of evil in a whole new way. Although the prophecy is short, it deals with the complexity of sin and divine punishment and the struggle to maintain godly behavior and perspectives in a twisted and compromised world.

Proper 27 / Pentecost 25 / Ordinary Time 32
Haggai 1:15b—2:9
2 Thessalonians 2:1-5, 13-17
Luke 20:27-38
David Kalas

A bright forecast

Primitive people, even more than we, were at the mercy of the weather. They were considerably less sheltered than we are. And they did not have the wide variety of resources that we do to compensate for a crop-killing frost or drought. Plus, for them, the weather had that extra element of mystery. It was beyond their knowledge and beyond their control. They did not know what tomorrow might bring, and they couldn't do anything to guarantee it.

Our relationship to the weather is somewhat different. We certainly still find ourselves overwhelmed by the forces of nature from time to time. We can't offer significant relief to whole regions devastated by heat. Our biggest cities can still be shut down by snow and ice, and we can't ward off the tornadoes or hurricanes that come our way.

On the other hand, we generally know when such things are coming our way. High-tech meteorology combines with high-tech communication to make the weather forecast perpetually accessible, and now we often know what tomorrow will bring — at least in terms of the weather.

When it comes to the rest of the future, though, we are in the very same situation as our ancestors thousands of years ago. Apart from the weather, we do not know what tomorrow may bring. And many of the people in our pews can bear witness to that. For as we come to the end of this calendar year, how many of us would raise our hands and say, "I had no idea back in the first part of January that by this time..."? Our lives can change in an instant. So can our world.

Apart from the weather, we lack a television channel, website, or government agency that is able to tell us what tomorrow may bring, we are often at odds about the forecast. The pessimist is quite certain of the gloom he sees (constantly) on the horizon. The optimist is equally sure that better days are still ahead. The worriers and the ambitious employ their imaginations in the service of their future paradigm. But no one knows.

There have always been a few in every generation who have believed that they could do something or other to affect or control the weather. There have been more than a few in every generation who have sought to control their own future. Both endeavors, however, inevitably prove futile.

Our three lections this morning are all about the future. The Lord speaks a hopeful word about it to the discouraged people of Haggai's day. Paul wrote to the Christians in Thessalonica, who were unsure about it. Jesus taught the Sadducees a thing or two they did not know about it. This week, we turn our attention to the forecast.

Haggai 1:15b—2:9

When this passage is read aloud in most of our churches, it will not likely sound familiar. This episode comes near the end of Old Testament history's time line, and most of our people are more familiar with the beginning and the middle. The stories of Adam and Abraham, Moses and Joshua, David and Solomon — these are all widely recognizable. But this episode comes from one of the post-exilic prophets and that may seem like foreign territory. Except for Daniel, Jonah, and a few cherished passages from Isaiah, the Old Testament prophets are just a confusing blur in the minds of so many.

It will be necessary for us, therefore, to set the stage for the hearing of this word. And that stage is the temple mount in Jerusalem.

Scene one must come about a decade into the reign of King Solomon, the son and successor of King David. When the throne passed from father to son, the united twelve tribes of Israel were strong and secure. They were, for the moment, the dominant power in the region. In time, Solomon gained the reputation of being one of the wisest men in the world. His reign was marked by peace, prosperity, and building.

After years of amassing the finest materials and constructing on the grandest scale, Solomon dedicated to God the temple that he had built there in Jerusalem. It was an epic event. The magnificent temple, combined with Solomon's fabulous offerings, made for a great spectacle in the eyes of the assembled people. Then God himself made his own awesome contribution to the spectacle and to the occasion.

Scene two comes some 400 years later. All the hallmarks of Solomon's era — the splendor, the wisdom, the peace, the security — are gone. Jerusalem is overrun by the unstoppable troops of the Babylonian army. The kings of Babylon have been calling the shots for Judah and Jerusalem for some years, and now they have exercised their force to put an end to all thought of rebellion. Jerusalem is decimated, and the temple — Solomon's masterpiece to the glory of God — lies in ruins.

Finally, scene three comes with our Old Testament lection. It is just forty-some years after scene two. That suggests there may be a few people in the cast who were present in both scenes.

The exiles who have returned from Babylon had begun the painful task of rebuilding the ruined temple. It is an easier thing, we know, to start fresh than to rebuild what has fallen down. The internal and external obstacles conspired to halt the work that those first folks had begun. After a few years of inactivity, the prophet Haggai appears on the scene: first, to challenge the people to resume the project and second, in our passage, to encourage them in the midst of the difficult and discouraging task.

What they started with were memories — burdensome memories. The glorious recollection of all that the former temple had been, plus the painful memories of its destruction. As they set out to rebuild, they recognized the inferiority of their effort. So the Lord asked them, "Who is left among you that saw this house in its former glory? How does it look to you now? Is it not in your sight as nothing?"

It is to that difficult situation and disheartened crowd that God speaks his powerful and reassuring word.

First, there is the magnificent promise of God's presence: "I am with you" and "my spirit abides among you." To those who know best, this is the real issue. For a glorious temple without his presence becomes a terrible and vulnerable thing. But even a simple place inhabited by his glory becomes a setting of inexpressible beauty. Indeed, we discover in Revelation that, when God is fully present, no temple is necessary at all (Revelation 21:22).

Second, when God promises to "shake the heavens" and the like, we are rightly reminded of the vast difference between what we can do and what he can do. The people would have been right to underestimate the project if its success and beauty depended entirely upon them; but it does not.

That truth leads, finally, to God's promise that "the latter splendor of this house shall be greater than the former." Is that because Zerubbabel has more resources than Solomon or that Joshua will be a better designer or builder? Not at all. Rather, it is by God's graciousness and good pleasure that the beauty of the future will eclipse even the best of the past.

Perhaps, then, that blessed prospect becomes scene four.

2 Thessalonians 2:1-5, 13-17

Most scholars agree that the Thessalonian epistles are probably the earliest of Paul's letters. In these two pieces, we discover that the return of Christ is a recurring theme. For his return was no doubt expected to be imminent by the first generation of believers, and so his seeming delay raised some practical and theological questions.

We and our people may not be immediately sympathetic to the Thessalonians' plight. After all, we have lived for generations with the problem that was completely new to them: namely, the long postponement of Christ's return. While those believers fully expected Christ's return any day, our level of expectation — and therefore, too, our level of disappointment — may be comparatively quite low.

The fact is that from the time Jesus first warned his disciples what would happen to him in Jerusalem, it was only a matter of months until it all took place. When he told them that he would rise again, or that he would go before them into Galilee, those things took place within a few days. When he instructed them to tarry in Jerusalem until he sent the Spirit, the time between instruction and fulfillment was only a few weeks. It was quite natural, therefore, for the earliest Christians to assume that his promised return would, likewise, come in very short order.

At the time of this writing, it had probably been some twenty years since Christ's ascension, and still he had not come back yet. That became the source of assorted theological and practical challenges, several of which we see Paul address in his two Thessalonian epistles.

Among the theological challenges, evidently, was the rumor that the anticipated "day of the Lord is already here." That teaching had the Thessalonians understandably concerned, for all that was anticipated to accompany that day had not transpired, at least in their experience.

Paul reassures the unsettled believers that they hadn't missed their flight. They should still wait patiently and hopefully. Then the apostle reminded them about what manner of opponent must first stride across the stage of history before Christ would return. Finally, having discussed the rebellion and apostasy that will necessarily precede Christ's coming, Paul affirms the Thessalonians in their faith, their calling, and their good future in Christ.

Luke 20:27-38

In order to set the context for this passage from Luke 20, we should observe that Luke 19 features the story of Palm Sunday. In other words, when we come to this particular dialogue between Jesus and the Sadducees, we are in the midst of that eventful, final week in Jerusalem. Accordingly, this particular discussion is just one of a handful of deliberate challenges that the Jewish leaders brought to Jesus. Immediately prior to this episode comes the touchy question about paying taxes to the Roman emperor. Prior to that was the question challenging Jesus' authority. Added to these, we find in the larger context several pointed teachings and parables by Jesus, which implicated those same Jewish leaders.

The other essential element for setting the stage is a little background information about the Sadducees. The Sadducees were one of the four main sects within Judaism at the time of Jesus (along with the Pharisees, the Zealots, and the Essenes). The Sadducees were theologically distinctive in their opposition to the oral tradition that was so important to the Pharisees, as well as their rejection of "resurrection, future rewards and punishments, angels and spirits, and providence" (John Bowdon, *A Source Book of the Bible for Teachers*, Robert C. Walton, editor [London: SCM Press Ltd., 1970], p. 227). Their characteristic emphases were on the five books of Moses and on the temple.

The basis for the Sadducees' question was the regulation in the Old Testament law that the brother of a man who died without having a son, was duty-bound to marry the widow and produce a son for his deceased sibling (Deuteronomy 25:5-10). It appears from the story of Onan (Genesis 38:1-10) that, even before the matter was codified in Deuteronomic law, the same expectation was already a part of the culture in the time of the patriarchs.

The Sadducees' endeavor, of course, was to make the idea of the resurrection seem like foolishness. It is standard fare in argumentation to try to make the opponent's position seem ridiculous. By their calculation, a resurrection of the dead would result in a most unsightly scandal in heaven: namely, a woman with seven different husbands waiting for her when she died. They no doubt expected that their clever proposal, based on scripture, would present Jesus with an embarrassing theological conundrum.

The advantage always goes to the questioner, of course, in a setting like this. It's an easy thing to play the part of the skeptic. He puts his opponent on the defensive, and he positions himself in such a place where he himself does not need to know much, but his opponent must be prepared to know everything. So the questioning skeptic is permitted to tear down someone else's construct, though without any obligation to offer something stable and viable in its place.

This was the simple and strategic role of the Sadducees in our story. But Jesus and his paradigm are undisturbed by their skepticism. The problem did not lie either in the regulations of the Old Testament law or in the future promise of the resurrection. Rather, the problem lay in the Sadducees themselves and their misunderstanding (see Matthew 22:29).

Jesus' answer makes a distinction between two ages: "this age" and "that age." What we are and what we do in this age are, not surprisingly, different from what we will be and what we will do in that age. Simple. So the conundrum that the Sadducees had proposed was an exclusively earthly problem. It would be no problem at all "in that age and in the resurrection."

In addition to making that simple, decisive distinction, Jesus adds a tantalizing caveat, "Those who are considered worthy of a place in that age." The tables are subtly turned. The Sadducees had, for a moment, sat as judges, passing down their uncharitable verdicts on Jesus and his foolish notion of a resurrection. In the turn of a phrase, they suddenly become the ones awaiting a verdict. What if there is such a resurrection? And what if it will not include everyone? At the outset, the Sadducees were certain that there was no future resurrection; but if there is a resurrection, then it becomes the Sadducees' future that is uncertain.

Application

The historical situations of our three selected passages are all quite different. Haggai preached to the Jews of sixth-century BC Palestine, just a generation removed from conquest and exile. Paul wrote to the first-century AD Christians of Macedonia, just twenty years removed from the earthly life and ministry of Jesus. Jesus himself conversed with the obstinate Sadducees of Jerusalem, who did not see clearly and thus opposed Jesus and the resurrection.

Likewise, the futures being contemplated in these several contexts are different. For Haggai's audience, both the splendors and the defeats of the past made it difficult for them to focus on the future, though God endeavored to point their faith to a glorious future, indeed. For Paul's congregation in Thessalonica, the future at issue was the return of Christ, with its uncertain (and debatable) timing. For Jesus and the Sadducees, the subject of a one-day resurrection was the disputed future.

For all of the differences, however, one great theme remains the same. Namely, the companion truths that the future is in God's hands and that he intends it to be very good.

The people of post-exilic Jerusalem were not the ones who could "shake the heavens and the earth and the sea and the dry land." But God could and he promised to do it. Similarly, the believers in ancient Macedonia were encouraged to trust God's timing for the day of the Lord, when he would make all things right. And the Sadducees had to be corrected, for they had underestimated the power of God and the full goodness of the future he has in store.

An Alternative Application

Haggai 1:15b—2:9. "Holy Prescription." We know what it is to read the instructions on a bottle of medicine. Perhaps it's the ordinary stuff of over-the-counter pain relief. In that instance, the diagnosis is left up to us. We identify the "indications" — headache, fever, congestion — and the bottle promises "temporary relief" or some such. Or, in the more rarefied business of prescription drugs, a doctor has made the diagnosis, and he has prescribed the cure. Whatever the case, the instructions on the bottle tell us what to take and when to take it.

In Jerusalem at the time of Haggai, see what the indications and symptoms were. The people and their country had been devastated. Their nation had been overrun and occupied by enemy forces, while their leaders, along with their best and brightest, had been carried off into exile. Their capital city had been laid waste and the temple of their God had been left in ruins. Indeed, if they didn't know better (thanks to the prophets), they might have been tempted to think that their God himself had been defeated by the gods of Babylon.

Now, a generation or so later, they were back in their homeland: somewhat free, somewhat prosperous, as they tried to establish new lives for themselves. In their midst stood a half-begun project — the rebuilding of the temple. But the sight of it bore duel witness to the rubble that preceded it and to the unmatchable glory of a day long gone by.

What do you take in that situation of feebleness, fear, and despair? God knew and he prescribed just what they needed. "Take courage, O Zerubbabel... take courage, O Joshua... take courage, all you people of the land."

We are sometimes inclined to think that courage is something that we feel or don't feel. Here it is not so passive. Rather, it is a conscious decision and deliberate action: take courage!

How? Well, we certainly know how to "take" discouragement. We focus on the troubles that surround us, the regrets of the past, the uncertainties of the future, and soon we are quite discouraged.

Conversely, we take courage by focusing elsewhere. We focus on the goodness, grace, love, and power of the one who is before us, beyond us, and all around us. "For I am with you, says the Lord of hosts... My spirit abides among you; do not fear."

Proper 28 / Pentecost 26 / Ordinary Time 33
Isaiah 65:17-25
2 Thessalonians 3:6-13
Luke 21:5-19
Craig MacCreary

What's new?

Life can be quite onerous depending on the answer given to this question. Many of us find ourselves perpetually overwhelmed by a steady stream of newness that is getting the best of us. Just when many of us have mastered one computer software, we find ourselves lusting after the newest operating system. I often feel that I spend a lifetime of unlearning the lessons I learned in seminary: It is now as legitimate to speak of thinking locally to act globally as the other way around; expectations are now that the preacher will insert personal illustrations lest they seem inauthentic, one will lead the sacraments in a personal tone of voice. There are days when there are just too many new heavens and earths to contend with. If this is what God is up to, then I must admit that I feel like my C-drive is beginning to fill up as I am being thrust into overdrive by the promise of a variety of new approaches to ministry. My prayer becomes, "O Lord, give it thou a rest for mine eyes grow weary and my congregation grows faint at all the fads. Let thou thy people depart in peace to process and reflect before thy preacher goes off to another workshop."

Of course, on the other end of the scale there are days when the congregation pleads for the pastor to get off his or her hobbyhorse and get with what is happening in the world. I now see congregations flinch when a pastor uses sexist language, for it is no longer the *lingua franca* of the day. Church school children do a duck and cover drill at the thought of having to walk where Jesus walked using a sixty-year-old flannel board. In what I thought was a brilliant move, I used the film *Good Will Hunting* with my confirmation class believing the popularity of Robin Williams would win the day, only to be asked, "Who is Robin Williams?" My prayer is also, "O Lord, do not let me shame myself in front of the confirmation class, spare me those flat seasons when my parishioners can mouth my sermons as I preach them. If thou cannot grant me a new heaven or earth at least spare me the hell of people avoiding me because I have become a 'Johnny One Note.' Save me from having my head in a book, from being stuck trying to balance the books, or trying to book the youth group for another fun event, when your new heaven and earth breaks out."

The problem with change is that we can have either too much of it or too little of it. We can either be overwhelmed by too much new heaven or earth or be left underwhelmed in our impact on life by the hellishness that comes from being out to lunch missing the great feast of newness that God is serving up. The text from Isaiah serves up the menu of what God is up to and gives some suggestions as to how we may partake of what God is attempting to do in our lives and in the world.

Well, why bother with the passage from 2 Thessalonians at all? We know where it is headed right from the start. Of course, the problem in our musty reading of this text might be that we are not open to the fresh implications in and between its lines. Or, do we favor the seeming reinforcement that this text offers to the middle-class lifestyles that many of us share and that not a few of us compulsively pursue as part of our redemption?

To paraphrase the old saying, "When all you have is a hammer then you are not likely to enjoy having your handiwork undone." The Luke texts suggest that many of us have been able to cobble together some pretty fancy work that would rival anything seen on PBS's *This Old House*. "When some were speaking about the temple, how it was adorned with beautiful stones and gifts dedicated to God, he said..." (Luke 21:5). The text offers a path to follow that will lead beyond survival to thriving in the midst of what God is bringing about.

Each of these texts suggests how much is at stake in answers we give to the question, "What's new?"

Isaiah 65:17-25

God is going to do a new thing. Well, the Hebrews must have thought it is about time. They are immersed in the rebuilding work following their exile in Babylon. Things have not gone quite as expected: the work is hard, the friction great, and their bad theology abundant. Bring on the newness.

Like us, I am sure they expected the newness to either conform to reasonable, manageable proportions or that it would be so sweeping that it would elevate them beyond the normal constraints and difficulties of human existence. Couples preparing for marriage often seem to be ready for a newness that will sweep away all obstacles in their lives. However, even in the heavenly city there are streets to be swept and no doubt garbage to be taken out and left at the curb of the golden streets. Or the young couple expects that they, much like Prince Charles and Camilla, will carry on life without much significant change to major parts of their former life. However, note that the text does not say that God will do away with all things, only make all things new. Neither does the text say that all things will be restored to the way they once were nor that people will live happily ever after. While infants do survive in the new order of things, there are still infants who need care and nurturing. While those who don't make it to 100 feel robbed, there will still be senior citizens whose needs must be addressed. While the order of one building and another inhabiting is overturned there is still much building to be done.

The new order of things will demand more than just sitting idly by. It will require actively participating in the new order by following a new set of blueprints, a new diet plan, and a new economic order of things. Of course, immediately we are presented with a bit of a chicken and the egg kind of issue. Is it the new blueprint, diet, and economic order that makes for the newness or is it the newness that makes it possible for this trinity? Of course, the really new thing is recognizing that it is both. Whichever end of the stick you pick up, it will lead you to the fulfillment of where God wants you to be.

Certainly, from whichever place we begin, there is going to be a lot of serious challenging change if these scenarios are enacted. Imagine if people did live to 100 on a routine basis. They would need to live with the consequences of much that they had planned for and worked for in ways they never had before. Visualize what it might mean to a family system's theory for people to regularly interact with their great, great, great, great, grandchildren. Certainly, our political life would take on quite a different coloration if politicians knew that they would be answerable to future generations in more than a metaphorical sense. Can you imagine a nation where the food supply is not controlled by huge corporate interests? "They shall not build and another inhabit; they shall not plant and another eat" (Isaiah 65:22). This vision would turn around the current energy crises if food was produced locally instead of needing to be shipped long distances. "They shall build houses and inhabit them; they shall plant vineyards and eat their fruit" (Isaiah 65:21). Here is a stunning vision of an alternative world that takes one's breath away.

2 Thessalonians 3:6-13

There are few texts in scripture that are more likely to send chills up and down my spine than this one. It is not so much because I find its rebuke of idleness addressed to me. Rather, it is the way that it has been interpreted and used over the years to reinforce a fairly prosaic moralistic stance toward life. "No work, no eat," do we really need this text to bring out this particular truth? If anything, this text tends to reinforce a pride in pulling one's own weight that belies the true interdependent human reality. The text becomes a little bit more comfortable if what is meant here is that I do my part that others may do their part just as their work makes it possible for me to do mine.

It is one thing to address this text to the well-educated, able-bodied, upwardly mobile with interesting jobs. It is quite another to address this text to those who haven't been able to find work in six months or who grind away at mind-numbing, soul-searing jobs.

If one examines the text closely, it is addressed to those who have been using their beliefs about the world to come or, in essence, to drop out of the world that is. Many Christians have advocated less than a spirited care of the environment because the issue of this life will soon be addressed by the second coming. Bill Moyers has commented on Glenn Scherer's *The Road to Environmental Apocalypse*. Read it and you will see how millions of Christian fundamentalists may believe that environmental destruction is not only to be disregarded but actually welcomed — even hastened — as a sign of the coming apocalypse.

Paul is saying here that whatever one's beliefs about the world to come, disengagement from the world that is likely to lead to an aridness of soul and dullness of mind is to be avoided. It is one thing to address this passage to a single working mom whose world weariness has come from the day in and day out struggle to keep human and to keep food on the table. It is quite another to address it to those whose disengagement from the world comes from their ability to live off their investments that free them from participating in the daily struggles that most of us must face. Something more is suggested here than the simple failure to work for a living. The King James Version, as it renders verse 6, highlights what Paul is after, "Now we command you, brethren, in the name of our Lord Jesus Christ that ye withdraw yourselves from every brother that walketh disorderly, and not after the tradition which he received of us." Often in scripture the phrase disorderly connotes those who have fallen out of military discipline: those who have gotten out of step or those who have fallen from the ranks. I am reminded of the price that George H.W. Bush paid for the political misstep of not knowing what the electronic price code bars were for on the items that he purchased. In the minds of many it demonstrated that he was not to be ranked among the people he sought to lead. Fairly or unfairly, the impression was given that somehow he was not one of us. Certainly this is to be avoided by Christians if they proclaim a gospel of redemption of the world as it is so that it can be what God intended it to be.

For Aristotle, the first task of persuasive rhetoric was to establish a fundamental rapport with the audience in which they recognized the speaker as basically one of them. It was for Aristotle the most important of the fundamental persuasive elements of speech: *ethnos*, *pathos*, and *logos*. How can we proclaim the redemption of the world if we are not seen as, like most others, taking the world that is very seriously? Certainly if we live in idleness we will not be understood to be taking the world very seriously. Work is to be redeemed not eliminated. Paul is adamant about this for there will be some serious missteps ahead if the church is seen as the people who are out of step with the way that most people must live their lives. The church will be seen as not only having nothing new to say to the world but nothing to say at all.

Luke 21:5-19

Having stood looking across the Kidron Valley toward the temple, I know the truth of Jesus' words. "When some were speaking about the temple, how it was adorned with beautiful stones and gifts dedicated to God, he said, 'As for these things that you see, the days will come when not one stone will be left upon another; all will be thrown down' " (Luke 21:5-6). All that one can see of the ruins of the temple is the retaining wall that Herod installed and that has become known world wide as the Wailing Wall. Occasionally, one can see the Israeli Arab conflict acted out in the clash of those who have come to the Wailing Wall and those who have come to visit the Dome of the Rock, the third holiest site in Islam that is only a few hundred yards away.

They asked Jesus, "Teacher, when will this be, and what will be the sign that this is about to take place?" In many ways, in the age that we live in, we have grown skeptical, not about the end time but that there could be anything ahead that will look like sustained good times. Energy crises, global warming, war, have all left us quite suspicious about anyone claiming that there could be an age of abundance ahead for us in any meaningful sense. Newness does not come easily for human beings in the first place. Fly by wire aircraft, which operated like an electronic organ console by making electronic connections instead of like a tracker organ where there is physical connection with the control surfaces, posed a serious problem for pilots who had been trained on older planes. Flying without an actual wheel in front of them that gave a physical sense of the plane was well outside of the comfort zone of most pilots. The pilots were only pacified when a fake wheel was installed that they could hold onto during the flight. Newness does not come easily. Well into WWII, the British still trained their artillery crews to hold the horses as the guns fired even though they no longer used the animals to move the guns. Newness does not come easily. We come to terms and find ourselves not expecting anything more than nations rising up against nation and the general run of plagues and famines that make up the nightly news.

Many will come claiming that they know when these events will have taken a turn from which there is no return as the heavens either close up on our future or when will they open up a new future for us.

What is new here is that it seems the option to just retreat into our shell will be foreclosed. "But before all this occurs, they will arrest you and persecute you; they will hand you over to synagogues and prisons, and you will be brought before kings and governors because of my name. This will give you an opportunity to testify" (Luke 21:12-13). Along with the opportunity to testify, there will be family divisions and public opposition. Yet Jesus says that the community will get through these things even though we cannot imagine beforehand how. As a matter of fact, we will not only survive but will find ourselves thriving as we gain our souls.

There is much to be gained as we handle family divisions, face public opposition, and find ourselves giving public account of our faith. We gain soul power and a depth of soul that will not perish. It is certainly new to see a time of internal division, external opposition, and a general accounting as the place where we need to be. I don't see this presented in much of the church renewal literature as the way we ought to go. However, our attempts to either paper over differences or cut ourselves off from each other, along with our unwillingness to endure real hatred for the sake of deeper relationships, may be preventing us from going anywhere.

Application

Let us be clear about what the Hebrew text says here. It is God who will be making a new heaven and a new earth. If God is doing this in our age, it is certainly rearranging our understanding of what heaven and earth is about. At this point, many of us find ourselves saying, "Check, please!" We are hard-pressed to see how a new heaven or a new earth can be carved out of the mess that we are in. Yet, look around and there are signs that this just may be what is happening. Certainly, something new is brewing when a group of evangelical leaders unite to take global warming seriously.

My home conference of the United Church of Christ devoted its latest annual meeting to the themes of evangelism and prayer. Michael Ignatieff, deputy leader of the Liberal party of Canada, recently wrote an apology in the *New York Times* for having backed the Iraq War. What struck me was not so much his new position as the model he chose to emulate in his thinking. Daring leaders can be trusted as long as they give some inkling of knowing what it is to fail. They must be men of sorrow acquainted with grief, as the prophet Isaiah says, "Something is going on here that reflects a new heaven and earth."

Of course, this is going to cause some problems for some people as they discover that this new heaven and new earth may burst the bounds of old churches, theologies, and understandings. This newness sounds familiar, "And no one puts new wine into old wineskins; otherwise, the wine will burst the skins, and the wine is lost, and so are the skins; but one puts new wine into fresh wineskins" (Mark 2:22). Indeed, it may be that "the old, old story" is what makes all things new. Perhaps in the church we get all bollixed up over change because we fall short of offering a new heaven and a new earth. To many people it seems that the church is about the same pettiness and narrowness of vision and self-serving pursuit that they see in the rest of the world.

Yet, what always haunts and can often help is that it has always been such people that surrounded Jesus.

An Alternative Application
2 Thessalonians 3:6-13. Part of the Hippocratic Oath is the pledge, "to do no harm." It might not be a bad thing for a similar pledge to be part of ordination and confirmation vows, as well as membership commitments. For all our high-minded theology, visionary statements, and impassioned mission we find ourselves all too often falling into hurtful patterns in the life of the church. I know of no pastor who does not find him or herself engaged from time to time in a ministry to those who are seeking transformed lives but are church-phobic. They fear that they will find the same abusive patterns in church that they see in the outside world.

Our fear to offend or embarrass ourselves often overtakes us when we are given an opportunity to testify and are afraid to enter into the openness to what God can do with those opportunities that, according to Jesus, will be given us to testify.

Unlike Paul, all too often we have been a burden for we have not done the work of making our congregations free of sexual abuse. We have done harm because we have not done the work of examining our life to see to what degree it partakes of a sexual understanding that have left the weakest and most vulnerable among us exposed to hurt. Like Paul, who knew he needed to work to earn his keep and keep his credibility, we have to do our homework in order to maintain our credibility as a source of vitality in our society.

I wonder to what degree our slavishness to expediency, a survival mentality, and the desire to draw lines between each other rather than draw circles that include each other prevents us from being a joy and our people a delight.

Perhaps the new thing that God is doing among us is the call to do no harm. If we begin there, we will end up where "the wolf and the lamb shall feed together, the lion shall eat straw like the ox; but the serpent — its food shall be dust! They shall not hurt or destroy on all my holy mountain, says the Lord" (Isaiah 65:25).

Christ the King (Proper 29)
Jeremiah 23:1-6
Colossians 1:11-20
Luke 23:33-43
David Kalas

A week to preach up

I was still just a boy when I felt my call to the ministry. At the time, my father gave me a couple of books he thought would be helpful to me as I explored and pursued my call. In one of those books, I came across a quote that penetrated my heart and mind. It has remained with me for over thirty years since I first read the book.

The quote was a bit of counsel from John Berridge, an eighteenth-century British preacher, who said: "Avoid all controversy in preaching, talking, or writing; preach nothing down but the devil, and nothing up but Jesus Christ." (From "John Berridge," *Preacher and Prayer*, by E.M. Bounds [Grand Rapids: Zondervan, 1946], p. 65.)

Some colleagues, I know, would think it cowardice to avoid all controversy in preaching. They would say that such a policy would be disobedient to their call. That said, however, we should also readily concede that some preachers may relish controversial preaching, but not by reason of their calling so much as by reason of their temperament. These are opinionated and bellicose people, who take pleasure in tweaking, disturbing, and provoking others — and since they are not talented enough to write a syndicated column, they hold a pulpit hostage, instead.

Furthermore, in some instances, controversial preaching may be its own sort of cowardice. Most of our pulpits, after all, furnish us with more protection than risk. It would be a far more courageous thing to say some things one-on-one, in dialogue, or in honest debate, than to hide behind the sacred, public monologue of the pulpit.

Whatever we think of the merits and demerits of controversy in preaching, I believe that Berridge's conclusion is inarguably wise. "Preach... nothing up but Jesus Christ."

It is tempting to "preach up" all sorts of things: causes and movements, issues and candidates, needs and opportunities — all sorts of things that you and I may believe in. But in doing so, we may reduce the overall value of the pulpit. For as people perceive that only some of what comes from the pulpit is of eternal value, while the rest is rather ordinary and temporal, then the whole enterprise is diminished. And if I preach such an assortment of things that I believe in — one Sunday, I preach about the Savior I believe in and the next Sunday I preach about some cause that I believe in — then I have given equal weight to Christ and to some cause. But could any cause deserve equal billing with him?

This week's lections remind me of Berridge's sage counsel. For our selected passages invite us to preach Christ up this Sunday.

Jeremiah 23:1-6

Shepherds are the theme du jour.

Shepherds and sheep are common, familiar, and cherished images in the pages of the Old and New Testament. We are, perhaps, best acquainted with — and most fond of — the use of the image in which the Lord himself is the shepherd (Psalm 23; Luke 15:1-7; John 10:1-18). In this particular passage from the Old Testament prophet Jeremiah, however, someone else plays the part of the shepherd. Surely our understanding of a good shepherd will be informed by seeing the Lord in that role. But in this passage, the sheep represent God's people collectively, and the shepherds represent their human leaders. It is a use of the sheep-and-shepherd imagery similarly used by the prophet Ezekiel (ch. 34).

The prophetic word begins as a sober one: "woe." The underlying Hebrew word, *hoy*, should not be read strictly as a scolding exclamation. In 1 Kings 13:30 and Jeremiah 22:18, it is clearly used as a lament, an expression of grief. In Isaiah 55:1, it is a more positive attention-getting exclamation. In many of its appearances in the Old Testament prophecies, it seems to convey a weary quality — like the mother of bickering youngsters who sighs, "Can't we just have two minutes of peace?"

The "woe" is addressed to the shepherds of God's people. We detect God's displeasure and grief with the situation. Consequently, the grief will soon belong to the shepherds.

Judgment is not the only response of God's displeasure. He will not only displace the current, inadequate shepherds; he will replace them with shepherds who will properly lead the people.

Thus we have juxtaposed pictures of the bad and good shepherds. We are told what the former are doing, as well as what the latter will do. And then, beyond that, there is a still better picture: "a righteous branch" for David, who "shall reign as king and deal wisely, and shall execute justice and righteousness in the land. In his days, Judah will be saved and Israel will live in safety."

In the good future promised by God, "they shall be fruitful and multiply," which recalls the beauty and perfection of Eden. Meanwhile, the reference to David recalls Israel's greatest (human) shepherd.

The anticipated "righteous branch" from David, of course, is a messianic image, which we understand to be fulfilled in Jesus Christ. Within the original context of the prophet's speech, it suggests a third era. The present is the era of the bad shepherds, "who destroy and scatter." In the future era, God "will raise up shepherds over them" who will properly tend his flock. But those shepherds — plural — are succeeded and eclipsed by one particular leader. His reign, as described here, surely has the hallmarks of a messianic era.

So it is that, in the end, we return again to the most cherished sheep-and-shepherd image: namely, when the Lord, himself, is the shepherd.

Finally, it is worth noting the combination of "justice and righteousness." It's a combination that we see over two dozen times in the Old Testament, from God's purpose for Abraham (Genesis 18:19) to high praise for Solomon (1 Kings 10:9); from attributes associated with God (Psalm 33:5; 97:2) to an ethical emphasis in Proverbs (21:3) and the prophets (Jeremiah 22:3; Amos 5:24). Loosely speaking, we might characterize righteousness as the chief desire of God in an individual or society, and justice is the necessary antidote where individual or societal righteousness fails.

Colossians 1:11-20

As with all of the New Testament epistles, the modern reader is like someone overhearing just half of a telephone conversation. We can infer some things about who is on the other end and what their situation is, but we have to depend entirely upon the half to which we are privy.

Here, in the case of Paul's letter to the Colossians, we depend upon these four chapters from Paul's end to glean some information about the people on the other end. The scholarly consensus about the church and the situation to which Paul wrote is that the Colossian Christians were in the midst of a doctrinal crisis. Specifically, the false teaching to which they had been exposed and evidently by which they had been influenced — suggested a low Christology. Paul undertook to write to the Christians in Colossae about no less a theme than the person and work of Christ.

On this Christ the King Sunday, we are rightly directed to this marvelous opening passage from Paul's letter to the Colossians. We are reminded, along with those first-century believers, about all that Jesus is and does.

While Paul's statement about Christ in this selected lection seems more extemporaneous than systematic, we might take what he says and organize it into five categories. Or, more precisely, five relationships.

First, there is Christ's relationship to God the Father. It might be worth considering, individually, which of these five relationships we preach most often or most seldom. It may be that many of us should preach this part of the truth about Jesus Christ more, for surely the pluralism of our day has caused an erosion in American Christology. Therefore, we do well to explicate and affirm that "he is the image of the invisible God" and that "in him all the fullness of God was pleased to dwell."

Second, there is Christ's relationship to us. This is where the gospel's rubber meets the road. Jesus is the one "in whom we have redemption" and "the forgiveness of sins." Of course, this part of the good news has been somewhat discounted by our society's discontinuance of the word "sin." The whole concept has been subtly dismissed as judgmental and archaic, and so we have gradually eliminated it from the American lexicon. Of course, calling cancer by some other name is not the same thing as curing cancer. Our many euphemisms and redefinitions of sin have not eliminated the problem. It has just made the diagnosis more difficult. But the cure remains available in the same place as always — in him — and that is what you and I are called to proclaim.

Third, there is Christ's relationship to creation. This may be an underemphasized truth in our day, for contemporary American Christianity — unlike the ancient church — has not had the need (or perceived the need) to affirm vigorously the divinity and pre-existence of Christ. But his status as "firstborn of all creation," in whom and for whom "all things in heaven and on earth were created" and in whom "all things hold together," is a recurring assertion and theme through the pages of the New Testament.

Fourth, there is Christ's relationship to the church. This is a recurring theme and image (Ephesians 1:22-23, 5:23-30; Colossians 1:24) and, of course, Paul offers a fuller picture of the church as Christ's body in 1 Corinthians 12:12ff. The matter is not much elaborated here, but Paul's brief reference invites our explication of the lovely truth that Jesus is "the head of the body, the church."

Finally, there is Christ's relationship to, shall we say, the re-creation. Just as the New Testament reveals Christ's central role in the original creation of the world and the universe, it also looks forward to God's perfect recreation and restoration of all things. Once again, Christ is central to that work, for he is "the firstborn from the dead," which anticipates the resurrection. "Through him God was pleased to reconcile to himself all things," which is an essential part of God's loving redemption of all creation.

The Christians in Colossae had a problem with their Christology, and so the apostle Paul wrote to remind them that Jesus Christ is unique and supreme. In our day, when there are so many cultural efforts to marginalize or domesticate Jesus, we would do well to remind our congregations, too, of all that he — and only he — is.

Luke 23:33-43

"Did you turn to the wrong page, preacher?" some church member might ask this Sunday. "Doesn't that passage belong in the spring?"

The scene at the cross may surprise the people in our pews this week. After all, we're looking ahead to the Christmas season, with all the festivities that it entails. Why, at this juncture in the holiday seasons, would we preach the scene at the cross?

Why? "Because it's Christ the King Sunday," we reply. Yet, still the quizzical look on the congregant's face remains. Even with the liturgical holiday identified, the passage does not seem, at the surface, a natural match. What does the cross have to do with the king?

Give me a passage from Easter Sunday, with the stone rolled triumphantly away and the guards mortified. Give me a parable of Jesus in which he anticipates his glorious and victorious return. Even give me, a few weeks early, the story of the wise men looking for the one born to be king, but naked and helpless on a cross? A victim at best, and a criminal at worst? What does the cross have to do with the king?

Ask that question of the thief on the right.

"Jesus, remember me when you come into your kingdom," he said.

These are not the words of one who has sidled up next to Jesus amidst the ticker-tape parade on Palm Sunday. This request does not come on the heels of the transfiguration or the booming affirmation from heaven at Jesus' baptism. The request does not come from Lazarus after he has been raised or a leper after he has been cleansed.

Rather, this is the gasping request of one dying man to another. And as such, it represents a most improbable faith. The writer of Hebrews famously defines faith as "the conviction of things not seen" (Hebrews 11:1). Surely the dying thief exemplified that faith, for the kingship and kingdom of Jesus must have been entirely out of sight at that moment.

That Jesus would one day rule over a kingdom might have seemed likely in any of the other aforementioned scenarios. But here, in this moment of apparent defeat, who could have believed it?

Notice that everyone else in this passage got it wrong. "If he is the Messiah," the Jewish leaders scoffed, "let him save himself." Likewise, the soldiers challenged, "If you are the king of the Jews, save yourself!" And the other criminal, too, bought into the same, errant paradigm, "Are you not the Messiah? Save yourself."

Such is the fallen human presumption about power, authority, and status. If Jesus really were the Messiah, the king, then surely he would exercise his power to save himself. But they had completely misunderstood. For while they sought proof of who he was in a display of power that was self-serving, they overlooked the proof of who he was in a display of love that was self-sacrificing.

Somehow that one remarkable criminal perceived the truth. Though all reasonable signs seemed to point in the other direction, he recognized that a king hung on the cross next to him. And not a king whose reign was past and ending. Rather, amazingly, he perceived that Jesus' kingdom was still ahead.

On this Christ the King Sunday, we affirm the faith of that anonymous, paradise-bound criminal. And we celebrate the king, whom we recognize even on a cross.

Application

Here is a frustrated artist who can't seem to make a living by using his skill for noble purposes. Instead, he works at an amusement park, drawing quick, ten-minute caricatures of people and their friends. The onlookers marvel; the recipients have a good laugh. He turns out dozens a day. His work is rolled up and taken home along with gaudy carnival prizes.

Here is another artist whose skill is recognized. He is at the right place at the right time, and he is commissioned to paint the portraits of corporate CEOs, wealthy benefactors, and even a United States president or two. His work is framed and it hangs in the dignified settings of conference rooms, libraries, universities, and even the White House.

You and I are not relegated to the first artist's plight, and we must not choose his path. For we need not devote our craft to silly and temporary things. The sermon does not belong in the company of carnival trinkets. Instead, we are called upon to devote ourselves this Sunday to the noblest subject of all.

Consider the one who sits for us to paint his portrait this week — every week. He is no less than "the image of the invisible God," "the head of the body," and "the firstborn of all creation" in Paul's letter to the Colossians. He is the promised shepherd and ruler in Jeremiah. He is the dying Savior and the anticipated king of Matthew's lection.

Every week, it is our privilege to portray him to our congregations — especially this week. God grant that our skill and effort do justice to the task at hand!

An Alternative Application
Luke 23:33-43. "Strange Bedfellows." Sift through the cacophony that day on Golgotha. Strain out the moaning of those being executed and the weeping of those who loved them. Remove the sounds of

donkeys, camels, and such along the nearby road. Eliminate the routine conversation of passersby and soldiers. Excerpt out the marvelous words of Jesus and of the thief who said, "Remember me."

What's left?

Taunting — mocking — and most of the mocking seems to be directed at one particular person. He is rightly placed on the middle cross, for he seems to be the great center of attention.

But see *whose* attention. Take note of *who* mocks Jesus.

"The leaders scoffed at him" (v. 35). "The soldiers also mocked him" (v. 36). "One of the criminals who were hanged there kept deriding him" (v. 39).

What a strange group picture. Is there any other time or place where those particular individuals — the Jewish leaders, the Roman soldiers, and a condemned criminal — would be allied? We can think of a dozen circumstances in which there would be animosity among those parties. In what other situation would they be cheering for the same thing?

Jesus makes strange bedfellows. He brings unity among his followers, even when they are unlikely companions for one another (such as Simon the Zealot and Matthew the tax collector). And he evokes a certain unity, too, among those who oppose him.

That is as it should be, for it bears witness to the significance of Christ. To be blasé about him is to be uninformed or intellectually dishonest. As C.S. Lewis wrote, "Either this man was, and is, the Son of God or else a madman or something worse. You can shut him up for a fool, you can spit at him and kill him as a demon; or you can fall at his feet and call him Lord and God. But let us not come with any patronizing nonsense about his being a great human teacher. He has not left that open to us. He did not intend to." (From C.S. Lewis, *The Best of C.S. Lewis* [New York: Iverson Brother Associates, 1969], p. 440.)

That all sorts of different people come together to follow and worship him testifies to who he is. And, likewise, the fact that all sorts of different people come together to oppose him also bears inadvertent witness to who he is.

Thanksgiving Day
Deuteronomy 26:1-11
Philippians 4:4-9
John 6:25-35
Wayne Brouwer

The secret of a perfect Thanksgiving

Mehmed II was the great Ottoman conqueror who captured Constantinople in 1453. Because of his uncertain parentage, unhappy childhood, and turbulent adolescence while his royal status was challenged, Mehmed became known for his great secretiveness. Once when asked what he was planning to do, he replied, "If a hair of my beard knew, I would pluck it out."

Most of us live lives more open than that, but we have all felt the pull of secrets. Secrets can be a source of power when knowledge is shared by only a few. Secrets can form a bond among friends who know intimate details that others are not privy to. Secrets are sometimes necessary in international negotiations in order to ensure that outcomes will not be sabotaged by information received and acted upon too quickly by others.

In fact, Jesus seemed somewhat secretive at times. On a number of occasions, particularly as recorded in the gospel of Mark, we are told that when Jesus performed a miracle or cast out a demon, he would instruct those who witnessed it not to tell anyone else. We might be mystified about that, thinking everybody should immediately hear the wonders of Jesus' divine skills. But at the time, Jesus appeared to have been concerned that some people might too quickly misinterpret his power and try, by force, to make him a human king, when his actual destiny was so much greater. Sometimes secrets are a good thing.

The secret of a perfect thanksgiving is both open and hidden. On the one hand, as Moses tells the Israelites in Deuteronomy, thanksgiving is best lived out in the community. At the same time, as Paul reminds the Philippian congregation, thankful hearts are honed in the secret places of remembered history. Finally, there is the teaching of Jesus, who turns the world of his hearers upside down, until the things they think they need are hidden away and until that which they don't know they need emerges from its secret place.

Deuteronomy 26:1-11

The idea of first fruit offerings is a pervasive scriptural concept. Abel appears to have brought the first fruits of his flocks, while Cain did not do the same from his garden (Genesis 4), indicating the level of investment each had in their acts of worship. "First fruits" was declared by God at Sinai to be one of the major religious and social holidays of the Israelite year (Leviticus 23:9-14). Its location on the calendar showed its heightened significance, for it took place on Abib 16 (the first month of the year), during the weeklong Feast of Unleavened Bread (Abib 15-21) that amplified the people's yearly celebration of the high and holy event of Passover (Abib 14). Since the Passover was one of the three pilgrim feasts that brought the entire population together at the tabernacle and later the temple, the Feast of First Fruits was indeed a national celebration.

On the Feast of First Fruits, each household was to gather into a sheaf the first cutting of grain in the barley harvest. This was to be taken to the altar of burnt offerings in the courtyard of the tabernacle or temple, waved before the Lord with ritual prayers of thanks, and then burned so that Yahweh could enjoy the first feast from the crop. The implications were several. First, the land and its produce belonged to God and were only granted by way of stewardship to the people. Second, the highest devotion of the people was to worship Yahweh of the Sinai Covenant and no other alliances or allegiances were to come in between. Third, this first fruit offering was also a matter of trust: Those who brought it believed that God would provide the complete harvest and that they need not worry about it.

Moses broadens the impact of the Feast of First Fruits here in Deuteronomy 26. For one thing, he calls on the Israelites to go beyond the barley harvest and think about all aspects of their agricultural existence when making offerings of thanks to God. Grains did not grow well in all parts of Palestine and many homes would focus their energies on vineyard crops, olive groves, or cattle care. Moses' instructions take all of those into account and encourage every branch of agricultural production to practice its own type of first fruit celebration.

Second, Moses removes the limits of the specific festival red-lettered into the yearly liturgical calendar of the people by making first fruit offerings a year-round expression of piety and devotion. Since the barley harvest occurred very early in the year, the institutional Feast of First Fruits was situated perfectly to mark the beginning of that season. But agricultural cycles produced various crops throughout the year, and animal husbandry knew of animals born on numerous occasions during the changing months, and Moses' instructions about first fruit offerings that are not limited to the feast of that name encourages year-round thank-offerings.

Third, Moses ties these ongoing first fruit offerings to a social consciousness. He instructs the people that when they bring their first fruit offerings they must make a public testimony reciting their history as slaves, the deliverance brought by Yahweh, their current state of landowner wealth, and the plight of those who are not as fortunate. In so ordering, Moses perpetuates among the people a historical rootedness that undergirds thankfulness and an eye for benevolence. They are never to take their possessions or opportunities for granted or become self-important with false notions of entitlement. Nor were they to become insulated or isolated in their riches so that they began to live in ghettoed suburbs or gated communities where they could escape the bothersome annoyance of seeing poor people. In fact, as the verses that follow today's lesson indicate, a portion of the first fruit offerings were to be shared with the poor in the towns where those who were bringing the gifts themselves resided. First fruit offerings were an active investment in social care.

The implications for Thanksgiving Day are huge. First, true thankfulness is an acknowledgment that life itself, along with the treasures that have accreted to each person along the way, is a gift. When life is taken for granted, it is desacralized and robbed of any significance. If thankfulness is taken out of the picture, atheistic evolutionism wins, and the result is the not-very-pretty carnage of the survival of the fittest, all of whom deserve exactly what they get.

Second, Thanksgiving cannot be limited to a single day, nor is it the primary provenance of a particular type of agricultural community. As Moses indicated, the first fruit offerings need to be made from all forms of livelihood. Barley is not the only crop of blessing, nor are farmers the only people dependent on the graciousness of God. Since Moses did not write the official Feast of First Fruits out of the national calendar, he was not saying that it was a trite and meaningless celebration. Instead, Moses was affirming the good of a single day on which there was a national thankful focus, and then using that celebration to build recurring acts of gratitude into the general life of the population.

Third, in Moses' instructions is a reminder of the meta-narratives that drive life and nurture its meaning. Busy lives and time-crunching planners atomize and fragment our lives into smaller and smaller chunks of efficiency. Our increased productiveness does not necessarily broaden or deepen our sense of meaning and self, however. So it is that festivals like first fruits or Thanksgiving give us opportunities to step away from the minutiae and re-engage the big testimonies of our lives or our cultures or our faith. Almost none of the people hearing Moses' words for the first time in Deuteronomy 26 could recall the hardships of slavery in Egypt. That entire generation had died during the forty years of wilderness wanderings. Along with that, none of those present had firsthand knowledge of the lives of the patriarchs who were "wandering Arameans." When they owned these histories, they were bound together again in a camaraderie of identity and purpose. So, too, in today's Thanksgiving celebrations. From our many little tales we are gathered again to enter the big sweep of redemptive history so that we remember again who we are and whose we are.

Fourth, Moses reminds us that Thanksgiving is a very social holiday. It is not about turkey and football, nor primarily about gathering with one's relatives and friends, although these things can be very important. True thankfulness sees the marginalized of society and seeks to do something about the injustices that make some scramble for crumbs while others don't know what to do with their waste. Thanksgiving may begin for many in the church, but it does not continue as thankfulness if it ends there.

Philippians 4:4-9

Paul would never forget his first time at Philippi. He was coming off the high of endorsement and influential success that had happened at the Jerusalem Council (Acts 15). There his church-planting work with Barnabas in Antioch had been affirmed, and the intense struggles of their first mission journey had been vindicated over against some in the church who wanted Gentiles to become Jews before they became Christians. Paul was on the road again to bring this news of hope and liberation to others. He had already stopped at the congregations of the first mission journey in central Asia Minor and was heading out into new territory.

At the same time, Paul was likely still smarting under the pain of separation from his old mentor and friend, Barnabas. During their first mission journey they had taken young John Mark along as an aid. Mark was Barnabas' cousin, and someone who had come under the older man's care since Mary, Mark's mother, had lost her husband. So Mark joined the team with a spirit of adventure but lost heart when the trip was longer and harder than expected. Halfway through, he left them to return home to Jerusalem. Now when Paul and Barnabas wanted to take the positive results of the Jerusalem Council back to their friends in Asia Minor, Barnabas thought Mark ought to be given a chance to redeem himself. Paul thought such a move was madness, and in a huff of angry words, these two great leaders split.

One more thing was likely in Paul's mind when he arrived at Philippi on the first occasion. Recently he had received the services of Dr. Luke, over in Troas, and had gained a friend and an ally in the process. At the same time, Paul had experienced a clear and unmistakable vision calling him and the others to venture into new European territory, well beyond the limits of typical Jewish settlement. When Paul stumbled into Philippi, he was entering with new friends and sensing the excitement of a divinely initiated missional challenge.

It began to unfold quickly. In a city with almost no Jews (ten Jewish males were required, at minimum, in any city in order to form a synagogue; there was no synagogue in Philippi, so Paul and Silas found a few Jewish believers down by the river at a place for ritual purifications), the first to believe their message of Jesus as Messiah was an independently wealthy business woman named Lydia (Acts 16). Her gracious hospitality provided them with a base of operations from which to roam Philippi's streets, preaching about Jesus. In short order, they got into trouble, however, when a demon-possessed slave girl rattled them with her accusations and then lost her unusual fortune-telling voice as Paul restored her spiritual wholeness. Angered by his tampering into their financial affairs, the girl's owners threw Paul and Silas into prison. The oddness of the events continued to spiral as an earthquake destroyed the facility, the crusty old pensioned Roman soldier who owned the place nearly committed suicide, and after a midnight revival meeting, the place was turned into a church.

With such a strange history, and in a church organized by this incredibly variegated initial group of believers, it would not be hard to imagine a tough survival rate for its membership. Unlike the Corinthian congregation, the church in Philippi seemed to thrive and became one of Paul's favorites among his key congregations. This letter, written by Paul from prison in Rome around 59-60 AD (see Acts 28), bubbles with delight and resonates with goodwill.

While there seems to have been a few relational issues to challenge the stability of the team in Philippi (see Philippians 4:2-3), for the most part, Paul exudes joy and graciousness when thinking about these folks. He himself is facing uncertainty in this appeal process to Caesar and that comes through in the verses that follow today's reading. All in all, the message of Philippians 4:4-9 is one of enthusiasm, encouragement, strength, and delight.

Paul's words are not so much to be preached as they are to be chanted, cheered, and championed. They are not a teaching but a testimony. They have not the weight of instruction so much as they carry themselves with illumination and insight. They need to be sung in choral enthusiasm as "To God Be the Glory, Great Things He Has Done," or blasted through the speakers in a stirring rendition of "Shout to the Lord." This is thanksgiving that stirs the passions and challenges the emotions to come alive with dancing.

John 6:25-35

Jesus is the greatest spokesperson of all times for understanding the blessings of God. No one experienced more of the richness of divine wealth or power than he or understood more fully the intent of God toward human development and fulfillment. As the incarnation of deity into the human race, Jesus could have configured his own existence in such a way that material possessions or social standing were his at a mere whim or grasp. Yet he makes very clear that these are not the beginning, ending, or meaning of human existence.

Furthermore, in his very life, Jesus made clear that our personal desires are not always fulfilled and that there is a deeper purpose for our existence than the accumulation of wealth or power. When tempted by the devil in the wilderness at the start of his ministry, Jesus resisted efforts to be drawn into the game of "If I want it, I can have it." When urged by the crowds to rule as king in Galilee, he set aside these honors to chart a course to the cross. Even when wrestling in the Garden of Gethsemane with his Father for a way to step back from pain and difficulty, Jesus admitted that his desires ought not rule the day.

Jesus' lifestyle is itself a negation of the secret of the popular book, *The Secret*. His teaching here makes it very clear that our priorities ought to shape our desires and that our desires are best focused when they look beyond ourselves to the things of the kingdom of God.

As the people come out to see him and to seek from him some kind of blessing, he challenges their very assumptions about the cravings inside. If one surveys the idea of "blessing" in the Bible, several core concepts come to mind. To bless is to take note of someone with love and pleasure, wish that person well, and then to do what one can to participate in bringing about that person's welfare and good fortunes. Thus "blessing," in scripture, is always at heart a relational idea. It is based upon the commitments of people to people (such as parents who bless their children), God to people (as when the priests would pronounce the blessing of God over the people — see Numbers 6:22-27), and even people to God (notice the language of Psalm 103 in the King James Bible — "Bless the Lord, O my soul!"). Any material benefits that might flow out of such relationships of tenderness and commitment are secondary to the essence of the blessing itself.

For that reason, mere desire for food can actually take the focus off the issues of real need in life. So if one desires to be blessed in this life, the wrong place to begin is visualizing material possessions or career advancement opportunities. These, in fact, may serve to cloud our horizons and keep us from seeing the real values of our existence. This is always the danger on Thanksgiving Day, where the mythical abundance of food, and people who are "stuffed" with too much turkey, can make the day less religious than it ought to be. Thankfulness is not always engendered by full bellies.

Years ago Madeleine L'Engle was "Writer in Residence" at St. John's Cathedral in New York City. She and the bishop often talked about creativity, and after one conversation they concluded that it had usually come in both their lives through times of difficulty and pain. As he left her office, the bishop turned to make his farewell and said, "I don't know quite how to say this, Madeleine, but have a bad day!" They both laughed but she knew what he meant; sometimes for the creative grace of God to be deeply experienced, it would flow out of difficult circumstances.

In this manner, Jesus' words about eating the divine manna are prophetic of his own coming bad day. For those who would receive the blessings of heaven must first remember the cost that fell on Jesus.

Application

The message today might start out with sharing "secret recipes" for Thanksgiving meal dishes. How might one set the perfect Thanksgiving table? What would Martha or Oprah say is the secret to a perfect holiday celebration? Then it might be possible to transition into the scripture themes noted above that give picture-perfect thankfulness a different twist.

An Alternative Application

Deuteronomy 26:1-11. The Deuteronomy passage is marvelous. Call out the themes from that section of the study and a great thanksgiving message leaps to life.

About the Authors

Wayne Brouwer teaches Religion, Theology, and Ministry Studies at both Hope College and Western Theological Seminary in Holland, Michigan. He holds degrees from Dordt College (A.B.), Calvin Theological Seminary (M.Div., Th.M.), and McMaster University (M.A., Ph.D.), and spent three decades as a pastor and international missionary teacher. Along with hundreds of published articles, Wayne Brouwer has authored thirteen books, including *Covenant Documents: Reading the Bible Again for the First Time* (Cognella), *The Literary Development of John 13-17: A Chiastic Reading* (SBL), and *Being a Believer in an Unbelieving World* (Hendrickson).

Timothy B. Cargal currently serves as Associate for Preparation for Ministry with the General Assembly of the Presbyterian Church (USA). For some twenty years he combined pastoral ministry with teaching biblical studies in universities and seminaries. He is the author of two books, including *Hearing a Film, Seeing a Sermon: Preaching and Popular Movies* (Westminster John Knox Press), and has contributed to several other books, study bibles, dictionaries, and journals in the areas of New Testament studies and preaching. He holds a Ph.D. in Religious Studies from Vanderbilt University.

David Kalas is the pastor of First United Methodist Church in Green Bay, Wisconsin. Before moving to Green Bay, he pastored churches in Whitewater, Wisconsin; Appleton, Wisconsin; and Hurt, Virginia. He also led youth ministries in Cleveland, Ohio, and Richmond, Virginia. David earned his undergraduate degree from the University of Virginia in Charlottesville and his Master of Divinity degree from Union Theological Seminary in Richmond, Virginia. He has also done coursework at Pittsburgh Theological Seminary and Asbury Theological Seminary.

In addition to the present volume, David has also contributed to other preaching resources published by CSS, is a regular contributor to *Emphasis: A Lectionary Preaching Journal* (CSS Publishing Company, Inc.), and has also written curriculum materials for the United Methodist Publishing House. David and his wife, Karen, have been married nearly 30 years and have three daughters, Angela, Lydia, and Susanna.

The late **R. Craig MacCreary** was pastor of South Congregational Church, United Church of Christ in Newport, New Hampshire. He held pastorates in Pennsylvania, West Virginia, and Massachusetts. He earned degrees from Elon University (B.A.), Lancaster Theological Seminary (M. Div.), and Hartford Seminary (D. Min.). His work appeared in *Colleague*, *Pulpit Digest*, and *The United Church News*. He was a guest on National Public Radio and was a contributor to *Candles in the Dark: Preaching and Poetry in Times of Crises*, edited by James Randolph.

Mark Molldrem has served as a pastor in the Evangelical Lutheran Church in America for 37 years. He has had parishes in Cobb/Edmund, Wisconsin; Beaver Dam, Wisconsin; Mondovi/Modena, Wisconsin; and Saginaw, Michigan. Currently he is Senior Pastor at First Lutheran Church in Beaver Dam, Wisconsin. Molldrem has written previously for CSS. He has authored numerous articles in various national magazines and journals. He received his Master of Divinity and also his Doctor of Ministry degrees from Luther Theological Seminary, St. Paul, Minnesota. He is very involved in his community, supporting People Against a Violent Environment (domestic violence) and developing community leadership through the Chamber of Commerce. Throughout the years, he has enjoyed art glass, martial arts, landscaping, preaching and teaching in the Lutheran Church in Liberia (West Africa), playing with his grandchildren, and vacationing with his wife, Shirley, with whom he has raised two children.

If You Like This Book...

Please go to **www.csspub.com** or call **800-241-4056** to order any of the below titles.

David Kalas contributed to each of the following books: **Sermons on the First Readings**, Series II, Cycle A (978-0-7880-2451-1) (printed book $37.95, e-book $29.95), **Sermons on the First Readings**, Series III, Cycle C (978-0-7880-2619-5) (printed book $37.95, e-book $29.95), and **Sermons on the Gospel Readings**, Series I, Cycle C (978-0-7880-1968-5) (printed book $38.95, e-book $29.95).

Craig MacCreary has pieces from **Emphasis** published in the 2011 **Navigating the Sermon**, Cycle B (978-0-7880-2670-6) (printed book $39.95, e-book $29.95).

Mark Molldrem wrote **The Victory of Faith**, New Testament Sermons for Lent and Easter (978-0-7880-1005-7) (printed book $11.95, e-book $8.95).

Timothy Cargal has pieces from **Emphasis** published in the 2011 **Navigating the Sermon**, Cycle B (978-0-7880-2670-6) (printed book $39.95, e-book $29.95).

Wayne Brouwer wrote **Humming Till the Music Returns**, Second Lesson Sermons for Advent/Christmas/Epiphany, Cycle B (978-0-7880-1506-9) (printed book $17.95, e-book $9.95) and contributed to **Sermons on the Gospel Readings**, Series II, Cycle A (978-0-7880-2453-5) (printed book $37.95, e-book $29.95).

Prices are subject to change without notice.